4/26/06

Something Dangerous

Emergent and Changing Illicit Drug Use and Community Health

MERRILL SINGER

Hispanic Health Council

WAVELAND

PRESS, INC.

Long Grove, Illinois

062136

$17.95

For information about this book, contact:
Waveland Press, Inc.
4180 IL Route 83, Suite 101
Long Grove, IL 60047-9580
(847) 634-0081
info@waveland.com
www.waveland.com

ISBN 1-57766-376-4

Printed in the United States of America

7   6   5   4   3   2   1

Contents

Acknowledgments   vi

Introduction   1
The Hispanic Health Council   2
The Role of the Social Science of Health   4
Organization of the Book   7

1 Assessing Emergent and Changing Drug Use Practices   9
The Importance of Understanding Drug Use Dynamics   10
A Typology of Drug Use Dynamics   14
Emergent Drug Trends, Emergent Health Risk   16
Engines of Change: Explanatory Models of Drug Use   22
The Critical Medical Anthropology (CMA) Approach   25
Conclusion   34

2 The Colonial Era to Drug Criminalization   35
Forgotten Drug Histories   35
Drug Voyages: Columbus and the Other Conquerors   36
First Waves: The Impact of Tobacco
   on Europe and the New World   38
The Other Colonial Drugs   41
Explanatory Factors in the Age of Drug Exploration   52
Conclusion   53

**3   The Era of Drug Criminalization
to the 1960s**   **55**
Criminalizing Drug Use and the
   Rise of the Underground Drug Scene   55
In the Shadow of Criminalization   59
Paint It Black: 1940–1959   63
Conclusion   71

**4   The '60s Drug Transition
to the Time of AIDS**   **73**
The Rising Numbers of Drug Users   74
The Middle-Class Drug Counterculture   74
New Drugs, New Visions   79
From the Counterculture to the Rise of AIDS   87
Understanding Evolutionary Aspects
   of Drug Use Dynamics   94
Conclusion   97

**5   The Role of Youth in
New Drug Use Practices**   **99**
Identifiable Patterns of Youth Drug Use   100
Coming of Age   107
Drug Use Innovation and Diffusion   111
The Functions of Social Networks   116
Trends in Youthful Drug Use   117
Conclusion   120

6   Club Drugs and Beyond   **123**
The Club Drugs   126
Drugs, Sex, and Predation   132
New Diseases, New Drugs   136
Old Drugs, New Twists   138
Conclusion   146

**7   Dealers on the Street:
The Impact of Drug Marketing**   **149**
Players and Practices   150
Social Relations among Adult Drug Users   154
The Impact of World War II on Drug Production   155
The Drug Business   156
Conclusion   164

8 The War on Drugs   **167**
Deconstructing the War on Drugs   167
The War Goes On, and On   173
Costs and Benefits   176
A Health Perspective Strategy   183
Conclusion   185

**9 Health Consequences of
  Changing Drug Use Patterns**   **187**
The Spread of HIV/AIDS   188
Other Risks Associated with Drug Use   193
Limiting Risk   214
Syndemics   216
Conclusion   218

**10 Emergent Drug-Related Risk
   and Public Health Responses**   **219**
Fear: An Unauthentic Response   220
Thinking about Trends   222
Studying Change: Methods for Monitoring
    Emergent Drug-related Risk   224
Rapid Assessment and Monitoring   229
Ethnography as a Monitoring Method   232
Multiyear Monitoring   234
Conclusion   235

References   237
Index   263

Acknowledgments

This book was inspired by the standards for anthropology set by James Spradley and is dedicated to Jim, Hans, Mariann, Alayne, Arachu, Grace, Roberta, Bob, Bryan, Patty, Peg, Jay, Herns, Robert, Scott, Kim, Dan and many more, because friendship makes the journey worth taking. I want to thank all of my colleagues over the years at the Hispanic Health Council for their many contributions large and small to the contents of this book. Special thanks to Joan Cruz for her assistance and to Bryan Page and Alisse Waterston for their helpful comments on an earlier draft of the book. Also special thanks to my editors at Waveland Press, Tom Curtin and Jeni Ogilvie.

Introduction

Instead of attempting to halt the onslaught of change, we should try to understand how to usher it in with the least pain and turmoil.

—Erich Goode, *Drugs in American Society*

This book—a historic examination of the nature and health effects of changing illicit drug use practices in U.S. society—grew out of 15 years of ethnographic and epidemiological research on street drug use. I have been involved in this work in various ways, initially as an ethnographer, then as a project director, and finally in my current role as the director of research at the Hispanic Health Council's Center for Community Health Research, in Hartford, Connecticut. My involvement in drug research began even earlier, when, in 1979, I arrived fresh out of graduate school to serve a one-year postdoctoral fellowship on family factors in alcoholism at the Center for Family Research, George Washington University Medical Center in Washington, D.C. Prior to beginning this fellowship, I had no particular academic interest in the issue of psychoactive substance use; since completing the fellowship it has been the focus of much of my professional work as an applied medical anthropologist.

Like most anthropologists before the era of AIDS, I did not specifically choose to become an applied drug abuse researcher because of long-held intellectual interest; rather, I inadvertently stumbled into the field only to discover that as someone trained in doing naturalistic participant-observational research on social behavior there was something I had to offer and much I had to learn. During my time in Washington, D.C., I realized that chemical dependency is a complex issue that is best understood in terms of cultural factors, social relationships, and social structures and not solely within the narrow realm of individual genetic or psychological propensity. By way of analogy, the anthropologist Eric Wolf (1982) once said that you could add up

1

Opium poppy, the source of heroin. Courtesy of Drug Enforcement Administration.

all the reasons that individual soldiers go off to fight in wars and it would never explain war itself. So too, drug abuse. The clearest indicators of this fact are the trends and patterns in drug use explored in this book.

The Hispanic Health Council

My transition from a focus on the study of drinking behavior to one on illicit drug use occurred at the Hispanic Health Council (HHC).

The HHC is a unique organization. It was founded in 1978 through a fortuitous meeting and resulting collaboration that developed between a group of Puerto Rican and other Latino community health activists who recognized that the health-care system was not meeting community needs and several action-oriented anthropologists interested in working with communities in the application of anthropology to the solving of human social problems. Through conversations between these community and scholarly activists there emerged a desire to create a community-based research and advocacy center devoted to the improvement of the health of Puerto Ricans and other medically underserved populations in and around the capital city of Hartford, Connecticut. Funding from the National Institute on Mental Health and the Hartford Foundation for Public Giving gave structure and substance to these desires, leading to the incorporation of the HHC and its subsequent occupancy of a time-worn and rodent-infested storefront office in the heart of Hartford's burgeoning Puerto Rican community.

I joined the HHC when the organization was five years old and have remained on the staff for the last 22 years. Coming with an admittedly limited understanding but nonetheless quite energized interest in drinking behavior born of my "postdoc," I was able to write several grants to the National Institute on Alcohol Abuse and Alcoholism early in my stay at the HHC that allowed me to begin studies of drinking behavior among Puerto Rican adolescents, mothers of adolescents, and adult men. These studies, in turn, led to the development of a set of prevention programs—which later served as the foundation for the launching of the HHC's Center for Family Health and Youth Development—designed to assist Puerto Rican and other inner-city youth to avoid abusive drinking patterns.

Over the years, in part through its work on drinking, and later on drug abuse and its health consequences, the HHC has become a nationally recognized organization committed to developing and providing a comprehensive approach to improving the health and social well-being of Latinos and other low-income, inner-city and rural populations. The distinctiveness of the HHC lies in its successful track record of translating the social science of health research findings into prevention, intervention, and community education

The Hispanic Health Council. Photograph by Alberto Bonello.

programs. As a result, the HHC has developed into the largest Latino social service organization in the state of Connecticut, with special expertise in culturally sensitive drug treatment for inner-city women, AIDS prevention for those engaged in high-risk behavior, intervention in high-risk pregnancy, women's reproductive health, youth development, family nutrition, and multimedia community health education.

The central mission of the HHC, in short, is to reverse existing inadequacies in the quality and accessibility of health services being provided to the urban and rural poor and to empower low-income communities and groups through direct services, health education, social support, self-efficacy training, community health development, and research. In order to achieve these broad goals, the HHC uses a combination of strategies, including: case management and assisted referral, community-based quantitative and qualitative evaluation, information dissemination, educational materials development, community education and training, technical assistance, and health advocacy. The HHC is especially committed to building and maintaining community-based consortia to pool facilities and resources, reach the various underserved sectors of the community, and effectively respond to community health crises among disparity populations. Research helps to drive this work, providing new insights, direct experience, and useable findings.

With the beginning of the AIDS epidemic, much of the research carried out by the HHC, and much of my own work as well, has focused on HIV/AIDS risk and prevention. Building on the experience gained in the investigation of Puerto Rican drinking behavior, the HHC has conducted a series of ethnographic and epidemiological studies aimed at understanding subcultures and behaviors of drug-using populations, the social and contextual factors that shape their drug use, and the drug-related and other health risks they encounter (Singer 1999a).

While the HHC utilizes a multidisciplinary approach, anthropology, with its ethnographic methodology, has long been the lead discipline in the HHC's research program. In this work, participant-observation ethnographic techniques are merged with epidemiological surveys, surveillance methods, and psychosocial/behavioral assessment to form the HHC's unique ethnoepidemiological and psychosocial approach to applied community-based health research. In the case of illicit drug use or abusive drinking, this has involved direct field observation of the acquisition and use of mind-altering substances in social contexts, including attempting to understand the causes and consequences of abusive drug use.

The Role of the Social Science of Health

It is not unreasonable to assert that if you ask the average woman or man "on the street" what medical research is, odds are good you will get a reasonably accurate and positive response. Medical research, you're likely to be told, studies diseases and new treatments for them. Moreover, although admittedly not universally, your respondents will tend to think that medical research is a good thing, even if the specific new medicines, surgeries, or other treatments it produces are seen as painfully overpriced (or under covered by health insurance). By contrast, ask the same passersby about the kind of social and behavioral health research that we do at the HHC (and is reported on in this book) and you are likely to produce a furrowed brow, a blank look, and a fumbled answer that veers off-target by a wide margin.

What is wrong with this picture? Plenty, because medical research is often extremely expensive, especially if its focus is the clinical treatment of an existing disease. Moreover, the key elements in the development and spread of many diseases (e.g., substance abuse, AIDS, sexually transmitted diseases, many cancers, pulmonary and cardiovascular problems, diabetes, etc.) are human beliefs and behaviors, social relationships, and socially constructed living and working conditions. Consequently, social and behavioral patterns are the critical arenas for the development of preventive interventions, many of which are far less costly (both in terms of dollars and human suffering) than medical treatment. And, in cases where medical treatment is not available, prevention is the only medicine!

If people are concerned about improving health and cutting health costs, and every poll says they are, why is social and behavioral health research so obscure, undervalued, and often denigrated? This is a question my colleagues and I at the Hispanic Health Council grapple with every day as we conduct social and behavior studies of pressing public health issues like the causes of malnutrition among inner-city youth or the attitudes about pregnancy among pregnant teenagers and their family members. If we are to address the mental health problems of youth, is it not imperative to assess the obstructions to accessing mental health care faced by young people? If we know that barrier methods (like condoms) are very effective in preventing sexually transmitted diseases (including AIDS), is it not essential to know why people avoid using them? If rates of asthma are far higher among one inner-city population than another, would finding out why provide insight for slowing the significant spread of this dangerous, breath-robbing disease? If we are to stop the spread of AIDS, we ask, is it not vital to know the precise behaviors and social contexts that propel the movement of HIV from one person to another? If people are made aware of HIV/AIDS risk behavior, why does such behavior persist?

When the HHC began, AIDS was unheard of, as were some of the behaviors (such as exchanging sex for crack cocaine) that have contributed to its rise as a major cause of illness and death locally and beyond. By sharply focusing research attention on identifying and carefully describing the on-the-ground behavioral and social factors that put people at risk for HIV infection, HHC researchers, along with our colleagues and collaborators in numerous universities and research centers, have identified a series of preventable behaviors that contribute to the spread of HIV. Moreover, because this kind of research is not carried out with the narrow goal of developing new knowledge for knowledge's sake, but is fundamentally concerned with putting that knowledge to immediate use for the public good, applied social and behavioral health research has helped to establish approaches for lowering risk and for slowing the spread of disease.

In Hartford, where this work began for the HHC (and has since been carried out as well in our research projects in China, the Virgin Islands, and Brazil), drug use has long been the primary source of new HIV infections. Consequently, drug abuse became a primary focus of HHC prevention research in the HIV/AIDS epidemic. While documenting the ways in which drug use contributes to the spread of HIV, this work also drew our attention to significant other health-related risks of drug abuse. Concern with the role of emergent drug use practices on health—the topic of this volume—exemplifies this broadened focus.

Growing awareness of the changing drug scene has impacted the direction of HHC research. Two HHC studies in particular have specifically focused our attention on drug use dynamics and their health impacts. The first study, funded by and operated in conjunction with the Connecticut Department of Public Health and the Institute for Community Research was called the Drug Monitoring Study. It was designed to spot and assess new drug use practices (i.e., new locally, even if they have diffused from other places where they are no longer new).

The second was a CDC (Centers for Disease Control)-funded study called Building Community Responses to Risks of Emergent Drug Use, which was designed to use ethnographic and epidemiological methods to identify and track emergent drug use trends; analyze selected drug use patterns in terms of key sociodemographic traits, such as age, gender, ethnicity, and neighborhood of residence; and use a participatory action research model, which is guided by key health-care policy makers and providers, to implement public health responses to the health risks associated with identified emergent drug use behaviors. These two studies, as well as several other HHC research projects, will be called on in this book as sources of information about changing drug use practices and their health sequelae.

Again and again since the appearance of AIDS in the early 1980s, our sense of security has been rattled by the sudden, seemingly unexpected appearance of emergent infections, each more exotic in origin than the last. The rate new diseases are showing up and spreading around the globe has been accelerating steadily. These new infections hold a simple lesson: with the spread of denser populations to new geographic zones, the extensive and rapid movement of individuals and groups around the world, and the existence of a global market system, the world is much smaller than it used to be. In terms of disease—but also in terms of the composition of its residents, the goods they consume, and the issues that affect their lives—all cities have become global cities. Certainly, most of the drugs consumed locally have their origins elsewhere, indeed usually at great distance geographically and socially. Nonetheless, all cities are not the same city, even in our world of rapid communication, global production, and population movement.

This point holds two lessons for the issues of concern in this volume. The first lesson is that there is a need for close and continual monitoring of drug use as this behavior can be an important source of disease spread in a population. This is so for two reasons. On the one hand, drug use can be a route of direct blood-to-blood contact between individuals, even though contact is mediated by drug equipment like syringes, drug cooking containers, filtering cotton, crack pipes, and various syringe parts. Drug paraphernalia facilitate the transmission of blood-borne pathogens like HIV or HBV (hepatitis B). On the other hand, illicit drug use and abusive drinking are known to promote sexual contact, including unprotected sexual contact, which is another vector of disease spread. The second lesson is that differences in local context factors (e.g., which groups control illicit drug sales and where they acquire the drugs they sell, police practices relative to drug users, access to both housing and medical and social services, the nature of drug transport, conflicts among turf-holding street gangs, and a range of other variables), between cities, among regions, and even between neighborhoods, necessitates local tracking of drug use changes and the community responses to the health risks they generate.

While this book is concerned with the health and social consequences of changing drug use patterns, it is *not* written in what might be called the prevailing "drug panic" style: that is, it is not the intention of this book to overstate the "drug problem" in U.S. society. As David Musto (1987:244) observes, "The bad results of drug use and the number of drug users have often been exaggerated for partisan advantage." Most people in the United States do not use illicit drugs; many who have used them in their youth no longer use them; most people who do use illicit substances use marijuana rather than more powerful drugs like heroin, cocaine, or methamphetamine; and most of the direct public health consequences of illicit drug use pale by comparison with those wrought by abusive drinking. Nonetheless, the contemporary AIDS and hepatitis epidemics are closely tied to illicit drug use, and a wide range of other damaging health and social consequences befall many drug users and the people in their lives. Consequently, changing patterns of drug use are of significant public health and community importance.

Organization of the Book

The remainder of the book contains ten chapters. The first chapter presents an overview of the issues of concern with a specific focus on the shifting nature of illicit drug use behavior. Additionally, the chapter offers an introduction to the theoretical framework—known as Critical Medical Anthropology (Singer 2004a)—that organizes this analysis of emergent drug use. The next chapter begins an exploration of the history of changing drug use practices in the United States from the precolonial era to the criminalization of drug use early in the twentieth century. Chapter 3 continues this historic review of drug use up to the '60s drug transition. Chapter 4 presents features that mark significant changes in drug use dynamics in the 1960s and early 1970s. Chapter 5 examines the special role that youth and young adults play as drug experimenters, testing new drugs and methods of consumption. The sixth chapter considers drug use patterns that diffuse beyond youth to wider social fields of drug users. In the seventh chapter, changing drug use practices are analyzed as a consequence of shifting profit-seeking strategies among drug producers and dealers. Chapter 8 deconstructs the War on Drugs by examining the reasoning behind its creation and its impact on drug use practices and minority communities. Chapter 9 examines the relationship between changing drug use patterns and changing disease patterns, including contemporary syndemics (intertwined, structurally linked epidemics) like drug use/AIDS/hepatitis. The final chapter of the book shifts to the need for drug use behavior monitoring systems that identify, assess, and respond to emergent drug-related public health threats before they take an extensive toll on community health and well-being.

Writing of emergent diseases, the medical anthropologist and physician Paul Farmer (1999:5) noted that "all models of disease emergence need to be dynamic, systemic, and critical. They need to be critical of facile claims of causality, particularly those that scant the pathogenic role of social inequality." This is the approach taken here in examining emergent drug use practices and their health consequences.

CHAPTER 1

Assessing Emergent and Changing Drug Use Practices

I have in me something dangerous

—William Shakespeare, *Hamlet*

Edmund Spenser, a sixteenth-century poet, wrote of "the ever-whirling wheel of change," presaging the kinds of world-transforming changes that have swept across the stage of modern history. Though not Spenser's intent, this phrase serves as an apt label for the illicit drug scene in the United States and globally at the beginning of the twenty-first century. Like the complex social world around it—a world of rapidly changing technologies, mobile populations, frequent market-driven introductions of "newer" and "better" consumer products, and a fluctuating array of global producers and distributors—the underground world of illegal drug use is in constant and consequential flux. As James Inciardi, Dorothy Lockwood, and Anne Pottieger (1993:1) keenly observe, "If anything has been learned from the history of drug use in America it is that 'drug problems' are ever-shifting and changing phenomena. There are fads and fashions, rages and crazes, and alternative trends in drugs of choice and patterns of use." In a similar tone, Lawrence Ouellet, Wayne Wiebel, and Antonio Jimenez (1995:182) remark:

> Illicit drug use is dynamic. Within neighborhoods and across the United States the popularity of any one drug waxes and wanes, a drug's availability fluctuates, the forms and modes of ingestion of drugs change, new drugs are introduced, and people vary in their willingness to try and continue using various types of drugs.

9

The Importance of Understanding Drug Use Dynamics

In this book, processes and patterns of change and transformation in illicit drug consumption—the fads and fashions, rages and crazes, and alternative trends noted by Inciardi and his colleagues—are referred to as *drug use dynamics*. Understanding drug use dynamics is important for several reasons.

First, while drug use is in constant motion, drug treatment and prevention efforts tend to get frozen in time. Once treatment systems are established, their procedures routinized, and their philosophies extolled, they tend to be resistant to change. For example, in the midst of the AIDS epidemic among drug users, a disease that was debilitating and killing thousands of drug users, many treatment programs refused to recognize AIDS risk and infection as issues that had to be addressed in drug treatment. Similarly, prevention programs tend to get stuck implementing models that may have proved effective at a particular time and place but are no longer useful due to changes that have occurred in the drug scene. Whether it be drug prevention or treatment, there is a critical need to reconceptualize drug use as a dynamic process with changing practices, substances, populations, contexts, equipment, and threats to health and well-being.

Second, a close reading of the antidrug legislation that has been passed since the original Harrison Narcotic Act of 1914 reveals an ongoing effort to impose punishments on newly identified drug use practices, especially the use of new drugs, and also on (real or imagined) new populations of drug users. Ironically, new drug laws and how they are enforced have been engines that drive changes in drug use, as users seek to avoid detection, drug seizure, and arrest by changing their behaviors. At the same time, such laws reflect societal fears and panics, as well as underlying prejudices. Initial social concern about cocaine, for example, was shaped as much or more by fear that the drug would embolden African American resistance to social subordination than by the negative health effects of cocaine addiction. Similarly, the first laws and court decisions banning opium reflected anti-Asian sentiment more so than they did a public health concern about harmful aspects of drug use. Studying emergent drug use and the response to it of legislative bodies, law enforcement, and the courts, in short, provides a unique window on the U.S. criminal justice system and its role in society.

Third, drug use dynamics and societal responses to them illuminate the quandary of poor and working-class communities and communities of color, most of which feel the painful impact of drug use, drug-related crimes, and the enforcement of changing drug laws by the police and courts. For example, while studies show that 15 percent of the nation's cocaine users are African American, they account for approximately 40 percent of those charged with powder cocaine violations and 90 percent of those convicted on crack cocaine charges (Davidson 1999). Overall, African Americans, who comprise 12 percent of the population of the United States, make up 55 percent of those convicted for illicit drug possession. One in 15 African American males currently is incarcerated, primarily as a result of drug laws. Moreover, in 1995, approximately 30 percent of African American males between the ages of 20 and 29 years were under some form of criminal justice supervision, up from 23 percent in 1990 (Singer 2004b), and in midyear 2003, Blacks comprised 46 percent of males age 20–29 in federal prisons and local jails (Harrison and Karberg 2004). In 2001, 79 percent of state inmates convicted for drug offenses were African American (Harrison and Beck 2003). Relative to the issue of emergent drug use trends, the significantly higher proportion of African Americans charged specifically with crack cocaine offenses is "the single most important difference accounting for the overall longer sentences imposed on blacks, relative to other groups" according to a 1993 Justice Department report (Muwakkil 1996:21). Penalties for crack possession are greater than for powder cocaine possession, even though, from a chemical standpoint, there is no significant difference between the two substances (Singer 2004b). As William James and Stephen Johnson (1996:149) emphasize:

> Since the early 1900s drug possession and drug dealing have consistently resulted in longer sentences for African American offenders and also in different kinds of penalties. . . . The impact of such sentencing practices on the African American community has been horrendous. . . . The trauma and loss of dignity such imprisonment causes communities, families, and individuals is a key factor in the growth of gangs, teen violence, and child abuse.

At the same time, communities of color equally feel the weight and are often just as angered by the presence of drug users and drug dealers, especially the succumbing of new generations of their youth to the torments of new waves of drugs and drug addiction. As Philippe Bourgois (1995:261), who lived among and studied East Harlem drug sellers, observed:

> On a personal level, the most stressful dimension of living in El Barrio's street scene was witnessing the wholesale destruction of the children of my friends and neighbors. . . . Within five short years, my little neighbor Gigi metamorphosed from being an outgoing, cute, eager-to-please eight year old who gave me a construction paper Valentine's card every year, into becoming a homeless, pregnant, crack-using thirteen-year-old "teenager."

Fourth, as is discussed in chapter 5, because youth play a big role in drug experimentation, society has witnessed a series of historic waves of concern about drug use dynamics among parents. During the 1960s and 1970s, for example, parental concern about the use of marijuana, LSD, and several other substances among white, middle-class youth was particularly marked. More recently, the explosion of the club drug scene, and the widespread use of Ecstasy and a laundry list of other substances in music/dance and party settings among youth, has led to another wave of parental concern. These episodic and often high-pitched social reactions—expressed in sudden pressure on school systems to tighten up on drug detection; in angry and upset letters to newspaper editors or, today, in emotional exchanges in chat rooms and other online electronic outlets; and in demands on policy makers for better drug laws—can be read as indicators of changing social awareness of and values concerning drug use dynamics. At the same time, they provide another window on the structure of U.S. society in that they reflect the markedly different ways the country responds to new drug epidemics in white communities versus those of color. For example, the rampant rise in drug use among primarily African American and Puerto Rican youth in the inner city after World War II did not attract much attention or real concern from the dominant society, except to the degree that drug users were mentioned as either psychologically damaged or as criminal deviants in need of harsh punishment. By contrast, 20 years later, the appearance of growing drug use among white youth became a cause of general societal alarm.

Finally, and most significantly, emergent and changing drug use behaviors are important because of the public health issues and challenges they raise. It is evident that as drug use practices are modified, society is confronted with new diseases or disease expressions, renewed diseases (i.e., new epidemics of older diseases), and other health and social consequences (e.g., overdose cases, injury-causing drug-related violence, and other drug-related crimes).

In our drug use research at the Hispanic Health Council in Hartford, for example, we have begun to find increases in the numbers of individuals who report use of "black tar" heroin (BTH). The most widely available type of heroin found in the western regions of the country, black tar has not been common in the Northeast, in no small part because of the traditional control of eastern drug markets by dealers who specialize in white powder heroin imported first from Asia and later from South America.

Black tar heroin, which is produced in Mexico, has the appearance of sticky roofing tar or hard coal, varying in color from dark brown to black. Unlike refined powder heroin, black tar is a product of rough-and-ready processing methods and, as a result, generally contains manufacture by-products, including poppy plant sugars, sterols, and fatty acids, as well as residual processing acids. To inject BTH it must first be melted, usually by adding a small amount of water and then heating it over a flame. Once the black tar melts, the resulting brownish liquid is drawn up in a syringe and injected by a user (although black tar can also be snorted).

From a public health standpoint, concern about the introduction of this drug to a new population stems from several factors (Ciccarone and Bourgois 2003). First, because of the many impurities it contains, BTH is commonly associated with vein damage and collapse. Long-term black tar users, in fact, have trouble finding a vein that can be used for injection, and thus they must inject it into a muscle. Second, BTH is known to be associated with various skin and wound infections, including abscesses and cellulitis and, as discussed in chapter 9 in terms of cumulative cases, to be one of the most costly causes of emergency room visits (Ciccarone et al. 2001). Moreover, it has been linked with deadly infections like "flesh-eating" bacteria and botulism. Third, as Sperry (1988) reports, based on the detection of a dramatic jump in the number of heroin-related deaths among injection drug users (IDUs) in New Mexico a number of years ago, BTH may become the source of drug overdoses as it is adopted by populations that are unfamiliar with this type of heroin and the difficulties of diluting nonpowdered heroin to tolerable levels.

Counterbalancing these concerns is the fact that heating BTH to melt it for injection may, at the same time, kill HIV present in the drug solution. Also, intramuscular injection may not be as likely to transmit HIV as intravenous injection. As Daniel Ciccarone and Philippe Bourgois (2003:2054–2055) argue:

> We posit that the lower HIV prevalence among Midwest and Western IDUs can be largely explained by the fact that the chemical properties of BTH oblige IDUs to modify their drug-using behavior. A triangulation of evidence from epidemiological as well as clinical and ethnographical observations suggests that at least three mechanisms in concert potentially reduce HIV survival and transmission. Firstly, and probably most importantly, BTH obliges IDUs to thoroughly rinse their syringes following each injection in order to prevent the syringe mechanism from becoming obstructed. This has the unintended consequence of reducing residual blood volume and its potential HIV load. Secondly, heating is necessary to enhance drug solubility. This reduces the probability of transmitting HIV indirectly through paraphernalia (e.g., cookers) sharing. . . . Thirdly, BTH promotes rapid venous sclerosis among injectors, leading them to seek alternative routes of injection (subcutaneous and intramuscular), which may transmit less blood-borne virus. . . .

The lesson to be learned from this example is that changes in drug use can both heighten as well as lower the health risks associated with drug use (or, as in this case, heighten concerns about some health risks while lowering them for others).

As this discussion suggests, there are multiple reasons for paying close attention to drug use dynamics. To this endeavor, this book brings a social science of health perspective. The key questions around which it is framed are: (1) why do drug use patterns change; (2) what kinds of change occur; (3) whom do they affect; and (4) what are the emergent threats to public health (and needed public health responses) associated with such change? As demonstrated below, a number of different kinds of factors—some international, some national, some local—interact to fuel processes of change in the drug scene. Also, the engines of change can be found in: (1) *structural factors* such as competition in the illicit drug industry or the effects of police pressure (e.g., through drug user street sweeps and sting operations); (2) *social factors*, such as the patterning of drug users' social networks; (3) *cultural factors*, such as changing beliefs and values; and (4) *biological factors*, such a the mutation of a pathogen allowing a new mode of transmission or transmission from an animal species to humans. Before examining these issues, we begin this exploration of drug use dynamics by reviewing the various and potentially risky types of changes that tend to occur in the drug scene.

A Typology of Drug Use Dynamics

A careful examination of illicit drug use reveals that there are number of different kinds of change that are possible, and that, in fact, occur. The primary kinds of change in the drug scene include:

1. the introduction of brand new drugs, exemplified by the mid-1960s appearance of d-lysergic acid diethalamide (LSD or "acid");

2. the diversion of pharmaceuticals to street use, such as the mid-1970s adoption of phencyclidine (PCP or "angel dust"), an animal tranquilizer, among youthful drug users, or the appearance of both "street methadone" (diverted by methadone patients who spit out their medication and sell it on the street), and "street Ritalin" (methylphenidate, a stimulant used to treat attention deficit disorder) diverted by youthful patients to sell to their peers;

3. the marketing of new forms of older drugs, such as the early 1980s appearance of crack cocaine (powder cocaine mixed with water and sodium bicarbonate and heated until a smokable "rock" is formed) or the late 1980s spread from Asia to the United States of "ice" (a potent, more crystalline and smokable type of methamphetamine);

4. the mixing of new drug combinations, such as the lacing of methamphetamine drugs like Ecstasy with heroin among youthful after-hours club goers or the older shift to "speedballing" (mixing heroin and cocaine) among drug injectors;

5. the transition in a user population from focus on a single drug and route of consumption to the regular incorporation of one or more additional drugs, often with differing routes of consumption, such as the 1980s movement from "thoroughbred" heroin injection (or at least use of a narrow range of heroin and other drugs) to the contemporary polydrug use pattern;

6. the adoption of specific drugs because of their enhancing effects on other activities, such as the use of "poppers" during club dancing;

7. the use of new substances to "cut" or adulterate drugs in order to increase profits from drug sales, such as the occasional use of toxins like strychnine to cut heroin;

8. the use of one drug to cut another to increase potency;

9. adoption of new drug use equipment, such as the use of plastic alcohol "nip" bottles and a plastic straw to construct crack cocaine pipes,

or the earlier shift from homemade syringes or glass syringes with disposal needles to plastic diabetic syringes with fixed needles;

10. the discovery of new ways to consume existing drugs, such as the mid-1990s advent of crack cocaine injection (through a chemical procedure to reliquefy the crack cocaine rock), the 1930s initiation of intravenous drug injection, the switch to liquefying heroin without heating that followed the introduction of purer "dope" in the 1990s, or the appearance of alcohol injection in Latin America;

11. the emergence of new drug use settings, such as the anonymous "shooting gallery" among drug injectors or the medically controlled "injection room" in parts of Europe and in Canada;

12. the appearance of new behaviors linked to drug use, such as the development of "crack house" sex-for-drugs transactions or the use of vaporous rubs among Ecstasy users;

13. the restructuring of drug production processes and distribution patterns leading to changes in drug purity, availability, price, and composition, such as refinements in South American heroin production that led to much purer forms of the drug hitting the streets of U.S. cities and towns;

14. the development of new populations of drug users, such as homeless street youth in U.S. cities or the growing pattern of heroin use among suburban teens;

15. the sudden risk enhancement of established drug-related behaviors, such as the spread of HIV associated with syringe transfer and reuse (including syringe sharing, lending, and selling, and use of discarded syringes); and

16. risks associated with the production of new drugs, such as explosions resulting from the use of solvents in some types of drug making.

These 16 areas of possible change can be grouped together to form a typology of drug use dynamics, as displayed in figure 1.

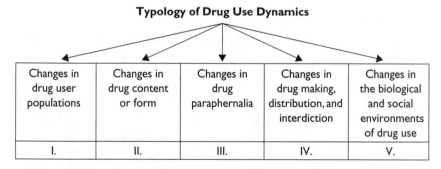

Typology of Drug Use Dynamics

Changes in drug user populations	Changes in drug content or form	Changes in drug paraphernalia	Changes in drug making, distribution, and interdiction	Changes in the biological and social environments of drug use
I.	II.	III.	IV.	V.

Figure 1 Categories of change in drug use

The five categories of change in drug use all have potential health implications for drug users, those in their kin and social networks, the broader communities in which they live, and society as a whole. The general public health aspects of these several different types of change are discussed below; examinations of the relationship between specific changes and resulting changes in public health are discussed in subsequent chapters.

Emergent Drug Trends, Emergent Health Risk

From a targeted public health and health social science perspective, early-bird spotting and understanding the specific changes that occur in the patterns of drug use are of vital importance for a simple reason: different drugs and different ways of consuming drugs, including different conditions under which drugs are consumed, have varying epidemiological implications. Some of them are of critical global public health importance, while others are of great national, regional, or local significance. Although there always have been health effects associated with drug consumption, the reasons for paying closer attention to drug use trends have *multiplied* by several fold in recent years with the emergence of a new set of blood-borne pathogens, like HIV, and with their pathogenic linkage with older infectious threats to human well-being, like hepatitis, botulism, and sexually transmitted diseases.

Beyond the spread of HIV through syringe-sharing among IDUs, changes in the way drug users consume drugs or in the particular drugs or drug combinations they consume can have a range of health consequences. While chapter 9 will more closely review many of the health and social consequences that can be associated with drug use in some detail, three recent examples of change—increases in the use of illicit drugs among pregnant women; the intimate connection that has developed among crack cocaine, oral-sex-for-drugs transactions, and sexually transmitted diseases; and the sudden periodic rash of drug overdose cases associated with the distribution of new laboratory-produced designer drugs—suggest some of the ways emergent drug use patterns can have significant public health impacts.

Drug Use and Pregnancy

The first of the changes cited above—increases in illicit drug use among pregnant women—is an example from the typology of drug dynamics of the emergence of a new drug using population. At the HHC, this development came to our attention through our Comadrona Program. This intervention began in 1983 as a federally funded model demonstration project designed to translate to urban Hartford the social support role of the *comadrona*, "lay midwife," common to rural areas of Puerto Rico. Through this ongoing program, staff are trained to conduct outreach to the target community (specifically, two Hartford neighborhoods with large Puerto Rican populations): to find pregnant women and to engage these women to insure their early access to perinatal and infant health care, maternal and child health-care information, and pre- and postnatal social support.

During the early 1990s, outreach workers from the comadrona program began to return to the office from trips to the community with upsetting reports of drug use among pregnant women. This discovery surprised them because it had been their experience that women who had been using drugs prior to pregnancy had tended, in the past, to curtail this practice during pregnancy for fear of harm that might be caused to their unborn child. Indeed, the outreach workers were aptly concerned about the changes they were seeing in drug use behaviors. Substance use during pregnancy is associated with multiple medical complications; for the pregnant women these include anemia, cardiac disease, cellulitis, edema, hepatitis, phlebitis, HIV, and pneumonia. For the unborn child, drug exposure *in utero* can cause developmental delays, birth defects, and fetal death. Major effects on the fetus include overwhelming infection, chorioamnionitis, premature rupture of membranes, poor fetal growth, mental retardation, infection, and low-birth weight with accompanying complications for the newborn.

Shiegla Murphy and Marsha Rosenbaum (1999), who study pregnancy and drug use, describe the case of a young woman they called Krista. Krista began smoking marijuana at age nine, not long after her mother died. Soon she was introduced to marijuana laced with "angel dust" (PCP). She reported to Murphy and Rosenbaum that she had moved on to methamphetamine three years later. Raped at 15, her drug of choice switched afterward to injected cocaine and heroin. The man who introduced her to drug injection was the father of her first child. She views her relationship with him as being primarily about getting high together. It also involved his periodic violent abuse of her. Because sex and drugs often mix, she soon found herself pregnant. Since so much of her life and her social relationships with others focused on drug use, it never occurred to her to change this pattern during pregnancy, at least not until years later (during her pregnancy with her sixth child).

What is most noteworthy about Krista's case is not that it is an exception, but rather that it is typical of poor and working-class women who wind up using drugs during pregnancy (which, it should be emphasized, are a minority of women in poverty). As we have found in our own research at the HHC (Singer and Snipes 1992; Duke et al. 2004), women who continue to use illicit drugs during pregnancy tend to come from troubled and possibly violent homes, experience early sexual abuse, are introduced to drugs just before or early into their teen years, and tend to enter into relationships with abusive men who are themselves drug users and often are the women's drug suppliers. Drug use in such cases is connected to both personal and psychological needs as well as to the women's network of social ties. Often birth control is not practiced and pregnancies are not planned; drug use, not the pregnancy, is the primary focus of the women's attention during much of their pregnancy.

While it is certainly true that the issue of drug abuse during pregnancy can create undue public reaction, including the passage of harm-enhancing legislation that equates drug use during pregnancy with child abuse, or that generates public alarm without scientific support (e.g., the "crack baby" scare), it is evident that the emergence of this new population of drug users brings with it significant public health concerns for the welfare of the mother and the child.

Sex for Crack and Disease

The second example of the emergence of a new drug use trend involves several of the categories included in the typology, including changes in drug form, in drug-using populations, and in the environment of drug consumption. Crack, the drug of concern here, is a form of cocaine, an alkaloid found in leaves of the South American coca plant known scientifically as *Erythroxylon coca*. Cocaine is a powerfully reinforcing stimulant that produces an intense sense of euphoria, primarily by hindering the brain's uptake of the neurotransmitter chemical known as dopamine.

Leaves of the coca shrub have long been chewed among the Indians of the Andes as a mild stimulant that eases breathing at high altitudes while producing no health or social consequences. The ancient Inca revered coca and worshiped a god named Mother Coca. Arrival of the Spanish colonial invaders set off an attempt to eliminate the chewing of coca leaves, probably more because of its pagan religious ties than because of antidrug sentiment. Nonetheless, returning Spanish *conquistadores* introduced coca to Europe, launching a long history of periodic reintroductions of cocaine in new forms, each with its own public health sequelae, as described in chapter 2.

One such example was the discovery of cocaine base or freebase. Freebase is the treatment of processed cocaine with chemicals that free the cocaine from hydrochloride while lowering the temperature at which cocaine melts. Initially, it was produced using highly volatile solvents, such as ether. While this new form proved popular among some users, it soon became clear that there were notable risks involved in mixing solvents and fire. To overcome this problem, drug experimenters tested other methods of producing base. During the early 1980s, they discovered that by heating cocaine in a solution of baking soda they could remove the hydrochloride. The solution is boiled, and a solid substance separates from the boiling mixture. The solid substance is crack cocaine, which is removed and allowed to dry. It is then broken or cut into smaller "rocks," each typically weighing from one-tenth to one-half of a gram. The term "crack" developed because of the crackling sound produced when the mixture is smoked, probably because of the sodium bicarbonate.

One gram of pure cocaine powder converts into about 0.89 grams of crack. The Drug Enforcement Administration (DEA) estimates that crack cocaine rocks are between 75 and 90 percent pure cocaine. Because crack vaporizes at a low temperature, it can easily be inhaled with a heated pipe or stem, the standard route of consumption. Smoking crack allows high doses of cocaine to reach the brain very swiftly and to trigger an intense and extremely pleasurable, if short-lived, high. It takes less than 20 seconds for cocaine to reach the brain, even though only 30–60 percent is actually absorbed because of incomplete inhalation of the cocaine fumes and variations in the heating temperature.

As Mitchell Ratner (1993:2) notes, crack eventually garnered considerable public attention:

> In the late 1980s, the widespread sale and use of crack cocaine became a major public issue; few if any health related topics received such widespread media attention. [C]rack cocaine use, especially in poor and minority communities appeared to be epidemic. Arrestees in major cities presented the clearest indicators of skyrocketing cocaine use. . . . National concern about crack use began to center not only on the devastation experienced by users but by their families and well.

One consequence of the crack cocaine epidemic was the appearance of "crack-addicted sex workers" who trade sex for drugs, individuals who are given a variety of deprecating names on the street (Sterk 1999). Those who have studied the relationship between drug use and prostitution point out that the appearance of crack was associated with a turn toward desperateness in street behavior, including decreased prices for sex, less control over sex activities by sex workers and hence an increase in riskier behaviors, and an increase in the degradation and humiliation of sex workers by dealers who control the drug supply. For example, in a seven-city ethnographic examination of HIV transmission in crack use and sex-for-crack exchanges funded by the National Institute on Drug Abuse (NIDA), researchers interviewed a sample of 340 active crack users concerning their drug use and sexual behaviors. The study reported close linkages between crack use and risky sexual practices (Ratner 1993). Women comprised two-thirds of the survey sample, with those engaged in the provision of sexual services reporting 30 or more customers a day. Of the 107 men in the sample, 27 percent were engaged in sex-for-drugs/money exchanges, almost solely with other men. Typical of the larger study, the Miami site found that only 23 percent of women involved in sex-for-crack/money exchanges always used condoms during vaginal intercourse, and only 14 percent always used condoms during oral sex. James Inciardi (1993:59) presents this account by one crack "house girl" from the Miami site:

> [A]fter awhile I just wanted to be high all the time, and I saw what was going on at the time. . . . So I asked the house man one night if I could work for him. He calls in this guy Stoney. He was working "lookout" across the street. And right there he says, "Sit down on his chair and do Stoney, let Stoney come in your mouth." He wanted me to do it right there, in front of five, six people. And Stoney was real happy, because he

was just a green kid, was happy to have me get off his nut [make him climax]. And after Stoney, I did three others in the room, and by midnight I had done 30 more.

Claire Sterk (2000:70) presents a similar case, that of Peep, a 27-year-old crack sex worker from Atlanta:

The guys think about us as their fucking property. Like they own us because they give us some smoke. . . . You see this black eye? . . . I got beat up because he couldn't get it up. I had been rubbing and sucking him for a long time. He was bleeding, and he wanted to go on. . . . Finally he gave up and made me have sex with this other girl.

The turn to sex-for-crack prostitution is not random and may be predicated on prior life experiences rather than the chemical effects of the drug. As a participant in the HHC's study of drug use and intimate partner violence among women told us:

I was suffering from depression, you know [since being raped by her stepfather], and I never got help for it so. Then I had my oldest son, after my oldest son, I moved out. . . . I left my apartment, went into a shelter and got me another apartment . . . had another baby from another man. Then I started doing drugs. That's when I got into doing drugs . . . doing dope, I started doing dope. I was already twenty-one. First I was sniffing then I got into doing shooting up. . . . I started hanging around with people that was shooting and stuff. So let me try it . . . that's when I really got into the heavy, doing dope. I started learning how to [do] crack cocaine, I started smoking it. I lost my apartment, I went through a lot, you know. I started even selling myself, just to get the drugs, drug money for the cocaine, for my habit and stuff. (HHC taped interview, SAVA 2 study)

Under such conditions of disempowerment, these addicted sex workers are subject to both high levels of violence and regular exposure to disease. Sex-for-crack transactions thus have become important engines propelling the AIDS epidemic in the United States, with studies finding that crack users are 5–7 times more likely to be infected with HIV than nonusers. To assess crack-associated risk, T. K. Logan, Carl Leukefeld, and David Farabee (1998) initiated a study designed to compare women crack users who reported exchanging sex for drugs and money with women crack users who did not report involvement in such exchanges. They found that both women crack users who exchanged sex for drugs and those who did not had unprotected sexual intercourse as often, had similar drug use patterns, and had initiated drug use at similar ages. However, the women who exchanged sex had more sexual partners, had unprotected oral sex more often, used drugs before and during sex more often, and had a higher rate of sexually transmitted diseases than those women who did not exchange sex. This study revealed that not all women who use crack become commercial sex workers, but those who do have significantly increased health risks.

Designer Drugs and Drug User Death

Periodically, there is a sudden rash of overdose death cases among drug users. One occurred in Hartford in the early 1990s. Within a few days, five known IDUs died, suddenly and without warning. All, it turned out, had purchased "heroin" from the same dealer. The police identified the "drug brand" stamped on the glassine bags sold by this dealer (to differentiate their product, dealers will often stamp a name, usually intended to suggest the potency of the drug or to link it with a popular movie or other meaningful social symbol). They sent out police cars with loud speakers to warn drug users that the bags labeled "Tango and Cash" did not contain heroin but instead were filled with alpha-methylfentanyl (fentanyl), a synthetic designer drug that exists in 12 somewhat different chemically engineered forms and produces a heroin-like high at a fraction of the dose. As a result, when injectors who purchased "Tango and Cash" used their usual drug dose, they overdosed with tragic consequence. Ironically, when other drug users learned about fentanyl from the police announcements they flocked to buy it rather than shy away from it, on the assumption that they could handle it and it would give them a powerful high, as the craving for a re-experience of one's initial experiences is a potent psychological motivator of continued drug use. The incident described above is not unique. Similar occurrences of deadly designer drug overdoses have been reported from other cities. Designer drugs have become widely used, producing more than their share of negative consequences, and is the third of our examples of effects of change in drug use patterns on health.

Designer drugs were initially developed in an attempt to get around the very specific language of earlier drug laws. By slightly modifying the chemical properties of a drug—something that can be accomplished in an average kitchen—drug dealers sought to create new substances that had psychoactive properties but were not covered by legal restrictions. For example, one of the most extensively studied classes of mind-altering drugs is the phenylethylamines (analogues of mescaline). Various alterations of the phenylethylamine molecule gave rise to amphetamine, methamphetamine, 3,4-methylenedioxyamphetamine (MDA, nicknamed the "love drug"), and 3,4-methylenedioxymethamphetamine (MDMA), each of which has set off a new drug use craze. As a group, this class of drugs has been connected to a large number of deadly overdoses due to heart arrhythmias, hyperthermia, or brain hemorrhage.

As the three cases of drug use dynamics described above affirm, there are, as discussed in greater detail in chapter 10, important public health reasons for establishing effective monitoring systems to identify, track, and assess the development and use of new drugs or the adoption of new drug use behaviors, drug paraphernalia, and drug-using populations. Failure to monitor changes in drug use patterns—a tendency driven by the false conception that drug users constitute an isolated and epidemiologically insignificant population—also can have major health consequences. The very rapid spread of HIV in some populations of drug users (and from them to their lovers, spouses, sex partners, and children) is one recent consequence of inattention to health implications of changing drug use dynamics (Des Jarlais et al. 1995).

Engines of Change: Explanatory Models of Drug Use

As the accounts above suggest, drug use patterns change in a variety of ways. Change, however, is not automatic, and thus it is appropriate to ask: Why do drug use patterns change? What propels drug use dynamics?

A review of the extensive illicit drug use literature suggests the existence of a number of competing explanatory models, all of which may have a bearing on understanding emergent and changing drug use patterns. These models include the following.

- *Psychological Model.* This perspective views involvement in illicit drug use as a reflection of underlying psychological problems; stated simply: the abuse of illicit substances is an expression of damaged personality. Researchers have reported that 48–90 percent of opiate-dependent patients in drug treatment suffer from psychiatric disorders, with anxiety and depression being the most frequently reported diagnoses (Rounsaville et al. 1982a, Rounsaville et al. 1982b; Grant 1997). For example, 60 percent of drug users in methadone treatment at San Francisco General Hospital were found to have moderate to high levels of depression and the majority also had moderate or higher levels of hopelessness (Sorensen et al. 1991). The shortcomings of this approach are: (1) it overemphasizes individual mental health while inadequately addressing trends, patterns, and transformations in drug use that affect many individuals with heterogeneous personalities and wide-ranging mental health statuses; and (2) it deemphasizes social context and learned behavior (e.g., learning about drugs and how to get and use them from peers, which are social rather than psychological factors).

- *Social Pathology or Deviance Model.* As contrasted with much of the anthropological literature, which tends to view the use of psychoactive drugs in cultural context, sociological theory has tended to emphasize a deviance model of drug use (Becker 1963). For example, Mark Fleisher (1995:118) argues that drug-involved youth caught up in the criminal justice system "have little control over their feelings, emotions and behaviors." Over time, "[d]eviance becomes a group norm for these boys and a life trajectory acted out on the margins of society is set in motion" (119). While this model recognizes that drug use is a social behavior, and that social networks merit attention, it fails to locate subgroup drug use within the context of broader societal patterns of drug consumption as well within the context of the social contradictions (e.g., barriers to social equality) and structural violence (e.g., poverty) that shape the life experience of so-called "deviants."

- *Brain Disease Model.* This relatively new model holds that addiction is a brain disease that develops over time as a result of what is initially voluntary drug use (Leshner 2001). From this perspective, using psychoactive substances changes the physical structure of the brain and the functioning therein in fundamental and long-lasting ways that appear to persist even after the individual stops using illicit substances. Argues Alan Leshner (2001:75), "Addiction comes about through an array of neuroadaptive changes and the laying down and strengthening of new memory connections in various circuits in the brain." This reordering of brain anatomy and biochemistry, which is believed to involve a number of cellular and molecular changes, produces an uncontrollable compulsion or craving to acquire and reuse drugs. Neuroscientists involved in brain studies of addiction generally do not deny the importance of social factors in creating the life conditions that lead some individuals and not others to begin using psychoactive substances. However, while recognizing that social factors play a role in the development of addiction, they do not tend to explore the actual interplay between biology, social experience, and the social conditions that underlie obsessive desire.

- *Subcultural Model.* Within sociology, and to some degree within anthropology, one reaction to what were seen as problematic attempts to create a psychological explanation of illicit drug use was the development of the culturalogical or culture determinist concept of "drug subculture." From this perspective, drug use is not so much a reflection of psychopathology as it is a product of socialization within an alternative cultural pattern. Drug users are not driven by an assortment of individual psychological problems but by their shared knowledge, values, and goals. For example, Erich Goode (2005) argues that there are distinct alcohol, marijuana, cocaine, heroin-injecting, and polydrug use subcultures. From the standpoint of change, however, fixed notions of distinct subcultures appear questionable. Groups that at one point in time primarily are using one drug have been found at later points to have changed to a new and different drug of choice (e.g., going from heroin to crack use), or they have added a second drug to their repertoire. The subcultural approach, like the deviance model, tends to overemphasize the boundaries between illicit drug users and nondrug users, ignoring the ways these are intimately connected and mutually dependent.

For example, in our studies of street drug users in Hartford we have found that a common survival strategy is to "boost" (shoplift) small items like batteries or cans of baby formula from one store and to sell them at discount prices to the proprietor of another store, who in turn can make a bigger profit off items bought cheaply on the street. On a much larger scale, well-respected banking institutions have been found to be involved in drug money laundering, while the police in various places have been implicated in taking payoffs to allow local drug use. Drug users and drug use, in short, are not as disconnected from the wider society as is sometimes asserted. Moreover, there is considerable local variation in drug use behavior. Marijuana users in one place may be quite different from marijuana users in another location. As Ed Knipe (1995:172) stresses, "To place the use of marihuana by Rastafarians [in Jamaica] and by American adolescents into a single cultural category is an obscene misapplication of the concept of culture." For these reasons, while it is evident that some subcultural patterns do exist among drug users (e.g., knowledge about how to "score" and prepare drugs for use), an overemphasis on this feature of the drug scene deflects attention from both the fluid nature of culture and group boundaries and identities as well as the social structures and processes that crosscut and unite disparate groups.

- **Trend Theory Model.** This is an approach for assessing multiple factors that shape the trajectory of use of particular drugs over time (Agar and Reisinger 2002). The goal of this approach is to anticipate increases and decreases in the popularity of specific drugs of interest during specified time periods. Factors that are seen as being of critical importance to take into consideration include an array of social connections and contingencies, such as the nature of the chemical and physical properties of the drug in question, the experiences of the users with the drug, the array of historic conditions that produce populations that begin using the drug, the distribution systems for moving the drug from producer to consumer, and the policies and practices involved in state efforts to control the drug. While this approach shows promise, it remains unclear how to do a trend analysis (what do you do first, what do you do second, etc.), how much emphasis to place on each of the various factors noted above, and how to actually predict the next phase in a drug use trend.

- **Macrostructural Model.** This approach focuses analytic attention on the often overlooked significant role of political and economic forces in shaping broad patterns of drug abuse. Standard interpretations from this perspective "are based on class analysis, exploitation, and the contradictions of the capitalist system" (Thoumi 1995:68). Despite this needed corrective to much of the literature on illicit drug use, a major shortcoming of this approach is its failure to investigate the interaction between large-scale, macroforces in society (e.g., institutional racism) and the kinds of rich variation found by ethnographic research to exist across local cases.

The Critical Medical Anthropology (CMA) Approach

As noted earlier, explaining drug use dynamics requires an examination of at least four different areas of possible influence: (1) structural; (2) interpersonal/social; (3) cultural; and (4) biological. Accounting for the influence of multiple factors on behavior calls for a complex, broadly hewn theoretical model, a model designed to examine interaction across discrete levels of analysis (Singer 1999b). The model followed in this book is known as Critical Medical Anthropology (CMA) (Baer, Singer, and Susser 2004; Singer and Baer 1995) and constitutes an alternative to existing models of drug use.

The CMA perspective developed in the early 1980s among a group of medical anthropologists who were critical of the way health issues were being analyzed and explained by the reigning theoretical models of medical ecology, cognitive and meaning-centered theory, and culturalogical approaches. Missing from the analysis, in the view of these anthropologists—several of whom had a specific interest in substance use and abuse (e.g., Bourgois 1995; Waterston 1993)—were efforts to account fully for the impact of social inequality and the exercise of differential levels of power in society (Castro and Singer 2004; Farmer 1999). From the perspective of CMA, health came to be defined as *access to and control over the basic material and nonmaterial resources that sustain and promote life at a high level of satisfaction.* Health, in other words, is not an absolute state of being but rather an elastic quality that is highly sensitive to social context, social relationships, and state of mind.

With specific regard to the issue of human interaction with psychoactive chemicals and the impact of this behavior on health, critical medical anthropologists ask questions like: What is the role of the multinational corporation with its vast advertising apparatus, ability to influence government policy, and control of scientific knowledge about how to manipulate the chemical properties of its products on changing patterns of consumption? How do social inequality, structural violence, social marginalization and stigma, and resultant social suffering contribute to the appeal of various mind/mood altering substances? What impact do state institutions of social control (e.g., the police, the courts, prisons), dominant social ideologies and values (e.g., our cultural emphasis on achievement and personal responsibility for success and failure), and social networks of support and coping have on drug use dynamics? How do drug chemistry, socially and historically shaped human biology, and socially structured life experience interact to shape drug-related experience and consequence?

Beyond the structural level, CMA as an anthropological perspective is concerned with variation across local cases and the agency of individuals and groups in creating the social events and processes in which they participate. As this suggests, central to CMA is the development of analyses that fully see the individual and the social group engaged in day-to-day processes of decision making and action, while identifying the impact of often extralocal forces, such as the exercise of power by dominant groups in society, on the ideas, options, and contexts that define human social life and experience in the health arena. For example, writing on the issue of unwanted pregnancies among Euro-American women in southern California within a CMA perspective, Marcia Ellison (2003:324) notes that the "dense interplay of agency and social forces . . . underscores that women are, ineluctably, neither free agents nor passive victims." By viewing those who suffer illness or administer care as neither free agents nor doormats to structural forces and oppression, CMA seeks to develop understandings that illuminate the processes of interaction across macro- and microlevels of social process.

Additionally, and equally important, CMA is concerned with developing a critical biocultural synthesis. However, unlike traditional bioculturalist perspectives, CMA does not treat biology or components of the environment as independent variables. While so-called "forces of nature" obviously preexist and operate independently from human society, increasingly we inhabit a physical world and have physical bodies that are reshaped (often unconsciously) by the effects of political and economic forces (e.g., economically prompted migrations of human populations and subsequent mixing with other populations). It is for this reason that explanations of biology that ignore the effects of human social, economic, and political forces tend to be narrowly reductionistic (i.e., the equivalent of studying Central Park in New York City as an "untouched" expression of natural forces while ignoring the enormous effects of human intentions and actions on the composition of the flora, fauna, and inanimate objects that comprise the park). Human bodies and the physical environments they inhabit, in short, bear the imprint of human social history and hence cannot be treated as independent, natural factors, but neither can they be ignored in understanding human behavior and health.

As a result of these concerns, the CMA model of explanation incorporates structural factors, social factors, cultural factors, and biological factors in its explanation of health issues—as explored in this book—including the consequences for community health of emergent drug use practices. Each of these components of the CMA model is elaborated below.

Structural Factors

In his classic study of the American experience with drug use and its prevention, David Musto (1987:253) notes that:

> The use of illegal drugs increased astoundingly in the 1960s. Drugs thought safely interred with the past, marijuana and heroin, rapidly

resurfaced at the same time that new drugs such as LSD materialized and attained tremendous popularity. . . . *This rapid turnaround occurred amid massive changes in American society, which we must appreciate in order to understand the reactions drug use evoked.* (emphasis added)

As this statement indicates, and the previous discussion of crack and HIV in Hartford implies, changes in drug use patterns, and hence changes in the health threats associated with them, reflect changes in encompassing social structures and processes. In other words, to fully understand particular drug use dynamics requires an examination of changes in the structure of political and social relations in society (at various levels); the organization, operation, and impact of changes in the economy on the daily lives of societal members; and further, transformations of society's political and economic relations globally.

What are the structural changes Musto credits with playing a critical role in the surge of new drugs and new populations of drug users during the 1960s? He identifies two primary factors. First, the United States experienced an enormous growth in wealth, with the gross national product doubling between 1960 and 1970. As a result, middle-class families began to experience an increase in disposable income. Behind this increase in wealth was a growth in the global position of U.S.-based multinational corporations. Of the 7,000 multinational companies in the world in 1970, more than half were centered in either the United States or Britain (that percentage is far lower today, a change with its own ramifications on drug use dynamics). Major corporations like IBM, GM, and Pfizer were positioned to control the emerging global economy, while, in many lands, resentment began to build against the New World's "Coca-colonization of the Old World" (Barnet and Cavanagh 1994:423). In the United States the benefits of global economic dominance began to be realized in the lives and lifestyles of people from the upper class, and, to a degree, some of this new wealth trickled down to suburban families in the middle class.

Second, Musto points to the emergence of the "baby boom" generation. Between 1960 and 1979, the number of 15–24-year-olds jumped by 50 percent. Shaping the sentiments and values of the boomer generation was the Vietnam War, a conflict that produced intense alienation among youth, in particular, with lasting effects. One expression of this disaffection was the adoption of an emergent youth counterculture, of which drug use—a practice that was shocking and repulsive to the prior generation—was an integral component. While the causes of the Vietnam War have been debated for decades, it is clear that the war was closely tied to efforts to maintain the newly achieved corporate dominance of the global economy (to which the feared spread of communism in Southeast Asia and elsewhere was seen as a looming threat). One of the unintended, and indeed initially unimagined, consequences of this failed war, however, was its impact on drug use dynamics, namely the "1960s transition" in adolescent and young adult middle-class drug use.

Rapid changes in drug use patterns have continued to sweep across the U.S. social landscape ever since the 1960s. The appearance and widespread adoption of crack cocaine, beginning in the mid-1980s, the emergence of the club drug phenomenon in the 1990s, the continuing spread of methamphetamine use nationwide, and the growing practice of diverting several kinds of psychoactive pharmaceutical drugs for illicit use are four notable examples of the kinds of changes in drug use that have followed in the wake of the 1960s transition. Once firmly established during the mid- to late-1960s as meeting various social needs (e.g., palliation of oppressive conditions among the poor, relief from work drudgery and limited options among the working classes, escape from monotony and convention among young people of all social classes), illicit drug use has remained a significant if constantly evolving feature of U.S. social life ever since.

In recent years, the term *structural violence* has been used to label the negative impact of power on health (Farmer 1999). Structural violence refers to "large-scale forces—ranging from gender inequality and racism to poverty—which structure unequal access to goods and services" (Farmer, Connors and Simmons 1996:369). These domineering forces bring into being the social, emotional, and physical conditions that promote emergent drug use practices. From the CMA perspective, drug use is understood, in part, as "the epiphenomenonal expression of deeper, structural dilemmas" (Bourgois 1995:319). These dilemmas, experienced in different ways in different social sectors and classes, have common taproots in a restructuring global political economy.

One effect of this restructuring is the loss of many traditional pathways to dignified employment among inner-city populations, with many jobs moving out of the country to foreign shores—while distributional inequality has opened a widening and more experientially painful chasm between the top and bottom of the U.S. economic pyramid. Class disparities, and the power inequalities that support them, are further enhanced and maintained through racial and gender discrimination, creating the opening for "multiple subordination" (Friedman et al. 1998) and the resulting appeal of chemical "solutions" to the painful experiences of alienation, anger, and hopelessness.

Like physical violence (which it can unleash), structural violence directly causes much human pain and suffering. While experienced individually, structural violence targets classes of people and subjects them to common forms of lived oppression. Hence the experience of structural violence has been called "social suffering" (Bourgois, Lettiere, and Quesada 1997). Some social suffering is overt and finds expression in countless indicators of health, mental health, nutrition, and health-care inequality. For example, there is a condition we have referred to in our work at the Hispanic Health Council as "oppression illness" (Baer, Singer, and Susser 2004), which we define as a traumatic stress disorder produced by the combined effects of being subject over time to intense social opprobrium (e.g., in the form of racial hatred, sexism, class discrimination, homophobia) and the internalization of this reproach in the form of depression, self-hatred, and a sense of powerlessness. Other forms of social misery are less visible and consist of daily, structurally imposed insults, indignities, and emotional injuries stemming from the experience of status inequalities. These psychological wounds, which, borrowing from Richard Sennett and Jonathan Cobb (1973), are referred to in critical medical anthropology as "hidden injuries of oppression," include both repeated exposure to disrespect (across class, race/ethnicity, sexual identity, and gender lines) and the enduring frustrations of prolonged social failure in the U.S. culture of personal achievement. For example, each time persons of color walk into a store and feel that they are being unduly scrutinized by white store employees, the resulting feeling of indignity is a hidden injury of oppression. For the inner-city poor such experiences, in varied form and social location, are a recurrent component of everyday oppression.

In short, there are a number of interacting structural factors that play a significant role in creating social conditions that are conducive to the emergence and spread of new drug use practices in different social sectors. However, structural factors do not act alone in shaping drug use dynamics. Several other factors also are critical.

Social Factors

Drug user peer social networks are also an important factor in drug use dynamics. For example, with reference to the development and spread of injection drug use in working-class neighborhoods of Madrid, Spain, Juan Gamella (1994:1399) notes that the transmission of injection knowledge tends to flow within "groups of equals, in a climate of trust, emulation, and peer influence." Social suffering, because of its shared nature, helps to produce the kinds of common experiences of marginalization, alienation, and resistance and associated social bonds of shared experience that act as the conveyor belts of drug injection technical knowledge and encouragement. Increasingly, drug researchers have turned their attention to social networks among drug users, realizing that drug users do not exist or operate as social isolates but, rather, maintain important webs of emotional, sexual, economic, and defensive social connection with other drug users and with nonusers as well (Dei 2002). Importantly, as Gamella suggests, social networks appear to play pivotal roles in diffusing new drug use information and practices.

Gamella's observation is consistent with the literature on peer influence on behavior. Summarizing seventy-five years of adolescent research, Dana Haynie (2001:1014) succinctly notes, "adolescents are likely to behave in a manner consistent with their friends." She goes on to raise questions about the relative influence of different kinds of peer social networks, asking, for example, whether close-knit friendship networks have greater influence on adolescent behavior than less cohesive friendship networks. Haynie answers this question in the affirmative; existing research indicates that network density—the number of actual one-to-one personal ties found in a group of people divided by the number of possible ties in the group—is an important influence on peer behavior, including drug use behavior. Simply put, network characteristics influence drug use dynamics.

Moreover, as will be elaborated on later, there are a number of specific roles within social networks that are particularly important in emergent drug use. Individuals who fill these roles first gain an entrée to new drugs (e.g., by discovering them in some fashion) and then spread information about them (as well as samples of them) to widening circles of social network connections.

Cultural Factors

Unpacking U.S. cultural values, and ethnic or class-based versions or subgroup variations of these values, relative to drug use, is a vital step in explaining drug use dynamics in U.S. society. Notably, the concept of culture, which traditionally has been the hallmark of the anthropological approach to social and behavioral research, has become hotly contested of late. While anthropologists never achieved a single, universally accepted definition of culture, it has commonly been understood to mean an enduring set of beliefs, values, and way of life shared among a group of people that is handed down from generation to generation. With reference to drug use, Goode (1984:9–10) points out the role of culture:

> Social groups and cultures define what kind of drug-taking is appropriate. They define which drugs are acceptable and which are not. They define who takes drugs and why. They decide what amounts of each drug are socially acceptable. They spell out which social institutions are approved for drug use and which are not. They define what drugs do, what their actions and effects upon people will be.

This traditional understanding of culture—while a significant improvement over simply ignoring the cultural influence on human behavior—has come to be seen as highly problematic. The primary shortcomings of traditional notions of culture are two: (1) they essentialize and reify culture (i.e., make it seem as if cultures rather than people are the actors in human social drama) while freezing human social processes, including those concerned with self-definition; and (2) they create and maintain false differences among peoples.

The first of these points is that actual observation of human social life reveals that culture is a lived process rather than a static, homogenizing code; cultural elements may be handed down from one generation to the next, but rarely in unchanged form, intensity, or set of meanings. In other words, culture is not a prison that forces people to conform to a set routines; rather, it is a resource people use creatively to confront challenges and exploit opportunities. Certainly behaviors may be prescribed, but this practice never reveals what people actually do "in the moment," nor does it tell us much about how people select a course of action, make specific decisions, operationalize their plans, or respond to contingency. In the case of drug use dynamics, it would be hard to account for changes in drug use (e.g., the appearance and diffusion of a new drug) if the culture of drug users narrowly determined and limited innovative behaviors.

There are alternative approaches however. As Lila Abu-Lughod (1991:53) points out:

> Anthropologists commonly generalize about communities by saying that they are characterized by certain institutions, rules or ways of doing things. For example, we can and often do say things like "The Bongo-Bongo are polygamous." Yet one could refuse to generalize in this way, instead asking how a particular set of individuals . . . live the "institution" that we call polygamy.

By adhering to the approach proposed by Abu-Lughod, accounts of culture move from generalized statements of what culture is to processual and particular accounts of how a culture is manifest in specific instances. Adds Abu-Lughod (1991:154), "By focusing closely on particular individuals and their changing relationships, one would necessarily subvert the problematic connotations of culture: homogeneity, coherence, and timeless."

The second problem is that the culture concept often is used to freeze differences between groups of people rather than to see overriding processes and intertwined histories. For example, descriptions of an emergent drug use pattern solely in terms of local culture imagines that cultures are isolated local phenomena. In Eric Wolf's (1982:114) words, they "assume the autonomy and boundedness" of local social groups rather than "take cognizance of processes [like colonialism, class structure, labor markets, advertising, the mass media] that transcend separate cases." Rather than use the culture concept to show how group "X" is different from group "Y," critics of fixed notions of culture have urged that we pay closer attention to "studying the relationships between whatever unit one undertakes to study and the larger social and cultural universe within which it operates" (Ortner 1991:186). This is, however, no easy task. As Philippe Bourgois (1995:17) noted in his study of crack dealers in Spanish Harlem, "Structures of power and history cannot be touched or talked to. . . . Embroiled in what seemed like a whirlpool of suffering during my ethnographic research, it was often hard for me to see the larger relationships structuring the jumble of human interaction all around me." Despite the challenges, attempting to understand how particular beliefs and practices, including lack of emergent ideas and behaviors, fit into a much broader structure of relationships that reaches far beyond what is immediately observable "on the ground" allows us to see historic connections in human behavior across time, place, and peoples.

Examination of illicit drug users in this book does not start with the assumption that they necessarily embrace cultural values that are radically distinct from those of non-drug users. In an action-oriented culture, like that found in the United States, which forcefully and publicly promotes the value of individualism, the need for instant gratification, pain intolerance, and the benevolence of chemical intervention, drug use (legal or illicit) is a commonly selected solution to life's burdens, stresses, and abuse across social groupings. As Stuart Hills (1980:118) observes:

> Physicians and the pharmacological industry have combined to hold out the promise of putting an end to personal distress through chemistry. Drug manufacturers seeking new markets and bigger profits urge everyone to feel better fast ("relief is only a swallow away"), and attempt to persuade physicians and the public that *unpleasant human feelings are abnormal*—an "illness" that should be corrected with drugs.

Selection of a chemical solution to a discomforting experience—whether that experience be the misery of domestic violence, the assault on one's dignity borne of prolonged unemployment, the internalized rage of injustice and racial discrimination, or the bland boredom of teen life in suburbia—is promoted by the ready availability of a changing array of powerful mood-altering drugs in many locations, legal and illicit. Therefore, the key question is not why do people use drugs but who uses which drugs for what purpose; when; with whom; how; and with what experiential, social, and health effects? For example, for many inner-city youth and young adults the "American dream" cannot be achieved through a prestigious job, material comfort, or social recognition in mainstream society; all of these are unavailable to most of them. By contrast, drugs and the kind of "dreams" they offer are highly available, continually alluring, and known on the street to be effective.

Illustratively, the crack users/dealers studied by Bourgois (1995:141) entered their teen years with hopes of the solid working-class lifestyle that once could be gained "working an eight-hour shift plus overtime," only to "find themselves propelled headlong into an explosive confrontation between their sense of cultural dignity versus the humiliating interpersonal subordination of service work." Like the alcohol and marijuana-using street corner men of an earlier generation described by Elliot Liebow (1967), they find it is hard to derive any dignity from low-level, dead-end, menial jobs that neither the employer nor society at-large much values or invests with much dignity. Deciding to use the newest psychoactive substance to hit the streets, even though it may already have been outlawed, may not be a sign of social deviance or of the existence of a distinctive subculture. Rather, it may be the expression of generally approved mainstream values operationalized under a given set of harsh social circumstances (i.e., poverty, social discrimination, lack of access to socially valued resources). This behavior "appears not so much as a way of realizing the distinctive values of [a drug] subculture, or of conforming to its models, but rather as [a] way of trying to achieve many of the goals and values of the larger society, of failing to do this, and of concealing [this] failure from others and from [oneself]" (Liebow 1967:222) in the culturally approved strategy for managing painful feelings—that is, by taking drugs.

Biological Factors

We already have mentioned the role of biological factors in discussing both the "brain disease model" and the health consequences of drug use dynamics. Obviously diseases are biological in nature. However, they are not *only* biological and are not best reduced—as is generally the practice in medical care—to their biological features. Consider the spread of HIV/AIDS. Drug users on the north end of Hartford have been found in our studies to be less likely to be drug injectors. Even among those who are injectors, they tend to inject drugs less frequently than drug users on the south end of the city. Yet north-end drug users have much higher rates of HIV infection. At first, this seems puzzling in light of the fact that multiperson use of syringes has been verified in many studies as a primary factor in the spread of HIV.

Although there remain those who dispute it, it is now fully established that AIDS is a consequence of bodily invasion and immunosystem destruction by a specific pathogen, the Human Immunodeficiency Virus. The same is true of other STDs like syphilis, in which a specific, known pathogen (a bacterium called *Treponema pallidum*) is the immediate cause. Moreover, it is known that syphilis leads to the development of lesions on the body's mucus membranes, which, in cases of coinfection with both HIV and syphilis, create opportunities for easier interpersonal transmission of HIV. Thus, bioassays of syphilitic lesions in coinfected individuals have revealed high concentrations of HIV available for transmission. Notably, the north end of Hartford has emerged as an epicenter of syphilis infection in the city. Thus, it is likely that the higher rate of HIV among drug users on the north end is a consequence of sexual transmission associated with the spread of syphilis. Linking the spread of HIV to the spread of syphilis reveals the biological factors underlying the higher rates of HIV among drug users on the north end of Hartford compared to their counterparts on the south end. However, left unexplained in this account is why syphilis has become a much more significant health problem on one end of town than on the other.

One of the important differences in the general pattern of drug use on north and south ends of the city is the frequency of use of crack cocaine, with crack users tending to be found on the north end. The rapid spread of syphilis in Hartford in recent years, in other words, appears to be a consequence of sex-for-drugs commercial exchanges tied especially to the introduction of crack. The spread of crack on the north end of Hartford—a socially depressed area that is predominantly African American—is, as Bourgois (1995:2) stresses, "a symptom . . . of deeper dynamics of social marginalization and alienation." In other words, while the spread of AIDS must be understood in terms of biological factors, it is only through examination of the complex, multistranded interplay of biology and sociocultural factors, including patterns of social inequality, that we can fully account for the AIDS epidemic (issues we shall return to in chapter 9).

Conclusion

In sum, it is the perspective of Critical Medical Anthropology and of this book that analysis of drug use trends and dynamics, including the spread of new drugs or drug use practices, requires a holistic approach that integrates analyses of structural, social, cultural, and biological factors into a single model. In this book, the focus is not on applying this model to this or that specific drug epidemic, but rather to the entire history of changing drug use trends in U.S. society.

The next three chapters examine the history of changing drug use in the United States in order to identify the primary features and causes of drug use dynamics in this society. Specifically, within the framework introduced in this chapter, chapters 2, 3, and 4 provide a detailed and socially contextualized chronology of key moments and processes in U.S. drug use. The arrival of Europeans in the New World in the fifteenth century to the beginning of the twenty-first century was a 500-year period that witnessed vast social changes, including the ways drugs were viewed and used, and their role as a source of health and social problems.

CHAPTER 2

The Colonial Era to Drug Criminalization

Not poppy, nor mandragore,
Nor all the drowsy syrups of the world
Shall ever medicine thee to that sweet sleep
Which though ow'dst yesterday

—William Shakespeare, *Othello*

Forgotten Drug Histories

There is a tendency to think of psychoactive drug use and drug-related problems as a modern phenomenon, a symptom of the impersonal, insensitive, and often jagged world that we come to know as much from images flashed on a TV screen or computer monitor as from our own personal experiences. Perhaps this is so, in part, because when we are taught the history of this country, drugs rarely, if ever, are included as part of the story. Alcohol finds mention at certain points, including the colonial rum trade and certainly because of Prohibition and its violation, but illicit drugs tend to be written out of history and treated as an embarrassing footnote unworthy of attention. In fact, however, a fairer account, one open to showing the darker sides of our collectivity that both scare and allure us, would reveal that drugs have played a distinct and not insignificant part in shaping U.S. history and the lives of people famous, infamous, and obscure throughout our over 400 years as a social formation within the modern world system. This and the two chapters that follow trace the changing kaleidoscope of psychoactive drug use back into American history, with the late nineteenth- and early twentieth-century transition from the era of legal to illegal drug use serving to bound this chapter from the next two.

U.S. history commonly is presented as beginning with Columbus' first voyage from the Old to the New World. This "world-turning" venture began

35

the comparatively swift process of tying the Eastern and Western hemispheres (as well as the Northern and Southern ones) together as a single world unit, creating thereafter an ultimately intertwined, multistranded global history and setting into motion the emergence of an evermore integrated international economy, a world-binding communication system, and the rapid flow across porous boundaries of peoples, ideas, goods, and diseases. If, as anthropologists tell us, humans as a species are five or more million years old, the time since the *Nina*, the *Pinta*, and the *Santa Maria* first set sail westward on August 3, 1492, from Palos, a small port city on the southwestern coast of Spain, is little more than the last second on the time clock of humanity.

While the general outcome of Columbus' journey is well known, what rarely is mentioned is that opium "was one of the products Columbus hoped to bring back" to Europe (Scott 1969:11). Also, rarely mentioned are the actual drugs Columbus encountered in the place that, because of his misunderstanding of where his caravel sailing ships had actually taken him, came to be called the West Indies. Nor do we often learn much historically about the powerful and highly dangerous drug Columbus brought back with him on his return voyages to Europe. In short, both the role of drugs in sparking Columbus' voyages and his role in subsequent European and U.S. drug use dynamics are not commonly included in the teaching of Columbus in the U.S. school system.

Also given short shrift in everyday public school pedagogy is the role of psychoactive drugs in the far-flung voyages of other explorers who, during the Age of Exploration, set sail from Europe and traveled to the far points of the globe. While, prior to this period, Europe was a region notably limited in its array of popularly used psychoactive substances, a group of intrepid adventurers quickly filled the continent's understocked pharmacological cupboard with a wide array of colonial products containing psychoactive properties. Wherever they found them, the explorers collected and carried back to Europe a diverse menu of drugs, including caffeine, tobacco, cocaine, opium, and hallucinogens, thereby sparking the first waves of emergent drug use in the comparatively virgin populations of Europe and, subsequently, colonial America, a process that continued through various crazes and trends up to the present. In retrospect, it is clear these drugs had a profound impact on the course of world events over the last 500 years.

Drug Voyages: Columbus and the Other Conquerors

The date of opium's original emergence as a drug used by humans is lost to us. Without doubt, it was early in human history, as Neolithic archeological sites containing opium-bearing poppy pods dating to the fourth millennium BC have been found in Switzerland. Opium poppy cultivation was carried out along the Tigris-Euphrates by the Sumerians—who called it *hul gil* (joy plant)—in 3400 BC. Given how much has been written about opium ever since, it is noteworthy that the Sumerians can be credited with giving the world both writing and the opiates (Booth 1996). In time, opium was known in many parts of Asia, and it was from Asia that Europeans first learned of the drug. When the Moors invaded Spain in 711, they brought opium with them. At the time, opium was culturally defined as a medicine. Indeed, it was seen as a very powerful and effective medicine and was highly desired as such. Consequently, when the Christians drove the Moors out of Spain—which occurred just before the Spanish royalty agreed to finance Columbus' voyage—they had just lost their supply of opium. By then, the Portuguese had invented the caravel, a ship sturdy enough to sail against the wind, and hoped to use it to reach Asia and its "riches" by sailing around Africa. The "riches" of concern were gold, silk, gems, and spices. The latter, which included cloves, nutmeg, mace, and opium, were valued as both medicines and as seasonings (except opium which, unlike the others, was not defined as a flavoring). In short, the Spanish wanted Moslem goods without the Moslems. Thus, in April 1492 when Columbus' bold plan suddenly received royal Spanish approval, opium was one of the commodities he was instructed to bring back with him.

Of course, Columbus did not find opium in the New World, as poppies are not indigenous to the region (although, over 500 years since the famous voyage, they are now grown in the New World in great quantities, to the chagrin of both Asian competitors and U.S. antidrug warriors). Columbus and his crew did find other psychoactive drugs in use among the peoples of the New World. Some of what Columbus found is known because of the careful records he and his crew maintained on New World geography, peoples, customs, and artifacts. The man Columbus specifically assigned to record information about the New World peoples they encountered upon their landing in the "Indies" was Friar Ramon Pane (Feldman and Aldrich 1990). Based on conversations with Taino Indians on the Caribbean island of Hispaniola (which today is parceled between the countries of Haiti and the Dominican Republic), Pane described Taino experience with a drug they called *cohoba*, which is now known to be an hallucinogenic extract (containing dimethyltryptamine and bufotenine) from the bean of the tree *Anadenanthera peregrina*. Additionally, as Richard Rudgley (1993:166) remarks, "When Columbus landed on the north coast of Cuba on 5 November 1492 he was not only discovering a New World for Europe but also a highly addictive stimulant—tobacco." Among the first Europeans to witness tobacco smoking, Pane presents a description of daily tobacco use among the Taino, a drug men and women smoked in huge cigars to comfort the limbs, enhance wakefulness, and lessen weariness.

In the period after Columbus, other explorers and European invaders (and their fellow travelers) observed other drugs new to European experience that were in common use among indigenous populations subject to colonial penetration. Amerigo Vespucci first described coca chewing in South America at the turn of the sixteenth century, beginning the multilayered history of cocaine as a substance repeatedly reintroduced in differing forms to new populations with varying expectations. When Hernando Cortés landed in Mexico in 1519, he and his crew encountered cacao. Used as a drink in the New World, cacao—the source of chocolate—contains theobromine, a chemical compound that has effects similar to caffeine. Drug use among the Aztecs, which was observed and recorded by a number of Spanish colonialists and clerics, included several substances such as Jimsonweed (*Datura meteloides*), which notably did not find a European or colonial American following, and peyote, which did, but not until later. Like Columbus, other explorers, including John Cabot (England) and Ferdinand Magellan and Vasco da Gama (Portugal), were specifically requested to seek out sources of opium by their respective colonial sponsors. Successfully navigating an ocean route around the horn of Africa, da Gama fulfilled this request, as he linked Portugal with opium producers in India and allowed his homeland to take the lead in importing this as well as various other desired spices and mendicants from the East.

First Waves: The Impact of Tobacco on Europe and the New World

Columbus' first return voyage from the Americas to Europe proved to be particularly harrowing. Some of the Taino people he brought back with him to parade before his royal benefactors died en route. After sailing for a month, the *Nina* and the *Pinta* were separated in a terrifying storm. The *Nina*, which Columbus captained, finally struck land on the Portuguese island of Santa Maria in the Azores. Assuming they had been trading illegally in Africa, the governor of the island was intent on arresting Columbus and his crew. Allowed at last to set sail once more, Columbus then ran into more stormy weather forcing him to seek safe harbor in Lisbon. Finally, on March 15, 1493, Columbus sailed into his home port at Palos, Spain. He reported directly to Ferdinand and Isabella in Barcelona, where he was celebrated with a royal reception. Columbus knew only too well that, except for his vivid stories of a world heretofore beyond European imagination, he had little to show for his seven months of New World exploration. He brought back a few gold ornaments, as well as those wearied Tainos who survived the cruel ocean voyage, and in addition, he displayed some dried, yellowish, peculiarly aromatic leaves of an unfamiliar plant that he said the Indians called *tabaco*.

Tobacco, of course, came to have a massive impact on Europe and ultimately on the whole world, including the United States. Columbus introduced tobacco as a medicinal drug, and it was at first cultivated in Europe for this purpose. European physicians of the sixteenth century became convinced that tobacco could be used to cure a wide assortment of diseases. Before long, however, people who were treated with tobacco, and probably their physicians as well, realized that it was a powerful mood-altering drug that had recreational value. By 1600, smoking was a common practice of working people in the port cities of England and Ireland (Brooks 1952).

As tobacco shifted from being primarily a medicine to an emergent mood-altering drug among the poor and working-classes of Europe, a backlash against its use was unleashed by the dominant social classes and the church. Sidney Mintz (1985:100), an anthropologist who has studied the consumable commodities brought to Europe as colonial trade, suggests that the reason for this hostile response lay in the distinct "visible, directly noticeable" physical reaction that smoking produces, especially for the new user. These changes in comportment in working people, he points out, were threatening to the wealthier classes, who preferred a more passive, servile, and controlled demeanor in the social strata they dominated. Thus, critics began to taint smoking as a lower-class habit, "of ryotous and disordered Persons of meane and base Condition" (Best 1983:175). Additionally, argues Mintz, unlike tobacco, tea, coffee, and rum, all of which are dark in color and all of which upon their introduction provoked opposition from powers that be in Europe, refined sugar, which is white, the symbolic color of purity, was warmly received. Racialist symbolism of this sort (involving mood-altering products that come from foreign lands with threatening, dark-skinned peoples), may have been an underlying cultural influence on the moralistic opposition to tobacco as well as to tea, coffee, and rum.

In a concerted attempt to build a moral argument against smoking, King James of England enacted a set of policies designed to restrict tobacco consumption, while other European countries enforced criminal penalties to punish smokers. Usually the punishment involved having to pay a small fine. Despite these efforts, illicit use of tobacco continued to be popular, and in the end, both government and moralist efforts to limit or prohibit smoking collapsed. By the end of the seventeenth century, the drug was legal throughout Europe. Underlying this radical shift was a reevaluation of smoking. What had been defined as a growing social problem came to be seen as an important source of tax revenue for an expanding state structure. In the English case, colonization of North America played an important role in this process.

To launch the British colony in Virginia, King James invested considerable sums of money. The objective was to reap the same kinds of benefits that Spain had in its greedy plundering of the mineral resources of Mexico, the Caribbean, and South America. However, while Spain extracted over seven million pounds of silver from its New World colonies between 1503 and 1660 (Wolf 1982), in Virginia no precious metals were found in any quantity, nor was the colony able to find other extractable sources of exportable wealth. Nonetheless, the colonists did find one item they could produce successfully and send to England in large quantities—tobacco.

The soil of Virginia proved to be a good medium for tobacco growth; dried tobacco was lightweight and therefore could be shipped across the ocean at comparatively low cost; the demand for it in England meant that it would bring a sale price far above production costs. Consequently, from an initial export of 2,500 pounds shipped to England in 1616, within fifteen years Virginia was exporting over 1.5 million pounds of tobacco, and by the end of the century this jumped to 30 million pounds (Price 1964). Tobacco, in short, became one of North America's first cash crops. Were it not for tobacco profits, it is likely that the British colonies, much like Jamestown, would have failed and Spanish would be the primary language of almost all the Americas.

The British, in turn, aggressively exported tobacco to other countries in Europe, further empowering Britain as a world power. Paradoxically, and as an indication of the impact of tobacco on world history, while the British helped to open the French market to tobacco, during the Revolutionary War against England Thomas Jefferson and Benjamin Franklin put up American tobacco as collateral for French war loans to fight and defeat the British.

Through these processes of social, political, economic, and cultural change, tobacco was transformed from an illegal and widely condemned drug into a legal and economically important force throughout Europe. It became a source of revenue that helped to fund the transformation from feudalist to capitalist production. Tobacco, in short, gained wide acceptance because of the role it eventually played as a commodity critical to the emergence of the global economy. Additionally, as Mintz (1985) points out, tobacco, like other colonial psychoactive substances such as coffee and tea, was among the "drug foods" that served as low-cost food substitutes for the laboring classes of Europe during the rise of colonialism and the subsequent rise of the capitalist mode of production. Increasing "the worker's energy output and productivity, such substitutes figured importantly in balancing the accounts of capitalism" (Mintz 1985:148) by lowering the cost of supporting a manual labor force while increasing production. As a result, while languages, customs, ideologies, and values differed sharply from nation to nation around the globe, almost all came to adopt a common cultural element, the secular smoking of the psychoactive leaves of the tobacco plant.

In colonial America, the impact of tobacco was immeasurable. In an era when peoples were defined (by those with the military and economic power to do so) in terms of a hierarchy that put whites at the top as civilized and Africans at the bottom as barbarian, it was tobacco production that sparked the demand in North America for slave labor. As Thomas Scharf (1967) stresses, in colonial America all the practices of government, society, and domestic life began and ended with tobacco. With gold and silver scarce on the eastern seaboard of North America, tobacco leaves served as money in colonial transactions, and colonists even paid their taxes in tobacco currency.

Of course, colonists also smoked tobacco, often in small-bowled clay pipes with long stems, the broken pieces of which can still be dug up in long-buried colonial garbage dumps. Snuff was another method of consumption. Then in the early nineteenth century, chewing tobacco, or "chaw," as it was known, and regularly spitting out tobacco-colored saliva, emerged and became popular practice, one that helped to confirm to Europeans their view of Americans as lowly in their habits and as lacking sophistication. By mid-century, yet another consumption strategy, the cigarette, was introduced and rapidly caught on. Although by the early 1790s tobacco ceased to be the most valuable item of export from the colonies, production continued to grow. By 1860, the United States was producing more than twice as much tobacco as it had in 1775, but by then the primary market was domestic and increasingly thereafter cigarettes were the primary mode of consumption, with cigars, snuffs, and chewing tobaccos fading in and out of popularity as is the common pattern for established psychoactive substances.

The Other Colonial Drugs

The term "drug" is used widely to refer to illicit consumable substances, although this was not always the case. Prior to the First World War, before the United States and other countries began defining some substances as problems, the term generally was not linked with the notion of illicit consumption, nor was it tied to the concepts of "abuse" and "addiction." In fact, in the original edition of the *Oxford English Dictionary* (published in 1897), the noun "drug" was defined as a "simple medicinal substance" without any reference to narcotics. In fact, after the First World War, pharmacists in the United States (who in time stopped calling themselves "druggists" to disassociate their work from illicit drug consumption) launched a struggle to convince newspapers not to use the term "drugs" to refer to nonmedicinal substances used without prescription because of their psychoactive effects. They failed, and thus we inherit a term whose meaning has changed to label a set of substances, methods of using them, and populations of users that are themselves in constant flux. The term "drug," of course, still adheres to pharmaceuticals sold for their medicinal value, further complicating the linguistics of consumption while presaging the later street diversion of some types of pharmaceutical products (e.g., painkillers, tranquilizers) because of their psychotropic properties.

In the early years of U.S. history, three psychoactive drugs that were later to be outlawed—the opiates, marijuana, and cocaine—were common items of legal, everyday trade and consumption (alcohol too, the drinking of which was particularly intense during the colonial period and has been a mainstay of altering consciousness in North America ever since, had its own brief period of legal sanction, but compared to the drugs discussed below this was rather fleeting). Each of these, the trilogy of contemporary illicit American drug use, will be examined in turn in their respective sociohistoric and cultural contexts. Later chapters will focus on methamphetamines and illicit pharmaceuticals, emergent contenders for inclusion in an expanded menu of the most widely used illicit drugs in North America.

Opium

Although Columbus could find no opium in the Americas, whether one is in Columbus, Ohio, or in our nation's capital, the District of Columbia, today opiate drugs are not hard to find in America. It is as easy to buy heroin, a derivative of the opium produced by the Oriental poppy plant (*Papaver somniferum*)—specifically from the white sap that forms in the large bulb between the stem and the flower—on the streets of America as it is to buy sunglasses and music CDs, and for about the same price. The origin of opiate use in the United States is not completely clear, but it certainly occurred during the colonial period. The earliest English-language account of opium use was written during the colonial era by Thomas De Quincey. Having first taken opium to relieve a prolonged headache, De Quincey (1822:3) went on to use it for ten years "for the sake of creating an artificial state of pleasure." In fact, it would not be incorrect to say that the United States came into existence with opium use as a normal part of everyday life for many of its citizens. Critical to its introduction was the work of one of the best-known British doctors of the seventeenth century, a man named Thomas Sydenham.

Regarded as the founder of clinical medicine, Sydenham advocated the use of opium, primarily in the form of a tincture composed of the drug dissolved in wine (called laudanum), which was the most common way opium was used as a medicinal well into the nineteenth century. Opium, in Sydenham's view, was "one of the most valued medicines in the world [which] does more honor to medicine than any remedy whatsoever" (Musto 1987:69). Without opium, he maintained, "the healing arts would cease to exist" (Scott 1969:114).

Sydenham, of course, was not the first man of medicine to praise the ability of opium to produce feelings of contentment while numbing pain. Knowledge of these properties of poppy sap dates to at least 1,500 years ago in India and very likely well before that. A naturally occurring substance that, unlike even alcohol, requires no further processing after extraction, opium may be humankind's oldest drug.

Early in his career, Thomas Dover, a student of Sydenham, developed a form of opium known as Dover's Powder, which was in use until World War II. Developed

Harvesting raw opium. Courtesy of Drug Enforcement Administration.

as a treatment for gout, it contained equal parts of opium, ipecac, licorice, and lesser amounts of saltpeter, tartar, and wine. Dover put his product on the market for over-the-counter sale to the public in 1709. Interestingly, this was the same year that Dover, an enthusiastic adventurer, captained a ship that rescued the castaway Alexander Selkirk from the secluded Juan Fernandez Islands off the coast of Chile, an event that inspired Daniel Defoe's famous book *Robinson Crusoe*. Dover's Powder was shipped from London to the British colonies and became the most widely used opiate preparation in the New World for many decades. Its long-lasting popularity resulted in its specific mention under the general listing for "powder" in *Webster's Dictionary*.

Its considerable popularity notwithstanding, Dover's Powder was not without many competitors. Introduction of the drug, in fact, helped to launch the patent medicine business in the New World. By the end of the eighteenth century, patent medicines (which actually lacked any legal patents whatsoever) heavily dosed with opium were readily available and widely used. They could be purchased in pharmacies, from food venders, in general stores, at printers' offices, or through the mail, and were peddled by traveling medicine shows that crisscrossed the countryside visiting smaller towns and distant villages. These purported medicines were marketed directly to the public under a host of personalized labels, such as Ayer's Cherry Pectoral, Mrs. Winslow's Soothing Syrup, Dr. J. Collis Brownse's Chlorodyne, McMunn's Elixir, Godfrey's Cordial, Hooper's Anodyne, the Infant's Friend, Scott's Emulsion, and of course, Dover's Powder, labels reflecting a period before mass industrial capitalism depersonalized the relationship between products and their producers.

Opium potions were said to be nature's cure for a multitude of health concerns, including body pain, cough, nervousness, TB, diarrhea, dysentery, cholera, athlete's foot, baldness, and cancer. Some were marketed as "women's friends," drugs said to be effective in calming agitated women who were seen by many physicians during this era as emotionally unstable because of the deleterious effects of possessing a uterus. Others were advertised as soothing syrups for cranky babies suffering from colic. Until the Revolutionary War, most patent medicines sold in the American colonies were shipped from England, very likely arriving back aboard the same ships that had transported colonial tobacco to England.

After the war, American entrepreneurs launched their own opium-laced patent medicines. The emergence of the home-grown patent medicine industry was closely tied to the expansion of the American newspaper enterprise. Medicinal manufacturers were among the first to seek a national market for their products through advertising in newspapers. Developing a practice that has endured since, these companies used psychological lures to entice customers to buy their opium-based wares. By the latter part of the 1800s, some patent medicine manufacturers were spending hundreds of thousands of dollars on advertising. For example, Hamlins Wizard Oil Company of Chicago

Opium powder sold legally in the early twentieth century. Courtesy of Drug Enforcement Administration.

aggressively advertised its opium-infused oil as "the Great Medical Wonder—There is no sore it will not heal, no pain it will not subdue" (Inciardi 1986:5), while the makers of Scott's Emulsion were spending over $1 million a year on similar marketing efforts by the 1890s.

While patent medicines were widely used, the public did not have any clear idea what they were consuming (a pattern that continues today in the illicit drug market), but a study done in Boston in 1888 of the contents of prescriptions purchased from several pharmacies found that of the 10,200 prescriptions filled that year, 15 percent contained opiates and that opiate-based proprietary drugs had the highest sales (Eaton 1888). The end result was that during the 1800s, opium use was widespread in the United States; for the most part it was treated as a "normal" behavior that was both legal and integrated into everyday life. People of all walks of life became addicted. For example, Benjamin Franklin was a user and "was almost certainly addicted to opium in his declining years," as were other colonial leaders (Booth 1996:30). Other historically renowned Americans of the era were definitely opium users and possibly addicts. Edgar Allen Poe was an opium user. In one of his many emotional downturns Poe even swallowed a large quantity of laudanum in hopes of ending his life, but in this as in many of his literary endeavors, he failed (only to be honored posthumously as the greatest American poet). In fact, literary references to opium were not uncommon during this period. Even Dorothy in chapter 8 of the original *The Wonderful Wizard of Oz* novel (Baum 1990) falls for a time into a sleepy opium haze after wandering through a field of poppy flowers.

Addiction, in fact, was common during this period but was not defined as a health problem nor as a social ill; rather, it was "accepted as the price one paid for the relief of pain" (Booth 1996:30). The drug's popularity was not limited to the wealthy and well-known, as "there were many hundreds of thousands of common folk for whom opium was the only way out of the drudgery of a harsh life" (Booth 1996:49). Importantly, addiction was not recognized as such, since opium was readily available and easily acquired (and addicts could

Raw opium. Courtesy of Drug Enforcement Administration.

treat their withdrawal symptoms through continued drug consumption). Certainly users were not labeled criminals or treated as social deviants.

Not all opium use was seen as acceptable, however. As America stretched ever westward, becoming eventually a country that spanned from the Atlantic to the Pacific, a complex nation filled with diverse ethnic groups of far-flung origins, and a society grown increasingly tense with conflicted interests of differentially enriched and empowered social classes, acceptable and unacceptable drug use dynamics began to appear. Perhaps the earliest sign of the coming politicalization of drug use was the social attack on so-called opium dens that generally were located in the segregated Chinese sections of western cities, although frequented by Chinese and non-Chinese clients alike. Thus, the first antiopium law in the nation was passed in San Francisco in 1875, home to a large Chinese population. Smoking opium was labeled deviant and debilitating, but the real issue appears to have been anti-Asian racism. The primary concern was not drug use *per se* but rather *who* was using and *who* was profiting from the sale of the drugs. For example, in an Oregon court case involving the arrest and conviction of a Chinese man for opium sales, a legal review of the case concluded, "Smoking opium is not our vice, and therefore, it may be that this legislation proceeds more from a desire to vex and annoy the 'Heathen Chinese' in this respect, than to protect the people from the evil habit" (Bonnie and Whitebread 1970:997).

From this moment on, U.S. societal reactions to drug use and attitudes about particular racial/ethnic groups have been closely intertwined. Moreover, drug use, the emergence of new drug practices, and changes in drug use behaviors took a significant conceptual turn and before long came to be defined as problematic and of keen societal concern. Importantly, these two phenomena were closely connected: drug use dynamics became culturally constructed as a major social problem in American society in no small part because of who was using drugs rather than what drugs they were using or how severe the resulting health consequences were.

In the case of Chinese opium smoking, a major underlying factor motivating social condemnation was the economic depression that began in the 1860s and the resulting social redefinition of the Chinese as unwanted surplus labor. Originally, the Chinese were recruited to the United States to build the national railroad system that linked the eastern and western halves of the nation and to work the mines that were helping to pay for American nation building. Willing to perform types of labor that were unappealing to many American-born workers, the Chinese later became scapegoats of working-class frustration as the economy collapsed and people were pushed into unemployment. This example reveals an important aspect of U.S. experience with illicit drugs that is often hidden. As John Helmer asserts, "the conflict over social justice is what the story of narcotics in America is about" (1983:27).

Meanwhile, the place of opium use in American society had undergone a critical transition beginning in 1803 with the discovery of morphine. The discoverer was Frederick Serturner, a 23-year-old German pharmacist's assistant. Serturner, who, despite a lack of scientific training, successfully isolated the chief alkaloid of opium, a substance he named morphine, after Morpheus, the Greek god of sleep. Ten times more potent than raw opium, morphine was quickly put to work as a painkiller; morphine, in fact, remains one of the strongest chemical pain relievers available. Also given its considerable impact on the human body, one of its potential health effects was quickly realized: morphine could be used to commit suicide painlessly. As word of this property spread, the drug was adopted by a large number of people who wished to end their lives.

Morphine's painkilling capacity really gained attention during the American Civil War, a massively bloody conflict that threatened to overwhelm the capacity of the mid-nineteenth-century biomedical system. Physicians turned to morphine as a means of handling the incredible number of war-inflicted wounds and amputations, products of the massive quantities of lead bullets and cannon balls let fly by each side in the direction of their adversaries. Battlefield use of morphine was facilitated by the invention of the hypodermic needle, which allowed the rapid introduction of the drug into the bloodstream. These two developments set the stage for subsequent twentieth-century drug use dynamics involving opiate-based drugs (although two other changes, the discovery of another opiate that came to be called heroin and the criminalization of drug use, were critical to this process as well).

One product of the extensive use of morphine by physicians during and after the Civil War was the appearance of a new health problem that came to

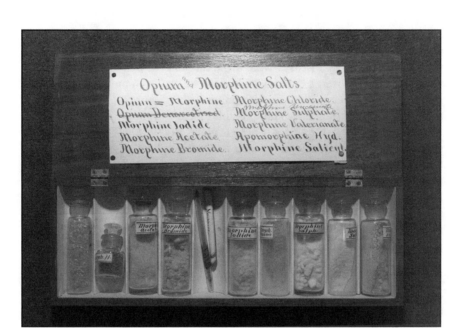

Doctor's opium and morphine kit, circa 1890. Courtesy of Drug Enforcement Administration.

be called "soldier's disease," a condition exclusive to those who were wounded in the war, treated with morphine for pain, and had as their primary symptom intense morphine craving. By the end of the war, it is estimated that as many as 400,000 people were suffering from "soldier's disease." Some estimate that as many as 10 million opium pills were issued by doctors to Union soldiers during the war, along with almost 3 million ounces of other opium preparations. In Europe, the Franco-Prussian War produced similar results. The treatment adopted by physicians was to continue morphine injections for those with soldier's disease. The frequency of morphine injection created a popular market for needles. The 1897 Sears Roebuck mail order catalogue responded to this need by advertising a hypodermic kit composed of a syringe, two detachable needles, two vials to hold morphine, and a carrying case, all for $1.50 (Inciardi 1986).

Serturner's profitable success in isolating a marketable product from opium prompted others to undertake similar research, leading to the discovery of several dozen other alkaloids in opium. This is why a British chemist by the name of C. R. A. Wright conducted a series of experiments during the 1870s that involved combining morphine with various acids. One of the chemicals Wright discovered was a compound he called diacetylmorphine. Twenty-four years later, a German man named Heinrich Dreser, a pharmacologist employed by the Bayer pharmaceutical company, used diacetylmorphine in a series of medical experiments and reported that it proved very effective in the treatment of coughs, chest pains, and discomforts associated with various other respiratory diseases. Antibiotics were unknown at the time, and respiratory diseases were a major cause of death in the Western world. Dreser discovered that diacetylmorphine was even more effective than morphine for this condition, and he (incorrectly) assumed that a fatal over-dose of diacetylmorphine was not possible (Inciardi 1986).

Seeing the opportunity for a new revenue stream, the Bayer laboratory began marketing its new wonder-drug under the upbeat trade name of "heroin," derived from the German word for heroic (*heroisch*). Before long, heroin was being promoted as a nonaddictive cure for morphine addiction. As a Bayer advertisement from this era stated: Heroin is "free from unpleasant after effect," an interesting euphemism for addiction (Inciardi 1986:10). This grievous error occurred because morphine addicts who were going through painful withdrawal stopped experiencing all of their symptoms when they were given heroin. At the time, people did not understand the phenomenon we now call "cross-addiction" (i.e., addiction to one opium product produces addiction to all opium products). Given its seemingly lofty attributes, heroin soon became a popular legal drug.

During this era of drug use legality—a period during which several hundred thousand Americans were addicted to opiates (Courtwright 1982)—the social composition of drug using and addicted populations is noteworthy, as Peter Conrad and Joseph Schneider (1980:116) comment:

> For those of us who are accustomed to thinking of the typical modern-day opiate addict as young, male, urban, lower-class, and a member of a minority group, 19th century addicts provide a sharp contrast. From all the data we have . . . it appears that the typical 19th century addict was middle-aged, female, rural, middle-class, and white.

Thus Conrad and Schneider report on the findings of an 1872 survey by the Massachusetts Board of Health, which found that among the ranks of opiate users there were many women (no doubt stemming from the tendency of physicians to prescribe opiates for "women's problems" and the targeting of women by the patent medicine industry) and rural dwellers. Similarly, they report on a study conducted in Chicago in 1880, which found that the vast majority of opium users were white.

Marijuana

Beyond the opiates, other psychoactive drugs also emerged during and just after the colonial era in America and became widely used substances. One of these was marijuana (*Cannabis sativa*). In use as a mood-altering drug for centuries, the marijuana plant also has been widely cultivated as a source of hemp fibers and seeds used to make fiber, paper, ropes, and lamp oil. By 1840, hemp production was one of the largest industries in the United States. Also during the nineteenth century there was a dramatic medical rediscovery of cannabis by physicians and others, resulting in marijuana (in the form of elixirs and patent medicines) becoming among the most widely prescribed drug prior to the Civil War. As suggested above, although its centrality in the medical armory for pain was displaced by morphine during the war between the states, marijuana remained the second most commonly prescribed pain medication until 1901 when it was replaced by aspirin. Beyond pain, it was prescribed for over 100 different illnesses, including recovery from alcoholism, insuring that exposure to marijuana was widespread. Moreover, the daily dosage levels of cannabis that were prescribed for adults, pregnant women, and children are similar to what contemporary illicit users might consume in a month. Popular American marriage guides from this period even recommended it as an aphrodisiac of extraordinary powers. Despite its growing popularity, the companies that marketed it (Lilly, Parke-Davis,

Marijuana pipes. Courtesy of Drug Enforcement Administration.

Squibb), the physicians who prescribed it, and the people who used it had no knowledge of its active ingredient.

Marijuana's unchallenged popularity continued through the 1920s when it ran headfirst into the same wall thrown up to protect society from another "foreign" population seen as dangerous and drug-crazed. In areas with large Mexican immigrant and Chicano populations, "the fear of marihuana was intense" (Musto 1987:219). As the Latino population of the L-shaped region from Washington State down through California and eastward to Louisiana increased through the early years of the twentieth century, the stereotype of the marijuana-smoking, violently criminal Mexican gained increasing acceptance among non-Hispanic white citizens. These prejudicial sentiments reached fever pitch as the Great Depression began to make its cruel intentions felt in the lives and livelihoods of the people of the greater Southwest. In a pattern that replicated anti-Chinese hostility in the wake of an economic crisis, anti-Mexican bigotry and the identification of deviant behavior among Mexicans having its roots in alleged rampant marijuana use fueled twin drives to control both marijuana use and Mexican immigration.

Cocaine

During the late 1800s, yet another drug emerged in America as a highly desired substance: cocaine. Its route to popular usage was initially quite different from that of the opiates or marijuana. Toward the end of the century, a Corsican winemaker, Angelo Mariani, began to import coca leaves from Peru to add to a new wine that he produced called Vin Coca Mariani. The wine was an instant success and was publicized as capable of lifting the spirits and eliminating fatigue. This new drink came to the attention of John Styth Pemberton of Atlanta, Georgia, who worked in the patent medicine business. In 1885, Pemberton developed a medicinal drink he registered as French Wine Coca, which he asserted was a nerve stimulant. The following year, he added other ingredients and began to market it as a soft drink called Coca-Cola. Eventually, over 40 soft drinks were enlivened with cocaine. By the 1890s, the patent medicine industry began marketing cocaine as a reliable cure for everything from alcoholism to venereal disease, even as a therapy for addiction to the opiate-based patent medicines.

Several researchers attempted to isolate the stimulant in the coca leaves. This objective was achieved finally in the 1860s by Albert Neimann. The Parke-Davis Company, "an exceptionally enthusiastic producer of cocaine, even sold coca-leaf cigarettes and coca cheroots to accompany their other products, which provided cocaine in a variety of media and routes such as a liqueurlike alcohol mixture called Coca Cordial, tablets, hypodermic injections, ointments, and sprays" (Musto 1987:7). These developments caught the attention of a Viennese neurologist named Sigmund Freud who experimented with the substance for awhile. Another experimenter was William Stewart Halsted, one of the founders of the Johns Hopkins Medical School, the prototype of the modern American medical school. He became addicted to cocaine while discovering its properties as an anesthetic.

As with the opiates and marijuana, societal attitudes about cocaine were colored by racism. Fear that if Blacks had access to cocaine they "might become oblivious of their prescribed bounds and attack white society" became a Southern obsession (Musto 1987:6). Asserting that "many of the horrible crimes committed in the Southern States by colored people can be traced directly to the cocaine habit" (Goode 1984:186), Colonel J. W. Watson of Georgia gave voice to this hate-fueled panic in a 1903 article in the *New York Tribune.* Similarly, the *New York Times* published an expose entitled "Negro Cocaine Fiends Are a New Southern Menace" that described Blacks as "running amuck in a cocaine frenzy" (Goode 1984:186). That African Americans were on the receiving end of most the racially motivated hate crimes committed in the South during this period was of little consequence. As Musto (1987:7) notes, the deep-seated "fear of the cocainized Blacks . . . coincided with the peak of lynchings, legal segregation, and voting laws all designed to

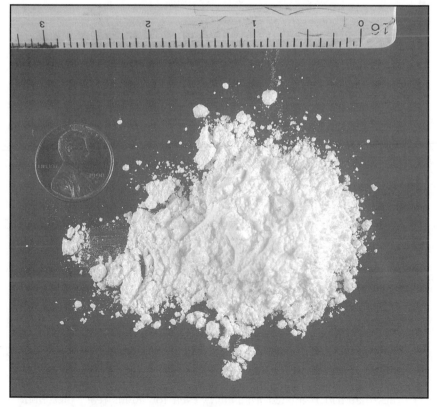

Powder cocaine. Courtesy of Drug Enforcement Administration.

remove political and social power from [Blacks]. . . ." One of the more peculiar beliefs about cocaine at the time was that it improved pistol marksmanship. "Another myth," adds Musto, "that cocaine made blacks almost unaffected by mere .32 caliber bullets, is said to have caused southern police departments to switch to .38 caliber revolvers" (1987:7). These dark fantasies propelled white fears far more than the biochemical reality of cocaine's actual effects, providing white society with one more excuse for Black repression.

Ironically, these politically motivated fears were not only misguided with respect to cocaine's effects, they were motivated by erroneous ideas about African American access to cocaine. In fact, the cost of the drug (twenty-five cents per grain in 1910) prohibited most African Americans in the South, the majority of whom were sharecroppers and notably poorer on average than whites, from acquiring it during this period. E. M. Green (1914), who examined admissions to Georgia State Sanitarium at the time, showed that rates of cocaine use by Blacks in the South were significantly lower than rates of cocaine use by whites. Nonetheless, to insure that cocaine in any form did not reach African Americans, it was dropped as an ingredient in Coca-Cola in 1903 and replaced by another colonial stimulant, caffeine.

Explanatory Factors in the Age of Drug Exploration

As Rudi Matthee (1995:24) succinctly concludes, "From the late sixteenth to the early eighteenth century substances with [psychoactive and] addictive properties, such as tobacco, coffee, cacao, tea and distilled liquor, were introduced, found acceptance, and spread with remarkable speed around the globe." Add to this list opium and cocaine, which also were ensnared in the rapid introduction of psychoactive substances that found new populations of users in various parts of the world during this era. Reception of the new substances varied, although it generally included some level of controversy and social conflict, with supporters and opponents clashing over the relative good or harm introduced by the new products. Commonly, condemnation of the new substances reflected a pattern that might be termed "differential opposition," in that opponents in any locale objected more stringently to some of the new drugs than to others. Consequently, over time, patterns of adoption and rejection varied by place; for example, tea came to be much more popular in England than did coffee, while the latter found a home in America (with coffee houses springing up in the colonies as early as the 1600s). At the same time, broader, cross-site patterns developed. Thus, David Courtwright (2001) differentiates four categories of societal response to the new drugs in what can be viewed as a continuum of acceptance, with key alternatives being: (1) drugs made freely available to all members of society (e.g., cocoa, caffeine); (2) drugs that were made freely available to adults only (e.g., tobacco, alcohol); (3) drugs that had regulated availability even for adults (e.g., prescription drugs, including, now, medical marijuana); and (4) drugs that were prohibited to everyone in society (heroin, cocaine). Key factors determining where on this continuum a drug might likely wind up include: the chemical capacity of a drug to support and extend labor productivity, the medicinal value of a drug, and the perceived chemical capacity of a drug to generate or help sustain social unrest, especially in an ethnic minority population.

Conclusion

While the historic period discussed in this chapter has been called by some the "age of exploration," from the perspective of this book it could just as well be labeled the "age of new drug exploration." The drugs introduced into what later came to be called the developed world during this period set the stage for many of the subsequent trends, fads, and crazes of psychoactive drug use in the United States. As discussed in the next two chapters, however, criminalization radically changed the pathways taken by various drugs as they emerged and reemerged in new forms, among new populations, in new drug combinations, and for some of them, in the spread of various new and renewed diseases of global significance like HIV/AIDS and hepatitis.

CHAPTER 3

The Era of Drug Criminalization to the 1960s

> Then there was the hatred and the concern regarding addicts and addiction. It's a lot of things: it's race and class; it's fear, the realization that addicts have to commit crimes to support their habits; and it's a resentment that people are feeling that good three, four times a day.
>
> —Robert Newman, quoted in *Addicts Who Survived*

Criminalizing Drug Use and the Rise of the Underground Drug Scene

The later part of the nineteenth century has been dubbed "a dope fiend's paradise" (Brecher 1972) because of the lack of legal restrictions and trouble-free availability of a smorgasbord of psychoactive substances in various forms and dosages. Just as importantly, during this era "[a]ddiction was not considered a major social problem, and there was no public moral devaluation of addicts . . ." (Conrad and Schneider 1980:119). "Victorian Americans," as David Courtwright, Herman Joseph, and Don Des Jarlais (1989:2) state, "were much less worried about drugs . . . than they were about drink." Being addicted to heroin at the time was similar to being addicted to caffeine today. People readily, if perhaps with a sheepish smile, can admit they are addicted to their morning cup of coffee without the least fear that their morality, sanity, or competence will be questioned or that they might face criminal charges and a potentially long prison sentence. In the nineteenth century, the same was true of heroin or cocaine addiction. All of this changed early in the twentieth century as a push for criminalization gained momentum. In the aftermath of this social restructuring, drug use continued unabated, but use patterns underwent a thorough transformation, including the development of new health consequences associated with the new behaviors and consumption contexts.

The criminalization of drug use was not achieved instantaneously through the dramatic passage of a single piece of legislation; rather, it was accomplished in a stepwise fashion through a series of legal and political maneuvers that included the enactment of a number of laws and required several court decisions affirming their legality and defining their limits. Interestingly, unlike the brief attempt at alcohol prohibition, the ban initially on cocaine and heroin, and later on marijuana and many other substances as well, was achieved without an amendment to the U.S. Constitution.

As we have seen in the case of morphine in chapter 2, the first antidrug laws were passed at the state level. Musto (1987), in his classic account of the rise of narcotics control policy, *The American Disease*, effectively shows that the movement by the states toward making drug use illegal usually was driven by social fears about the growth of a particular local minority ethnic group, be it African Americans in the southern states, the Chinese in the western states, or Mexicans in the Southwest. The hyperemotional language used by opponents of drug use makes it clear that their concern was dual: (1) fear of racial mixing that they believed could cause a dampening of American vigor and spirit, and (2) fear that minority drug use would disrupt the reigning structure of inequality that they regarded as the backbone of American society. These two themes easily intertwined to create popular images of evil drugs and dangerous ethnic groups driven to mayhem by drug use.

This complex dread reflects the emergence in U.S. culture of a belief in the connection of psychoactive substances and social disruption. The existence of this conceptual linkage in our cultural consciousness is further seen in efforts over time to marry drugs to any and all perceived threats to the status quo, including, eventually, both communism and terrorism. At the turn of the twentieth century, however, the real force driving this troublesome belief was the arrival on America's shores of massive numbers of immigrants combined with the migration of African Americans from rural, agricultural areas in the South to both southern and northeastern cities. Both groups of new arrivals, with their differing ways, languages, and appearances were perceived as dangerous threats to the American way of life.

Consequently, drugs that were not linked in the public's mind to any particular subordinated, and hence potentially dangerous, minority group were not given the same attention by those pushing for drug criminalization. Thus, tobacco and barbiturates, both very dangerous substances but neither of which was associated in the public's imagination *at the time* with any particular ethnic minority group (although barbiturates were later linked with Hispanic street gangs), escaped criminalization. In short, the development of public (as well as policy maker) concern about drug use, as reflected in the initial state laws limiting or banning *particular kinds of drug use*, was driven more by prejudicial social values and unequal social structures than by compassionate concern about public health.

At the federal level, an additional element was added to racial motivations. In 1909 and 1911, the United States convened an international conference on opium that produced a document called the *Hague Convention of 1912*. The focus of this early antidrug effort was to institute restrictions on international opium trade. Backing the leadership of William Jennings Bryan on the issue, Congress followed up on the convention with the passage of The Harrison Narcotic Act of 1914. This federal law placed explicit but far from total restriction on the sale of psychoactive substances. Notably, however, congressional debate over the passage of this bill did not put emphasis on the negative health effects of opium or cocaine use, nor was it infused with hand-wringing distress about the rising tide of addiction in the mainstream U.S. population. Instead, the primary cause of federal disquiet was the troublesome fact that the British were gaining a hefty economic windfall from their ability to force opium sales on China, gaining thereby a potent edge against U.S. business interests globally.

Swept along by these weighty structural dynamics, in the first decades of the twentieth century the legal and moral climate surrounding drug use reversed, with the drug user being transformed rather suddenly from an

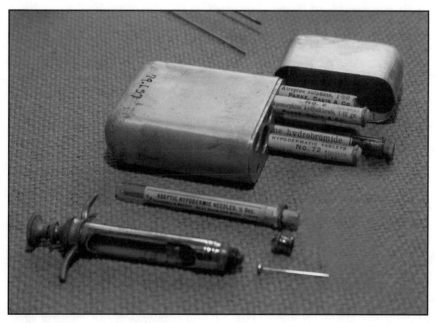

Glass hypodermic syringe with detachable needles from the early twentieth century. Courtesy of Drug Enforcement Administration.

unblemished if indulgent compatriot into a miscreant. As a result of newly forged social labels, use of some psychoactive drugs (but not others) came to be synonymous with deviance, lack of control, violence, and moral decay. As Goode (1984:218) aptly comments, "By the 1920s the public image of the addict had become that of a criminal, a willful degenerate, a hedonistic thrill-seeker in need of imprisonment and stiff punishment." It is estimated that at the time there were over 200,000 American drug addicts (not counting those addicted to nonstigmatized yet no less addictive drugs like caffeine and nicotine), and possibly as many as half a million (McCoy, Read, and Adams 1986; Goode 1984). Whatever the exact number, all were targeted as enemies of "normal society" and moral righteousness.

In response to The Harrison Act, physicians around the country set up clinics to medically dispense psychoactive drugs to patients who suffered from the disease of addiction, a therapeutic relationship that was not banned by the new law. As a survival strategy, some drug users manipulated this system to gain access to their allotted dose plus additional doses for resale on the street to other addicts. Thus began the underground narcotics industry. Initially, enforcing the new drug restrictions fell to the U.S. Treasury Department. Central to Treasury's drive to stomp out illicit drug taking was the growing concern that the practice would spread again "into the higher social ranks of the country" (Helmer 1983:16), a group that had shied away from drugs like cocaine and the opiates in response to new drug laws and the recast and denigrated image of drug users. Then, in 1919, in *Webb v. United States*, the Supreme Court ruled that a physician could not prescribe a "narcotic" (a term that included cocaine) to addicts simply to protect them from the pain of withdrawal. Three years later, in *United States v. Behrman*, the Supreme Court ruled that narcotics could not be prescribed even as part of a cure. In light of these Court decisions, it became all but impossible for an addict to obtain needed drugs legally: "The clinics shut their doors and a new figure appeared on the American scene—the pusher" (McCoy, Read, and Adams 1986:110).

These radical changes not withstanding, the number of new drug addicts did not suddenly decline. Over 1,000 people were charged with drug possession in 1919; six years later, the annual arrest rate was 10,000. What did change, however, was the population of drug users and, as noted, the primary sources of supply. Gone were the self-medicating middle-class female addicts who purchased heroin legally as a drinkable tincture or smokable cheroot at their local pharmacy; they were replaced by young male heroin snorters, often inhabitants of immigrant slums, who began using drugs in the bars and brothels that were concentrated in poorer areas. Often violent street gangs emerged in impoverished neighborhoods in response to threats from outsiders and hindered access to social success and upward mobility. They explored alternative, criminal routes of getting by, including distribution of drugs to poor and working-class youth seeking escape and excitement.

In the Shadow of Criminalization

Systematic illicit drug research in the United States began in Chicago during the 1930s, in the aftermath of the criminalization of narcotics. This body of work began with a study by University of Chicago sociology student Bingham Dai (1937:123), who was concerned with understanding drug addicts as a social group in terms of "the social and cultural environment which was immediately connected with their addiction [as well as] that which was responsible for the formation of their personality traits." Dai viewed illicit drug use as social deviance. This theoretical orientation was developed by Robert E. Park, a student of the German sociologist Georg Simmel. Park believed that modern urban dwelling gave birth to a new way of life that encouraged drug use. Like his mentor, Park saw the city as an inherently stressful environment that produces a breakdown of healthy social bonds, leading to disorganization, individual isolation, depersonalization, and deviant behaviors. In short, life in cities is pathological and the behavior of urban dwellers, especially inner-city populations, reflects this urban social crisis. Drug abuse, consequently, is understood as one of the direct expressions of the deeply damaging effects of urban living. Nonetheless, Park and his colleagues recognized that most people who live in cities—even in the poorest and most derelict zones of American inner cities—do not use illegal drugs. Rather, they cope with the challenges of city life (or, more precisely, of being poor in the city) in other ways, which may or may not be sanctioned by the dominant society.

In *Opium Addiction in Chicago*, Dai reported findings from his observational fieldwork and life history interviewing with two populations: individuals with an iatrogenic addiction to morphine as a result of medical treatment (e.g., soldier's disease or accidental injury), and those who acquired their addiction on the street through their involvement with other drug users. This division marks the two populations or generations of hard drug users, one fading off the drug scene, the other beginning to dominate it during the period of Dai's research. With reference to the latter group, Dai emphasized the importance of social networks in the diffusion of drug use; he argued, "it was through the association with drug users that they learned the properties of the drug they had been given and were initiated into the role of a drug addict. The influence of other addicts is also found to be the most common factor leading to relapse after a cure" (Dai 1937:122).

An important part of the drug use transition that began after criminalization, but that would not arrive in full force until after World War II and would significantly influence the public image of the street drug addict, was identified by Dai. He reported (1937) that in Chicago during the years 1928–1934, African Americans comprised 6.9 percent of the population but accounted for 17.3 percent of individuals addicted to drugs (and 22 percent of those who were unemployed). This pattern continued in subsequent years, not only in

Chicago but in other northern, midwestern, and western urban centers as well. African Americans "were using drugs in the 1940s and 1950s in a way they had not [previously]" (Courtwright, Joseph, and Des Jarlais 1989:14). Narcotic arrests among African Americans rose from 362 in 1933 to 4,262 by 1950 and to 11,815 by 1965, numbers that reflect both absolute and relative increases in arrest patterns. Harry Jacob Anslinger, who headed the U.S. Bureau of Narcotics from 1930–1962, noted in 1957, "Fifteen years ago, the Lexington and Forth Worth Hospitals [federal institutions that specialized in drug treatment] had mostly white patients. . . . Today, they are filled with Negro addicts" (quoted in Courtwright, Joseph, and Des Jarlais 1989:19).

There are a number of factors that contributed to new patterns of drug use and addiction in the African American population. For the most part, African Americans were relatively recent arrivals in the city, having migrated northward beginning in the early 1900s in one of the largest population shifts in U.S. history. In cities like Chicago—which has been called the most segregated city in America—they encountered intense racism, imposed social isolation, family disruption, broad-based structural discrimination, and urban poverty (which experientially was considerably more oppressive than the rural poverty most had known in the South prior to their migration). African Americans fled to the northern cities with hopes of social advancement and a desire to escape the stultifying Southern-style Jim Crow racism. For the most part, the migrants were young, single, and optimistic, but the urban environments that received them were anything but warm and welcoming.

As parts of northern cities filled up with African Americans, the dominant white society made a collective if unspoken decision to abandon these areas, leaving behind decaying schools, failing utilities and services, and few opportunities for legal employment, thereby condemning the inhabitants to perpetual poverty. Additionally, during Prohibition, African American neighborhoods "became the place where whites practiced their vices" (James and Johnson 1996:16). Black-owned jazz clubs, after-hours clubs, houses of prostitution, gambling halls, and dance clubs emerged as important social centers for the growing African American urban population. Whites, anxious for excitement and an escape from the depressing economy, flocked into the inner city "to hear African American music, to party, to patronize houses of prostitution, and to gamble" (James and Johnson 1996:17). For example, "Janet" (pseudonym), a Black drug user interviewed by Courtwright, Joseph, and Des Jarlais (1989:210), visited "coke joints" in Harlem during this period, describing them as apartments where you could order cocaine and the proprietor would put it on a saucer or mirror "and make these lines. . . . There were blacks and whites sniffing—the white people came up to Harlem in the thirties to connect. Some were show people, some were ordinary people." As a result, drugs were readily available for inner-city dwellers. Among those who patronized the urban clubs were African American soldiers who returned from the First World War having been exposed to drug use in

Europe or Northern Africa, as well as individuals with a more pecuniary interest in illicit drugs. As St. Clair Drake and Horace Cayton (1970:610) colorfully point out, these centers of congregation often became

> points of contact between the purveyors of pleasure "on the illigit" and their clientele—casual prostitutes, bootleggers, reefer peddlers, "pimps," and "freaks." Some of these places [were] merely "fronts" and "blinds" for the organized underworld. . . . The primary institutions of the underworld [were] the tougher taverns, the reefer pads, the gambling dens, the liquor joints, and the call houses and buffet-flats where professional prostitutes cater to the trade in an organized fashion.

These associations, and the racist sentiments that helped to fuel them, contributed to the identification and demonization of the drug addict as the ultimate deviant, the very embodiment of things strange and threatening to the dominant society: the Black drug user. Increasingly, in the minds of "middle Americans" inner-city ghettos were "filled with black men mugging whites for money to pay for heroin and then injecting this evil drug so that they can spend the rest of the day nodding away in a blissful vacuum" (Iiyama, Nishi, and Johnson 1976:17). So powerful was this image, and so ill-fitting was it to the realities of street drug use, that a later generation of naturalist drug researchers would make their names professionally showing the high degree of hard work and planning that was involved in being a drug addict (e.g., Agar 1973; Johnson et al. 1985; Preble and Casey 1969; Singer 1999c). Drug addiction, they would argue, takes many of the attributes—commitment, diligence, discipline—valued by the dominant society.

Supply and cost were additional factors propelling the new patterns of Black drug use. During the 1940s, "a dollar would buy enough for a good high for several people and $2.00-per-day habits were common" (James and Johnson 1996:19). As the number of addicted individuals increased and demand shot up, cost followed suit. Soon a thoroughbred heroin addiction was too costly for the average denizen of the inner city, leading to new forms of drug use behavior. Mixing substances became more common, with alcohol-based cough syrups and prescription sedatives and barbiturates being used in combination with or instead of heroin (when the latter was not affordable). Furthermore, the quality of heroin diminished as a new generation of illicit dealers increased the share of adulterants (e.g., baby laxative) they used to fatten their supply of saleable powder.

In this context, Dai launched his field study of opium addiction, bringing to the task a psychoanalytic perspective on the underlying causes of individual behavior. While an ethnographic methodology, which by design is geared to the study of social process and performance in context, may seem ill-suited to a highly individualized, inwardly focused orientation like psychoanalysis, the combination (known, somewhat tongue-in-cheek, as the "couch in the field" approach) has guided a number of researchers (see Levine 1971:203–

214). As Harvey Feldman and Michael Aldrich (1990:18) note, given Dai's approach it is not surprising to find that his observations were "cast in terms like 'infantile' personalities, excessive dependence on others, and a tendency to withdraw or escape from social responsibility." Use of these constructs was further reinforced through the recruitment of many study participants through the Psychopathic Hospital in Chicago.

In addition, as noted, Dai's work helped to usher in the social deviance approach to drug studies. This understanding, which was suggested but never fully developed in Dai's work, depicts the drug user as caught up in "an all-consuming life-style" (Waterston 1993) or total way of life (Bell 1971; Inciardi 1986). Some researchers have referred to the existence of a "deviance syndrome" among impoverished inner-city drug users (McGee and Newcomb 1992). For example, Gillies Bibeau (1989) asserted that regular intravenous drug use "quickly leads to a lifestyle often associated with social marginality, a lifestyle where risk-taking and danger play central roles." Thus, Dai (1937:136), in discussing the link between drug use and prostitution, asserted: "That the pimp in his attempt to entice a girl to his service not seldom 'dopes' her and makes her an addict so that she will have to depend on him for her drug and thereby becomes his woman is a matter of common knowledge." (It bears mentioning that if "common knowledge" were a fully dependable window on nonstandard behavior, no specialized social scientific knowledge would be needed.) Once addicted, from the perspective of the deviance model, drug users come to view "themselves as culturally and socially detached from the life style and everyday preoccupations of members of the conventional world" (Rettig 1999:244). In other words, addiction is not just a simple consequence of pharmacological effects of drugs on the human brain. Rather, the deviance model asserts that "[a]ddicts become addicted not only to drugs but to a way of life" (Lindesmith, Strauss, and Denzin 1975:571).

Not surprisingly, later researchers have questioned the deviance model, arguing that it "leads to an exaggerated picture of [drug] users' lives, as well as an overstatement of differences between users and nonusers. . . . [Indeed] the deviant subculture seems to insert itself in the middle of the metropolis, and we have no sense of it being part of anything larger than its own demi-world" (Waterston 1993:14–15). For example, the Heroin Lifestyle Study (HLS) (Hanson et al. 1985), which was carried out in the inner-city areas of Chicago, New York, Washington, D.C., and Philadelphia several decades after Dai's project was completed and he had left research for a career in therapy, questioned the validity of assuming that there is a distinctive heroin lifestyle that is separate from the basic lifestyle pattern of the surrounding inner-city community. As two members of the HLS research team note:

> An unexpected finding is that the HLS men live rather structured lives in which successive daily time periods are spent engaging in a variety of fairly predictable and even conventional activities. Like men in straight society, they arise early in order to spend many of their waking hours "on

the job"—but in their case, this usually means hustling in pursuit of the wherewithal to maintain their once-a-day, relatively controlled heroin habits. (Bovelle and Taylor 1985:175–176)

Importantly, it was the "pursuit of normality" (under conditions of marked social inequality and lack of opportunity) rather than escape or exhilaration that was found to drive the continued use of heroin among study participants. Also noteworthy was the control participants exercised over their drug habits, a refutation of the common assertion that regular heroin users "have an insatiable and uncontrollable appetite for heroin and that they therefore shoot up as many times as possible each day" (Bovelle and Taylor 1985:177). In short, the HLS identified a strata of daily heroin users whose behaviors and values did not fit reigning stereotypes about this population, revealing both the changing nature of the heroin scene and a notable degree of heterogeneity among drug using populations.

Interviews with inner-city heroin users by Alfred Lindesmith (1968), a noted drug researcher and advocate who helped Dai recruit his sample, found a range of experiences associated with the injection of heroin, with some users reporting pleasurable responses and others indicating that the pleasure was very limited. All respondents, however, affirmed that continued use protected them from the painful discomfort of withdrawal. Addiction, in Lindesmith's view, is not simply a physical need for a particular drug but also comprises a body of shared cultural knowledge about the drug and its effects. Additionally, Lindesmith, like Dai, argued that drug users become entangled in a set of social relationships with other drug users and life patterns that are organized around the getting and using of drugs, which along with the chemical properties of the drug, drive the drug use process. In other words, as stressed in chapter 1, understanding drug use dynamics requires an examination of structural factors (like racism), social factors (like the network of social relationships maintained by drug users), cultural factors (such as knowledge of drug use practices and beliefs about drug effects), and biological factors (including the impact of drugs on the human brain and body).

Paint It Black: 1940–1959

The growth during the 1930s in the number of hard drug users came to a sudden halt with the outbreak of the Second World War. The battle at sea, especially the German torpedoing of ships crossing the Atlantic, effectively blocked the flow of many drugs into the United States—leading to a significant drop in the frequency of drug use and the number of drug users. Illicit drug use did not end (e.g., the writer William S. Burroughs began using morphine during the war), but a limited supply of foreign drugs significantly slowed the level and frequency of use and the recruitment of new drug-using populations. Among existing users, it pushed them to explore new ways to get high, insuring a continued dynamism in drug use practice. In the immediate post–World War II years, a period during which heroin and other drugs began flowing back into the United States in ever-increasing quantities, the inner city once again became an epicenter of illicit drug trade and the number of inner-city drug users began to mount quickly once again.

Yet rampant drug use in the core of U.S. urban centers after the Second World War did not attract much attention or real concern from the dominant society, or even from social scientists concerned with explaining this behavior, except to the degree that drug users were described in various reports as either psychologically damaged individuals or as criminal deviants in need of harsh punishment. Often in the social and behavioral science literature, drug addicts were portrayed as being "either psychotic or neurotic casualties" (Inciardi 1992:30). Typical was the description of Arnold Chien and coworkers (1964:14), who argued that

> all addicts suffer from deep-rooted personality disorders. . . . They are not able to enter into prolonged, close, friendly relationships with . . . peers; they have difficulty assuming a masculine role; they are frequently overcome by a sense of futility, expectations of failure, and general depression; they are easily frustrated and made anxious, and they find frustrations and anxiety intolerable.

Among policy makers, drug users were primarily of interest because of their involvement in crime and because they were assumed to come primarily from ethnic minority communities, sectors of the population that seemed in the eyes of the powerful to hold endless potential for drug-inspired social upheaval. As the typical opium addict at mid-twentieth century became increasingly a "young, lower-class black male . . . moral hostility increased proportionately" (Conrad and Schneider 1980:127).

Strengthening the criminal justice approach to drug addiction, the Congressional Kefauver Committee on Crime held a series of televised hearings that drew public attention to the role of drug use in criminal behavior. Meanwhile, a number of widely read popular magazines published alarmist articles about the rising peril of drug use. In light of the reigning McCarthyite beliefs of this era, drug use soon was linked not only with property crimes but also with communism, just as in the contemporary moment it is being closely linked, with equal dubiousness, to international terrorism (as discussed in chapter 10).

Sources of information on drug use during and just after the Second World War are limited, as researchers who might have been involved in the study of drug consumption and its consequences were drawn away by the war effort. In addition to a set of retrospective life history interviews with drug users (Courtwright, Joseph, and Des Jarlais 1989), several autobiographies by men who came of age during this era and experienced drug use spreading in their communities, including their own initiation and involvement in the use of psychoactive substances, provide windows on the drug use dynamics of the period.

Prior to his life-changing conversion to Islam and his subsequent emergence as a charismatic and militant African American leader, Malcolm X spent a number of years, beginning during the Second World War, as a drug dealer. He specialized in the sale of marijuana, a drug that had been, in effect, criminalized by the Marijuana Tax Act of 1937. He would travel a set circuit, carrying a jar filled with marijuana "sticks" for sale to musicians in various East Coast cities. This association between the arts and drug use helped to create a street image of the drug user as a glamorous "hip" role worthy of emulation.

> In every band, a least half of the musicians smoked reefers. . . . I kept turning over my profit, increasing my supplies, and I sold reefers like a wild man. I scarcely slept; I was everywhere musicians congregated. A roll of money was in my pocket. Every day, I cleared at least fifty or sixty dollars. In those days . . . this was a fortune to a seventeen-year-old Negro. I felt, for the first time in my life, that great feeling of free! Suddenly, now, I was the peer of the other young hustlers I had admired. (Malcolm X 1965:99)

Before long, Malcolm caught the eye of the police. Under increasingly intense police pressure, he gave up selling marijuana and turned to other hustles. But he continued to smoke marijuana and developed a dependence on cocaine.

> Just satisfying my cocaine habit alone cost me about twenty dollars a day. I guess another five dollars a day could have been added for reefers and plain tobacco cigarettes that I smoked; besides getting high on drugs, I chain-smoked as many as four packs a day. (Malcolm X 1965:139)

Supporting himself and his addiction through burglary, he initiated a dangerous yet common cycle of avoiding having to worry about getting caught by sniffing more cocaine and smoking another stick of marijuana, behaviors that put him further at risk for arrest.

> Drugs helped me push the thought to the back of my mind. They were the center of my life. I had gotten to the stage where every day I used enough drugs—reefer, cocaine, or both—so that I felt above any worries or any strain. (Malcolm X 1965:143)

Then in February 1946, when Malcolm X was 20 years of age, he was arrested for robbery, convicted, and sentenced to 8–10 years in prison. There he continued to use whatever psychoactive substances that he could get his hands on—including items stolen from the prison kitchen like nutmeg—until his conversion to Islam, at which point he forswore all drug use for the rest of his life.

One consequence of his religious conversion was that Malcolm X was never swallowed up by the postwar heroin boom in New York City. For Claude Brown, who was a few years younger than Malcolm X, heroin became such a powerful attractant that by age 13 he could hardly contain his mounting desire to try it. Like Malcolm X, Brown was introduced to drug use by his friends, especially a social network of older boys whom he greatly admired. They first taught him how to roll and smoke marijuana. When they moved on to heroin, which, among other names was called "horse" at that time, he tried to emulate them. For several months during 1950 all Brown (1965) could think about was his craving for heroin:

> Horse was a new thing, not only in our neighborhood but in Brooklyn, the Bronx, and everyplace I went, uptown and downtown. It was like horse had just taken over. Everybody was talking about it. All the hip people were using it and snorting it and getting this new high. . . . I had been smoking reefers and had gotten high a lot of times, but I had the feeling that this horse was out of this world. (109)

Ultimately, Brown got his chance to try heroin.

> I couldn't believe it was really happening. I almost wanted to break out and laugh for joy, but I held back, and I snorted. . . . Something hit me right in the top of the head. It felt like a little spray of pepper on my brain. . . . Everything was getting rosy, beautiful. The sun got brighter in the sky and the whole day lit up and was twice as bright as it was before. . . . Everything was so slo-o-ow. (110–111)

While some heroin users report that their first exposure to the drug is overwhelmingly pleasurable, like love at first sight, leading to a long-term effort to relive the initial euphoric experience, Brown had a different reaction:

> My head seemed to stretch, and I thought my brain was going to burst. It was like a headache taking place all over the head at once and trying to break its way out. And then it seemed to get hot and hot and hot. And I was so slow . . . I got scared. I'd never felt this way before in my life. . . . My guts felt like they were going to come out. Everything was bursting out all at once, and there was nothing I could do. . . . And I said, "O Lawd, if you'll just give me one more chance, one more chance, I'll never get high again." (111)

While Brown continued to use marijuana, he never again dared to sample heroin. He did, however, begin to deal marijuana and cocaine, a course that soon led to an incident in which he was robbed of his drugs and money at gunpoint by a heroin addict.

> I knew that I would have to get a gun, and that when cats heard about it . . . they would want to hear that the guy had been killed. This was the way the people in our set did things. You didn't go around letting anybody stick you up. Shit, if you let somebody stick you up and go on living behind it, you didn't have any business dealing drugs. (176)

Before Brown could find the addict who robbed him, the man was shot several times by the police, which "took the heat off" of Brown to settle the score. As a result, however, Brown gave up drug dealing and was able to escape the emergent heroin epidemic of the post–World War II era in Harlem. Many of his friends were not so lucky.

> But then it seemed like drugs were coming in so strong with the younger generation that it was almost overshadowing numbers. A lot of younger cats who were taking numbers would start using drugs, and then they would start fucking with people's money. . . . People started to get shot and things like that over their money because cats needed it to get drugs. A lot of junkies started sticking up the numbers writers and sticking up the controllers. . . . Peddling drugs had become a popular vocation in Harlem. . . . If the plague didn't hit you directly, it hit you indirectly. It seemed as though nobody could really get away from it. There were a lot of guys trying to get young girls started on drugs so they could put them on the corner. (178)

During these years, in nearby in Spanish Harlem, Piri Thomas, a boy of mixed Puerto Rican and African American heritage, was a member of the younger generation that was coming of age and coming into contact with drugs in the shadow of the Second World War. He recalled one of his earliest encounters with marijuana at age 13. While drinking whiskey with several friends, one of them produced a "stick" of marijuana and asked if he would like some.

> I felt its size. It was king-sized, a bomber. I put it to my lips and began to hiss my reserve away. It was going, going, going. I was gonna get a gone high. I inhaled. I held my nose, stopped up my mouth. I was gonna get a gone high . . . a gone high . . . a gone high . . . and then the stick was gone, burnt to a little bit of a roach. (Thomas 1967:58)

Like Malcolm X and Claude Brown, within a few years Thomas (1967) was not only using but selling marijuana. But his initial reaction to heroin, which was becoming widely used by his peers, was negative. At age 16 watching friends use heroin, he recalled:

> I smoked marijuana, which was just like smoking cigarettes, but I was down on drugs. I had seen the young-old cats that dope [heroin] had messed up, the poor chumps who would try and hustle a buck or steal anything that would bring the price of a cap, a fix, to drive that mean devil away for awhile. (109)

But Thomas' resolve to avoid heroin was overwhelmed by his need to prove he was not a "punk." When a peer, Alfredo, held up a dollar cap of heroin and a folded matchbook to use in sniffing the powder, Thomas felt compelled to prove himself a worthy companion: "All for the feeling of belonging, for the price of being called 'one of us.'" (Thomas 1967:204):

> Looking dead at Alfredo, I inhaled, first through one nostril, then through the other. Then, turning quickly, away I went into the cold street. Almost immediately I felt a burning sensation in my nose, like a sneeze coming. I pulled out my handkerchief and had barely enough time to put it to my nose when blood came pouring out. . . . Now the night lights seemed to get duller and duller, my awareness of things grew delayed.

> But the music was clearer and I felt no pain, nothing at all. I seemed sort
> of detached. (110)

The power of heroin to wash away all pain, misery, and rejection made the
drug instantly appealing to Thomas: "All your troubles become a bunch of
bleary blurred memories . . ." (Thomas 1967:200). Before long, Thomas' life
was centered on the drug. He'd "go to bed thinking about [heroin] and wake
up in the morning thinking about it" (207):

> Heroin does a lot for one—and it's all bad. It becomes your whole life
> once you allow it to sink its white teeth in your blood stream. I never fig-
> ured on getting hooked all the way. I was only gonna play it for a Pepsi-
> Cola kick. Only was gonna use it like every seven days, that is until the
> day I woke up and dug that I was using it seven times a day instead. I had
> jumped from being a careful snorter, content to take my kicks of sniffing
> through my nose, to a not-so-careful skin-popper, and now was a full-
> grown mainliner. (200)

With a drug habit to support, Thomas realized he needed to develop a
hustle to make money. An inner-city youth with no job skills and unlikely, as
a Black Puerto Rican, to find legitimate employment even if he had work
experience, he felt he had only two options: stealing or selling drugs. He
chose the drug trade. Like Malcolm X, Thomas soon found himself in prison,
where his habit switched to benzedrine, phenobarbital, alcohol, strained shel-
lac, and whatever else the inmates could get their hands on that could free
them, however temporarily, from the stone cold reality of prison life. Ultimately, also like Malcolm X, Thomas overcame his addiction. He became an
author and an active proponent of drug rehabilitation.

Another literary example can be found in the life history of Manual
Torres, whose story mirrors the accounts of others from this era. A gang
member from his early teens during the 1950s, Torres tried heroin under circumstance not much different from those of Claude Brown, and like Brown
his first experience of heroin was uniformly unpleasant. But his role model
was his uncle, and he encouraged Torres to try heroin a second time.

> So I snort again and hey, it's like the shit really hit the fan . . . you can't
> describe it. All the colors of Times Square tumble right over your fore-
> head and explode in your eyeballs like a million, jillion shooting
> stars. . . . Everything's beautiful, and it's like nothing's happening baby
> but clear, crisp light. (Rettig 1999:33–34)

Soon Torres was snorting heroin daily. Then his uncle, who he looked to as a
role model, showed him how to skinpop (i.e., subcutaneous drug injection).

> I thought that I'd be satisfied with skinpopping forever. But everybody
> else around was mainlining it, sticking it in the vein. Now I'm scoring
> every day, and some days using a lot of stuff. It gets to be easier and easier
> to think about mainlining, until one day I decide to try it, just once. Hell,
> yes, just once. Shit, man, from that day on it was straight shooting for

> me. . . . You know, it's hard to explain the rush. It just knocks you completely into another dimension. . . . The feeling is *that* good. So good that once hooked you never really live the feeling down. (Rettig 1999:34–35)

Before long, Torres was injecting heroin four times a day, not to achieve a rush, but "just to maintain" (Rettig 1999:33). He began to shoplift to support his drug habit and then turned to armed robbery, which led to arrest and imprisonment.

Many years later, having stopped drug use and started college, Torres, in reflecting on his life, emphasized the political-economic origin of involvement with drugs among inner-city youth. Responding to a statement about Durkheim's theory that the social role of criminals is to set the boundaries of acceptable behavior for the rest of society, Torres stated:

> That's fine if you're on the right side of the tracks. But what if you are locked into the streets and locked out of the jobs because of your background or your dope habit? Hell, man, its simple for me to see, because I've been there. The social order created the drug problem and anything that comes of heroin addiction is their fault. *Personal breakdowns are an aspect of social breakdowns.* (Rettig 1999:175; emphasis added)

Torres goes on to ask the same question raised by the political theorist and social activist Frederick Engels over a hundred years earlier. Having carefully toured the wretched working-class sectors of Manchester, England, and having painfully witnessed drunkenness and opiate use at every turn among men, women, and children, Engels asked: who is to be blamed for this sorry state of affairs? His answer: "They who have degraded the working-man to a mere object have the responsibility to bear" (Engels 1969:134). By this, he meant members of the privileged class who own the factories and other institutions of employment, supply the liquor and drugs as a means of making profit, control the agencies of law enforcement and criminal justice, and establish and enforce social policies. In his own voice, Torres (Rettig 1999:182) similarly asks:

> Who are the real criminals? Most of the people of my generation in the Bronx turned out so-called bad. They either became crooks, or dopers, or they dropped out. One way or another they were wasted. . . . All I know is that I never had the opportunities someone else had to grow up on the hill in suburbia. . . . They created the habit, and they're still creating habits for sixteen-year-old kids.

These four autobiographical accounts reveal the development of the post–World War II drug scene in the inner city among African American and Puerto Rican youth. Building on the image of the "cool" marijuana user of the Depression and war years, the end of the war ushered in a period of significant increase in heroin use and heroin addiction. The street addict became a common sight in inner-city neighborhoods, as each new generation of youth, boys and girls alike, sought to prove their worth to their peers and to themselves by adopting the celebrated image of a fearless drug adventurer. Other options and role models were scarce, and none seemed to offer as much opportunity to impoverished youth who felt they had to demonstrate their "heart" or face rejection in the one arena—the streets—that offered any potential life validation. In Torres' words (Rettig 1999:181), "I wanted to be a stand-up cat too, you know." However, in the wake of the heroin "plague," Harlem and other U.S. inner cities changed. The sense of community miraculously had survived the migration of African Americans from the South and Puerto Ricans from their home island. But, the grinding poverty these groups encountered in their new northern and midwestern homes, and the fierce and punishing racial discrimination, undercut self-esteem and self-worth. Swiftly they became impoverished individuals who fell victim to widespread drug addiction with nowhere to turn for drug money except robbery, burglary, prostitution, and other crimes against themselves, their families, and their neighbors.

These patterns are seen in the life and words of Ramon Colon (pseudonym), a Puerto Rican man, interviewed in a Hispanic Health Council study during the 1990s. Born in East Harlem in 1939, Ramon first began to hear about heroin from his friends in about 1947. He recalls:

> When heroin came into our neighborhood, we were 13 or 14 years old, in middle school. Latinos, African Americans, and Italians all started using at the same time. We would play stick ball in the street and pass a bag around to get loaded. We didn't know anything about addiction. Heroin was as easy to get as candy then, it was everywhere and it was pure. One time the baseball player, Frankie Robinson, came to our school to talk and I bet every kid in that room had a bag of dope in his pocket. I learned about it first from a neighbor who lived upstairs in our building. I began to dip into his stuff. We frowned on guys that were shooting up then. For the first six months it was just snorting. My brother put it up his nose for four years before he started shooting. My cousin snorted for seven years. But I told them they were wasting their dope and got them into shooting. I watched some older boys shoot up on the roof at first. They would skin pop me. People in our building would stash "works" [syringes and cookers] in the basement of the building. I would find them. That was how I got my first set of works. Before dope, it was really a nice neighborhood, nobody locked their doors. But with drugs, everything deteriorated, it became mean. (Singer and Jia 1993:231)

Of course, not all addicts from this era were African American or Latino. Another autobiographical source on drug use during this era was written by the alto saxophone jazz musician, Art Pepper, who began injecting heroin in 1950. Of mixed European background, his introduction to heroin, through a singer he was involved with sexually at the time, began with snorting the drug through a rolled up dollar bill. The first time he tried heroin, he recalled "I felt this peace like a kind of warmth" (Pepper and Pepper 1994:84). The feeling was so strong and so contrary to his usual sense of self-loathing that he concluded, "This is it. This is the only answer for me" (Pepper and Pepper 1994:85). Three months later, already addicted, he injected for the first time. Like many lifelong addicts, this experience became an ideal he craved for years: "I've never felt any better than that again" (Pepper and Pepper 1994:96). As he traveled from town to town performing concerts, he kept his heroin and drug paraphernalia in a small carrying case in the inside pocket of his suit. "I would set up my outfit [drug equipment] next to the bed in the hotel with my stuff [heroin] in a condom . . . to keep it from getting wet" (Pepper and Pepper 1994:97). Pepper, whose fame as a musician soared after his autobiography first appeared in 1979, died still addicted to heroin in 1982.

Conclusion

Most of the cases presented above fall into the category of "addicts who survived" (Courtwright, Joseph, and Des Jarlais 1989) and went on to tell their story to others, in their own writing or in oral history interviews. Some addicts eventually stop drug use. Many others, however, do not survive, falling victim to overdose, street violence, the elements, and disease. The enduring irony of illicit drug use is the jagged contradiction between the appeal (be it escape, feeling valued among peers, experiencing adventure) and the danger (of suffering, disease, and death) that are so intimately wrapped together under the influence of drugs. In part, this contradiction between dread and desire helps propel drug use dynamics across time and place, leading to the end of one drug era and the beginning of another.

CHAPTER 4

The '60s Drug Transition to the Time of AIDS

It was not just that there were large numbers of adolescents in the 1960s and 1970s who were willing to experiment with drugs, it was that they had the wherewithal to do so.

—David Courtwright, Herman Joseph, Don Des Jarlais,
Addicts Who Survived

The 1960s and early 1970s marked an important new turning point in drug use dynamics in the United States. Aptly referred to by some as the "'60s drug transition," this period is distinguished by three features: (1) a huge increase in the number of illicit drug users in the country; (2) the addition of new populations of drug users, particularly youth and young adults from the white middle and even upper classes; and (3) the popular rise of a new set of drugs, including, but not limited to, a strong emphasis on a class of drugs known as the hallucinogens. As Ralph Salerno noted about this development, based on his 20 years of experience with the New York City Police Department:

> I would say that the biggest change in narcotics trafficking since 1946 has been the expansion of the market. . . . Drug abuse used to be regarded and treated as a very limited problem, engaged in by people in the entertainment world and by some people in the lower socioeconomic classes. That changed radically. It became recognized as much wider problem that had invaded the middle class, and even the more affluent and better-educated people in our society. (Courtwright, Joseph, and Des Jarlais 1989:202)

Each of the three main changes that comprise the '60s drug transition will be examined in turn.

The Rising Numbers of Drug Users

Without question, one of the dramatic changes in drug use dynamics introduced as part of the transition was the size of the population that became actively involved in illicit drug use during the 1960s and 1970s. By 1979, it is estimated that 50 million people living in the United States at that time had tried marijuana at least once. Notably, this included two-thirds of all young adults. Equally jarring, the number of 12–17-year-olds who had ever smoked marijuana jumped from close to zero in 1960 to 30 percent by 1979 (Institute of Medicine 1982). Parallel increases occurred in the use of hallucinogenic drugs, with Gallup survey findings showing that in 1967 only 1 percent of college students reported having ever used a hallucinogenic substance compared to 18 percent a mere four years later (Johnson 1973). The radical increase in drug use among youth during the 1960s and early 1970s led to a series of studies designed to understand why adolescents use such drugs. This research found that regular marijuana users tended to value nonconventionality and sensation-seeking, but the studies did not find evidence of greater psychopathology among adolescent heavy users. Also, these studies did not identify a single factor—like pursuit of pleasure, relief of boredom, psychic distress, peer influence, or family problems—that could account for the widespread experimentation with drugs (Jessor 1979). Drug exploration, in effect, was becoming the norm during this era, but why this was so was not clear and the uncertainty weighed on the minds of social analysts and researchers.

The Middle-Class Drug Counterculture

In 1957, Harry Anslinger, head of the Federal Bureau of Narcotics, and his coauthor, Kenneth Chapman, in commenting on the rise in drug addiction among African Americans during the 1950s, raised the question: "What happened to white addicts? You don't see them" (Anslinger and Chapman 1957:182). Had Anslinger and Chapman waited just a few years, the unexpected answer to their bewildered question would have to be: everywhere! The '60s drug transition was marked not just by a startling increase in the absolute number of people using illicit drugs but also by the sociodemographic status of these new drug users. Quite simply, they were people who were not expected to use illegal, psychoactive substances! The head wave of the new population of drug users was composed especially of white, middleclass youth and young adults, often still in college, recently dropped out, or having just graduated, who were to some degree, from mild to extreme, alienated from the values and life goals of the prior generation. In time, their values, lifestyle, and drug use practices would be described as a counterculture, an alternative to mainstream America.

Some have described this period as a backlash against the straight-laced post–World War II years in U.S. society. During the 1950s, a generation of Americans who had experienced the uncertainties of the Great Depression, fought against the evils of fascism, and recently won a degree of stability and prosperity in the quiet, tree-lined suburbs were having children of their own, and lots of them (e.g., between 1950 and 1960 alone, the U.S. population grew by about 28 million). The prevailing atmosphere in suburbia was a contradictory and tension-filled mix of material comfort and fear. The sense of rising good fortune was a product of a general pattern of economic upswing. The sources of social anxiety were more complex but involved two factors.

First, the United States was in the midst of an intensely hostile cold war with the Soviet Union and other nation-states whose governments looked to Karl Marx's ideology of collectivism as inspiration for social development rather than to the capitalist marketplace. From the McCarthy hearings, designed to find communist agents lurking in Hollywood or in the house next door, to the door-to-door bomb shelter salesmen out to profit from national anxieties, to the sudden appearance of a morbid suburban fear of germs and insects invading the home, society, and the bodies that composed it seemed under attack from secretive enemies with evil intensions. Second, the new government-constructed highways that took whites by car to the new government-financed suburbs still led back to the abandoned cities, where the poor and people of color—who also had suffered, largely in silence, throughout the Great Depression and fought with noted bravery in the Second World War—were denied access to the new prosperity. Social inequality was the hidden but never fully forgettable flip side of the shinny penny of prosperity. This set of intertwined tensions provided the rationale for the emergence of what has been called the 1950's "culture of conformity."

According to Bernard Siegel (1970:11), societies "whose members attempt to establish and preserve a cultural identity in the face of what they feel are external threats to that identity" tend to develop a set of traits that he calls "defensive adaptation." Members of defensive societies see the social and physical environment, internally and externally, as hostile and threatening. In response, they develop a set of protective strategies to defend against their ever-present if shadowy enemies. Features of such strategies include centralized authority, emphasis on conformity, distinctive badges of in-group membership, and acceptance of social inequality as the steep price of stability in the face of imminent danger. The United States, during the 1950s, exhibited many of these traits. Its culture, which no doubt has been oversimplified as comprising conventional Ozzie and Harriet family values, cookie-cutter tract home lifestyles, and socially imposed constraint, nonetheless displayed a comparatively heavy emphasis on structure, security, and uniformity. Thus, based on a poll among youth during the mid-1950s, Bemmers and Radler

(1958:28) concluded that "A need and craving to be liked; drifting with the crowd; conformity, a kind of passive anti-intellectualism—these seem to be outstanding characteristics of the present-day younger generation as it has expressed itself in our poll."

Beneath the calm surface of 1950s society, however, an intense social struggle was brewing. In 1955, Martin Luther King, Jr., and a group of supporters began organizing against racial discrimination in the South. By 1963, the civil rights movement was in full swing and was actively and aggressively challenging structural racism, the dark side of the American success story. At the same time, the war in Vietnam had begun, with the first antiwar demonstration occurring in 1962. As a result of these and related social movements that in time mobilized women, various ethnic minorities, gays, the disabled, the elderly, and others on the margins of power and approval, the stultifying mood of the 1950s was broken. Opposition to the war, a sense of betrayal rooted in an awareness of racial injustice, and uneasiness with the prevailing social emphasis on materialism merged into a countercultural critique of the American way of life. A willingness to challenge authority in one sphere of life led to challenges in other areas as well, including a rejection of dominant attitudes about drug use. Drugs, in fact, took on specific roles in the counterculture that produced a level of curiosity about them that was unprecedented among prior generations of American youth.

As part of the questioning of dominant values, drugs were seen by some as a toll-free road to "self-discovery," a countercultural value that, according to William Partridge (1973), was continually brought up in discussions before and during group drug taking during the 1960s. As Goode (1984:145) indicates, drugs quickly came to be understood as a way to "strip away the impediments to direct confrontation with reality; they allowed the drug user to see things clearly, without society's lies." The "quest for self-knowledge" and self-exploration ran directly counter to dominant societal emphasis on conformity to institutional norms and grey flannel uniformity during the 1950s (Whyte 1956). Drug use also was rationalized by the countercultural valuing of "experimentation with alternatives to life in the larger society" (Partridge 1973:65). Other cultures, such as some New World Indian populations, in which drug use was socially accepted and ritualized, were of keen interest among card-carrying counterculturalists, leading to the popularity of drug-experience writers like Carlos Castaneda. Interest in alternative ways of living and a desire for simpler, less conflict-laden ways of being led to rural migrations and communalism, and allowed the cultivation of some of the drugs that were most valued by the new generation.

At the same time, a spiritual emphasis on transcending the strictures of materiality and of "expanding one's consciousness" also developed as primary motivations to take drugs. Also, consuming psychoactive substances was viewed in the counterculture as a method of building intimacy in romantic as well as general group relations; sharing drugs was seen as a "prelude to meaningful verbal communication" (Partridge 1973:65) and the building of trustworthy social bonds (a theme to be reactivated along with various related ideas over 25 years later with the appearance of so-called club drugs like Ecstasy). Finally, drug use—along with unconventional appearance—had value as a way of defining membership in the counterculture and of demarcating differences with and a critique of the parental generation. All of these sentiments, including seeing drug use as personally and socially beneficial, found expression in the rock-and-roll music that infused countercultural activities and gave voice to the core values of this social movement.

While not all who participated in some aspects of the counterculture would have felt comfortable with the title "hippie," it was a term that commonly was applied, often by outsiders, to those who fit a particular image and lifestyle, despite a level of heterogeneity that was belied by some shared values and behaviors. Exemplary is Partridge's (1973:14) description of a small social network of drug-using friends from this era:

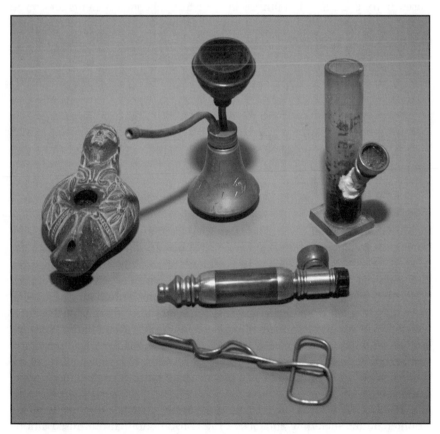

Marijuana pipes and clip. Courtesy of Drug Enforcement Administration.

> Most observers would agree that Jesus, his wife, Chuck, Martin, Patrick
> and Carol were hippies. They made their living making sandals and sell-
> ing drugs. They used LSD, marijuana, and opium in addition to heroin,
> cocaine, and morphine. They dressed in sandals, bell-bottom jeans, and
> so on. Both sexes wore their hair shoulder-length or longer. Their apart-
> ments flickered with neon lights, strobe lights, and day-glow posters; a
> stereo record player continually droned in the background and a water
> pipe with multiple hoses and mouthpieces for smoking marijuana occu-
> pied a central location on the living room floor.

Not surprisingly, individuals who embraced mainstream values viewed
many aspects of the counterculture as pointless, unpatriotic, and destructive
of America's moral order. Nonetheless, many countercultural ideals, clothing styles, and certainly the use of drugs diffused broadly in U.S. society, even
as the counterculture as a distinct social development lost steam and faded
from sight.

Thus, by the mid-1970s, illicit drugs—especially snorted cocaine—diffused beyond alienated youth to their far-from-alienated parents and on to
highbrow social circles, from the stars of Hollywood to the denizens of the
high-roller music industry, and from the weekend heroes of the sports field to
the well-heeled decision makers with penthouse keys and plush executive
suites. Popular newsstand magazines began running Alice in Wonderland
stories about "the 'smart set' offering coke spoons along with the caviar at
fashionable gatherings in Manhattan and Hollywood" (Gray 2000:99). The
New York Times Magazine (1975) called cocaine the new "champagne of
drugs," while *People* magazine (1978:16) announced: "In Showbiz, the Celebs
with a Nose for What's New Say the New High is Cocaine." Cocaine had
returned big time, but dressed up this time in high fashion with a whole new
clientele. The paraphernalia of cocaine snorting—such as tiny spoons and
double-edged razor blades—were iconized as gold-plated jewelry, "risqué
symbols of conspicuous consumption. Suddenly, cocaine was *au courant"*
(Courtwright, Joseph, and Des Jarlais 1989:354). Almost effortlessly, it
seems, an illegal substance that carried stiff penalties for possession and use
was absorbed into the upper-class armory of weapons of social display.
"Doing a line" (i.e., snorting) of cocaine powder with a tightly rolled hundred
dollar bill at an A-list party became a public statement about one's social
class standing, an ironic turn of events for a substance that just a few short
years previously had represented pathetic immorality, hard-bitten illegality,
and social failure. Furthermore, the ever-race-conscious American mind notwithstanding, like other cultural commodities before and since, a drug of the
Black underclass was usurped as a psychoactive pastime of the largely white
ruling class.

Hidden by the glamour of chic drug users, various components of the
counterculture, including enhanced drug consumption, also diffused among
younger members of the white working class, diminishing one arena of differ-

ence in the most multiracial and ethnically diverse social strata in U.S. society. Increased demand for cocaine led to extensive increases in the number of acres of South American soil devoted to coca cultivation. Replicating common cycles of capitalist production, the resulting glut of saleable cocaine led to a significant drop in the street price of the drug in 1983, making cocaine an affordable high for the working class.

New Drugs, New Visions

The drugs that have been mentioned in this book can be classified into four subtypes (Emboden 1974), based on their reported effects on users (although it should be emphasized that the same drug can have quite varied effects on different users or the same user at different times or during different phases of a single occasion of use):

- *Inebriants* are substances that cause intoxication, including temporary diminished control over physical and mental abilities, marked in the case of some substances by initial exhilaration and disinhibition and, with sufficient dosage, loss of consciousness. Alcohol is the widest known inebriant, others include ether, chloroform, benzine, and other inhaled solvents like glue or volatile chemicals like gasoline.

- *Hypnotics* are substances that cause tranquility, sleepiness, lethargy, and stupor, including tranquilizers and narcotics (e.g., heroin, morphine).

- *Stimulants* are substances that cause a heightened sense of wakefulness and the experience of enhanced cognitive and bodily tempo, including coffee, tea, tobacco, cocaine, and amphetamines.

- *Hallucinogens* are substances that cause visual, auditory, or other artificial sensory experiences and include drugs like LSD, peyote, various kinds of mushrooms, cannabis, and mescaline.

While all of these categories of drugs found new users during the '60s drug transition, it was, as noted, the hallucinogens that stand out as the initial drugs of choice of the broad wave of new drug users during this era. Many of the people during the 1960s who used drugs that fit into this category would not have agreed that the term hallucinogen accurately described drugs like LSD or mescaline, as they did not view the effects they produced as illusory or false. Rather the term psychedelic was in common use, as this term implies the user can "see more clearly, more acutely, more deeply" (Goode 1984:145).

Additionally, it would not be inaccurate to say that the '60s drug transition opened the floodgates of illicit drug use. Thus, while there was an emphasis on hallucinogens, representatives of the other classes of psychoactive drugs also emerged and diffused during this period. To get a better sense of the drug use dynamics of the transition years, the emergence (or reemergence) and diffusion of two hallucinogenic drugs (marijuana and LSD) plus one hypnotic (angel dust) and one stimulant (the amphetamine group) that came into widespread use during the 1960s/1970s, are examined in more detail below, while inhalant use is examined in the following chapter.

Marijuana Goes Mainstream

During the 1960s and 1970s, marijuana changed from being a drug that primarily could only be found in African American and Latino/a inner-city areas (even if all who came there to use or buy it were not African American and Latino/a) to a drug that was widely available and readily used in suburbia, especially among college and high school youth. Between 1962 and 1980, the percentage of young adults aged 18–25 years who used marijuana on a *daily basis* doubled, from 4 percent to 8 percent (Johnson et al. 1985). By 1982, almost one-third of 18–25-year-olds reported using the drug in the one-month period prior to being interviewed (Miller 1983). Gallup survey findings on college students who had ever tried marijuana showed a rapid rise during this era: 1967 (5 percent), 1969 (22 percent), 1970 (42 percent), and 1971 (51 percent) (Johnson 1973). The relatively sudden rise in marijuana use among economically and socially privileged youth led to widely voiced concern about a growing drug problem "in American society." Social concern about marijuana is not new, but marijuana's rapid rise to being the illicit drug

Harvested marijuana. Courtesy of Drug Enforcement Administration.

most commonly used by all sectors of society, including adolescents, significantly intensified the attention it has received in the media, among policy makers, from the criminal justice system, and elsewhere.

Partridge (1973:45–48) provides one account of marijuana use within the context of a long list of drugs, old and new, that found sudden favor among '60s drug users:

> The evening ritual begins with the passing of a joint, each person in succession drawing the marijuana smoke deeply into his lungs, holding it there, and passing the joint to the next person. Marijuana, smoked either in cigarette form or in a pipe, is the drug of choice . . . LSD, peyote, mescaline, psilocybin, amphetamines, barbiturates, and cocaine are not used with anything approaching regularity. . . . Even when there is an abundance of grass [marijuana], people follow this pattern of communally sharing [it]. After each individual receives the cigarette or pipe, inhales it deeply, and passes it on to the next person, he leans back and concentrates on retaining the smoke. It is felt that this action heightens the effects of smoking.

While not all marijuana smoking was communal during this period, nor was it always ritually segregated from other life activities, the pattern described by Partridge could be found in small gatherings across the country; even at large gatherings, like music concerts, passing a "joint" among strangers was not uncommon. Users reported that marijuana was favored because it was comparatively inexpensive, quite abundant and hence relatively easily acquired, and created feelings of "adequacy, well-being and euphoria" (Partridge 1973:49). Other reported effects included relaxation, loss of inhibition, greater openness, and enhanced sexuality. The mixing of marijuana and sex became a key factor in sudden jumps in sexually transmitted diseases during the 1960s and 1970s, a factor that contributed to the development of the free-clinic movement designed to provide no-cost medical response to the drug use- and lifestyle-related diseases and injuries of the counterculture.

Remarkably, one drug use dynamic that has been alleged many times—the assertion that marijuana is a natural stepping stone or gateway to harder drugs—did *not* occur for most users: "Of the seventy million Americans who smoked the weed, 98 percent didn't wind up on anything harder than martinis. Only a tiny fraction went on to become heroin or cocaine addicts, and the cause-effect connection to reefer for this group was no more evident than was the connection to coffee" (Gray 2000:187). However, as discussed in chapter 5, for those who moved to "harder drugs," use of marijuana almost always preceded the use of opiates, cocaine, and other illicit drugs, just as the use of tobacco and alcohol preceded the use of marijuana.

Tuning in to LSD

Lysergic acid diethylamide, or "acid" as it came to be known on the street, is one of several alkaloids derived from a parasitic fungus (*Claviceps pur-*

purea) that grows on cereal grains and grasses. Taken in its natural state, the fungus is quite poisonous, as evidenced by several very deadly epidemics in Europe during the Middle Ages caused by the consumption of rye bread infected with the ergot fungus. Poisoning of grazing animals is not uncommon also, causing a disease called ergotism, which is characterized by a number of striking symptoms including hyperexcitability, belligerence, staggering, falling down, convulsions, backward arching of the back, and gangrene of the nose, ears, tail, and limbs. In 1938, Albert Hoffman, a Swiss chemist, synthesized the LSD alkaloid but had no sense of its potential effects. He found out, however, five years later when in his lab he accidentally inhaled the substance (or got some on his hands, one of many controversial small details that make the study of drug use history a lively endeavor). He soon felt restless and dizzy and went home. There he lay down and later recorded that he "sank into a not unpleasant delirium which was marked by an extreme degree of fantasy [that included] fantastic visions of extraordinary vividness accompanied by a kaleidoscopic play of intense coloration continuously swirling about me" (Goode 1984:146). Hoffman later concluded that LSD causes psychosis.

During World War II, Hoffman's writings on LSD came to the attention of several psychiatrists in the U.S. military and the CIA, who conducted a number of LSD experiments with human subjects. No potential medical or military benefits were identified, and the testing ended. However, early in the 1960s this work was read by two up-and-coming Harvard University researchers, Timothy Leary and Richard Albert, who were concerned with understanding human consciousness. Leary and Albert also conducted human LSD experiments, and included themselves as subjects. Leary, who first tried hallucinogens (specifically, the mushroom psilocybin, which he later used in prison experiments) in 1960 during a study of folk healers in Mexico, described taking LSD as the most shattering experience of his life. Becoming an outspoken and articulate advocate of drug use, Leary (along with Albert) was fired from Harvard. He nonetheless continued enthusiastically to urge drug-induced "expansion of consciousness," a commitment that both attracted a significant following, including many luminaries from the arts (e.g., the Beatles), and landed him in trouble with the criminal justice system, leading to a jail sentence, a bold escape with the assistance of underground radicals, and political exile outside of the United States for much of the 1970s. His slogan, "Turn on, Tune in, Drop out" became an anthem during the '60s countercultural rebellion, which embraced the use of psychoactive drugs including LSD. Leary, wearing a t-shirt that read "If you only have one wish, make it BIG," died in his California home in 1996 (with some of his cremated remains later being launched into space, affirming that even in death he still had bold wishes).

Although counterculture suppliers learned how to produce LSD, production tended to be on a limited scale compared to the massive production of other psychoactive substances. It was distributed in several forms, including pills or dripped onto sugar cubes or paper. Even very tiny amounts were quite powerful; however, the effects were always unpredictable. Users differentiated most importantly between "good trips" and "bad trips." During the former, adherents described a blurring of sensory input (hearing colors, seeing sounds), intense hues, a Daliesque fluidity in the objects around them, mood swings and a sense of timelessness, as well as a feeling that they were seeing unveiled reality for the first time. By contrast, bad trips could be extremely dark and frightening, causing some users to question their sanity. The latter was enhanced by the tendency of LSD use to produce "flashbacks" or sudden LSD-like experiences even when users were not consuming the drug. Like most drugs that have come into popular use, LSD was praised by some users and damned by others, but its impact even among nonusers was significant. While the Beatles—who admitted LSD use—denied that their hit song "Lucy in the Sky with Diamonds" was about LSD, no one, especially anyone who listened to the song's lyrics, believed them.

PCP

One of the substances that emerged during the 1960s drug transition that is not a hallucinogen but nonetheless gained some followers is PCP (phencyclidine), a tranquilizer first developed in the 1950s. PCP began entering youth drug networks in a number of U.S. cities in the 1960s and gained in popularity through 1974. Thereafter, however, it began to lose its appeal, although it never completely disappeared from the post-1970s youth drug scene and, as noted in the next chapter, has in fact increased in popularity in recent years, in its own name or under the guise of other drug labels (Holland et al. 1998).

There has always been something elusive about angel dust (as it is known on the streets), a quality that is even implied in its street name. The name is also a product of its appearance—usually a white crystalline powder. The powder easily dissolves in either water or alcohol and has a distinctive bitter chemical taste. However, it turns up on the illicit drug market in a variety of forms, including tablets, capsules, liquid, and colored powders, and can be snorted, smoked, or swallowed as a pill. When users want to smoke PCP, they sprinkle it on mint, parsley, oregano, or marijuana, which they then roll into a cigarette paper or pour into a cut-open cigar that is then rewrapped.

As Harvey Feldman and Michael Aldrich (1990:22) remark, "The PCP phenomenon entered the world of youth and diminished without the [national drug monitoring systems] ever identifying it." When questions about PCP were finally added to the federally sponsored Monitoring the Future Study in 1979, lifetime prevalence for use among twelfth graders was found to be 2.4 percent, falling over the years to 1.4 percent by 1991 (Johnston, O'Malley, and Bachman 1997), but increasing to 2.5 percent in 2003 (National Institute on Drug Abuse, 2004a). The National Institute on Drug Abuse organized a study of angel dust and found that exclusive PCP use was rare and that its greatest appeal was among especially restless youth who experienced life as generally boring and uninteresting. The participants

Packets containing PCP. Courtesy of Drug Enforcement Administration.

in the study appeared to be quite familiar with the drug's effects and how to modulate them by controlling dosage levels. Of special concern to regular PCP users was a state they referred to as "burnout," in which the user exhibits memory loss and incoherent thoughts. Cutting back on consumption of PCP emerged as the folk cure for burnout.

At low to moderate doses, the physiological effects of PCP include a mild increase in breathing rate combined with a pronounced rise in blood pressure and pulse rate. Users report feelings of strength, power, and invulnerability that have contributed to increases in risky behavior among users, who, with continued use, become addicted to the drug. Overdose is fairly common and scary for users, and as a result, PCP leads to a large number of emergency room visits in which patients exhibit a comparatively high rate of violent and suicidal behaviors. These features contribute to many onetime PCP users who, having experienced the drug, forswear all future use. Yet, PCP, having gained a place on the U.S. illicit drug menu, still finds new users.

Speed Kills: Amphetamine

Amphetamine is a semisynthetic drug (i.e., a drug created through laboratory manipulation of a natural substance), that has been marketed as Benzedrine, Dexedrine, and other pharmaceutical names.

Amphetamine originally was derived from ephedrine, a natural stimulant found in the country mallow plant. The mallows, a large family of herbs, shrubs, and trees with fused stamens (the male reproductive part of the plant), include the flowering hibiscus bush, hollyhock, cotton, and okra. The drug is structurally related to adrenaline, the body's natural "fight or flight" hormone. Ephedrine is one of the world's oldest medicines, having been discovered by the Chinese as a cure for respiratory problems like asthma more than 5,000 years ago. Modern laboratory research has shown that ephedrine increases body metabolism, promotes perspiration, and helps stop asthmatic reactions to environmental triggers.

Amphetamine was first synthesized in Germany in 1887, but its medicinal potential as a stimulant was not recognized in Western biomedicine until the late 1920s, about the time Japanese scientists were discovering methamphetamine. Like ephedrine, amphetamine enlarges the bronchial small sacs of the lungs, allowing individuals with lung disease like asthma to take in larger quantities of needed air. In 1932, the pharmaceutical company Smith, Kline, and French began marketing the famous Benzedrine Inhaler, which provided a spray of Benzedrine (amphetamine sulphate) to relieve the symptoms of nasal congestion, asthma, hay fever, and the common cold. Jazz musician Art Pepper reported in his autobiography that in the early 1940s, he and other musicians would remove the drug strips from the inside of the inhalers and "put these strips in our mouths, behind our teeth. They really got you roaring as an upper. Your scalp would tingle and you'd get chills all over, and then it would center in your head and start ringing around. You'd feel as if your whole head was lifting off" (Pepper and Pepper 194:43). Amphetamine also has been prescribed for a wide range of health problems such as narcolepsy (compulsive sleepiness), depression, alcoholism, Parkinson's disease, schizophrenia, obesity, and, paradoxically, hyperactivity in children (among whom it produces calming rather than stimulating effects).

The experiential effects of amphetamine reported by users include euphoria, wakefulness, enhanced self-confidence, a feeling of strength, aggressiveness, chattiness, loss of appetite, prolonged initiative, and frenetic busyness. Reproducing these desired effects tends to require larger doses over time. After use, as the drug is metabolized by the body, withdrawal symptoms begin to set in, including intense craving, deep melancholy, a sense of meaninglessness, fatigue, lack of initiative, and unprovoked fear. Prolonged use is associated with significant weight loss, muscle and joint pain, and the obsessive performance of repetitive small tasks (e.g., continually looking for a lost item). Suspicion of others and hostility are commonly reported by those associated with heavy amphetamine users. Other health consequences, of which there are many, are examined in chapter 9.

As an effective stimulant that opens the adrenergic receptor sites of the heart and lungs, allowing an increase in the body's metabolic rate and the burning of calories, and as a result producing greater energy and wakefulness, amphetamine quickly drew the interest of military leaders. Both Allied and Axis soldiers were administered amphetamine tablets during World War II, which on occasion were found to set off instances of psychotic aggression among combatants. Even Hitler received daily injections of the drug from his personal physician, Dr. Theodore Morell, a practice that is believed over time to have damaged his capacity for effective judgment and to have weakened his overall health (Heston and Heston 2000). Battlefield use of amphetamine continues. In the bloody 1991–2002 insurrection in Sierra Leone, for example, rebel leader Foday Sankoh freely distributed amphetamine, as well as marijuana and cocaine, to his young soldiers (many of whom were teenagers or preteens), a factor in their gruesome assault with AK-47s and machetes on the citizenry of the country.

In that amphetamine produces a sudden sense of euphoria, called a "rush" by users, these pharmaceutical drugs began to be diverted for recreational consumption during the 1940s and 1950s and, with the initiation of illicit production in underground laboratories, had become by the 1960s "one of the half-dozen most popular street drugs" (Goode 1984:176), especially in the western sector of the United States. Street names for amphetamine and a group of chemically linked if structurally varying drugs include: crank, ice, bennies, pep pills, speed, uppers, meth, crystal, and wakeups. Differences among these entities include their actual chemical makeup, the form in which they are consumed, their appearance, and their purity. For example, both "crank" and "ice" are methamphetamines, but the former is a powder that can be smoked, snorted, or injected, while the latter is a crystalline substance that is most commonly smoked. All of these substances are central nervous system stimulants.

During the 1960s and 1970s, daily amphetamine injection (every 4–8 hours) became common in a population of younger users who called themselves and were called by others "speed freaks" or "meth-heads." After binging on the drug for several days, a routine that was called "a run," users learned to bring themselves back down by using barbiturates or heroin, which, in turn, led to many "speed freaks" becoming addicted to the latter and eventually switching to primary heroin use because its effects were easier to manage and less stressful on the body. An example at the individual level of how this kind of "emergent drug dissatisfaction" occurs can be seen in the case of Paul, a 28-year-old drug user interviewed in a HHC study, who told us:

> Sometimes, when I was doing the coke, I do the coke and to calm down I was doing heroin. When I started smoking cocaine, I would see monsters. I see people that was not there, boy I was seeing people, I was seeing monsters. I started running. I don't know, its crazy. . . . [W]hen I do heroin, it's like down, everything is cool, everything's slow, you know, I'm relaxed. And I feel happy, and you know, comfortable. (HHC taped interview, SAVA 1 study)

The sudden jump in amphetamine use provoked legislative response, with greater restraint being imposed on amphetamine prescribing, a move that eventually led to a 90 percent drop in legal production of the drug. As access dried up, amphetamine use was replaced by another pharmaceutical: methaqualone or "ludes," a drug that was introduced as an alternative to barbiturates. This drug's initial appeal was in part its reputation (promoted by the pharmaceutical industry), as a "safe drug." By 1972, "luding out," which involved taking methaqualone with wine, had become a popular college pastime. Before long there were a growing number of reports of acute reactions and fatal overdoses. Congress again imposed strong measures to control access, leading to a decline in both medical and recreational use. The drug came to be used unknowingly by many heroin addicts, as it has been a common adulterant of powder heroin.

From the Counterculture to the Rise of AIDS

The last quarter of the twentieth century witnessed various new waves of drug use and startling new consequences of drug consumption, with AIDS emerging as the most significant drug-related epidemic in human history. While the role of drug use in the spread of AIDS in the United States will be discussed in chapter 9, a number of other important changes occurred in the U.S. drug scene during the closing decades of the last century. Several of these, in fact, contributed to the spread of the AIDS epidemic. While some drug use changes, such as the conversion of cocaine powder into crack or the return to older "chasing the dragon" forms of heroin smoking have led to less syringe use (although not to a decline in the AIDS epidemic because of drug-influenced sexual risk), one change has moved consumption in the opposite direction. During the 1990s, drug users learned how to convert crack back into an injectable solution (by mixing it with vinegar or lemon juice), a strategy that users claim eliminates impurities, is cheaper, and provides a stronger high than smoking crack (Carlson, Falck, and Siegal 2000).

In Connecticut, we have tracked the movement of this practice up the coast from New York along Highway 95 to Bridgeport, from there to New Haven, and from New Haven up through the middle of the state along Highway 91 to Hartford and beyond to Springfield, Massachusetts. At each of the cities along this course, rates of awareness of the practice and involvement in crack cocaine conversion diminish the further one moves away from New York. This pattern suggests crack conversion knowledge and practice moves along drug user social networks that are comprised of individuals who are linked to two or more networks, and this linkage is critical to the movement across social geography. Also, this conversion practice was found to be much more common among white drug users than African American or Latino/a drug users, suggesting the ethnic-specific nature of many drug use social networks.

The Rise of Methamphetamine

In the late 1980s, a new wave of stimulant use developed, coming this time especially in the form of "crank" (methamphetamine). Initially, the drug was produced in "illegal laboratories in California, trafficked by [the] Hell's Angels and other biker and prison gangs and sold primarily to members of the white working class" (Inciardi 1992:51). From California and the Northwest coast, methamphetamine use spread across the country throughout the 1990s and into the twenty-first century. For example, in February 2003 members of the Soldiers of the Aryan Culture, a Utah gang, were arrested on various charges including operating a methamphetamine ring throughout the state. The gang is run as a military unit among inmates in the Utah prison system as well as on the street. Referred to as "soldiers," members adhere to a strict code of conduct that requires them to study white supremacy literature and participate in the gang's drug production and distribution system. Some of defendants in the cases were accused of attempting to kill seven individuals, one of whom was badly maimed, and of making violent threats in order to maintain their control of drug trafficking in the state. Increasingly throughout the 1990s, biker gangs had to compete with Mexican gangs for control of the methamphetamine trade, a conflict that Mexican gangs have tended to win.

Mexico-based drug trafficking gangs entered the illicit methamphetamine trade in about 1995 and moved quickly to control drug production and distribution. The advantage these groups had was access on the international market to large quantities of the various chemicals needed produce the drug (possession of which in the U.S. was outlawed by Congress with the passage

Bag of methamphetamine. Courtesy of Drug Enforcement Administration.

of the Methamphetamine Control Act) and their access to already existing heroin, cocaine, and marijuana smuggling and distribution networks, especially in the western United States but increasingly across the Midwest and South as well. To increase production, the Mexican gangs gained control over large laboratories in Mexico capable of turning out significant quantities of very pure methamphetamine.

From the labs the drug is smuggled into the United States and then transported using various means, including semitrailers, private cars, and motorcycles ridden by outlaw motorcycle gangs. At times, couriers who board commercial airlines and package delivery services are also used. When the drugs reach their destination, they are sold wholesale to local dealers, including local street gangs. These groups, in turn, dilute the relatively pure Mexican methamphetamine at "cut houses," which are usually private residences where methamphetamine is mixed with caffeine, methylsulfonylmethane (a nutritional supplement) or other adulterants to increase profits. The meth is then packaged in various quantities for sale by street dealers.

Not all production occurs in Mexico, however. There are "super labs" in California and smaller, clandestine meth labs have been found in many parts of the United States in recent years. Producers use various solvents, chemicals, and over-the-counter medicines to make the drug. Because of the solvents used, meth labs can easily catch fire or explode. Often labs are detected because of the odor they give off; also, producers need large quantities of coffee filters, acetone, camp fuel, lye, cold pills, and matches. One clear tip-off for the police that a meth lab is operating in an area is that large quantities of these items are suddenly being shoplifted from local stores. Expecting eventual police detection, methamphetamine laboratory operators have often been found to be well armed, and their laboratories are sometimes booby-trapped and equipped with cameras for scanning the surrounding area.

As contrasted with prior drug trends, rural areas have been heavily hit by meth. For example, Sioux City, Iowa, with a total population of only 84,000, has emerged as a regional center for meth trafficking because it sits at the intersection of Iowa, Nebraska, and South Dakota. Although Mexican drug gangs control the meth trade in Sioux City, small-time independent producers, called "cooks," operate labs in more rural parts of the state. Small labs produce less than an ounce at a time, but the number of these labs has been growing. Iowa police found two meth labs in 1994; in 1999 they raided 803 labs. "For every one that learns to cook, they teach 10," says Marti Reilly, a police drug task force spokesman. "It's kind of the Amway pyramid thing" (Bonne 2001:1).

In addition to attracting white urban and rural working-class users, methamphetamines diffused to various minority populations. For example, Tooru Nemoto and colleagues (2002) at the Center for AIDS Prevention Studies at the University of California, San Francisco, have studied methamphetamine use among Filipino drug users in the Bay Area. The second largest Asian and

Meth pipe. Courtesy of Drug Enforcement Administration.

Pacific Islander (API) population in the United States (after the Chinese), Filipinos have been found to initiate drug use at an earlier age than other API populations in the country. Among Filipinos in California, methamphetamine is known as *shabu*. Sold on the street as a white, odorless, crystalline power, shabu is smoked among Filipinos "for the energy and general feeling of well-being it induces" (Nemoto, Operario, and Soma 2002:531). Polydrug use was the most common pattern in Nemoto's sample, with most participants using at least one other drug besides shabu in the last 30 days, including 87 percent who also used cocaine and 42 percent who also used hallucinogens.

Michael Gorman and Robert Carroll (2000) reported on the use of methamphetamines among men who have sex with men (MSM) in Puget Sound, Washington. They identified a number of user subgroups, including men who used meth as part of their involvement in party circuits, those who used it in gay baths and sex clubs, a distinct group of transgender/transsexual meth users, and a group of HIV+ men who use meth to self-medicate HIV symptoms. Similarly, Rafael Diaz (1998:78) has described meth use among gay Latino men who favor it "as a way to deal with ambivalent feelings regarding anal intercourse. For some the drug facilitates taking the passive role."

As this list of meth-using populations suggests, the drug is now widely used across regions and social strata, with different groups having different motivations for their use of the drug. In other words, the fast-paced methamphetamine wave sweeping across the United States consists of multiple smaller waves at the regional, local, and social group levels. From western ultra-rightwing biker gangs to the party crowd at late-night gay dance clubs in New York City, meth has become the common drug of choice of groups that would otherwise claim little or nothing in common. This type of diffusion pattern, across not only regions but social groups with highly diverse cultural, ethnic, and sexual identities and lifestyles as well, provides a useful social gauge of the national significance of a drug use trend. By this measure, the methamphetamine wave is historically significant.

As will be explored in chapter 6, another significant drug use trend of the last quarter century has been the arrival of the club drug transition, which, like the '60s drug transition, has involved a variety of drugs (including Ecstasy, the most commonly used "club drug," and, of note, a form of methamphetamine), several different drug-using populations, and the appearance of new consumption settings, drug paraphernalia sets, and social meanings attached to drug use.

Pharmaceutical Diversion

The diversion of pharmaceuticals to street use, what might be called the production of "under-the-counter drugs" (Vivian et al. in press), has, in its own right, become big business, reaping huge profits for giant pharmaceutical companies, physicians, pharmacies, and illicit distributors alike. It is estimated that pharmaceutically produced drugs that are sidetracked for illicit use now account for 30 percent of the illegally consumed drugs in U.S. society, and collectively are *among the most commonly used illicit substances*. Diversion takes a number of different forms.

One method is for drug seekers to fake a medical condition in order to convince a physician to prescribe desired pharmaceutical drugs, a ploy that exploits high-volume, short-visit doctor–patient encounters that are especially common in public clinic settings. Fraudulent patients have learned to convincingly, if falsely, display a variety of health problems. For patients seeking narcotic drugs, the three most commonly faked illnesses are renal colic (achieved by feigning pain on the left side of the body—to rule out appendicitis—combined with a burning sensation during urination), toothache (and being new in town and not yet having a dentist), and tic douloureux (which is used because it lacks clinical signs and diagnosis is made on the basis of patient reported symptoms of recurring, intense episodes of facial pain).

A second strategy, and probably the most common, is the use of forged prescriptions. This can be achieved by stealing and filling in blank prescription pads (a scam that is often directed at busy emergency rooms and crowded clinics), altering a legally obtained prescription (e.g., by significantly increasing the dosage prescribed), or using computers and photocopy machines to forge legitimate appearing prescriptions. Increasingly, drug users also are using pharmacy "doctor lines" to telephone in prescriptions as if they were a physician, and then visit the pharmacy to pick up their prescription as the patient.

Doctor shopping is another strategy. It entails visiting multiple doctors with the same health complaint in the hopes of getting multiple prescriptions. Moreover, drugs are stolen outright, with break-ins at institutions that store or dispense pharmaceuticals, a practice that also has produced an increase in the rate of break-ins in health-related institutions like the Hispanic Health Council that do not actually have any medicines. In addition to the efforts of drug users, some physicians and pharmacists have become active "pill pushers," reaping great financial gain. Professionals who are willing to go down this path get to be well-known among drug users and can wind up distributing incredibly large quantities of pharmaceutical drugs. For example, in March 2003, police raided the office of a Tucson physician and accused her of operating a pain medication "pill mill," including over 350 counts of dispensing a controlled substance outside the normal practice of medicine (Kaufman 2003).

Another diversion strategy is to identify the chemical structure of a pharmaceutical drug and find a laboratory that can produce it. For example, Joan Moore (1978) found that barbiturate-dealing Chicano street gangs not only steal drugs from pharmacies or pharmacy warehouses, they also contract with manufacturers in Mexico to produce "bootleg" barbiturates for street sales. Finally, Internet Web sites are becoming busy sources for the purchase of diverted pharmaceutically controlled substances. Adware, an insidious form of computer program that can be attached to an Internet site and then be disseminated in the form of uninvited pop-ups on the computer screens of all who visit the booby-trapped site, has become an increasingly common way to advertise under-the-counter pharmaceuticals. Whatever the route of diversion, the most sought after pharmaceuticals in diversion schemes include: Vicodin, Lortab, Lorcet, Norco, Tylenol #3 and #4, Diazepam, Xanax, Stadol, Valium, Phenergan with Codeine, Tussionex, Ultram, Ultracet, Soma, and OxyContin.

The last drug on this list, OxyContin, was introduced in recent years as a longer-lasting, time-released form (e.g., for up to 12 hours) of the effective painkilling drug oxycodone (the active ingredient in combination pharmaceutical medicines like Percocet, Percodan, and Tylox). A semisynthetic opioid drug, OxyContin is derived from the opium alkaloid called thebaine, which is similar to codeine, methadone, and morphine in its effects. It was developed to address the longer-term pain-prevention needs of ambulatory patients with diseases like rheumatoid arthritis or cancer, and soon became one of the most commonly prescribed medical narcotics. Not long after being put on the market, data from the Drug Abuse Warning Network (DAWN—a national system for collecting emergency room patient reports of drug use) showed that it also was involved in an increasing number of emergency department overdose cases and deaths.

Diverted to illicit use under street names like Oxy's, OC's, Killers, Poor Man's Heroin, and Hillbilly Heroin, illicit efforts to acquire the drug led to notable increases in burglaries, thefts, and robberies of both private residences and pharmacies. Interestingly, the diversion of "Oxy" to the street is most common where illicit methamphetamine use is lowest: the Northeast sector of the United States, although it is spreading nationally. For example, in 2001, the Center for Behavioral Health in Louisiana reported that 40 percent of new treatment admissions throughout the state were for the abuse of Oxy-Contin. As of 2001, the Office of Diversion Control reported that medical examiners in 31 states have documented 1,096 overdose deaths involving oxycodone, 117 of these deaths involving OxyContin (Drug Enforcement Administration 2002).

OxyContin was developed for oral administration in tablet form; street users, however, discovered that they could crush the tablets (with tablet crushers sold at pharmacies) and snort the powder, defeating the intended time-release action mechanism and hastening the body's rapid absorption of the entire tablet. Injection of the crushed tablet, which also facilitates body absorption, is possible but it requires removing the tablet's outer coating, either by sucking on it or scraping it off, followed by melting the remainder in a cooker, adding water, mixing, and injecting the resulting drug solution. Users report a euphoric high but without, they claim, the debilitating withdrawal symptoms associated with heroin use. However, some OxyContin users are, in fact, moving to heroin. Researchers affiliated with the Ohio Substance Abuse Monitoring Network (OSAM) operated by Wright State University School of Medicine have studied recent heroin initiators (Siegal et al. 2000). Half of the individuals in their small opportunistic sample, aged 18–33 years, reported they had ended OxyContin just prior to beginning heroin injection. Participants indicated that heroin was more readily available and less expensive than OxyContin. Importantly, they also reported that they would never have tried heroin if they had not first become addicted to OxyContin.

Another group of drugs that has played a major role in pharmacy drug diversion are the benzodiazepines (BZDs), a relatively new family of anxiety-reducing tranquilizers that was discovered in 1957 and was being sold throughout the world by the 1960s and 1970s. One of the BZDs, valium, was at one time the best-selling prescription drug in the United States. Currently the top-selling tranquilizer is Xanax, also a BZD. Halcion, yet another BZD, is one of the most widely prescribed sleeping pills. Over 60 million prescriptions a year are written in the United States for these and other BZDs. These drugs target receptors in the limbic or emotional regulation region of the brain instead of depressing activity throughout the central nervous system.

In addition to their medicinal uses, BZDs have become popular with various populations of drug users. In our studies of heroin injectors in Hartford, Connecticut, for example, we have found that mixing heroin and Xanax or another BZD is quite common. Studies by George Yacoubian and coworkers (2002) in Houston found that the rate of benzodiazepine use jumped from 4.8 percent of individuals arrested for drug use in 1994 to 14.1 percent of those arrested in 1997. In several parts of the country, the BZDs have displaced the opiates in frequency of use among arrestees. In other words, BZDs and narcotic analgetics like oxycodone are rapidly joining heroin, cocaine, and methamphetamine as the "big boys" of street drug use in the United States, after marijuana, which is far and away the most frequently used and enduring illegal psychoactive drug in the country.

Remarkably, even AIDS medicines are being diverted for their psychoactive effects. Dronabinol (sold under the brand name Marinol), a drug prescribed for people living with AIDS to help stimulate their often sagging appetites, has found an underground market. The prescription contains delta-9-tetrahydrocannabinol (THC), which is the active ingredient in marijuana. Another AIDS medication, efavirenze (sold as Sistiva), prescribed to help keep viral infections in check, is said by some illicit users to have psychoactive properties.

Understanding Evolutionary Aspects of Drug Use Dynamics

As review of drug use dynamics from the founding of America to the contemporary period reveals, the emergence of new drugs and new forms of old drugs involves the social and physical *movement of drug materials and knowledge* from: (1) indigenous sources, such the awareness of the stimulative properties of plants like coca among pre-Columbian Native American populations or familiarity with medicinal value of the country mallow plant in traditional Chinese medicine; (2) scientific laboratory purification, alteration, and/or synthesis, or, in cases of laboratory drugs that had no indigenous predecessors, discovery; (3) street diversion and/or underground production; and (4) illicit consumption. While in their original unpurified and less-concentrated form in indigenous societies, and in light of their ritually regulated use, most of the traditional psychoactive substances produced limited if any negative social consequences or health problems, a point that Dwight Heath (1988) has argued as well for indigenous alcohol consumption. Freed of most socially imposable constraints, made available in potent form, and driven by nonritual motivations for consumption, including self-medication for the injuries of social inequality or the boredom of perceived dead-end lifestyles, the capacity of psychoactive drugs to do harm was magnified many times, an issue to which we return in chapter 9.

Under these conditions, over the course of U.S. history, new drug use patterns have emerged periodically and spread across the social landscape, along social networks of connected individuals. Like irregular ripples on a pond from their point of origin, new drug use patterns move in a series of waves (Becker 1967), which Bruce Johnson (Johnson and Manwar 1991; Johnson and Golub 1998) has called "drug eras" (intervals characterized by the emergence and spread of a new drug). Johnson and coworkers identify four stages in the development of a drug era: (1) incubation (after a new drug is first introduced but it has very limited use); (2) expansion (diffusion of the drug to a wider network of users); (3) plateau (established use of the drug, with some individuals starting use and relatively equal numbers curtailing use); and finally (4) decline (current users curtail use, while fewer and fewer new users adopt the drug). As Bruce Johnson and Ali Manwar (1991:2) affirm, there has been a "relative absence of concepts to understand why and how declines in drug use occur after a peak" in use, and this is a poorly researched topic (in part, because it is not of top priority for policy makers who are concerned about new rather than fading waves of drug use). While most drug waves reach a peak and then decline in popularity, an episodic pattern may emerge as a fading drug is replaced or at least joined by a "renewed form" of itself, such as the two-century-long broad-based waves of cocaine use, consisting of the following original and renewed forms:

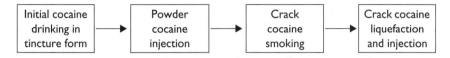

Figure 2 Evolutionary pathway of cocaine use

At the local level, many variants and branches multiplied the complexity of this "evolutionary course" (e.g., the mixing of cocaine with Viagra or with Ecstasy) in a manner similar to the complex general course and local branching found in biological evolution. Moreover, it must be noted that powder cocaine injection has continued to the present, as has crack smoking, producing an evolution branching into at least three contemporary "subspecies" (i.e., forms) of cocaine in use (for an interesting comparative case for changing cocaine use patterns in Argentina, see Epele 2003). Along the way, cocaine freebasing branched off from powder cocaine use as a new drug use practice, but it was largely driven to "extinction" by the appearance on the street of crack. It must be stressed, however, unlike biological species, "extinct" drug forms can always be renewed, as appears to have occurred with PCP.

The Johnson model calls attention as well to what might be called "intergenerational drug switching," that is, drug patterns that change as one generation of drug users dies out (including actual death as well as stopping drug use) and is not replaced by a younger generation with the same drug use practices. Another process that contributes to drug use dynamics is "intragenerational drug switching," that is, individuals and groups actually changing their drug use patterns over time.

Change in the popularity of a drug within or across drug use generations is effected by a number of factors, including (1) loss of regular access to it (e.g., because of changing legislation and police focus on making arrests for possession, such as what happened with amphetamine and quaaludes); (2) growing dissatisfaction with unpleasant side effects (e.g., bad trips and flashbacks among LSD users); (3) changes in the user population and its wider community (e.g., antiheroin addict sentiments that developed in the African American community that facilitated transition to cocaine use); (4) the arrival on the drug scene of a new drug with more appealing attributes including a lower price (e.g., the movement from amphetamine to heroin in California); and (5) growing fear of risks associated with a drug or a method of using the drug (e.g., transition from injecting to inhaling or smoking heroin to avoid the health risks associated with injection). For example, one form of drug switching that occurs, here termed "effects switching," involves either movement to a new drug that is felt to be more potent (because users find they are not enjoying an older drug as much as they used to) or switching to a drug that is felt to have smoother effects, including fewer unpleasant or undesirable side effects. Peca, a participant in a HHC study (SAVA 1) of Puerto Rican drug users, for example, reported the following about his personal drug switching:

> I changed to a stronger drug. I changed from reefer [marijuana] to cocaine because the high I was getting from the reefer I wasn't liking it. I didn't like the high from the reefer because I was getting drowsy, hungry, tired. I was getting silly, so I changed from the reefer to cocaine because the cocaine kept me awake, active.

While individual switching is no doubt common, groups within the same social network may begin to share their ideas and experiences, as well as new drug sources, leading to more general local switching patterns. Widespread, intra- and intergenerational switching throughout a region or even beyond one region of the country is likely to reflect changes in broader social and economic patterns within or beyond the drug scene (e.g., changing values and cultural attitudes, drug supply issues), as seen in the '60s drug transition.

The methamphetamine wave reveals another drug use dynamic, namely the social diversification of use. We are seeing certain drugs successfully dif-

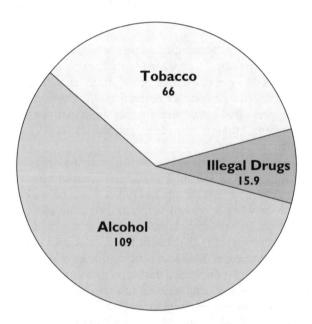

Source: 2001 National Household Survey on Drug Abuse [online] http://www.oas.samhsa.gov/NHSDA/2k1NHSDA/vol2/appendixh_2.htm and http://www.oas.samhsa.gov/NHSDA/2k1NHSDA/vol2/appendixh_1.htm

Figure 3   Comparative number of alcohol, tobacco, and illicit drug users (in millions)

fuse across the social links that bridge different ethnic, lifestyle, cultural, or identity groups. In the process, a particular drug is adapted by users, both in terms of what the drug means to them and how they consume it, so that it fits into (conceptually, experientially, and in terms of the emotions its use triggers) the set of ideas, sentiments, and behavioral patterns that demarcates each group of users. Consider the following question: Does heroin that is "mixed" (dissolved in water) and injected rapidly in an abscessed vein by a nervous junky in the decrepit hallway of an abandoned building hold the same meaning for its user as the heroin that is smoked by a group of adventure-seeking, middle-class college students in the comfort and privacy of their college dorm room? Very likely not, although chemically there need not be any difference at all.

Some drugs, it is clear, diffuse widely across social groups, others do not. Alcohol, without doubt, is the reigning king of diversification. Wine, for example, which ranges from very costly French imports served in polished crystal at the finest restaurants to cheap rotgut passed under the concealment of a rumpled paper bag among bottle gangs on U.S. skid rows, possesses quite varied social meanings and use practices across religious groups, social classes, ethnic groups, and regionally. Chemically, whatever the price, the label, or the design of the container, wine is ethanol. Culturally, however, it is many, quite distinct things to the quite different groups who consume it. So, too, with widely diffused illicit drugs.

Conclusion

As we have seen, the '60s drug transition radically reshaped drug use patterns in the United States. These changes, which have endured into the twenty-first century, have included: (1) a generalization of illicit drug use across multiple sectors of the U.S. population; (2) a jump in the number of illicit drugs in use; and (3) the ever more rapid introduction and spread of new or renewed drugs.

As the preceding account suggests as well, drug use dynamics are propelled (to varying extents) along a regional and even multiregional course, with sometimes small, sometimes considerable local variations in timing and detail, by various forces, including drug use innovation. As described in chapters 5 and 6, one sector of the population—youth—play a particularly important role in this process of change.

CHAPTER 5

The Role of Youth in New Drug Use Practices

One of the problems with conventional drug education is the notion that we have the ability to prevent experimentation with drugs among teenagers.

—Marsha Rosenbaum, "'Just Say Know' to Teenagers and Marijuana"

The "k-hole" is a drug-induced state of disassociation that has come to be the sought-after goal of a new generation of mobile young drug users. When users achieve the k-hole, time bends, space distorts, and intense dreamlike hallucinations follow. Lasting from 10 minutes up to an hour, the k-hole is so appealing that young users will shoot up the powerful and potentially deadly anesthetic that causes it 8–10 times in a drug use session, reinjecting each time the body successfully metabolizes the drug and its effects fall away. Ketamine, one of the so-called new-wave club drugs, is the drug used to produce the k-hole. While most ketamine users sniff or smoke it as they listen or dance to techno or other music in clubs, some youth drug users, through experimentation, found that injecting the drug produced a much more intense psychological and physical effect, including the prized mental state— the k-hole (Lankenau and Clatts 2002).

The practice of injecting ketamine or "Special K," as it is popularly known, caught on among youth, many of whom already had tried injecting other drugs like cocaine or heroin, but also among others who had never injected drugs before. The practice gained adherents particularly with a stratum of homeless youth who travel alone and in small groups from city to city around the country, panhandling, selling sex, or dealing drugs, including ketamine, to new users who may not be familiar with the drug. To study these nomads, drug researchers have had to invent new research methodologies. One approach that has proven successful is the "call-in" strategy. Partici-

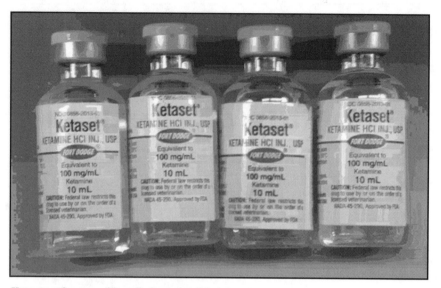

Ketamine. Courtesy of Drug Enforcement Administration.

pants enrolled in such a study are asked periodically to call collect to a project telephone number and respond to a set of computer questions about where they are, what they are doing, current drug use practices, and related matters. As incentive to continue their involvement, participants are given an ATM card; after each call-in, a payment is deposited into the participant's individual ATM account, and they can withdraw the money at a bank anywhere in the country.

While the number of ketamine injectors is comparatively small at this point, the initiation and spread of this practice suggests why the period of adolescence and young adulthood is pivotal to the fickle nature of the illicit drug use scene (Schensul et al. 2000).

Identifiable Patterns of Youth Drug Use

Youth play a critical role in the discovery of new drug use behaviors and the diffusion of many new psychoactive drugs, drug combinations, and methods of drug use for four reasons: (1) longer-term drug use patterns tend to begin during adolescence; (2) an experimental attitude is more common among youth; (3) most illicit drug use occurs during the teen and young adult years; and (4) risk behaviors cluster among some youth.

Setting the Stage for Longer-Term Drug Patterns

It is known from a number of seminal studies that patterns of longer-term drug use generally begin before the age of 21. Individuals who start using illicit drugs prior to this age are far more likely to move on to polydrug and hard drug use compared to their non-drug using teen peers. For example, in studies of twins in which one sibling smoked marijuana before the age of 17 and the other did not, the early marijuana smoker was twice as likely as the sibling to go on to use drugs in the opium family, three times as likely to use cocaine, three times as likely to use sedatives, and almost four times as likely to use hallucinogens. Moreover, the sibling who used marijuana before age 17 was between 1.6 and 6 times more likely to report alcohol and/or drug abuse or dependence than the twin, although the majority of even the early marijuana using individuals did not later develop drug or alcohol use or dependence (Lynskey et al. 2003). Long-term drug use patterns, in short, are established during the teen and young adult years, as reflected in many of our interviews with drug users at the Hispanic Health Council. Consistently, when asked about when they started illicit drug use or the use of specific illegal drugs, our participants—many of whom have 10 or more years of polydrug use histories—report beginning their involvement with drugs in their early or midteens.

For example, in the HHC's CDC-funded Building Community Responses to Risks of Emergent Drug Use study, we recruited a sample of drug users through street outreach in Hartford. Recruitment was restricted to individuals who were actively using drugs and had not been in drug treatment for the last 30 days. Among the questions asked of these individuals was the age at which they first tried all of the types of drugs they had ever used. As displayed in the table below, the average age at which participants in this study began drug use was 13 years, with 14 being the age at which the highest number began drug use. While on average these individuals started using marijuana a little before they began drinking alcoholic beverages (which is also an illegal drug for teenagers), these two substances appear to have been the primary drugs used until the late teens, at which point they began snorting cocaine, followed one or two years later by snorting heroin, and eventually moving on, in many cases, to injecting heroin. We have found that this pattern is quite common for individuals who go on to become heroin and/or cocaine injectors.

Table 1   Age of First Use Psychoactive Substances

Drug	Mean	Median
Marijuana	13.16	14
Alcohol	13.47	14
Cocaine (snorted)	17.94	18
Heroin (snorted)	20.93	19
Heroin (injected)	21.10	19.50

Typical of participants in our studies is Amanda, a Puerto Rican woman who was 27-years-old at the time we interviewed her. She told us:

> When I started [illicit drug use] at 15 it was cause I saw a lot of violence at home, with my mom, my dad, they were always fighting and arguing. . . . At 13 years old I was going into the fridge and drinking beer, that's when my addiction started. Then when I was about 15, I tried smoking pot and I liked it, and then at the same time I started doing coke. (Romero-Daza, Weeks, and Singer 2003:244)

Gloria, a participant in another of our studies, reported to us that she started smoking cigarettes and sniffing cocaine at age 13.

> My mother used to go out dancing every weekend and drink, so we used to be in the house and the neighborhood was real bad. So we just started hanging out with the neighborhood, with guys, and we used to do all kinds of stuff, drink and everything before my mother got home. (Singer 1999a:46)

An Experimental Attitude and Hunger for Novelty

Youth play a pivotal role in drug use dynamics due to their well-known propensity (on average) toward comparatively high levels of curiosity, adventurousness, and a sense of invulnerability. As Marsha Rosenbaum (1998:199) observes:

> Risk-taking is a normal part of adolescence. Many teenagers feel immortal, and as a consequence take part in activities that strike fear in the hearts of adults (especially their parents). For example, it is no wonder that teenagers learn to drive so easily. They are able to learn how to operate a motor vehicle while oblivious to the dangers of the road (watch a 35-year-old learning to drive and moving painfully slowly and you'll understand the difference).

This behavioral response to perceived risk underlies the willingness among many youth to experiment with new drugs, mix psychoactive substances to assess effects, and use alternative consumption methods to achieve "a better high"—behaviors that contribute to the emergence of new drug use patterns.

For example, in the year 2000, a number of students at a private liberal arts college in Connecticut began experimenting with drug mixing. The group combined various drugs. One of the cocktails they produced led to the death of one member of their group and the intensive-care hospitalization of another. On the day this occurred, local police reported that the deceased student and his three roommates mixed prescription antianxiety drugs like Xanax, sleeping pills, and a migraine medication. In addition, police reported, the students may have taken heroin and may have been drinking (Byron 2000:B1). The mixing of odd combinations of drugs like this is not uncommon among youthful drug users and reflects a stronger inclination toward drug experimentation than is found in other age groups. In a similar incident in Connecticut a few years later, a 19-year-old died of a drug overdose in his bedroom a few hours after attending a party at a friend's house. Apparently, drugs were abundant at the party, which was held at the home of a wealthy family when the parents were away: "Participants told police there were two $20 bags of cocaine. A bowl of marijuana dusted with cocaine was passed around. Prescription pills—Prozac and Clonezepam, an antiseizure medication—also were being handed out at the party" (Tuohy 2004:7).

Another expression of the experimental attitude of youth is the investigation of possible new psychoactive drugs of diverse origin. For example, teenagers in various cities have been reported in recent years to be experimenting with over-the-counter cough medications that contain the drug dextromethorphan (DXM). DXM, a semisynthetic narcotic, is an ingredient in over a hundred different over-the-counter cold medications. It is sought by young drug experimenters because in large doses it is known to produce psychedelic effects, heightened perceptual awareness, lethargy, perceptual distortion, and dissociation. DXM is also believed by some youth to extend and intensify the psychoactive effects of other drugs, a capacity that is of keen interest to drug experimenters (Community Epidemiological Work Group 2000). Called "robotripping" (possibly a play on the movie *Robocop* but also tied to the anti-coughing medication Robitussin), the practice is now widespread around the country. For example, in 2001 the New Hampshire Poison Information Center received 292 reports of cold medicine overdoses resulting in hospitalization, 25 of these involved preparations that included DXM. The following year, the center reported 246 cold medicine overdoses, 46 of which were attributed to DXM. While liquid cough medications contain a chemical that will cause vomiting if taken in large doses, cough suppressant pills, like Coricidin HBP Cold and Cough Medicine, which is known as Triple-C among youthful drug abusers, lacks this chemical. As reported by a 16-year-old girl in Detroit who consumed an entire box of Triple-C:

> The room turned different colors and everything swirled together. . . . I couldn't stay awake, but I couldn't fall asleep, either. I honestly thought that it would all be over soon, and I would be dead. (Hall 2002:1)

Some youth may be particularly primed for drug experimentation. These youth are strongly inclined to seek novelty in their lives more so than other youth. For example, research has shown that youth who are particularly focused on new experiences and novel sensations are more receptive to the promotional campaigns of the tobacco industry than youth who are less inclined to seek novelty. Generally, novelty-hungry youth find greater excitement in new experiences, are more impulsive, and exhibit higher levels of risk taking than other youth. Youth with these personality traits tend to be the first in peer groups to begin using tobacco and possibly other drugs as well. One study, conducted by researchers at the University of Pennsylvania and Georgetown University under the direction of Janet Audrain-McGovern (Audrain-McGovern et al. 2003), collected survey data from over 1,000 youth enrolled in the ninth grade in several northern Virginia high schools. The survey included questions on three main topics: (1) sociodemographic characteristics and family and peer smoking patterns; (2) personality traits, including novelty seeking; and (3) receptivity to tobacco advertising. About 33 percent of the participants reported a high level of receptivity to tobacco advertising while another 20 percent reported very low levels of receptivity. Notably, about half of those youth who were receptive to tobacco advertising also had high scores for novelty seeking, while only about a fourth of those youth who had low levels of receptivity to the advertisements scored high on novelty seeking.

In a second study, Audrain-McGovern and her colleague Kenneth Tercyak (2003) surveyed over 1,000 tenth graders who were going to school in the Mid-Atlantic region to explore (1) the relationship between novelty seeking; (2) symptoms of attention deficit hyperactivity disorder (ADHD); (3) lifetime cigarette smoking; and (4) and age of first cigarette use. Their findings show that teenagers who reported several symptoms of ADHD and who have already smoked cigarettes tend to have higher scores for novelty seeking than other teens in the sample. Youth with ADHD and novelty-seeking personalities, the researchers concluded, are at highest risk to begin smoking. In sum, these two studies suggest that youth vary in their degree of desire for novel experiences. Those who crave novelty are highly vulnerable to tobacco use and very likely to subsequent experimentation with other drugs as well.

Importantly, since the 1970s (Kandel and Jessor 2002), the notion has existed that adolescent drug use tends to begin with certain "starter" drugs that serve as the gateway to an identifiable developmental sequence of other classes and categories of drugs. This notion, which developed out of research on youth, has been called the "gateway hypothesis." The exact origin of the term "gateway drug" is not clear, although it is believed to have been coined by Robert Dupont when he was the Director of the National Institute on Drug Abuse. He and others pointed out that the usual starting points of drug use for most adolescents are tobacco and alcohol. The hypothesis asserts that these drugs, readily available to and legal for adults, are the psychoactive doors through which most adolescents who go on to become regular illicit drug users usually pass (which is not to imply that once a drug is used it does not continue as part of the user's drug repertoire). The hypothesis further asserts that the gateway to full illicit drug use—that is, a drug that is illegal for both adolescents and adults to use—is marijuana. In other words, according to this hypothesis, adolescents who go on to use heroin, cocaine, methamphetamines, and many other powerful drugs, tend to use marijuana—a highly diversified drug—before they move on to these other drugs. Again, this does not mean they stop using marijuana as they add other drugs to their repertoire.

What the hypothesis ignores is *that not every youth who starts using marijuana will automatically go on to use another drug;* most marijuana users don't! Ironically, misinformation provided in scare-based drug prevention efforts can be a factor in youth viewing all prevention information as untrustworthy because they have tried marijuana and found it to be nothing like what they had been told. Marsha Rosenbaum (1998:200), for example, presents the case of an imprisoned heroin addict who had been raised in an upper-middle-class suburb who told her:

> When I was in high school they had these so-called drug education classes. They told us if we used heroin we would become addicted. They told us if we used marijuana we would become addicted. Well, we all tried marijuana and found we did not become addicted, so we figured the entire message was b.s. I then tried heroin, got strung out, and here I am.

Built into the gateway hypothesis is an even older notion—sometimes called the "stepping stone" theory—that asserts that individuals adopt new substances into their drug use repertoires in a predictable order. While the sequencing tenets of the gateway hypothesis have been strongly supported by numerous studies in the United States, at different periods in the country's history different drugs have been in popular usage. Hence, after marijuana there is no identifiable order in which specific drugs tend to be added to adolescent drug use inventories. Additionally, the use of certain drugs may vary among different subgroups of adolescents or among adolescents in different parts of the country.

Despite its limitations, the gateway hypothesis predicts that the youth who are most likely to adopt an emergent illicit drug or drug use behavior (e.g., novelty cravers) are those who have already transitioned first to the use of alcohol and tobacco and subsequently to the use marijuana. These adolescents have made a decision to use psychoactive substances. What the gateway hypothesis will not tell us is which drugs adolescents will eventually go on to try or incorporate (for a short or a long time) into their drug use patterns, or which drugs will prove to be popular in regional or other populations of youth. Adding the notion of novelty-seeking personality to this model, however, suggests who in a group of youth are the most likely to be first to try new drugs and to share their experiences with close friends.

A Time for Drugs

The phase in life during which the use of illicit drugs is most common tends to be from the mid-teens to the mid-20s. In our society, adolescence is socially defined as a time for self-exploration, trying new things, and having fun before the burdensome responsibilities of adulthood arrive. Adolescents try drugs for various reasons, including curiosity, because they think they will like the experience, to reduce stress and avoid negative moods and feeling, to act in opposition to parental and adult authority, to feel grown up, and to fit in with and be admired by select peers. For example, the National Household Survey on Drug Abuse (Substance Abuse and Mental Health Services Administration 2001) found that the age group most likely to report using any illicit drug in the last 30 days was 18–25-year-olds (18.8 percent), followed by 12–17-year olds (10.8 percent). By contrast, for those over the age of 35 the percentage who had taken an illicit substance during the previous month was approximately 3 percent.

The extent of drug consumption among youth is exemplified by a police sting operation implemented by the Los Angeles Police Department at local high schools during 2002, a practice that has been implemented by other police departments as well. The operation involved youthful-looking police officers adopting the clothing and other accoutrements of youth, some of which were identified during school drive-bys by undercover officers, enrolling for an entire semester in high school, and passing as teenage students. The undercover police officers attended classes and mingled publicly with students, learning through casual conversation and observation who was buying and using drugs at the schools and where dealers could be found. Identified dealers included both students and nonstudents. During the course of the operation, the police bought drugs 227 times from 162 different dealers on school campuses or in areas adjacent to the school grounds. Marijuana was the drug of choice for most student drug purchasers, the police found, but cocaine, LSD, Ecstasy, methamphetamine, mushrooms, and prescription drugs were also available. One of the police involved, Dolores Martinez, a 25-year-old undercover officer, reported that drug use was rampant in area high schools. "It's wide open," Martinez reported. "The second day I was there I

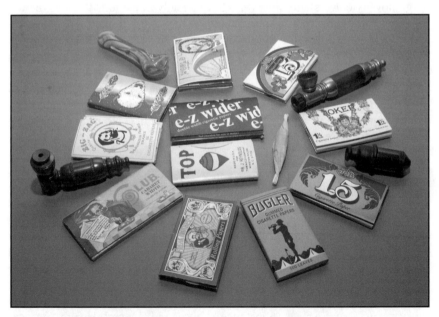

Marijuana paraphernalia, including rolling papers, pipes, and a joint. Courtesy of Drug Enforcement Administration.

saw these kids rolling it [marijuana] into a joint and smoking it on campus" (*Metropolitan News-Enterprise* 2002). To wrap up the operation, the police arrested 136 dealers on their "hit list."

The Syndrome Assumption

Some adolescents are particularly subject to the development of risky drug use careers. Teens who smoke cigarettes, for example, are three times more likely than those who do not smoke to also use alcohol, eight times more likely to smoke marijuana, and 22 times more likely to use cocaine. Interestingly, teen smoking is associated with a host of other risky behaviors as well, such as fighting and engaging in unprotected sex. This phenomenon has been referred to as "the syndrome assumption" (Girodin and Groat 1989). In the perspective of Richard Jessor and Shirley Jessor (1977), this syndrome consists of a generalized tilt toward "unconventionality." While its full-blown expression shows up in only a small percentage of youth, the syndrome appears to significantly amplify rather than contradict the "testing the limits" behavioral patterns seen generally among teens and young adults.

As a result of the factors discussed above, the drug use scene remains in constant flux and motion. Sometimes this motion speeds up, at other times it slows down, but it rarely stops. Youth, including those with novelty-seeking personalities and inclinations toward being unconventional, appear to be especially important contributors to drug use dynamics, but they are far from solely responsible for this feature of illicit drug use. Other groups with considerably more power in the wider world, such as drug manufacturers and distributors, are also critical to changing patterns of drug use. Unlike drug producers, who are primarily driven to be innovative by two factors—increasing profits and eluding the police—youth primarily are motivated by a desire to access new or more easily acquired psychoactive effects and achieve particular social statuses among their peers. However, there are always some young people involved in the illicit drug trade who have profit as a motive as well. This fact reflects larger issues in the teen and young adult years, including psychosocial tensions and conflicts commonly seen as part of coming of age.

Coming of Age

The process of coming of age has garnered considerable attention from the psychological, social, and biological sciences, in no small part because the teen years generally are seen in U.S. culture as a troublesome and challenging age. In the past, the developmental phase known as adolescence, which is now often defined as beginning at age 10 and stretching to age 19, was understood as an inherently turbulent time involving rebelliousness, parental rejection, obsessive compliance with peer norms, identity crisis, mood swings, and risk taking. More recent thinking has led to the social construction of adolescence as "a time of transformation not upheaval" (Steinberg 2002:15) for the majority of youth. Analyses of adolescence as a transformative period suggests three important issues with reference to the role of youth as drug use innovators: (1) developmental processes during adolescence that contribute to youth involvement in novel drug use behaviors (e.g., identity formation, parent/peer issues, testing limits behaviors); (2) changing family and cultural patterns in U.S. society that have contributed to an increased appeal of illicit drug use and diminished parental supervision; and (3) the existence of oppositional pockets and sectors of youth for whom adolescence presents greater-than-average challenges and conflicts.

Developmental Processes of Adolescence

The socially constructed category known as adolescence—marking the passage from childhood to adulthood—brings with it a biological transition called puberty. In fact, the rapid hormonal changes that mark this process have often been held responsible for the behavioral disruptions seen among some youth. While this view is not supported by research, it is likely that adolescent struggles with identity formation and strivings for autonomy are factors that create an openness to new ideas, new behaviors, and new social involvements, all of which are conducive to creative exploration. Also characteristic of this stage of development within the context of U.S. culture is an age-defined personality feature that has been called *adolescent egocentrism* (Elkin 1978), which appears to have two distinct components: "embracing a personal fable" and "having an imaginary audience."

The first of these terms labels the tendency of youth raised in an individualizing cultural system like that found in our society to believe that their experiences are distinct from those of other people, including their parents. Beyond this, these youth believe that their uniqueness clothes them with a kind of protective invulnerability, shielding them from the consequences of actions that they know have caused pain and suffering to others (i.e., "it won't happen to me" beliefs). As one HHC ethnographer recorded in her field notes as part of a study led by the Institute for Community Research on younger drug users:

> Youth especially feel the need to try the things that seem dangerous or risky. There is always that bit of faith that you are the one person who won't lose out, who won't become addicted, who will be able to have the high but still be in control. It doesn't matter very much that there are obvious results from getting involved in harder drugs that can be observed just by walking down the streets. Youth have an enormous amount of faith and belief that they are stronger and more powerful than the rest of the world and all its evil temptations. (Pathways project ethnographic field notes, 5/19/99)

The second of these terms, "having an imaginary audience," refers to the heightened self-consciousness of this developmental stage, ultimately rooted in ego-centered child socialization practices that makes youth particularly subject to peer influence. One consequence of the adolescent tendency to believe their behaviors are closely watched and judged by peers may be a self-imposed pressure to conform to perceived group patterns, including, in some contexts, drug use behaviors.

Changing Cultural Patterns

The dynamism of drug use behavior reflects broader processes of cultural change. While at one time anthropologists avoided the study of culture change, focusing instead on trying to preserve (on paper) indigenous cultural forms that were rapidly disappearing as a result of capitalist economic and Western cultural penetration, it is now recognized within the discipline that in "the rough-and-tumble of social interaction, groups are known to exploit the ambiguities of inherited [cultural] forms, to impart new evaluations or valences to them, to borrow forms more expressive of their interests, or to create wholly new forms to answer to changed circumstances" (Wolf 1982:387). Moreover, processes of cultural change are neither random nor internally driven but rather are products of shifting political and economic (i.e., structural) alignments, social contestations, and transformations in balances of power. Of particular concern, here, are three among many cultural alterations since the mid-twentieth century: (1) reordering family structures; (2) modifying outlooks on self-control and pleasure; and (3) recalibrations of attitudes about general drinking and drug use behaviors, all of which have had direct impact on the contemporary post-baby-boom generation of young people, the so-called Generation X (or Gen X).

Redefining Families. While it is probably true that despite the popular stereotypes family relations do not necessarily deteriorate when children reach adolescence, there certainly are new strains and stresses in intergenerational relations. Research indicates that traditional, two-parent families, especially those in which access to employment allows adequate family resources and child supervision, generally endure the challenges of adolescent transition for the most part unscathed (Offer, Ostrov, and Howard 1981). However, fewer and fewer kids in any social strata experience their full childhood and adolescence in two-parent families. From 1900 to 1972 the number of children whose parents divorced grew by 700 percent. Moreover, from 1970 to 1996 the number of children living in two-parent families declined from 85 to 68 percent (Saluter and Lugaila 1998). While in the past, married couples with children tended to suppress their own needs in light of the perceived needs of their children, increasingly the needs of parents have been prioritized: many couples no longer stay together "for the sake of the children." As a result, many children and teens are subjected to the painful experience of family break-up and, significantly, to a subsequent lessening of parental monitoring of and involvement in their out-of-school activities. Parental involvement has been shown to be one of the strongest barriers to the development of significant problems during adolescence.

Fun Morality. Another significant change, which like the rise in divorce reflects a more general cultural shift from an emphasis on responsibility to one on personal satisfaction, is the emergence of what Martha Wolfenstein refers to as "fun morality." According to Wolfenstein (1975:400):

> Fun and play have assumed a new obligatory aspect. While gratification of forbidden impulses traditionally aroused guilt, failure to have fun currently occasions lowered self-esteem. One is apt to feel inadequate, impotent, and also unwanted.

Training for fun seeking, says Wolfenstein, has (under a continuous barrage of product advertisements that stress consumerism) now replaced an emphasis earlier in U.S. history on teaching children restraint and impulse control. Among youth the growing cultural emphasis on fun, in conjunction with the liminal, socially ill-defined role of adolescent, often takes the form of a fun/rebellious complex in which the best fun involves being adventurous and disobedient, a development that makes banned substance use rather inviting.

Social Shifts in Consumption. Since the 1960s there has been a somewhat general growth in the acceptance of drinking and drug use, and to a limited degree this extends as well to consumption among adolescents. This change is reflected in an examination of adult drug use patterns. In a study of over 7,500 adults in their 30s, Alicia Merline and coworkers (2004) found that more than 32 percent of the men in the sample drank heavily (i.e., they consumed five drinks or more at one time). Also, 13 percent of the men and 7 percent of the women reported that they used marijuana. Finally, the study showed that 8 percent of the women and 7 percent of the men misused prescription drugs. Adolescents hear about and see parents drinking and using drugs. These experiences run counter to and may well diminish the impact of exposure to antidrug messages present in the media, schools, and in other social institutions, including the family. Moreover, beyond their own use of drugs, adults are also more likely today to allow limited teen drinking within the home than in earlier decades. In short, while teenagers are exposed to many antidrug messages, they receive contradictory messages in the everyday lives of their families and the other people in their social worlds.

Oppositional Pockets and Sectors of Youth

For some individuals, adolescence is a period of upheaval that includes problems at school, dropping out of school, delinquency, early sexual activity, a perpetual oppositional attitude, and regular use of alcohol and other drugs (Steinberg 2002). Pockets of particularly troublesome youth are found in all social classes and are certainly not absent from the upper or middle strata of society. Suburban vandalism, shoplifting, breaking and entering, disturbing the peace, and extensive drug use among privileged youth, to have fun and test the outer limits of daring behavior, are not rarities in contemporary U.S. society.

Nonetheless, in lower-income, socially disadvantaged minority communities, where insults are many and positive options are few, the frequency of youthful oppositionalism may be the highest. For example, the adolescent school dropout rate in 1999 was almost 29 percent among Latino/a youth and 13 percent for Black youth, compared to about 7 percent among white youth. Similarly, rates for getting into a fight during the last 12 months among youth who have ever tried marijuana were 55 percent and 50 percent respectively for Latino/a and Black youth compared to 44 percent for white youth (National Institute on Drug Abuse 2001). Additionally, ethnic minority youth are more likely to become involved in drug sales as a means of survival and of earning some level of peer respect (Bourgois 1995; Dei 2002). All of these patterns are exacerbated by social discrimination in the criminal justice system that makes it more likely that minority youth rather than their white counterparts will attract police attention, be stopped and questioned on the street by the police, be arrested, be convicted, and be subject to incarceration.

Wherever they are found, small cliques of like-minded youth who are alienated from dominant social values and institutions, who come to value living at the edges of dominant society, and whose lives focus on thrill seeking and risk taking often readily serve as especially active centers of drug use innovation and dissemination. Their drug-related discoveries, in turn, find their way to other, perhaps less-troubled yet very drug-curious and fun-oriented youth, facilitating the spread of drug use along social networks of friendship and social encounter. Rather than inhibiting subsequent involvement in drug use, for some youth, because of the exposure it provides to drug networks, it only enhances drug involvement.

Drug Use Innovation and Diffusion

Cultural shifts like those described above have contributed to the emergence of adolescence and young adulthood as periods of drug exploration and experimentation. Fun seeking is a primary motivation among youth who, freed of parental supervision, are in a position to test new ways to enjoy getting high (even if, not infrequently, a trial-and-error approach leads to an upsetting error). An important part of this process is the sharing of their drug-related experiences as well as the drugs they have experimented with and liked with their peers. Some new drugs find an audience and are tried by other youth, and they may, in turn, diffuse further among circles of youth or even beyond youth to adult drug users. Conversely, the new psychoactive substance may prove undesirable and fail to spread, although merely having negative qualities does not necessarily block a drug from disseminating. Rather, there appears to be a weighing and balancing process involved, with cultur-

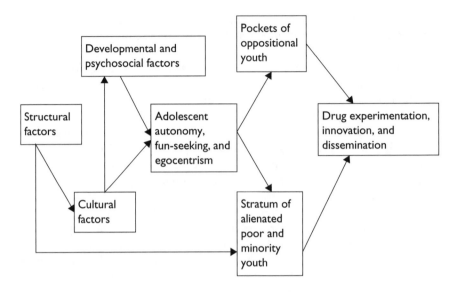

Figure 4   Factors in drug use innovation among youth

ally generated "good" (e.g., pleasant experiences) and "bad" (e.g., scary experiences) qualities being measured against each other (and against experiences with other drugs) in assessing the overall appeal of a new drug. Also important are the statuses and skills of those who discover and those who promote the new drug.

Social Epidemic Model

Early MDMA (Ecstasy) users have been found to be "conventional adolescents and young adults except in their tendency to be early risk takers and sensation seekers" (Baggott 2002:145). This finding is important in understanding how MDMA (and by extension other drugs) spread among adolescents and young adults. Malcolm Gladwell (2000), a student of processes of social change, argues that behaviors, ideas, and products, including illicit drugs, are spread person-to-person in widening fans of geometric progression, along preexistent word-of-mouth social networks, much like infectious disease epidemics. Hence, he refers to this type of change as a "social epidemic." To illustrate a social epidemic—how use of a product diffuses among networks to new users—consider the fax machine, which at first was only affordable to and used by a small number of corporations. There was a point in time when no homes had fax machines. Then, in 1984, the Sharp Electronics Corporation introduced the first low-priced fax model targeted for home use. Five years later, two million fax machines were being sold each year. During those five years, an important social change occurred, as companies, institutions, and individuals and families moved from not thinking they needed a fax machine to believing it was essential. The same is true for drug use. Gladwell's model suggests that the term "drug use epidemics" to label the diffusion component of the set of patterns termed "drug use dynamics" in this book.

Gladwell has identified three different kinds of people who are critical to the spread of social epidemics and whom he colloquially refers to as mavens, connectors, and salesmen: "Mavens are data banks [or trusted folk experts]. They provide the message. Connectors are the social glue; they spread it. . . . Salesmen [have] . . . the skills to persuade us . . ." (2000:70). Translating this conception to the world of emergent drug use and diffusion, Gladwell would refer to the individuals who have drug knowledge and test out new drug use possibilities (e.g., by searching the professional literature in biochemistry, pharmacy, anthropology, and other fields for possible new psychoactive substances) as *mavens*. Anthropologists and ethnobotanists have studied and written about indigenous drug use all over the world, including many substances that have never spread to the United States (Bennett and Cook 1996; Page 2004). Additionally, biochemists, pharmaceutical researchers, and their colleagues in various fields have conducted experiments and published reports of their findings on hundreds of substances in technical journals sitting on carefully labeled shelves in university libraries across the country. Drug mavens are individuals who explore these sources in hopes of finding the next big "high." Drug mavens may, in fact, be diploma-holding chemists or other professionals who—as a side interest—experiment with illicit drugs.

Further, argues Gladwell (2000:62), "The critical thing about Mavens . . . is that they aren't passive collectors of information. . . . They want to tell you about it too." But mavens may not be good persuaders or have widely dispersed social networks. Nonetheless, some of the individuals they talk to about their drug discoveries, individuals who are early risk takers and sensation seekers may be in a position to spread the word about the new drug and its appealing qualities. As seen in the figure below, individuals (represented by circles) who sit at critical nodes in social networks (like individual A) and are vital to the flow of information or objects (represented by the lines) between sectors of the network, especially between otherwise disconnected social groups, may be particularly important drug *connectors*. As Samuel Friedman and drug social network researchers at the National Research and Development Institutes, Inc., in New York (1999) indicate, when viewed in terms of social influence, the individual labeled A in the figure has the potential to be quite influential with the other network members as she is connected to everyone and likely knows something about their drug use behaviors.

People who are well connected in circles of youthful drug users no doubt vary in their persuasive capacity. Gladwell uses the term *salesman* to label charismatic individuals whose power of personality is especially persuasive. These "trend setters" tend to be particularly well liked and admired within their peer social networks. Their behaviors are watched and emulated by oth-

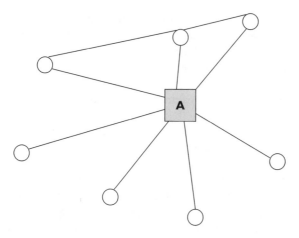

Figure 5   Schematic design of a social network

ers. In the case of a new drug with "market potential," these types of individuals may, quite literally, be salesmen who build markets by persuading others to try the new substance and sell it to them. According to Gladwell, through the efforts of mavens, connectors, and salesman, ideas and products spread in a population until, at a certain moment, the "tipping point" is reached and the ideas or products suddenly become generalized. Thus, with reference to MDMA, Matthew Baggott (2002:145) remarks that the spread of the drug to "well-adjusted individuals has led some to suggest that we are seeing a 'normalization' [of MDMA], with the drug becoming an accepted part of social life among the young." This has certainly occurred with marijuana, but whether it will be the case with MDMA remains to be seen.

Diffusion of Innovation Model

The broader dynamics of the diffusion of new drug use practices appears to fit what is called the "diffusion of innovation" model. For example, Andrew Golub and Bruce Johnson (1996) have suggested that the adoption of crack cocaine appears to follow a classic "diffusion of innovation" pattern. The diffusion of innovation model, first proposed by Everett Rogers (1962), defines diffusion as the process by which a new behavior or practice is communicated through the social connections linking members of a social system. Rogers identified four components of the diffusion process: (1) the innovation; (2) the communication channels that are used to move information about the innovation from person to person; (3) the time involved in the spread of an idea and the adoption of the behavior it is linked to; and (4) the social networks through which the innovation spreads. He further noted the existence of a number of roles and sectors of a social system that play critical roles in the diffusion of a behavioral innovation.

Rogers believed that the initial role that is crucial to a successful diffusion is the innovator (or to use Gladwell's term for the same thing, the maven). Successful innovators, Rogers maintained, tend to be daring, risky, and have a high capacity to cope with uncertainty. If diffusion is to be successful, innovators must converse about it with others, and in this way the practice must reach, be picked up by, and be incorporated by key opinion leaders who act as role models for other members of a social group. These "secondary adopters" (i.e., connectors and salesmen) tend to be influential because they embody key culturally defined features of ideals of the social group.

From these secondary adopters, Rogers saw innovation as passing through three stages within a social group. First, it is adopted by the "early majority," a large subgroup who tend to emulate the secondary adopters and to look to them consciously or otherwise as key trendsetters. The early majority tend to be individuals who like riding the waves of changing cultural practices (phrased variously in different eras as being modern, "with it," "hip," "cool, "kewl," "the bomb," etc.). From the early majority, practices eventually spread to a more cautious, more conservative group that is slower to accept change and tends to do so only because of distinct peer pressure, clearly identified advantage, or an inescapable restriction on other options. Finally, there are the "laggards," individuals who are highly suspicious of change and who are the last to adopt any innovation. These individuals are often described as being set in their ways, but, in time, may adopt an innovation if it endures among other members of their social group.

New drug use practices, of course, may not go through all of these stages, and few such behaviors are ever adopted by all members of a social group. As Rogers pointed out, an innovation may be rejected at any stage of the adoption process; hence, some drugs may disappear very quickly from the drug scene, long before they are spotted by researchers, because they have so few adopters after the initial innovator. Rejection, in Rogers' view, however, is not the same as discontinuance, which refers to the process by which individuals stop performing a behavior that they have already adopted (e.g., users abandoning drug injection to avoid contracting HIV infection). Rogers identified two types of discontinuance, both of which are seen among drug users.

The first, "disenchantment," refers to ending or greatly diminishing the frequency of a behavior because people are dissatisfied with it, such as the significant drop in PCP use during the 1980s because of user discomfort with some of its negative experiential effects. The second, "replacement," refers to patterns of ending or significantly diminishing the frequency of a behavior because a better, more favored behavior has been introduced (e.g., use of marijuana with lower levels of THC greatly diminished once the new "exotic" forms of marijuana with high THC levels became readily available). Importantly, in the U.S. drug scene, processes of *innovation, rejection, diffusion, disenchantment,* and *replacement,* as well as both the *rebirth* of an older drug use innovation and *diversification* across diverse subgroups are occurring simultaneously with various drug use behaviors (with one drug diversifying as another is being rejected and a third is being introduced). The sum total of all of these processes at any moment in time constitutes the drug use dynamics of a population and its various social class, ethnic, and other segments.

The Functions of Social Networks

As we have seen, social connections are critical to illicit drug use among youth (as well as adults) in at least three fundamental ways. First, emergent drugs readily diffuse through social network connections, with several types of individuals who occupy pivotal positions in the structure of social networks playing critical roles in the dissemination process. Second, social networks are the conveyor belts of much of what users know (and hence fail to know) about new drugs before they try them, including what effects to expect in many cases. Third, peer interaction and (material, emotional, and other) support are a critical part of drug use. Users report that club drugs, for example, tend to be used in smaller or larger group settings but do not tend to be consumed when alone. In the case of Ecstasy, which is sometimes called "the hug drug," interactions with supportive peers, including talking, touching, massaging, and sexual contact are considered part of the expected drug experience. The importance of these three social components of drug use in drug use dynamics are illustrated by the following interview extracts from drug using participants in the Hispanic Health Council's Building Community Responses to Risks of Emergent Drug Use project:

> Well I was in New York. . . . My friend and I used to go there to buy pot and we used to walk by certain places . . . and they used to call out certain names of the bags [of cocaine] and I wondered what the hell they were talking about. But one night we decided to go find out what it was, my friend and I split a bag and we were really wrecked.

> What I do is I team up. If I see myself that I'm in a tight situation [monetarily] when I know I cannot do it alone, I just team up with somebody and we hustle together to get the money.

> I got arrested once with an empty bag of heroin. It was major stupid. . . . And then I got charged for heroin possession. . . . My friends came up with half the money [for bail] and my relatives came up with half.

As these examples suggest, in addition to facilitating acquisition of drugs or introduction to new drugs and methods of use, social connections offer users a range of drug-related protections and resources, as well as affective and financial support.

One type of youth social network, the street gang, historically has played a particularly important role in local or even regional emergent drug distribution, both internally (within the gang) and externally (to other drug customers). As Joan Moore (1978:75), a long-time observer of Latino gangs, comments:

There are four points at which drugs and . . . gangs significantly intersect. First, the Chicano youth gangs have been consistently innovative in drugs—with marijuana, then with heroin, and most recently with inhalants and PCP. Second, most of the heroin use in Chicago's barrios begins with gangs. Third, a high proportion of all Chicano gang youth consistently become addicted. Fourth, the prison experience of Chicanos is predominantly within a context of narcotic offenses.

In a Chicago study, Ronald Glick (1990) traced the trajectory of changing drug use in a group of nine 16–18-year-old Puerto Rican members of a gang called the Division Street clique and in the West Town–Humboldt Park Puerto Rican community in which they lived. Glick saw this trajectory as including four phases. The initial phase, just prior to 1967, constituted the period of introduction, during which members of the clique, all of whom came from low-income, single-parent families, were given their first direct exposure to heroin by two young men who moved to the area from New York. They saw in the Division Street clique "a market for sales that could allow the New Yorkers to support their [own] habits" (Glick 1990:81). By the end of 1967, all members of the clique were addicted to heroin.

The second phase (1967–1973) was characterized by a significant growth in the number of Puerto Rican heroin injectors in the community, including most members of several youth gangs. During this period, the drug scene in Puerto Rican neighborhoods became increasingly competitive and violent. Glick (1990:86) found that individuals who became addicted during this period did not do so "as part of a hip or romantic lifestyle, but rather because drugs offered escape from their depression and feelings of failure."

The third period (1974–1982) was characterized by polydrug use, with comparative limited available quantities of diluted heroin, large quantities of cocaine, and a variety of other drugs. Clique members like their peers used a variety of drugs, based in part on availability. After 1982, cocaine, brought to the city from Miami, became the drug of choice among Chicago's Puerto Rican gang members and others and was widely available at comparatively low prices. According to Glick (1983:286), "One function of the Chicago Puerto Rican community has been to assume the heavy risks and absorb the social stigma of supplying drugs to higher status White outsiders."

Trends in Youthful Drug Use

While various correlates of drug use among youth have been identified, *no single factor* predicts a substantially large proportion of risk taking among youth (Miller et al. 1990). Furthermore, there has been less focus by researchers on the stages of progression of substance use from legal to illegal drugs on the pathway from childhood to adulthood (Brook et al. 1990; Brook, Richter, and Whiteman 2001). Nonetheless, studies show that identifiable developmental patterns exist for youth who start down the road of riskier behavior (Brook, Whiteman, and Gordon 1983; Kandel and Yamaguchi 1993), but less is known about the precise details of each of the many fads and trends in adolescent drug use that have occurred over time. A lack of information exists for the exact conditions under which specific new drugs or new ways of consuming them are identified, gain user approval, and are added to the repertoire of adolescent drug use, although the diffusion model presented above suggests the broad outlines of drug use dynamics of youth. However, it is clear that the motivations that drive youthful drug experimenters and innovators may be quite different than the driving forces that lead subsequent groups of youth (or adults) to try an increasingly popular new drug.

It is also clear that one factor that influences adolescent drug use is perception of drug availability. As part of the 2000 National Household Survey on Drug Abuse (Substance Abuse and Mental Health Services Administration 2001), youths aged 12–17 years were asked to indicate how much they agreed or disagreed with a set of statements about their neighborhood concerning drug selling, crime, and street fighting. The study found that more than one in four youths agreed with the statement: "There is a lot of drug selling in your neighborhood." Black youth were the most likely to agree with this statement; Hispanic youth were less likely than Blacks but more likely than whites or Asians to agree with the statement. Youths who lived in large metropolitan counties were more likely to perceive that their neighborhoods included a lot of drug selling than youth from smaller metropolitan or nonmetropolitan areas. These data suggest that many youth, especially minority youth and those in larger cities, view drug use and selling as quite common in their immediate social environments. These youth perceive their world as filled with psychoactive drugs and the people who use and sell them. Notably, the study found that marijuana use was more frequent among youth who perceived high rates of drug selling and crime in their neighborhoods.

Perception of availability, however, is not a sufficient cause of increases in use. Another critical component in the adoption of new drug use patterns is actual availability. New drugs spread among youth most rapidly when drug purchase is safe, easy, local, and cost effective. Local, "bath tub" manufacturing procedures produce a ready supply of accessible, inexpensive drugs—a factor that accounts for the rapid spread and use of drugs like methamphetamine as described in chapter 4. Local manufacturing procedures may result in products of uneven quality and unknown composition, but customers are more likely to know their distributors and can easily return to the point of purchase; thus quality control is necessary, a factor that may increase the popularity of a "homemade" product versus one produced elsewhere and distributed in large quantities, with unknown and questionable content. These factors are seen as critical to all of the specific recent adolescent drug trends discussed below.

Huffing

Ready availability and, in a sense, local production of the desired substance are key factors, for example, in the primarily youthful drug use practice of inhaling, also known as "huffing." This method of drug consumption involves inhaling the vapors given off by over a thousand commercial products, many but not all of which are common household items. Other drugs, such as heroin, can be inhaled, but substances included as inhalants are *only* consumed in this manner. The heterogeneous group of substances called "inhalants" (the only group of drugs defined by its method of use) includes at least four main types:

- *Volatile solvents*, including paint thinners and paint remover, dry-cleaning fluids, degreasers, gasoline, glue, typing correction fluids, and felt-tip marker fluids that give off fumes at room temperature
- *Aerosols*, such as spray paint (especially silver and gold), spray deodorant, hair sprays, vegetable oil sprays for cooking, shoe polish spray, and fabric protector sprays that contain both propellants and solvents
- *Gases* found in products that boost octane levels in cars, butane lighters, propane tanks, whipped cream dispensers (nitrous oxide or "laughing gas"), and refrigerants; as well as those used in medicine such as ether, chloroform, and halothane
- *Nitrites* such as cyclohexyl nitrite (from room deodorizers), amyl nitrite (a prescription drug for heart pain), and butyl nitrite (a street drug) that dilate blood vessels and produce relaxation (and hence their role as "sex drugs").

According to the National Household Survey on Drug Abuse (Substance Abuse and Mental Health Services Administration 1998) inhalants are so easily obtained at home that they often are among the first drugs used by adolescents. The survey found that approximately 6 percent of children in the U.S. have tried inhalants by the time they reach fourth grade. The practice tends to reach its peak among seventh through ninth graders. Huffing also tends to be more common among boys than girls, especially among longer-term users. It is found in both urban and rural settings, but poverty, a history of childhood abuse, and doing poorly in or dropping out of school all are statistically associated with inhalant abuse (Kozel, Sloboda, and De La Rosa 1995). It is also disproportionately found among Native American youth. The popularity of huffing changes each year. During the 1990s, there were major public health campaigns to draw attention to the risks of inhalant use, and inhalant use subsequently declined. By 2002, however, there were various indications that inhalant use among youth was once again on the rise; there was a 14 percent rise from 2002 to 2003 in inhalant use recorded on the Partnership for a Drug Free America survey of 8,000 sixth through twelfth graders in the United States (Reuters 2004). In January 2005, the head of the

National Institute on Drug Abuse issued a special community alert bulletin because of the continued growth in inhalant use among youth (Volkow 2005).

Polly Wants Another Drug

Another consequential trend in youthful drug use in recent years is the movement toward polydrug use, including both a significant expansion in the number of drugs being used among youth (and used by individual youth over time) and, perhaps even more important, in the mixing together of two or more drugs for simultaneous consumption. Polydrug use is known to be particularly risky because of the potential for synergistic chemical interaction with resulting increases in toxicity, greater psychomotor impairment, and overdosing (Starmer and Bird 1984; Jatlow et al. 1991). Part of the polydrug use trend among youthful drug users reflects the continued expansion in the number of different kinds of inhalants and hallucinogens currently in use, including powerful newer forms of marijuana. Another component of polydrug use among youth involves an experimental approach to "cocktailing," the blending of substances, like PCP and cocaine, to form new drug combinations.

Mixing It Up

Drug use dynamics involves more than the appearance of new drugs; they also involve the changing context of drug use. One such change of recent years involves social mixing and the diffusion of drug use patterns across social strata and groups. Youth from poor and middle-class backgrounds are not isolated to the degree that they once were. Shared music (e.g., hip-hop music, which is thickly laced with drug use references) and dance clubs that facilitate social mixing lead to a constant flow of information, values, and material items across porous ethnic and class lines, including drugs and knowledge of drug preparation and use procedures. At such clubs, suburban youth meet inner-city youth, individuals who they may see as leading comparatively more exciting and daring lives. Inner-city youth, in turn, may find suburban youth of interest because of their comparatively abundant resources and social status. Similarly, school busing, while not overcoming social segregation (e.g., the segregated school cafeteria), has created opportunities for the sharing of ideas, clothing styles, musical tastes, and drug use patterns. A key feature of drug-related social mixing of these sorts is that they often incorporate sex as well, doubling the opportunities for both valued pleasures and undesired consequences.

Conclusion

Despite differences in earlier and current drug use eras over time, large numbers of youth have used both illicit drugs and peer-oriented social settings—in which drug-influenced interaction is normative—to construct identity and community offstage from mainstream society (Buckland 2002). In other words, for some youth, drug use is an arena of self-definition. Prevention, as a result, is challenged to identify alternative spaces for adolescent identity formation. Additionally, it is clear that efforts to deglamorize drug use among youth have not worked. Illicit drugs continue to hold a dark appeal among youth. What has changed are the specific drugs that are popular among this age group.

An important window on drug use trends among youth is the Drug Abuse Warning Network (DAWN) monitoring of emergency room (ER) visits for drug-related health problems. This system monitors emergency room patient charts in sentinel hospitals around the United States and identifies any mention of drug use that is charted by health-care providers. From 2001 to 2002, total drug-related ER episodes increased 11 percent for patients 18 to 25 years of age (Substance Abuse and Mental Health Services Administration 2003:89). An examination of ER reports for specific drugs is also revealing. DAWN data show that emergency room mentions involving the club drug MDMA increased from 250 in 1994 to 2,850 in 1999, and jumped another 58 percent to 4,511 in the year 2000. About three-fourths of MDMA mentions in the DAWN ER data for 2002 involved people 25 years of age and younger. Emergency room mentions of another club drug increased from 56 in 1994 to just under 5,000 in the year 2000 (Substance Abuse and Mental Health Services Administration 2003:91).

To gain further insight to drug-use patterns among youth, in the next chapter we examine the phenomenon of clubs, the drugs associated with them, and their appeal. While some drugs, like LSD, spanned both the 1960s and 1990s drug use eras among youth and young adults, a range of new drugs entered the U.S. drug scene with the club drug transition.

CHAPTER 6

Club Drugs and Beyond

That unmatch'd form and figure of blown youth,
Blasted with ecstasy: O! Woe is me,
To have seen what I have seen, see what I see!

—William Shakespeare, *Hamlet*

Probably the most noticed change in adolescent drug use in recent years has involved the adoption of a wide and diverse set of drugs that have come to be called "club drugs" because of a common venue of consumption: youth-oriented dance clubs. The extent of concern about this development was signaled on December 2, 1999, when the National Institute on Drug Abuse (NIDA), in collaboration with the American Academy of Child and Adolescent Psychiatry, the Community Antidrug Coalitions of America, Join Together, and National Families in Action, issued a joint press release announcing a national initiative to combat the increasing use of club drugs among youth. In addition, NIDA launched a multimedia public education campaign targeted to youth, parents, educators, and the general public about the dangers of club drugs. These drugs, known to be popular at late-night, youth-oriented dance clubs and at all-night "raves" or dance parties, represent one of the important turn-of-the-century trends in the rapidly changing picture of youth and young adult drug use (Eiserman et al. in press). In their press release, NIDA and collaborators were not alarmed about the appearance of a particular new drug. Rather it was the appearance of a complex of drug use behaviors that generated the unusual step of issuing a multi-institute alert. These drug use behaviors included a number of drugs, old and new, being taken in various combinations; a cultural scene that supported drug use; a population of newer drug users; as well as the fact that these might be harbingers of a new 1960/1970s-style drug use transition, which caused trepidation at the nation's drug research headquarters.

Sharing NIDA's concern, researchers from the Hispanic Health Council participated in an examination of night-long raves and dance clubs (Eiserman et al. in press; Schensul et al. 2000, in press). During this study, a team of young ethnographers visited numerous dance clubs and rave parties in Connecticut and Massachusetts, participated in dancing while observing the behaviors of patrons and employees, engaged people in casual conversation, and attempted to recruit participants for more formal interviews at a later date. The characteristics of dance clubs that were repeatedly visited during the study are described in the field notes of one of the project ethnographers:

> We got to the club at 2 AM. It was already packed. . . . I went to the bathroom to see what was going on . . . and I walked in on four people ordering pills [Ecstasy] from a white guy named Tank. . . . He is collecting $20 per pill and in about two minutes he made $100. . . . I leave the bathroom and on my way back to the dance floor I meet up with Uno [a key informant]. I am standing with them and I see Uno speaking to a group of Puerto Rican guys. When he comes back over to me he says, "I just made $50. . . . He tells me that Tank gives him pills to "get rid of" [i.e., sell] and instead of charging $20 per pill, Uno ups the price to $30 per pill and keeps the $10 profit for himself. . . . Uno started doing E [Ecstasy] about three weeks ago. He tried it . . . with a friend at the club. He said he didn't feel much the first time except that touch [touching and being touched by others] felt indescribable and incredible. . . . [Later I see] Uno has his hands on a guy's face and their faces are almost nose to nose and from my perspective it looks at if they are kissing. When they pull apart, the other guy wipes his eyes cause they are tearing and he is smiling and saying how good he feels. I look at Uno and he has the base of a Vicks . . . inhaler in his mouth. . . . Not only does [the Vicks] make the person's eyes tear, it enhances the high of whatever you are on . . . tremendously. . . . A lot of what goes on at this club between [social] network members is incredibly intimate. . . . There is a lot of sexual attention given between women—touching, dancing really intimately, kissing and playing. . . . Everyone is so "touchy feely happy sharing" with everyone that throughout the night I get offered to share water with lots of people.

Based on this research, we identified five features of dance clubs that are important to contemporary drug use dynamics: (1) they are heavily attended by youth; (2) there is mixing across youth social groups and strata; (3) sexual contact is common; (4) various paraphernalia are used that are unique to the club drug scene; and (5) Ecstasy and many other drugs are openly discussed, used, shared, and sold. In addition, in light of the model of drug innovation and diffusion presented earlier, dance clubs are one of the stages on which drug connectors and salesmen perform, spreading ideas about and samples of emergent drugs to new users. Based on ethnographic observations by our research team over a number of months, the individual referred to in the excerpts above as Uno is a "salesman," both as that term is used by Malcolm Gladwell in his theory of social epidemics and as it is used conventionally as a vendor of commodities.

Another setting in which club drugs are commonly used are called raves. This type of intense youth gathering began in Europe and arrived in the United States in the later part of the 1990s. The rave appeals to the fun-morality orientation of Generation Xers as described by an ethnographer on the Pathways team (Eiserman et al. 2003:21):

> At one point, an MC was rapping about the negative effects of the drug, K [Ketamine]. I finally found a seat, and some of the people around me began to talk to me. I met a group of very friendly, white, high school kids. There was about five of them. One was . . . "rolling" very heavily on "E" [Ecstasy], and his friends were very caught up with giving him water and massages. He introduced me to a girl that he went to school with, and they said that they were engaged. As the night went on, he looked worse and worse. He sat in front of the speakers because he said he liked the way that the vibrations felt on his body. . . . Another guy they knew kept trying to sell me "Ephedrine" [which was legal at the time but has since been banned in the U.S.] for $10. He said that I would get a similar high to E, but that it was cheaper. When he left, the other kids told me not to buy it, that it was basically a caffeine pill.

These accounts confirm that the club drug phenomenon is not simply a set of drugs that have become popular among younger users, but, in addition, the club/rave scene constitutes a broader cultural development that includes several core values (sometime phrased as "peace, love, unity, and respect" or P.L.U.R.), key symbols of group membership and valuation, styles of social interaction, favored material artifacts, culturally meaningful activities (e.g., dancing, parties), certain musical genres, and acceptance of drug use and experimentation as valued activities.

To some degree these cultural elaborations (e.g., the centrality of music, the emphasis on bright and shifting colors, the idealistic tone) contain echoes of the hippie scene of the 1960s and 1970s (and thus several magazine articles have depicted the club scene as "The Second Summer of Love"), but differences are also observable, including (1) the hippie era emphasized outdoor gatherings and "back to the land" sentiments as opposed to the stronger indoor and urban emphasis of the club drug scene (e.g., structural music); (2) among the hippies there was a distinct communal and collectivist emphasis that appears to be lacking among party kids; (3) political activism and expressed desire for social change were significantly stronger among hippies than among party kids; and (4) party kids like Gen Xers generally have been found to be somewhat more materialistic in their orientation than their hippie predecessors.

The very appeal to Gen Xers of the social settings associated with club drug use according to Marsha Rosenbaum (2002:138) is that they offer "a sense of community they badly needed." Clubs and raves evolved not simply as places where a lot of drug use takes place (although they certainly are this as well), they are socially constructed spaces in which youth form themselves as individuals and as a collectivity through specific kinds of social behaviors and communication. Key components of these behaviors include tenderly supportive and highly tactile social interaction, intense dancing and physical exertion to pulsating, high-volume synthetic dance music, and frequent psychoactive drug use. From the standpoint of this book, what is of greatest interest about the identities and community constructed in raves, dance clubs, and related settings is the incorporation of pro-drug values that include mildly cautious but generally enthusiastic support of drug innovation and experimental use.

The new club drugs are only one facet of the current drug use phenomenon among youth. As noted later, old drugs also have found their way to new users, while some drugs have found new uses, affirming that drugs are reborn and drug use behaviors are reinvented by new generations.

The Club Drugs

From Empathy to Ecstasy

If LSD was the drug that came to symbolize the hippie era of the 1960s, for the club kids it is Ecstasy (3,4-methylenedioxymethamphetamine) also called "X," "E," or "MDMA" among its many folk names. Richard Hammersley and coworkers (2002:1) report that the label "'empathy' was field tested as a candidate name for the drug, but that 'Ecstasy' had more sales appeal," suggesting the bottom line of this "feel good" drug. It has been estimated that over six million people worldwide have tried Ecstasy, and most of them have been under 25 (Heilig 2002). Its sudden popularity is tied to its complex effects, combining the energetic jolt of a stimulant with the psychedelic embrace of a mild hallucinogen. The drug, a synthesized derivative of the bark of the sassafras tree, was patented by the German pharmaceutical company Merck in 1912, but was rarely seen until it began to be used for mood alteration of patients by a small group of psychotherapists in California in the late 1960s. Notes Rosenbaum (2002:138), "Calling it an 'entactogen' (meaning, to touch within), they found it reduced fear and promoted acceptance, thereby facilitating communication." Adoption of the drug in these circles was sparked by the work of Alexander Shulgin (1978), who experimented with the drug and became an enthusiastic endorser of its potential therapeutic effects. Its psychedelic capacity was also noted by Shulgin, who later wrote a preface for Timothy Leary's book *The Politics of Psychopharmacology* in his role as a trusted "communicator" on the drug scene.

The various mood-altering qualities of the drug soon led to MDMA seeping from therapeutic use to recreational use. As a street drug, MDMA appears to have first caught on in Texas, where it was sold as a legal "fun" drug at bars catering to young professionals. Growing popularity there led to interest from the Drug Enforcement Administration, which moved quickly and successfully to have the drug criminalized in 1986. In doing so, however, the DEA brought considerable media attention to what had up until then been a rather obscure item in the U.S. underground pharmacopeia. While therapists curtailed usage once the drug was illegal, Ecstasy attracted a rapidly growing set of recreational adherents. Those who began using the drug reported that it helped them to feel accepted, let go of their fears and anxieties, improve their ability to relate to and communicate with others, and feel affection for those around them—experiences that were not plentiful for users without the drug (Beck and Rosenbaum 1994). A magic bullet for loneliness seemed at hand. Studies of young MDMA users in Europe found both males and females (49 percent and 42 percent respectively) reported the drug helped them to feel less inhibited and, to a lesser degree, to fit into a social group (28 percent of boys and 36 percent of girls) (Calafat et al. 1999).

With such positive word-of-mouth publicity, the popularity of the drug accelerated. The 2001 Partnership Attitude Tracking Survey of 6,937 teens across the country (conducted by the Partnership for a Drug-free America) found that 12 percent of adolescents between 12 and 18 years of age reported using Ecstasy at least once, a 71 percent increase over the 1999 survey (Roper 2002). Based on these data, it was estimated that almost thee million teenagers had tried the drug. Researchers directing the study likened their findings to those for cocaine in the previous generation and reported that users viewed taking Ecstasy as a low-risk, high-benefit experience, one that could be shared with existing friends or used to make new ones. Sometimes these friends were in the public spotlight. In the year 2002, for example, internationally known German cyclist, Jan Ullrich, was not allowed to compete in the Tour de France after he tested positive for Ecstasy.

Those drawn to MDMA do not tend to use only this drug, but rather, as has become the norm among drug users, other drugs as well. Amador Calafat and colleagues (1999) found that 72 percent of Ecstasy users had also consumed marijuana in the last month in some locales, as high as 96 percent in others. Other drugs also used in the last 30 days in this sample (in order of frequency) were: cocaine, amphetamine, and LSD. Kellie Sherlock (1997) found that 14 percent of the British youth in his sample of Ecstasy users had also tried cocaine and heroin. Simultaneous use of MDMA and marijuana also is common, often mixed with other drugs as well.

Production of Ecstasy often occurs in small, sometimes makeshift laboratories called "kitchen labs," many of which are found in Belgium and the Netherlands, as well as in Eastern Europe and China where there are cheaper production facilities. A basic kitchen lab consists of several heaters, a number of distillation flasks and funnels, and access to running water, electricity, and a waste pipe. Many of the labs are mobile, being packed up into the back of a van and moved to a new location every few weeks in order to avoid detection by the police. The factories often are run by loosely organized crime groups, initially from Israel or Russia and later from other countries. The profits they have reaped from the drug are astronomical.

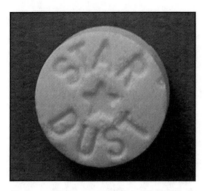

Ecstasy pill. Courtesy of Drug Enforcement Administration.

Ecstasy spread, friend to friend, peer group to peer group, city to city, country to country, becoming eventually a drug used worldwide especially among youth. Before long, however, users began to express concerns about what was actually in the pills being sold at clubs, parties, and other venues. While dealers claimed to be selling MDMA, questions about both the dosage-level of the pills (including concern about very large and very small doses) and the actual presence of any MDMA were raised by disgruntled customers.

This point of growing tension in the underground world of Ecstasy distribution raises a broader issue from the standpoint of research about drug content. When researchers interview drug users, they often hear detailed accounts of the drugs that informants consume. Unfortunately, researchers usually have no immediate way of knowing the accuracy of these reports, not because the informant is intentionally misreporting or even because accurate recall by a binging polydrug user with potential short- and longer-term memory loss from prolonged drug use may be difficult. In many instances users may not be able to discern the actual content of the drugs they consume (although most longer-term users would report otherwise). "Bogus innovations" (Johnson and Manwar 1991), drugs that are sold as one thing but are actually something else, like the attempt to sell what may have been bogus ephedrine to a member of our field team noted earlier, is common in the drug scene. For example, as a substitute for crack cocaine, one "popular bogus concoction . . . [is] a frozen blend of baking soda, candle wax and Oragel—which produces oral numbing and mimic[s] the consistency of crack" (Jacobs 1999:75). As a result of such practices, as well as the general variability of illicitly produced substances (and the potential health consequences associated with this pattern), researchers at the HHC have become very interested in laboratory testing the contents of the drugs used by people we interview.

In the case of Ecstasy, tests have shown a variety of substances in pills that were sold as MDMA. One of the chemicals sold sometimes as Ecstasy is PMA (paramethoxyamphetamine or 4-methoxyamphetamine), a drug that is chemically similar to but provides weaker psychotropic effects than MDMA. As a result, thinking they have purchased a "weak batch" of Ecstasy, unsuspecting users may take additional doses of the drug to achieve desired effects. PMA, however, can raise body temperature to dangerously high levels, producing dehydration and hyperthermia, seizure, and stroke, with potentially lethal results. Other substances that have been sold as Ecstasy include: MDE, MBDB, -2-butamine, ketamine, amphetamine, methamphetamine, caffeine,

LSD, and 2CB (although the actual list would undoubtedly be far longer). One examination of 107 pills sold as Ecstasy found that 29 percent contained no MDMA. Instead, the pills contained various substances, some with no identifiable drug content at all, but others were found to have the cough suppressant dextromethorphan in potentially dangerous quantities (Hayner 2002). The word on MDMA on the street has come to reflect the old marketplace adage: let the buyer beware.

In response to this dilemma for users, several consumer organizations began marketing drug test kits and several Web sites were constructed to report the contents (along with pictures and descriptions) of bogus Ecstasy. One of the frequently visited sites of this sort was established by DanceSafe, a nonprofit organization dedicated to promoting health and safety within the rave and nightclub community. Founded in 1999, DanceSafe developed 20 chapters across the United States and Canada. The organization has maintained an on-again, off-again program in which users can send in club drugs for testing. Notably, in one series of 25 pills submitted by diverse users to DanceSafe for testing, only eight were 100 percent MDMA, while another three had at least some MDMA. Other substances found in the pills included amphetamine, methamphetamine, caffeine, ephedrine, and DXM.

As reported in chapter 9, in addition to the problem of misrepresentation, Ecstasy users have also been exposed to increasing quantities of anti-drug messages, including findings on the health consequences of using the drug. In Europe, the dance club scene has begun to unravel, with some of the most famous clubs now attempting to rebrand themselves as more sedate settings as part of a movement away from Ecstasy. The same trend may be moving across the Atlantic, hastened as well by new federal drug legislation called the Illicit Drug Anti-Proliferation Act, also known as the RAVE Act, which strengthens existing laws under which property owners are deemed responsible for any drug use on their premises. The slowing of the Ecstasy wave is also suggested by the findings from the 2003 Partnership Attitude Tracking Study, which showed a decline in the percentage of adolescents who reported using the drug (compared to 2001 and 2002), as displayed in figure 5.

Whatever the vicissitudes of Ecstasy as a psychoactive club drug, interest in its therapeutic properties continues among some researchers. Most noteworthy among these is Rick Doblin, founder of the Multidisciplinary Association for Psychedelic Studies (MAPS) in Sarasota, Florida (Check 2004). In 2001, MAPS received initial U.S. Food and Drug Administration (FDA) approval for a clinical trial to test the effectiveness of MDMA in treating patients with post-traumatic stress disorder (PTSD). After a long delay, caused in part by unsettling findings from a Johns Hopkins University study on MDMA effects on monkeys (see chapter 9), on 24 February 2004, the FDA granted psychiatrist Michael Mithoefer a license to dispense MDMA. In the study, 20 patients diagnosed with PTSD will be given 11 hours of psy-

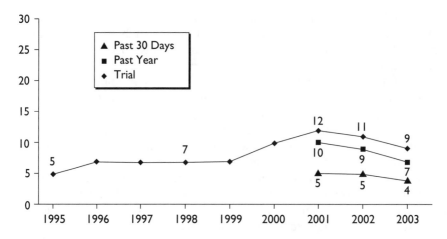

Source: Partnership for a Drug-Free America, *Partnership Attitude Tracking Study, Teens 2003*:10. [online] http://www.drugfreeamerica.org (accessed November 3, 2004).

Figure 6   Percentage of teens who report Ecstasy trial and use

chotherapy, followed by two eight-hour psychotherapeutic sessions about a month apart, after which the patients spend a night at Mithoefer's clinic in Charleston, South Carolina. While there, 12 of the patients will be given MDMA and the other 8 will receive a placebo. The study will compare the two groups in terms of their continued PTSD symptoms. Doblin, knowing the social and political barriers to the therapeutic use of psychotropic drugs once they have been labeled as drugs of abuse, is leery: "We are at the forefront of studying risk and benefit. We hope that there's enough respect for science that people will judge us on the basis of our data" (quoted in Check 2004:128). Other researchers, who assert there is ample evidence of the negative effects of MDMA question the ethics of the FDA's decision.

As the club scene began to slow down at the turn of the twenty-first century, a number of the so-called club drugs began hitting the streets, making the term "club drug" a misnomer for substances like Ecstasy, among others. In our research in Hartford in the Building Community Responses to Risks of Emergent Drug Use project, we found that most users we interviewed said that they purchased Ecstasy from street dealers and used it at home or on the street. Ecstasy increasingly is being used in the inner city, a finding reported in several sites around the country. Not surprisingly, as a result, mention of the drug is now found in the lyrics of a growing number of hip-hop songs by very successful performers, although not nearly as often as references to marijuana. In some of these lyrics, the use of Ecstasy for enhanced and prolonged or multiple-partner sex is emphasized.

Ketamine

The emergence of a new illicit drug often ushers forth other new illegal acts to facilitate drug production and use, as discussed in chapter 4 with the sudden appearance of focused shoplifting to procure the unusual set of items needed for methamphetamine production. In the case of ketamine, the drug discussed at the beginning of the last chapter, its growth in popularity has led to a rash of veterinary clinic burglaries. In addition to taking human users to the place they call the "k-hole," ketamine is still used commonly by veterinarians to sedate small animals.

Like many newer substances that end up as illicit "recreational" drugs, ketamine began its history in a laboratory. The drug was invented in 1962 by Calvin Stevens in the Parke-Davis laboratories in Michigan. Related to PCP, the drug was initially approved by the FDA as a battlefield anesthetic. It is still prescribed legally for human use under the name Ketalar, while it is sold for animal use under the trade name Ketaset. Its diversion into illicit use may have begun during the Vietnam War, when soldiers were exposed to its effects when wounded. From there, the drug found its way into the hands of several well-known drug adventurers. One of these was Marcia Moore, an author of New Age books on astrology, yoga, reincarnation, and other spiritual and occult fields, who died of exposure while using ketamine. Another early user was John Lilly, a physician—perhaps best known for his experiments with dolphins on interspecies communication—who was deeply and personally involved for much of his adult life in constant explorations of the mind, using sensory deprivation and drugs, as reported in his autobiography *The Scientist* and in other writings. Lilly, who was first given ketamine to (successfully) treat extremely painful migraine headaches, is legendary among ketamine users for allegedly injecting himself with the drug once an hour, twenty hours a day, for nearly a year.

The specific nature of the ketamine experience is striking according to users. James Kent (1996:1), former publisher of the psychedelic zine called *Trip Magazine*, and a regular ketamine user and advocate, explains:

> Ketamine begins to make itself known about 4 to 5 minutes after intramuscular injection. . . . The first signs are a warmish all-over body tingle, much like Nitrous Oxide [N_2O] inhalation. This initial effect grows in noticeable "waves" of penetration into the mind, and by the 10 minute mark, you will be in a very distant state from where you started. The Ketamine experience peaks at the 17 to 25 minute mark, hangs steady for about another 20 minutes, and then begins to drop you back down by the 45 minute to one hour mark. Residuals can be felt for a good hour afterward. Although Ketamine shares some qualities with both ether and N_2O—such as an anesthetic "tingle," ego suspension, suspension of pain and tactile feedback, perceptual reverberation (or phlanging), and loss of motor skills, it is quite unique in it's overall sub-anesthetic effects. In addition to all of the above effects on the body, there is also a profound

"emergence" phenomenon which accompanies Ketamine inebriation. The most profound impact of Ketamine is it's effect on time. When becoming "emergent," time begins to slow to a shuddering, thugging crawl—each moment stretches out into a sea of infinity and rolls sluggishly into the next.

During the early 1980s, ketamine remained a favored sacrament of a set of small yet sometimes high-profile literary, therapeutic, and New Age circles. Ketamine appears to have made its more public debut in the mid-1980s, coming out of the gilded closet in several of San Francisco's gay clubs. From there it diffused to the general club scene, sometimes initially being administered to those who thought they were receiving Ecstasy (Jansen 2000). The drug has since become increasingly popular among teenagers, who have added it to the long list of favored club drugs. A hallucinogen that at low doses is experienced like a stimulant, users say the drug makes them unable to feel their own bodies, an experience that puts them at risk for unrecognized bodily injury in fast-paced, highly mobile dance club settings. The drug has even been featured on a segment of the once very widely watched TV series, *The X-Files*, where it was used to help recapture lost memories (as revisiting lapsed memories is a feature of the ketamine experience). Some users who are movie buffs even claim that one of the pills offered by Morpheus to Neo in *The Matrix*, based on the context, was surely meant to be ketamine.

More recently, "Special K" has begun to diversify to street use, but in a unique context. Drug dealers have found that if their customers complain that a particular batch of heroin is weak, lacing the powder with "Special K" helps to mute customer dissatisfaction.

Drugs, Sex, and Predation

One of the issues commonly raised about some of the new drugs is whether they have contributed to enhanced sexual activity, and, as a result to increased risk for sexually transmitted infections or other threats to health. Mixing drugs and sex is common across many of the drug types, perhaps some more so than others. Cocaine, for example, has been described as a sexual stimulant and enhancer. During an interview on initiation into drug use as part of a Hispanic Health Council study, a young man relayed the following incident involving a girl that he had been attracted to for some time:

> I had my van at the time and no matter what . . . I tried with her I couldn't get my way with her, you know what I mean. So this one night, we were hanging out and she was like "Okay, you known me for like three months . . . and I know what you want . . . I want to give it to you but . . . do you freebase?" I said, "Hell no, I don't even know what that is." She says, "Well we go to my house and . . . we get our freak on and I'm gonna teach you how to freebase, show you how to really freebase." I said, "All right, sounds good to me," so we get to the house and [she]

cooks up the coke, you know, and I'm like "Wow." She comes back and says "Watch," and she smoked it and I see it smoking and sizzling and she blew the smoke out and . . . as soon as she did that she started fondling herself and stuff. . . . So I tried some, you know, she put some of it for me and I tried it. My first time getting high, I didn't even know what I was suppose to feel or anything. . . . I know I was feeling real up there and I felt this euphoria type feeling, you know. Next thing I know, we're doing all kinds of crazy things and . . . that kind of started a little something there. So we kind of made it a habit, you know, go hang out once or twice a week.

Researchers "have found considerable differences in sexual responses to the same dosage level of cocaine, depending primarily on the setting of use and the background experience of the user" (Auerbach, Wypijewski, and Brodie 1994:61). Among the club drugs, Ecstasy is described as a disinhibitor by many users and is often linked with increased sexual desire, erection (lubrication in women), orgasm, and heightened sexual intensity. Folk claims like this about the powers of particular drugs to magnify sexual experience, making sexuality a motivation for using drugs, have not always been supported by research findings. While studies do show that sexual desire and satisfaction are increased with drugs like Ecstasy, as is delayed but intensified orgasm, they also show that erection is impaired in many men who are "rolling on E."

To amplify the aphrodisiac qualities of Ecstasy, some club kids have taken to combining it with anti-impotence drugs like Viagra, creating a combination some call "sextasy." Used together, Ecstasy and Viagra allow users to engage in all-night dancing and marathon sex. Mixing sex and drugs has a long history and has certainly marked earlier drug eras. Having sex while using marijuana, LSD, and other drugs, for example, was commonplace during the 1960–1970s counterculture movement.

In recent years, in the gay community, younger gay men, have created a social gathering called the "circuit party," which often has involved elegant decorations, dancing, use of methamphetamine and other drugs, and sexual contact. A study by Gordon Mansergh and coworkers (2001) of 295 gay and bisexual male circuit partygoers in the San Francisco Bay Area who reported that they had attended at least one circuit party in the previous year found that almost all of them indicated the use of drugs during circuit party weekends, including Ecstasy (75 percent), ketamine (58 percent), crystal methamphetamine (36 percent), gamma hydroxybutyrate or gamma butyrolactone— GHB (25 percent), and Viagra (12 percent). Additionally, one-fourth of the men affirmed they had had a drug "overuse" experience during the previous year. Two-thirds of the men reported having sex (49 percent reported having anal sex and 28 percent reported having unprotected anal sex) during the three-day period prior to being interviewed. Data analysis revealed a statistical association between use of drugs and risky sexual behavior. In light of these findings and other data, circuit parties have been suggested as one venue contributing to the return of rising rates of HIV among younger gay men.

Aside from Ecstasy, a number of other club drugs are seen by users as enhancing sex, and as a result, club drug use has been found to be associated with increased levels of sexually transmitted disease. Additionally, ketamine and a number of the other new drugs commonly grouped under the rubric of club drugs, including GHB (also known as liquid Ecstasy) and Rohypnol (sometimes called the "date rape drug"), have gained notoriety for playing a role in facilitating sexual assault. These drugs have a reputation for reducing a victim's capacity to resist unwanted sexual advances or to recall them clearly after the event. Because they are invisible and odorless when dissolved, if a little salty in taste, they are indiscernible when dissolved in beverages such as sodas, juice, hard liquor, or beer; because of these characteristics it is possible to conceal from victims that they have consumed a drug. These drugs have greatest impact on the inexperienced user, among whom overdose is common, with potentially tragic outcomes. Some people who have been given the drug without knowing it have slipped into a long-term coma and a number have died.

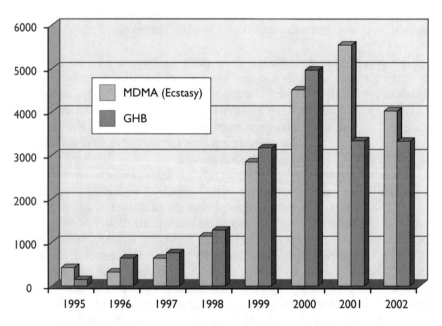

Source: ED Trends from DAWN, Table 2.2 [online] http://dawninfo.samhsa.gov/old_dawn/pubs_94_02/edpubs/2002final/

Figure 7   Use of GHB and MDMA (Ecstasy) based on emergency department visits

Although originally developed as an anesthetic, GHB (gamma hydroxy-butyric acid) first entered into popular use among aggressive bodybuilders seeking to stimulate muscle growth. In addition to its anabolic or bodybuilding traits (the drug causes the release of growth hormone), GHB produces both rapidly appearing euphoric and sedative effects. These traits led to its diffusion in about 1990 into gay clubs and from there into the general club scene as a recreational drug, where it is sometimes called "Grievous Bodily Harm." Another drug found in the club scene is BD (1,4-Butanediol), an ingredient in industrial cleaners, polyurethane, and spandex. Inside the human body, BD is transformed during the metabolic process into GHB. Both drugs, while quite popular in the illicit drug trade, are associated with sporadic cases of coma and death.

Rohypnol (flunitrazepam), better known as "roofies," is a benzodiazephine produced especially in Tijuana, Mexico, and marketed legally by Hoffman-LaRoche, Inc., worldwide (except in the United States, where it is banned) as a short-term treatment for insomnia. Users report effects similar to alcohol intoxication but without producing a hangover. One of its side effects, however, is a condition known as anterograde amnesia, which involves limited memory formation while the drug is acting on the brain. Because of its diversion into illicit use as a "date-rape" drug, the manufacturer has added a green dye intended to alert the unexpecting victim. One diversification of the drug in recent years is among high school youth who have begun using it regularly as a drug of choice.

Seen also at dance clubs and youth-oriented concerts is a drug sold under the street name of "Herbal Ecstasy" or ephedrine. Playing on the popularity of natural foods, it was at one time touted as a safe and legal alternative to Ecstasy. In 2004, however, the federal government banned the drug for sale in the United States as presenting an unreasonable risk of illness, following a common pattern seen many times before: (1) a new, initially obscure drug begins to become popular with a small, homogeneous group of users; (2) information about the effects of the drug spreads by word of mouth (and possibly before long, via the Internet); (3) the drug attracts new users (including some who ethnically or otherwise differ from the initial users), perhaps producing a number of emergency room cases and drawing media attention (perhaps being labeled as "the new cocaine" or the "dangerous new high"); (4) spread of the drug and publicity in the media about it draws the attention of both the new groups of users and eventually the DEA, which moves to have the drug added to the ever-growing list of controlled substances; and (5) the drug joins the menu of popular illegal chemicals that come and go in waves of use, often in modified form or carrying new street names.

In the early 1970s, Congress implemented the Controlled Substance Act, which established a system for classifying illicit drugs into one of five levels of schedules based on their reputed danger to users and society. Below is a summary:

Schedule I: These are drugs that have a high potential for abuse but no current medical value. Examples include Ecstasy, marijuana, and heroin.

Schedule II: These drugs have a high potential for abuse but some treatment value; however, they also have a propensity for physical or emotional dependence. Examples include PCP, oxycodone, cocaine, and methamphetamine.

Schedule III: These drugs have the same features as Schedule II drugs but are seen as having less potential for abuse as well as for dependence. These drugs include LSD, anabolic steroids, and ketamine.

Schedule IV: These drugs have a low potential for abuse, clear medicinal value, and only limited potential for dependence and include such drugs as tranquilizers.

Schedule V: These drugs have an even lower potential for abuse than Schedule IV drugs. While they have some potential for dependency, they have an established medical use, such as kapectolin PG, which contains some opium.

While a number of these designations have been disputed (e.g., the medical value of marijuana), they are used by the DEA to prioritize their antidrug efforts.

New Diseases, New Drugs

As revealed throughout this text, a range of drugs, legal and illegal, of diverse origins and kinds, has emerged in recent years and has proven popular with youth. Some of these drugs find their way into dance clubs, others do not or at least have not yet tended to be used regularly in clubs. In light of drug use dynamics, the movement of drugs from one location to another, one drug use venue to another, and one social group to another (the process that is here termed "drug diversification") is to be expected. The interesting questions are: Which drugs move where, why, how, and how fast? Which new cultural meanings are invested in them as their use spreads to new groups? How do the ways they are used change as they diversify? What new public health and social consequences are produced in their dynamic history of use?

Increasingly, a source of new street drugs is biomedicine. With high-technology laboratories and huge budgets, pharmaceutical companies and their collaborators in university science buildings are in a position to explore the properties of numerous substances at a pace that is unmatchable by lay experimenters. Consequently, understanding what kinds of new pharmaceutical drugs are likely to be in demand in biomedicine is an important arena in the contemporary study of illicit drug dynamics. In this regard, one of the lessons of medical anthropology is that diseases, somewhat like psychoactive drugs, come and go (although in the case of diseases it is sometimes with far greater finality). Thus, diseases of the past, such as drapetomania (the desire of freedom from slavery), dysaethesia aethipis (intentional acts of mischief by slaves), and onanism (masturbation), are no longer accepted as bonafide diseases; diseases of the present, similarly, may not be diseases among subsequent generations; and diseases that have not yet been imagined await future "discovery."

Diseases change for the same reason that drug use practices change: because the wider society changes in its organization, behaviors, and conceptions. In the case of disease, the advance of medical technology has contributed greatly to this process, penetrating new body barriers, significantly magnifying the details of body locations, and opening up new worlds to clinical gaze. From the perspective of medical anthropology, however, rather than natural entities discovered by medical science, diseases are understood as cultural constructions, linking material realities and cultural understandings and expectations to form categories of ailment that we think of as being "in nature" rather than having been assembled and given meaning by culture. Consequently, the diseases that are prominent at one stage in history may disappear or become minor phenomena, and new disease conceptions arise and are used to interpret the signs and symptoms of patients, creating a social demand for treatment (Baer, Singer, and Susser 2004).

One relevant example of the way diseases reflect the wider cultural system in which they are found is the ailment now called Attention Deficit Disorder (ADD) or Attention Deficit/Hyperactive Disorder (ADHD). The diagnosis of this disease has increased dramatically in recent years, especially since adults are beginning to be diagnosed with it as well. It is now described as one of the most common mental disorders among children, affecting 3–8 percent of all children, or as many as two million children in the United States. While this rate has sparked considerable public concern about whether the real issue is lack of school tolerance for natural human diversity in learning styles as individuals are being trained to fit in as employees of large corporate structures, there nonetheless has been a several-fold increase in the prescription of powerful stimulant medications for children diagnosed with ADD/ADHD during the past decade.

One of these drugs, manufactured by CIBA-Geigy Corporation, is called Ritalin. It comes in 5 mg., 10 mg., and 20 mg. tablets and is intended to be taken orally. Prescriptions for Ritalin increased more than 600 percent during the period 1998–2002. According to the DEA, however, a significant number of Ritalin and related prescriptions are diverted for illicit nonmedical use.

While Ritalin is produced as a tablet, it is water soluble, and when diverted into the illicit drug scene users often inject the liquefied drug or they crush the tablets and snort the powder. When purchased in pharmacies with a valid prescription, Ritalin tablets usually only cost between 25 to 50 cents each, while in the illicit street drug market tablets sell for as high as $3 to $15 each, with considerable regional variation. Outside of clinical use, Ritalin is listed by the government as a Schedule II Controlled Substance and cannot be used legally. Nonetheless, Ritalin has begun to diversify as a street drug and now shows up in varied settings from hard-core injection drug user networks to college dormitories. Among college students it is seen as a "study drug," because it assists users in staying highly focused on specific tasks like cramming for exams. Because the drug is so widely prescribed, all colleges and universities have students who have legal prescriptions for Ritalin but who become, by personal desire or peer pressure, underground distributors of the drug. As the example of Ritalin use suggests, as new diseases are "discovered" by a changing society and a changing medical system, new pharmaceuticals will enter the market, some of which will be found to have nonmedical mind/mood-altering appeal and become sources of future illicit drug emergence.

Old Drugs, New Twists

Cranking Up the THC

Despite the development of a virtual cornucopia of new drugs, marijuana continues to be the most frequently used illicit substance among youth (and adults). Contributing to the continued appeal of marijuana among users is the availability of a high potency product (containing delta-9-tetrahydrocannabinol or THC—the main psychoactive ingredient—at levels that are as much as five times those of the 1980s). We have studied marijuana distribution and use among inner-city youth in Hartford (Schensul et al. 2000). This research points to several factors that have contributed to the strong appeal of potent forms marijuana, including the ability of youth to make what they call "fast money" through participation in marijuana distribution and sales. The amount of money that can be made is much more than would be possible in any of the low-paying, entry-level jobs that are available to inner-city youth. Furthermore, new marijuana use intersects with other arenas of the corporation-driven "youth culture," such as the highly profitable rap and hip-hop music and youth-oriented clothing industries. Additionally, using and selling high potency marijuana is an available pathway to gain prestige among peers.

High-potency marijuana looks, smells, and tastes different than its low-potency counterpart and sells for a considerably higher price. As one of our participants explained, "Anybody that sells it, they could tell you the difference. It's a big difference. . . . [I]t is just a whole different ball game" (Schensul et al. 2000:397). Users often refer to high-THC marijuana as "bud," and they differentiate many subtypes based on where and how the plants were grown, the aroma, the look and color, and the effects produced. Compared to regular low-THC marijuana, bud has a deeper green color, lacks seeds, and has a chunky appearance. Distinct brands we have seen in Hartford include Hydro, Purple Haze, Redline, Arizona Red, and Brinson, but drug use names change even faster than drug use practices.

Our study participants emphasized that bud is usually smoked "with the boys" (i.e., one's social network members), being passed from person to person, rather than alone, because, they stressed, the best part of the "high" is that you are sharing it with others (a continuation of an older pattern of marijuana use found during the 1960s among hippies and before them among the 1950s beat generation of marijuana users). Usually the bud is loaded into a partially emptied blunt cigar called an "L." Notably, participants asserted they have no interest in "harder" drugs because they can get "really bent" (i.e., high) from a single "piece" or L.

Marijuana use has a long history of controversy; in recent years the most intense debates about marijuana have been about efforts to achieve its legalization as a medical treatment for a range of health problems. In fact, prior to its criminalization, marijuana had a long medical history, having been prescribed to relieve many distressful symptoms—such as menstrual cramps, as it was for Queen Victoria of Great Britain. Contemporary interest in "medical marijuana" has focused especially on relieving nausea, pain, glaucoma, migraines, and depression. An ardent supporter and spokesperson for the movement to legalize marijuana for medical purposes, Teresa Michalski, for example, lost her 29-year-old son to a rare form of blood cancer. She compellingly asserts, "Marijuana . . . helped quell my son's agony and made it possible for him to eat. . . . Because of marijuana, he was able to live his last days and die in relative comfort" (MacDonald 2004:1).

Being easy to grow, and because demand makes it quite profitable to do so, it is all but impossible for any group, however great their resources, to maintain control over the means of marijuana production. Unlike heroin or cocaine, whose production is largely controlled by a small number of "illicit companies," there are thousands of smaller local marijuana producers (as well as regional suppliers); some people produce for their own consumption, others approach marijuana production with an entrepreneurial attitude and the intention of making a considerable tax-free profit. The range of contemporary local marijuana production is suggested by the people arrested in two recent "drug busts" in towns not far from the Hispanic Health Council.

Antimarijuana poster from the mid-twentieth century. Courtesy of Drug Enforcement Administration.

In the first case, a police officer asked an older, middle-class couple if they would mind if he walked through their yard in search of a dog that he thought he might have hit with his car. The couple politely and readily agreed. To his surprise, the officer found that the couple was growing several quite tall marijuana plants in their neatly tended garden. The police nonetheless arrested the couple, who said that the marijuana was for their own use (and that they were so accustomed to growing it that they had forgotten it was illegal). In the second case, police were called to investigate the smell of smoke and an angry confrontation on the lawn of a home in a very upscale suburban neighborhood. Police found a man sitting on the lawn of the house with cuts on his legs. He said that he had been attacked by another man who had gone back into the house. The police caught the latter man when he tried to flee out of a back door and into a nearby forest. When they entered the house, the police found no furniture (except for two mattresses). The house was not empty however. In it were 225 marijuana plants "lined up in neat rows in pots like peas in a garden, thriving under growlights, fed through a tangle of irrigation pipes and supplied with fresh air by duct work that crossed the ceiling" (Byron and Stacom 2004:1). An investigation led to several other large, expensive houses held by the same owner that were also being used as indoor marijuana farms. In all, the police confiscated 1,200 marijuana plants with a street value of half a million dollars and arrested five people, all relatives.

Dusted

Although from Connecticut, Billie Smith was not a participant in any of our studies at the Hispanic Health Council. But he easily could have been. Like the majority of the participants in our research on drug use, he was an inner-city, gang-involved youth who smoked marijuana. On September 4, 1994, and on the previous evening, he was getting high on marijuana laced with a drug called "illy." When his stash of the drug dwindled, he decided to take a ride with some friends to resupply. Billie drove, and when they got near where they were going, one of the boys in Billie's car pointed to another car nearby and insisted that it belonged to members of a rival gang. Billie took off after the car and was able to pull alongside of it, at which point his friend in the passenger seat fired four shots into the other car. Two of the four occupants of the other car were killed. After the shooting, both cars careened out of control and crashed. Billie survived and was charged with complicity in a homicide. As a defense, he maintained that the illy he smoked nonstop for two days made him lose his mind temporarily. The court was not convinced and found Billie guilty. Ultimately the Connecticut Supreme Court affirmed the ruling, and so died the short-lived "illy defense." The question of illy's connection to violence, however, remains open, with mixed reports.

Illy is one of a number of street names, others being "dust," "tecal," "wet," and "fry," for a drug mixture said to contain embalming fluid and marijuana. In the last several years, there have been various reports of the use of embalming fluid as a psychoactive drug, especially among urban youth (Holland et al. 1998). Despite indications that in some locations, including at our research site in Hartford (Singer, Juvalis, and Weeks 2000), this drug has become very popular among younger street drug users, there has been considerable uncertainty as to its exact chemical composition. Some researchers and several Web sites assert that this substance is nothing other than PCP (phencyclidine, also called angel dust), an animal tranquilizer that has been wrapped up in a fancy new guise by drug producers in order to attract a new market for an old drug. For example, the Vaults of Erowid Web site—http://www.erowid.org/chemicals/pcp/pcp_info6.shtml—an online library of information about psychoactive plants and chemicals frequented by youth drug users—reports the following:

> [This drug is] sold in a variety of forms including cannabis joints or regular cigarettes dipped in liquid and cannabis leaf or tea leaves dipped in liquid. In all of these forms, the material is then smoked. Despite the variety of names, there is good reason to believe that these are all various preparations containing PCP.
>
> In most instances PCP is not mentioned when the substance is sold or discussed. In fact, there are constantly re-circulating rumors that substances being sold by these names do not contain PCP, but are instead actually the fluid (formaldehyde) used for embalming as would be used in a mortuary. But there is evidence to support that this is primarily a case of confused slang terms. "Embalming Fluid" is a common street slang term for PCP and has been for many years. PCP can come in liquid form, so the term "fluid" is fitting. It is entirely possible (actually quite likely) that the confusion between PCP and embalming fluid (formaldehyde) has gone so far as to cause a new trend where PCP is actually mixed with formaldehyde (or other "embalming fluids") and used as a recreational psychoactive. But there is little evidence that the formaldehyde itself causes any pleasant or desirable effects. (accessed November 4, 2004)

As this statement makes clear, a new drug (or an old drug with a new label) is now growing in popularity, but there is considerable confusion, including among users, about precisely what the drug is.

Reports of embalming fluid use as a recreational drug date as far back as the 1980s (Spector 1985; James and Johnson 1996), although the extent of ethnographic research on this drug continues to be quite limited. The first significant report on the use of embalming fluid as a psychoactive drug appeared in a brief issued by the Texas Commission on Alcohol and Drug Use (Elwood, 1998), which identified "fry" as marijuana with embalming fluid and PCP as an occasional additive. The National Institute on Drug Abuse's system for tracking trends in drug use reported on embalming fluid for the first time in the year 2000 (Community Epidemiology Work Group

2000). The reports for 2001 and 2002 (Community Epidemiology Work Group 2001, 2002) add only Minneapolis/St. Paul to the list of U.S. cities in which embalming fluid is said to be used, despite ethnographic evidence of broader use across the country (Fleisher 1998).

In our own research with illy in Hartford we have found that the vast majority (almost 90 percent) of the over 400 inner-city, 18–25-year-old drug-involved youth interviewed in the Pathway study (Singer et al. in press[a]) reported having ever used embalming fluid, always mixed with another substance, usually marijuana or mint leaves.

For the most part, these combinations are purchased ready-made in plastic bags from young street drug dealers, in two primary forms: wet and dry, but participants in our studies have expressed a degree of uncertainty about exactly what was in the bags they purchased. As one noted:

> The difference between the bags will be . . . depends on who gives you the dust, what they have in the dust. You don't ever know what is in the dust. You just buy it. You are hoping it is the same thing that you had the night before. (Singer et al. 2004)

Some participants also recognize that PCP may be added to embalming fluid mixtures (Elwood, 1998; Holland et al. 1998), although the name "dust" is said to come from the appearance of the drug and is not a derivative of "angel dust." Overall, participants were familiar with PCP and differentiated it, based on appearance, from illy. In qualitative interviews, some participants reported concurrent (i.e., in the same evening) use of embalming fluid mixtures with other drugs, including Ecstasy and other so-called club drugs.

More recently, in our Building Community Responses to Risks of Emergent Drug Use study, we asked a street-recruited sample of 150 not-in-treatment drug users about the composition of "dust." The drug most commonly listed by participants was embalming fluid (43 percent), followed by PCP (26 percent). Notably, 45 percent said they did not know what was in the drug. Similarly, when asked about the composition of "wet," 37 percent identified embalming fluid and 26 percent indicated PCP as components, but the majority (55 percent) said that they did not know. When asked about the difference between "dust" and "wet," 70 percent replied they were uncertain. Those who reported use of this drug did tend to believe (64 percent) unlike nonusers (30 percent) that dust contains embalming fluid and PCP. As one user told us, however, consumers of illy are not concerned about its contents, only its effects (Singer et al. in press[b]).

As previously noted, there is debate about whether illy causes violence. This is ironic since PCP has a long rap sheet as a drug of violence. It was PCP, for example, that members of the Los Angeles Police Department claimed Rodney King was using the day in 1992 that they beat him into submission on a city street. Only brutal force, the police claimed in their testimony, can subdue a resistant PCP user. Furthermore, we concluded from our study that PCP's presence in illy is likely to set off violent behavior. In conjunction with emergency room physicians and toxicology staff at Hartford Hospital, we recruited individuals who reported having used illy in the last 48 hours (the amount of time it takes the body to fully rid itself of PCP), and we tested their urine for the PCP. While not present in all cases—perhaps because some producers of illy do not use PCP but other drugs instead, or because it really had been longer than 48 hours since some study participants actually last used illy—PCP was found in the majority of cases in our sample, affirming that whatever the effects embalming fluid might have, the presence of PCP helps explain the experiences of some of the participants in our studies, such as the following:

> Fighting that is all. . . . Fist fighting, where there is pulling hair and everything . . . I don't know because if I am on E (Ecstasy) I am happy. If I do hemey [illy], I feel evil. My whole face is like . . . guys tell me the whole expression on your face changes. You look evil. And I start trouble. I start looking for trouble.
>
> It's a mind altering drug. If you're mad, you can kill somebody on dust; if you are upset and you're smoking. (tape recorded project interviews, Building Community Responses to Risks of Emergent Drug Use Project)

Some of our study participants were able to describe fully the procedures for turning embalming fluid into a consumable drug. One explained that the process of production involves heating mint leaves in a microwave oven until they turn dark black, and then sprinkling them with embalming fluid. The mint absorbs the fluid, turning it into a black dusty substance that is then poured into a blunt cigar that is split open, filled, and then rewrapped. Another reported soaking leaves (marijuana, mint, or tea leaves) in formaldehyde and freezing them. Freezing apparently acts as a dehydrator, and the leaves are crumbled to make a dry black powder, which is bagged, sold on the street, and sprinkled by the consumer into cigars or marijuana cigarettes.

The majority of participants (52 percent) said it is not hard to get illy on the street, and the majority of these (also 52 percent) said it is, in fact, very easy to access the drug (Singer et al. in press[b]). As for the embalming fluid needed to make illy, one participant noted, "Some people know people who work in the morgue. Some people get it over the Internet. It is basically who you know and how much you are willing to pay." Others reported that theft from funeral homes was the primary source of embalming fluid on the street. Awareness of this practice has appeared in the newsletters of funeral home operators, who have been warned to keep a close watch on their embalming fluid supplies.

Just as some drugs have moved from dance clubs and rave parties onto the street, some street drugs have moved in the opposite direction. In the Pathways study, 53 percent of the participants reported having ever used illy in a dance club, after-hours club, or a rave (Singer et al. 2005a). Additionally,

15 percent reported having sold the drug in a club, and 32 percent indicated they have purchased it in a club.

Heroin Hits Home

One of the lessons of drug research is that negative experiences with drugs do not transmit well between generations. That one generation of drug users became heavily involved with a drug, ultimately to realize that its costs far outweighed any benefits ascribed to it, does not mean that the next generation (or, perhaps, the one after it) will not wander down the same well-worn path, which has usually been dressed up in some fashion by drug distributors. New visitations of old drugs are especially common among newer, younger users, people who may have heard something about the lessons learned by previous generations of drug users but who tend not to see the relevance of those lessons to their own lives (a pattern described earlier as "adolescent egocentrism"). The consequences of what might be called "intergenerational drug amnesia" have been seen several times with heroin, a drug noted for its capacity to return again and again in new waves of use and addiction across multiple generations of drug users. While a new generation of users may know that heroin *can* be addictive, what they fail to absorb from prior generations of users is that it *will* be addictive.

Thus, during the late 1990s, drug treatment providers and others who work with drug-using populations began to notice a new trend in heroin use. In the city of Denver, for example, researchers were finding that "a younger, more affluent heroin-using population sees smoking or inhaling as more 'socially acceptable,' almost chic, like cocaine in the eighties" (Community Epidemiological Work Group 20002:32). By 2001, 15 cities around the country that participate in the Community Epidemiological Work Group (CEWG) reported increases in heroin use among younger populations, including in suburban neighborhoods and rural communities.

Erin Artigiani, coordinator of the Drug Early Warning System at the University of Maryland's Center for Substance Abuse Research, observed, "From 1998, we [began] seeing heroin starting to spread beyond the cities into the surrounding area with some dealers setting up shop in apartments in the suburbs and smaller towns" (Join Together 2001:1). This observation was borne out by several monitoring studies. In 1996, an estimated 171,000 people in the United States used heroin for the first time. The estimated number of new users and the rate of initiation for youth were hitting their highest levels in 30 years, with the use of heroin by high school seniors increasing by more than 100 percent from 1990 to 1997 (Monitoring the Future Study 1997; Substance Abuse and Mental Health Services Administration 1997). As a result, from the first six months of 1988 through the first six months of 1997, visits to hospital emergency rooms in which patients mentioned they had been using heroin increased by 99 percent (Drug Abuse Warning Network 1997); according to SAMHSA, from 1995 to 2002 heroin mentions increased 22 percent (Substance Abuse and Mental Health Services Administration 2003). While the largest increase took place in the first half of the 1990s, heroin use was still on the rise in the late 1990s and early 2000s. Smaller towns were taken totally by surprise by the rapid spread of the drug to local youth and were ill prepared to respond. "All of a sudden it blossomed," Captain Robert McLaughlin of the Huron County, Ohio, Sheriff's Department told reporters. "We're up to our eyeballs in it."

Thus, two decades into the AIDS epidemic, a disease that had already taken a massive toll on heroin users, the drug was making a comeback. It returned as a fashionable new "fun" drug, that—since it was in such pure form it could deliver a powerful high without resorting to injection—was not being defined as a risk for HIV infection among new users and was therefore deemed safe. Many new users believed that if they remained noninjecting users (NIUs) of heroin and only snorted, they would not develop an addiction to the drug.

Indeed the purity of heroin increased dramatically from the early 1980s on, yet the street price decreased. While in 1981 the average purity of a dose of heroin sold on the street was 5 percent (with the other 95 percent being composed of adulterants of diverse nature from baby laxative to toxic chemicals to other psychoactive drugs), it had risen to 24 percent by 1998. During this period the average price of one gram (.035 ounces) of pure heroin fell from $3,115 to $1,799 (Office of the National Drug Control Policy 2001). The increased purity and lowered price of white powder heroin reflected the growing competition between Asian and South American heroin producers.

Like many waves of new or renewed use of a drug, the 1990s rise in youthful heroin snorting and smoking had an identifiable "drug epicenter," the location where the drug or method of consumption reaches its highest level, often with the largest consequences. In this case, the location was Baltimore, Maryland. Within a few years of the start of the new wave of heroin use, the U.S. Drug Enforcement Administration reported that the Baltimore area had the highest per capita heroin addiction rate in the country. The Baltimore Department of Health estimated in 2001 that there were 48,000 heroin addicts in the city that has a population of 645,000; meaning that over 7 percent of the residents of the city were addicted to the drug, while the DEA, which put the figure at over 9 percent, designated the city as a High Intensity Drug Trafficking Area (Yang 2001a).

Based on interviews with youth and adults in the greater Baltimore area, as well as mass media and drug indicator analysis conducted during 1998, Agar and Reisinger (1999) found that the transition to heroin use in suburban Maryland began in 1995–96. Reviewing findings from the Maryland Adolescent Survey, a drug monitoring system run by the Maryland Department of Education and the Department of Mental Health and Hygiene every two years since 1973, Agar and Reisinger note, "In Baltimore County, the suburban areas immediately around the city, the percentage of high school seniors who have 'ever tried' heroin increased from 1.9 in 1992 to 3.9 in 1994 to 6.1 in 1996" (1999:367). They found basically similar patterns for nearby suburban Carroll and Howard Counties.

Where was all of the heroin flooding into Baltimore coming from? One potential source was Afghanistan. An unexpected consequence of the U.S. invasion of Afghanistan to overthrow the Taliban government was that Afghani farmers were no longer constrained by the ban imposed by the rigid Taliban regime on opium poppy cultivation, resulting in dramatic increases in the acreage being seeded with poppy flowers. However, it was actually Colombian sources, distributors who had controlled the Baltimore heroin market during the mid-1990s, who were primarily responsible for the increasing availability of inexpensive, very pure heroin on the streets of Baltimore. Most commonly sold in small gelatin capsules with a street price of $10–20, the DEA estimated that the Baltimore heroin market alone produced $1 billion a year in the underground drug economy. One consequence of the undiluted drug was overdose: in 2000 Baltimore experienced over 300 heroin overdose fatalities (Yang 2001b).

As with past waves of drug use, the spread of heroin use among suburban youth only captured public attention several years after the wave began. During February 2004, National Public Radio broadcast a week-long series highlighting concerns about heroin use among young suburbanites. The series caught the public's attention and generated considerable public discussion, although treatment providers and researchers were already well aware of the new wave. Central to the new concern was whether the "pure heroin" wave of the 1990s would produce a repetition of the old heroin pattern: a new generation of addicts engaged in heroin injection. The likelihood of this secondary wave—involving a change in method of consumption—was supported by several studies. For example, in a New York study of 560 NIUs, Alan Neaigus (1998) found that more than 15 percent already had transitioned from noninjection to injection within about a year of beginning heroin snorting. These researchers noted that socializing or having sex with injection drug users is a key predictor of moving to drug injection, including being in the presence of someone while they are injecting. This finding affirms the importance of social networks in the transfer of drug use knowledge and techniques. Another factor that influenced the transition to injection was level of addiction. Individuals who were snorting more heroin (e.g., several bags a day) were more likely to transition to injection than those who were less-frequent users (e.g., weekend snorters).

Conclusion

The notably long list of new and renewed, discovered and diverted, youth-only or generalized drugs used among contemporary youth has not sated the interest in finding new ways to have psychoactive "fun." The youthful mavens of drug exploration continue to explore potential new drugs and ways of using them. In recent years, for example, a still largely unknown candidate drug has attracted the attention of young drug experimenters. The drug known as Salvia (*Salvia divinorum*) is derived from a perennial plant from the mint family that grows in several parts of the Sierra Mazateca region of Oaxaca, Mexico. The plant is found in large stands that grow to over three feet high. Although Salvia is new to youth in the United States, its use as a psychoactive substance is not novel, as it is one of several vision-inducing plants used in religious rituals by the Mazatec Indians. Studies have shown that a dose of 200–500 micrograms produces intense hallucinations when smoked. Users report the drug causes effects similar to those experienced with ketamine, mescaline, or psilocybin. Being legal, it has been openly advertised on Internet sites aimed at young adults and adolescents eager to experiment with new substances.

Although the precise direction drug use dynamics will take in the twenty-first century is still unclear, the hidden seeds of the next dramatic "turning point" (Agar and Reisinger 1999:372) in drug use behaviors may already be planted. Very likely, an important influence will be conflicts played out at the macro level as discussed in chapters 7 and 8. Approaches for spotting the next turning point early in the process of transition—when rapid intervention could avert significant health and other social costs—are examined in chapter 10.

CHAPTER 7

Dealers on the Street
The Impact of Drug Marketing

We did not realize that the moment restrictive legislation made these drugs difficult to secure legitimately, the drugs would also be made profitable to illicit traffickers.

—Charles Terry, quoted in *Addicts Who Survived*

Although teenagers and young adults play pivotal roles in the discovery and diffusion of new drugs and modes of use, youth involved in drug use are only part of the story of emergent and changing drug use practices. Also critical to the fads, trends, and crazes of drug use are drug suppliers (both producers and street-level distributors) and government bodies that ostensibly seek to stop drug dealers and the use of drugs among all ages. These two seemingly opposing forces are really not independent entities but are closely intertwined on two levels. First, antidrug efforts lead to changes in the production and distribution of drugs; in turn, these new drug producer initiatives elicit countermeasures from the antidrug warriors. The end result is thrust-and-parry cycles that continue to reproduce themselves over time. Second, sometimes the boundaries between the "drug lords" and the "antidrug lords" get blurry because, from a cost/benefit standpoint, drugs can provide benefits for both illegitimate and legitimate sectors of society. Furthermore, the various maneuvers of the drug industry and their opposition have introduced significant changes in drug use dynamics, some with important health consequences. This chapter's focus is on the impact of drug production and marketing—the business of the drug lords—on changing patterns of drug use.

Players and Practices

As we have seen, with the criminalization of drug use early in the twentieth century, drugs like heroin and cocaine took on a new place in U.S. society. Making these drugs illegal did not remove the appeal of their powerful psychotropic effects. Rather, it created an opportunity for a new source of income for individuals and groups who were making their way in the rough and tumble of the American poor and working classes. Ultimately, as globalization took hold in the arena of illicit drug production—as well as in many other areas of production—a global set of players came to predominate in the shadow world of illicit drug capitalism.

The Jewish Connection

Initially, given the era in which it occurred, many of the individuals who first saw an exploitable opening for quick profits from the criminalization of a number of mood altering drugs were Jewish gangsters, as depicted in the 1984 Hollywood film *Once Upon a Time in America*. Inhabitants of immigrant Jewish enclaves in New York and other big cities, these individuals not only recognized a significant demand for psychoactive drugs, they also had the connections needed to buy drugs legally outside of the United States—as drugs like heroin, morphine, and cocaine were still being produced legally by European pharmaceutical companies—and smuggle them into the United States (Gosch and Hammer 1974). These early drug suppliers—men like Arnold Rothstein and Irving Wexler—set up distribution systems that continue as the models used for contemporary illicit drug sales.

Known in the underworld by various names, including "Mr. Big" and "The Brain," Arnold Rothstein is probably best known as the likely criminal mind behind the infamous "Black Socks" scandal involving the fixing of the 1919 World Series that left an indelible and enduring mark on baseball's sensitivity to gambling. Born in Manhattan in 1882 to a working-class Jewish family, Rothstein quit school at age 16 to make a life on the streets. He was initially attracted to gambling, a perennial domain of organized crime, and earned a reputation as a first-rate billiards player in the heavy-betting, smoke-filled pool halls around New York City. Rothstein also got quite involved in playing craps and other games of chance (Joselit 1983). Through these activities, he began to meet other young men who shared his attraction to illegal ways of making fast money while avoiding the kind of low-paying, low-status, dead-end jobs open to uneducated immigrant boys from the working class. No doubt, institutionalized anti-Semitism played an important role in the career path of Rothstein and his Jewish criminal counterparts. Rothstein began to build a reputation as a gambler and loan shark while still a teenager. Before long, he came under the wing of Timothy D. Sullivan, the political boss for Tammany Hall on New York's East Side. In exchange for insuring the democratic vote on Election Day, Sullivan took care of the people in his district, providing coal in winter and food and jobs for those in need. Rothstein became Sullivan's representative to the Jewish community while he explored various illicit moneymaking schemes.

With the passage of the Volstead Act that ushered in Prohibition in 1920, Rothstein became a rumrunner and bankrolled a number of bootleggers, providing them with trucks and drivers to transport illegal alcohol. Rothstein showed his greatest promise as a behind-the-scenes organizer and financier of illegal activities. One of Rothstein's associates from the Lower East Side of New York was Irving Wexler, who went by the name of "Waxey Gordon" (a nickname he picked up during his years as a pickpocket because he would wax his fingers to help ease a wallet from a victim's pocket). Rothstein, Gordon, and a Detroit bootlegger named Maxie Greenberg built a large rum-running operation that brought in alcohol from England for illicit sale in the United States. On the side, Gordon began purchasing speedboats to smuggle in diamonds and narcotics, the sales of which allowed him to build a huge mansion on the palisades in New Jersey. Gordon introduced Rothstein to the emergent drug smuggling field.

Recognizing the potential for an economic windfall, Rothstein decided to dedicate his energy to organizing an incipient drug trafficking industry in the United States. To insure a steady supply, he needed to set up an international operation. To this end, he brought in several criminals with international connections, including Louis Lepke, Harry Mather, "Dapper Dan" Collins, Sid Stager, George Uffner, and Jacob "Yasha" Katzenberg. Rothstein purchased a furniture import business in New York called "Vantines," which provided him with a legitimate cover for receiving shipments from Asia. He also purchased several antique shops and art galleries to provide other fronts for his growing drug business. While others had smuggled drugs into the United States before him, "it was a slapdash affair—not a business. Rothstein changed that" (Cohen 1999:132). Rothstein sent Katzenberg to Europe several times a year to visit the pharmaceutical companies and arrange large purchases (later, after Rothstein was murdered and Lepke took over the operation, Katzenberg would travel to China to build a heroin factory). Before long, waves of illicit narcotics were reaching New York and being farmed out by Rothstein's lieutenant, Lepke, to a new generation of young street drug dealers and street drug addicts. Through his success in the drug trade, Rothstein demonstrated to others in the underworld that narcotics importation and distribution was possible, hugely profitable, and, unlike bootlegging and rum-running, not likely to disappear soon because of legalization. Thus was born illicit drug capitalism, a sector of the global economy that must continually adapt to its special legal status.

Many other Jewish gangsters also were involved in the early illicit drug trade. One of them, Tolly Greenberg, came up with the idea of purchasing a pharmaceutical pill-making machine and using it to turn liquid heroin into pills. He primarily distributed these in the southern United States, a market not being tapped by other drug dealers. His scheme was enormously successful.

The Italian Connection

As a result of the success of Jewish gangsters in the drug trade, others soon wanted in on the action. One of these was Salvatore Luciana (who became known as Charles "Lucky" Luciano), a leader of the increasingly powerful Italian Mafia. While some members of the Mafia may have initially been somewhat ambivalent about involvement in narcotics, Luciano successfully pushed La Cosa Nostra to use the sale of heroin to expand its success in the sale of illegal alcohol.

While a teenager, Luciano, like Rothstein, was the type of individual described in the previous chapter as an oppositional youth, alienated both from mainstream institutions and prosocial behavioral norms. He was born in 1897 in the town of Lercardia Friddi, on the Mediterranean island of Sicily. His parents were so poor they struggled to put food on the family's dinner table. Luciano developed a knack for getting into trouble from an early age. How differently Luciano's life might have been if his family had stayed in Sicily is uncertain, but what happened to him after his parents immigrated to America in hopes that it truly was the promised land is well-known. The family arrived in their new home in 1906. Within a year, Luciano was arrested for the first time (for shoplifting). During his youth, Luciano befriended a Jewish youth from the neighborhood named Meyer Lansky, his future partner in the international narcotics trade (Katcher 1959).

By his teen years, Luciano became adept at various illicit activities, including dealing drugs. Consequently, by age 18 he was arrested and convicted of selling heroin and morphine and served six months in a reformatory. By 1916, Luciano was a leading member of the notorious Five Points Gang and was believed by the police to be responsible for several murders. Five years later, Luciano had become a powerful figure in the bootlegging trade in partnership with his old friend Meyer Lansky. Luciano came to the attention of the heads of the Mafia, one of whom, Frank Costello, introduced him to Arnold Rothstein.

This connection helped to propel Luciano further in the drug trade. Soon he was dispensing heroin to the 200 New York brothels and 1,200 prostitutes under his control. From there, distribution was extended to communities of color, although because of inner-city proximity, heroin use also spread to Italian and Jewish neighborhoods as well. The end result was a fresh wave of heroin addictions among new populations using new methods of drug consumption, all under a new set of social conditions (i.e., criminalization) that produced the potential for far greater drug-related suffering, disease, and death than occurred during America's first wave of (legal) drug addiction.

The Transition from Snorting to Injection

Desire among new suppliers to increase drug profits by diluting heroin played a direct role in a critical change in drug use practice. Dilution was possible because the Mafia gained more or less complete control over heroin within a few years of entering the trade. Referring to the point in time when the Mafia took over control of illicit drug distribution, an individual who was a heroin user at the time noted:

> They started thinking people were just a bunch of animals—just give them anything. They took out the true substance of the drug. They started diluting it to a weaker state. (Courtwright, Joseph, and Des Jarlais 1989:88)

Intravenous drug injection became a prominent mode of heroin use as users coped with an increasingly diluted drug supply; in the period between 1925 and 1930, it became standardized as the preferred method of heroin use. The origin of this technique of drug use has been traced by John O'Donnell and Judith Jones (1968). Interviews with old-time drug users suggest that intravenous injection was discovered several times by individuals who were attempting intramuscular injection and hit a vein accidentally. Some individuals who made this colossal mistake, and who were using large quantities of uncut heroin, paid for it with their lives in the resulting drug overdose. Others, who only had access to impure heroin, however, found that an intravenous shot "was more enjoyable, and . . . [there followed] a very rapid spread of the technique among addicts" (O'Donnell and Jones 1968:128). While other forms of heroin consumption did not completely disappear (and some were later to return to popularity), the general technological switch to injection would eventually have telling consequences.

As a user from the 1930s reported to David Courtwright and colleagues (1989:110):

> I didn't use the needle in Germany. I started using it in this country when the Italians [i.e., the Mafia] got the stuff [heroin] and they started to cut it. That was in 1929, when Arnold Rothstein got killed. . . . And when they got it and they started to cut it—not too base at first, it was still 40 percent [pure]. But gradually it got weaker, and weaker, and weaker.

The Mafia maintained primary control over the import of heroin, until, under intensive police pressure, Mafia drug dominance began to decline in the 1970s (Booth 1999). During the same period, between 1960 and 1995, the Chinese population of New York jumped dramatically from 20,000 to 400,000, providing a strong base for Chinese crime organizations or Triads, which began to compete for sectors of the Mafia drug trade. Later, control of heroin importation in the eastern United States shifted to Colombian hands, with Mexican gangs becoming primary suppliers in the West. With each restructuring of the drug industry, supplies of various drugs on the street peaked and fell, producing behavioral changes among drug users who were forced to cope with supply-side instabilities that were beyond their control.

Social Relations among Adult Drug Users

The role of social networks in the diffusion of drugs among younger users was explored in chapter 5. What is the nature of the social world of the adult users? Beginning with work done on the epidemiology of syphilis, there has been growing recognition of the importance of social networks in the spread of disease. In this research, social networks have come to be defined as the structure of one-to-another linkages between all of the individuals within a social group. These linkages can be used to share information (e.g., about new drugs), provide social support (e.g, in the case of a drug overdose), model social behaviors (e.g., new ways to use particular drugs), and pass resources (e.g., pooling money to purchase drugs). They may also be the conveyor belts of infection, and hence the nature of their configuration can be used to predict the way in which HIV or other diseases (or even drug use) will spread. For example, research has shown that drug user social networks that contain individuals who engage frequently in HIV risk behavior and have many links to members of the social network are more likely to have infected members than those social networks in which risk is only common among more fringe members of the group. As a result of findings like this, researchers have begun to pay greater attention to drug user social networks. Consequently, various studies have been conducted in which drug users are asked to name (often street or nicknames are used) all of the people they share drugs or have sex with. Participants in such studies may be asked to help recruit some of the individuals they mention so that they too can be interviewed about their network of drug use and sex partners. In this way, researchers are able to connect the reports of multiple drug users to produce complex maps of risk linkages in a social setting such as a neighborhood. Researchers engaged in this work have come to recognize the importance of certain social roles in networks—such as individuals who reside in the core of the network and are linked to many people within the broader network, as well as individuals who serve as the only link between two components of the network or are the connecting point between two or more otherwise independent networks.

It is likely that the nature of drug user social networks and the differences that exist in network structures from one locale to another reflect adaptations to local conditions. For example, comparison of Puerto Rican drug users in different geographic regions of the country by the Hispanic Health Council has found significant socioeconomic differences. When drug users are especially poor, they may be inclined to maintain broader networks to insure access to drugs despite limited resources. Police pressure can also affect drug user social networks. Broad networks may be difficult to maintain in areas where police have a bigger impact on the day-to-day lives of drug users. Additionally, as Friedman et al. (1999:223) note:

> We have been impressionistically struck by the extent to which most cities in the United States with high-seroprevalence rates among drug users

are cities in which the majority of the major drug injection neighborhoods are pedestrian-oriented rather than automobile-oriented. Thus in New York, Newark, San Juan, Miami and Chicago—cities in which 30% or more of drug injectors are infected—drug scenes are places where many people walk rather than drive. Many of the drug scenes in Los Angeles and Houston (cities with seroprevalence less than 10%), on the other hand, are places people drive to when they want to buy drugs.

The role of drugs in the social relations of drug users is a particularly intriguing domain because, put simply, *drugs make friends and drugs make enemies*. Drugs make friends in the classic sense intended by Marcel Mauss (2000) in his seminal book *The Gift*. As Mauss points out, gifts are representative of human relations; they stand for and embody social and emotional ties that extend far beyond the value of the gifts themselves. In the case of drugs, which are commonly given from one person to another in social networks of drug users, drug sharing sustains the social relationships that are needed to sustain drug use, a circular knot that makes it hard to quit using drugs. This does not mean that the relationships in drug-using social networks are any less real or meaningful or less emotionally important than relationships in non-drug-using social networks, because gifts of various sorts help to sustain all social bonds. At the same time, conflicts over drugs are ubiquitous among drug users and sellers and can be the cause of considerable violence of the most brutal and lethal forms. The latter has in part to do with the fact, as Mauss points out, that gifts like drugs, which have material value, are part of an economy in which any sense of loss may become the motivation for lethal revenge, a pattern that has led to the creation of the enforcer role in drug organizations around the world.

The Impact of World War II on Drug Production

Illicit drug use was significantly disrupted by the Second World War. Avenues of drug smuggling were blocked by the war, and the flow of drugs from Asia and Europe into the United States dropped to a trickle. Consequently, by the early 1940s, recorded rates of drug addiction in the United States took a sudden drop. The decline was short-lived, however. Soldiers who were introduced to drugs overseas brought their addictions and cultural knowledge of drug use home. And it was in the ghettos and barrios along the East and West coasts that drug injection found a new home after the war, especially among young men whose hopes, raised by a war against totalitarianism, were smashed by racism and the postwar economic downturn.

In addition to the press of social conditions, the postwar U.S. inner-city drug epidemic was the end result of several events, including the 1949 retreat of defeated Kuomintang Nationalist Chinese forces into eastern Burma and their takeover of opium production in the Golden Triangle poppy-growing region of Southeast Asia, the emergence of Hong Kong and Marseilles as

Mafia-controlled heroin-refining centers, and the reestablishment of Mafia dominated international drug trafficking networks (Inciardi 1986; Schultheis 1983). The individual particularly responsible for the latter was none other than Lucky Luciano. Arrested in 1936 on drug charges, from his jail cell he sent messages to Sicily directing the Mafia to support the U.S. Army during World War II. It is widely believed that in return for helping the Allied conquest of Sicily and for violently opposing the rise of communism in Italy after the war, the Mafia was made various promises by the U.S. government, including the return of weapons confiscated by Mussolini's Fascists.

In addition, in 1946, American military intelligence made one final gesture of thanks to the Mafia—they released Luciano from prison and deported him to Italy, freeing an experienced crime boss to rebuild the international heroin industry. For more than a decade his crime machine moved morphine base from the Middle East to labs in Europe, which transformed it into heroin and then exported it in considerable quantities to the United States, all without a major narcotics arrest or drug seizure. (McCoy, Read, and Adams 1986). As a result, the post–World War II heroin epidemic was born, beginning with kids on the streets of New York snorting "horse" from bags they kept in their pockets to relax after stickball games and ending with a generation of inner-city addicts, strung out, nodding out, and dropping out on China white.

The Drug Business

The drug trade is a for-profit business. The value of the global illicit drug market has been estimated to be over $400 billion a year. Despite being part of the underground economy, the drug trade is an example of a capitalist enterprise in which decision making is profit-driven. In order to make money, drug lords and their "illicit corporations" engage in strategies that are not dissimilar generally from other spheres of capitalist production and distribution, although, what might be called "illicit drug capitalism" has some unique commodity-specific features, as do other capitalist subtypes such as casinos or professional sports. For example, players in major league baseball may love what they do for a living, but as their hard-fought battle for higher salaries shows, they never deny that playing is their job and baseball is a business. The reason they can command salaries that make other workers turn green with envy is because of a unique feature of sports capitalism: the players are part of the working class in this industry and part of the product as well.

From the laundering of drug profits by mainstream banking institutions to the shopkeeper's purchase "on the cheap" of items shoplifted by drug addicts from competitors as a way to cut overhead, and from heroin chic designer clothes displayed on fashion runways in Paris to the reinvestment of drug profits in legal businesses, the aboveground mainstream economy and the belowground drug economy are, in the end, one economy that consists of two closely intertwined components. Both sectors are market driven and their main concern is making money with limited regard for nonmarket, social values, except to the degree that acting "socially conscious" is good for business (e.g., very wealthy capitalists, whether their riches come from above- or below-ground sectors of the economy, are often hailed as great philanthropists). Their market-driven attitudes promote commodification and the progressive destruction of "nonmarket values, such as commitment in relationships, solidarity, community, care, sacrifice, risk, and struggle. Market values encourage a preoccupation with the now, with the immediate" (West 1999:295). Ironically, it is the market destruction of social values and the personal and social consequences of this destruction that are the driving engines of much illicit drug use to begin with; drug use, which commodifies experience (a thing that can be bought for immediate consumption and sold for enormous gain), in turn replicates the dominance of market values.

Like corporate heads in other sectors of the business world, drug lords must develop systems of insuring regular delivery of new or updated products, opening new markets, protecting existing markets, maintaining control over labor, and increasing production and distribution. As a result of these economic dictates of capitalist production and distribution, the captains and foot soldiers of the drug industry have implemented changes that have significantly influenced drug use dynamics at a number of transitional moments, usually by introducing new drugs, bringing in large amounts of a particular drug in a specific region, changing the contents of drugs, or introducing new forms of older drugs.

South American Cocaine

Most of the cocaine consumed in the United States comes from three South American countries: Colombia, Bolivia, and Peru. The emergence of Colombia as a center of cocaine production dates to the mid-1970s, with rapid growth beginning a few years later (Thoumi 1995). Cocaine production in Colombia began as a cottage industry, with amateur equipment in makeshift laboratories, sometimes located in private homes, designed to convert small amounts of coca leaf into cocaine powder. Initially, transport systems were simple, with individual couriers (called "mules") carrying small quantities of cocaine hidden in luggage or other personal effects on commercial flights from Colombia for delivery to a buyer in the United States. Early in the industry, most of the initial founders of the Colombian cocaine cartels—drug dealers like Pablo Escobar; the Ochoa brothers, Jorge, Fabio, and Juan; Gonzalo Rodriguez Gacha; Carlos Lehder; and the Rodriguez Orejuela brothers—worked as couriers carrying their own cocaine to the United States for direct sale to a buyer. These men recognized the potential of the North American market and used their time during drop-offs in the United States to scout operatives for larger-scale smuggling and distribution networks. Jorge Ochoa explained his entrance as a youth into the drug trade during a *Frontline* (2000a) interview following his release from prison in 1996:

I was very young and I didn't have any experience, not even in life, or anything. By coincidence, I met a friend [during a trip to the U.S. in the late 1970s] who was in that [drug dealing]. We began a business that was very small. He introduced me to someone, and between the two of us, we sold him a small quantity. But it wasn't that I needed the money to live or anything. We were born in a wealthy family, to live well. We never needed anything. . . . The business started growing like any business. It becomes like a ball of snow. It grows by itself, and demand makes it grow. The business grows on its own—not because you want the business to grow, but it's that the business itself starts growing. It seemed like a game, and nobody paid any attention to it. Nobody, nobody. "That was something very easy," I thought.

As the U.S. demand for cocaine took off in the early 1980s, and cocaine increasingly claimed a place as the coolest drug on the scene, pressure was created on the producers to expand and consolidate their organizations and drastically increase production and distribution.

To meet the new demand and realize the unbelievable profits that could be made, groups of small-time producers living in the same city came together to form illicit corporations, entities that would become known worldwide as the Colombian drug cartels. Among themselves, these underground companies established a hierarchy, but there was no single leader; the cartels were actually confederations of smaller independent drug groups (often composed of family members, chemists, pilots, and other operatives) who came together for mutual benefit (e.g., to set wholesale prices, to share intelligence about common threats) and to profit from economies of scale. These "core organizations collaborate to improve smuggling logistics or to thwart government counternarcotic efforts" (Clawson and Lee 1998:19). Initially there were about ten of these confederations. Carlos Toro, a close associate of Carlos Lehder, (*Frontline* 2000b) recalls:

Carlos Lehder approached Pablo Escobar and he told him [about working together], he is the one who said to Escobar, we have to change the way we're doing business. . . . Carlos earned that elevation in his power when they saw that he had tremendous capabilities of getting organized and doing things. They saw that he was a man that could transport anything. He had alternative routes and he had connections where to scramble frequencies. He had radio people. Carlos became the most important ingredient of the whole pie. . . . And that's how the cartel got started. Carlos was a very good pilot. Carlos can fly anything. He can fly a helicopter, he can fly a Citation, a Turbo Commander, you name it. And he knew the islands extremely well. In addition to that, he had the charisma to convince these people in the islands and Cuba and other surrounding neighbors to support him and to give him what he needed: refueling opportunities; the protection of his people as they unloaded cocaine and needed refuge overnight; and so on and so forth.

As Toro's statement suggests, the individual mule was scrapped in favor of small aircraft and boats capable of hauling as much as 1,000 kilograms of cocaine. Larger laboratories, some on the scale of large factories, were built to process great quantities of coca leaves. Farmers by the tens of thousands were recruited to plant coca, which allowed them a somewhat better income than the coffee or other crops they had grown previously. Distribution systems were established. As Juan Ochoa (*Frontline* 2000c) explained:

> The business worked in the following way. The supply people would bring it initially from Peru and Bolivia, and they would process it in labs here in Colombia. From there, you would buy the cocaine and you would con-tract it with someone to send to the United States. Maybe it was through air or perhaps some maritime way, and there someone would receive it. It's this person who would receive it. That agent would be in charge of sending it to other clients, from California, from New York, from different states. The person in the United States would be in charge of receiving the money and sending it back to Colombia. That's the way it would work.

The cartels also brought in outside investors, usually businessmen from legal industries who would purchase a share in a cocaine shipment. In this arrangement the cartel "provided the cocaine and served as the shipping agent. If the shipment was successful everyone made money. If not, they were insured" (Duzan 1994:198). The insurance was provided by Pablo Escobar, who received about 10 percent of the U.S. price for each cocaine shipment. If the shipment was confiscated by the police or otherwise lost, Escobar replaced it.

With expansion came specialization. While the cartels provided overall management, many tasks (smuggling, sales, money laundering, police moni-toring and enforcement) were subcontracted to smaller groups and freelanc-ers. In Cali, Colombia, the drug lords paid $200,000 a month to set up and maintain a joint counterintelligence and enforcement operation (Sheridan 1995). Some of this money was used to bribe officials (including heads of state) and the police and to support a cadre of thugs to carry out cartel wishes. As Carlos Toro (*Frontline* 2000b) explained:

> The DEA was the greatest fear. The DEA was indeed the only force capable of . . . [putting] us out of business, and put us in jail and extradite us and do whatever was necessary. The American government, . . . the DEA. . . . [The] DEA knew about the operations. That was the paranoia that kept the group so well armed and so well protected. There were con-tingency plans of blowing airplanes and blowing the airstrip and dyna-miting the whole thing. . . . We [had] plans of escape and we [had] boats and speedboats and cigar boats and all kinds of equipment, as plan B or plan C to evacuate.

The cartels also maintained marketing cells in key cities in the United States. These cells were closely tied to their Colombian bosses, who made all

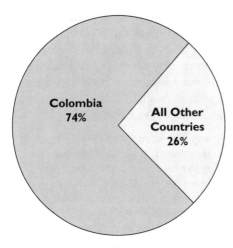

Source: DEA "The Drug Trade in Colombia," 2002

Figure 8   Comparative sources of cocaine

of the key marketing decisions, set prices, and approved high-end buyers of large shipments. Relations were also established with drug trafficking gangs in other countries to facilitate smuggling, including drugs for weapons exchanges. A number of Mexican organizations became key partners with the Colombian cartels, and later set up their own production and distributions systems as the Colombian groups came under military pressure from joint U.S./Colombia antidrug campaigns. This pressure forced changes in the South American cocaine production and distribution system, including decentralization. However, although many of the earlier drug kingpins were arrested, the industry itself, in changed form, has continued as a force shaping contemporary drug use dynamics. To quote Peter Lupsha's (1992) apt phrase, "The players change but the game continues."

Production and Marketing Dynamics

One debate among drug researchers concerns the degree to which the international drug trade has ever been controlled by a small set of very powerful criminal organizations with a global reach and monopolistic capacity or, instead, by numerous smaller groups with far from monopolistic control over any aspect of the industry. One pattern that appears to hold is that there have been moments of far greater concentration and control exercised on the production end of the drug trade than at the market level. Whether it be the Mafia with their Asian and European connections or the South American "narcotraficantes," upper echelons of the drug industry have, at times, achieved broad power over the production and shipment of drugs to user markets, while recognizing that the Mafia was always divided into sometimes warring, sometimes cooperative families, and the Colombian cartels were always independent entities.

Based on ethnographic work in the drug trade, Patricia Adler (1993:82) argues that "illicit markets are populated by individual entrepreneurs and small organizations rather than massive, centrally organized bureaucracies, and are therefore characterized by a competitive rather than monopolistic structure." Agar and Reisinger (1999) draw a similar conclusion based on their review of available information on Ecstasy production and distribution. They note that in the Netherlands, for example, Ecstasy producers lower their risk of being caught by segmenting production processes in different locations, mixing chemicals at one site, producing Ecstasy tablets at a second site, and preparing tablets for international shipment at a third site. Maintaining a "fluid and modular structure," Agar and Reisinger (1999:7) emphasize, within and across (possibly temporarily) allied drug dealing organizations, as well as globally across countries with players of diverse nationality (as contrasted with the ethnic-centered Mafia model), is the postmodern style of the Ecstasy industry. In its ability to continually change in response to external pressure, illicit drug capitalism has exhibited notable flexibility, no doubt a capacity fueled by the incredible profit produced by the drug trade.

Be it the upper or lower echelons of the industry, one way that drug suppliers impact drug use behavior is through the introduction of new products. In the case of the cocaine industry, the early-1980s introduction of crack cocaine is exemplary. As Craig Reinarman and Harry Levine (1997:2) indicate:

> Crack was a marketing innovation. It was a way of packing a relatively expensive and upscale commodity (powder cocaine) in small, inexpensive units. So packaged, this form of smokeable cocaine (crack) was then sold . . . to a whole new class of customers: residents of impoverished inner-city neighborhoods.

The invention of crack, or "ready rock" as it is called in some places, appears to have followed the pattern of drug innovation, whereby experimenters try new ways to consume cocaine and share their findings with others by word of mouth and through underground publications (Inciardi, Lockwood, and Pottieger 1993). Reinarman and Levine (1997) suggest several identifiable reasons why this innovation proved so devastatingly successful: (1) large numbers of unemployed youth in the inner city provide an available workforce for production and street sales, making crack readily and widely available; (2) the price is low enough ($2–$5 per "rock") to make crack easily accessible to lower-income populations; and (3) as a smoked drug that crosses the blood/brain barrier in only six seconds, crack offers an immediate, powerful (if short-lived) "high," making it clearly different than powder cocaine, which usually is snorted, produces longer-lasting, more subtle, and only limited immediate effects. Additionally, crack rocks are easily hidden, easily disposed of in a pinch, and accessible through simple paraphernalia that can be fabricated from readily available materials.

The conversion of powder cocaine into crack can occur at various levels in the complex world of drug manufacture, transport, and street-level sales. The precise nature of the social entities that prepare and market the drug are usually only revealed when police—commonly through the use of wiretaps— successfully penetrate a drug network and arrest its participants. In Hartford, for example, one of the largest such arrests or "takedowns" occurred in late

2004 through early 2005. Using a wiretap on the phone of a suspected street-level crack dealer, the police ultimately discovered four individuals at the top of a local network of Jamaican drug dealers. One of these, a former State Department of Corrections officer, co-owned a local café with his wife, another of the dealers. Together with two others they ran a crack "cookhouse" to convert powder cocaine into crack in the basement of a local apartment. When the police raided the cookhouse, they found dozens of coffee pots used to "cook" the cocaine with baking soda, 180 pounds of baking soda, face masks, gloves, and expensive security cameras hidden in smoke detectors that allowed the operators to monitor the production process (Brown 2005a).

One of the dealers arrested by police had set up a delivery service to take large quantities of crack to a network of suburban customers. One of these customers turned out to be a senior vice president for brand management at a major insurance company. Another member of the drug ring was caught in possession of almost a kilogram of crack, with a street value of approximately $25,000, which had been cooked into small cakes known as "cookies." At one of the homes used by the network, the police also seized $400,000 and numerous weapons. Ultimately, the police arrested 52 individuals and shut down a drug network that they realize will be replaced by other "players" in the drug trade before very long. Indeed, a day after the arrests, a reporter observed that "the effects of the crackdown was not evident on many Hartford street corners" where street-level crack dealers "appeared to be doing

Bags of crack. Courtesy of Drug Enforcement Administration.

business as usual" (Brown 2005b:B3). Police investigations revealed that the drug ring's source of supply was in Mexico, through a middleman distributor from the Los Angeles area. Plans to import 50–100 kilograms per month (with a street value of $1.5–$3 million) were uncovered by police.

Marketing Heroin to the Middle Class

Early in 2004, the Vienna-based International Narcotics Control Board (INCB), which monitors the international distribution of illicit drugs and is financed by the United Nations, announced that the changes in heroin marketing (described in chapter 6) for Baltimore and other U.S. cities had become a global phenomenon. The world, the INCB, reported, was facing a noticeable jump in middle-class heroin use as a result of a decision by drug manufacturers and distributors to go after this niche market with a tailor-made form of heroin targeted to this lucrative set of potential customers. With signs of a growing aversion to drug injection produced by the fear of contracting AIDS, the potential for a radical drop in heroin profits was brewing. In response, marketing-conscious heroin suppliers began selling a very pure, smokable form of heroin, accompanied by a sales pitch claiming snorted heroin was not addictive. Rainer Wolfgang Schmid, a representative of the INCB noted: "This shows how the illicit market operates in a very smart way by selling a drug to a new class of users by telling them, 'Use it in a different way and you won't become addicted.'" Illicit drug dealers, he said, "have a lot of intelligent ideas to keep production going and keep this business going" (Associated Press 2004).

Marketing Club Drugs Online

In recent years, with the surge in the use of home computers and the World Wide Web, more and more information about drugs flows independent of face-to-face social networks. Current estimates are that 85 percent of 12–24-year-olds in the United States have access to and use computers, and many youth use them to learn about new drugs and even to acquire them. Numerous Web sites, newsgroups, bulletin boards, and chat rooms are dedicated to "informing" Internet users about drugs and drug paraphernalia. Some of these sites are quite antidrug in their perspective and are primarily concerned with providing information about the negative consequences of drug use. Others, while possibly including a disclaimer about encouraging drug use, nonetheless appear to have a generally pro-drug-use tone and include information on the manufacture of drugs like Ecstasy, LSD, and GHB. For example, a number of Web sites have posted a description of the complex process of synthesizing Ecstasy that was originally published by Alexander and Ann Shulgin in their book *Phenethylamines I Have Known and Loved: A Chemical Love Story*. Various alternate approaches for producing Ecstasy and its analog drugs, like MDA, are readily found online. It is evident from our interviews with youthful drug users that they seek out desired drug information online including harm reduction information. As reflected in the two anonymous posts to drug information Web sites recorded below, youth may be exposed to conflicted information on the Web:

> *Post 1:* This E [Ecstasy] is so f***ing good. I love you guys. I understand why we were made, it's all about love, people, being, giving. . . .

> *Post 2:* I am in my mid 30s. From about March 1999 to June 2000 I rolled [used Ecstasy] almost every weekend night taking an average of 7 pills a weekend. I didn't take any steps to pre or post load to prevent neurotoxicity. Now, my short-term memory is really bad. In addition, I have been using the wrong word sometimes when I speak or taking time to find the right word. I find it very difficult to think, reason or concentrate. I had to leave my last job because I couldn't do my assignments. Finally, my sense of smell is almost completely gone.

In addition to pro and con drug information and harm reduction Web sites, drug dealers also have responded to the new marketing opportunities provided by computers and have made the Internet a new location for "copping" drugs. While a wide array of psychotropic substances can be purchased online, there is special emphasis on club drugs, as the primary consumers of this battery of drugs are more likely to have computer access than some other drug-using populations, such as street drug users. It cannot, however, be assumed that even hard-core homeless drug addicts are isolated from the cyber age, as we discovered in talking with a homeless woman who gave us her e-mail address.

One of the earliest Internet drug dealers ran an Amsterdam-based Web site known as Neuroroom, which began selling marijuana, hashish, and Ecstasy in 1996. Drugs were shipped through the regular postal service to 15 countries. Customers did not formally purchase the drugs, rather they made "donations" to the Web site hosts. To the chagrin of its users, Neuroroom was shut down by the Dutch police about a year after it was constructed. Undeterred, other Internet drug dealers jumped on the new bandwagon, and an explosion of drug Web sites followed.

Entering terms like MDMA and GHB on Web search engines produces sites that sell drugs, offer kits for drug production, and provide menus for creating drugs at home. GHB kits were popular online for a number of years, selling for $50–$200 and netting millions of dollars in profits for sellers. To avoid arrest, Web sites commonly advertise analogs of club drugs for sale— for example, GBL and 1,4-butanediol, legal chemicals with industrial uses that are converted by the body into GHB when consumed.

Conclusion

It has been the argument of this chapter that emergent and changing drug use patterns are heavily influenced by supply-side transitions and dynamics. In the realm of psychotropic drug use, the supply side is dominated by what here has been termed illicit drug capitalism. Underlying this concept is recognition that what defines an economy is not its legal status but rather its mode of production and distribution. While it is possible for individuals to grow a few marijuana plants for their own use and it is also possible to set up a methamphetamine lab in your kitchen, much of illicit drug production follows a capitalist mode of production and marketing.

The defining feature of capitalism is private ownership of the means of production and distribution. Certainly, on the production side, the workers who toil in laboratories that transform raw products into consumable drugs, as well as those who fly planes filled with drugs or swallow balloons filled with drugs and serve as "mules" to get drugs to the market, sell their labor as a means of survival. It is the surplus value of their labor—the amount of money the drugs bring in above the workers' wages and other production/distribution costs—that constitutes the profit reaped by the owners of the illicit drug trade. Consequently, it is accurate to say that illicit drug "corporations" are no less a part of contemporary capitalism than General Motors, Nabisco, or Microsoft. In fact, as described in this chapter, the licit and illicit sectors of the economy are extensively intertwined. In short, there is not a legal economy and a separate illegal economy; rather, there are divergent sectors of one capitalist economy.

All sectors of this economy face unique challenges shaped by the niches they fill in the larger system. In the case of the illicit drug industry, criminalization presents a significant, but seemingly manageable, challenge. In responding to this challenge in ways that do not threaten the bottom line, illicit drug manufacturers and distributors constantly introduce innovations, some of which impact the patterns and health consequences of drug use.

In addition to the efforts of drug producers and suppliers to offer new products, find new markets, and control new sources of profit, drug use dynamics are also strongly influenced by the counterefforts of the criminal justice system to interfere with the production of drugs, block their importation and transport, stop their sale, and arrest producers and users, adding up to a complex and costly set of strategies commonly known as the War on Drugs, discussed in the next chapter.

CHAPTER 8

The War on Drugs

The first casualty when war comes is truth.

—Hiram Johnson, Speech, U.S. Senate, 1917

The War on Drugs was publicly declared in 1969 by Richard Nixon early in his presidential term as part of his campaign to restore "law and order" to American society. As Musto (1987:254) asserted, "No President has equaled Nixon's antagonism to drug abuse, and he took an active role in organizing the federal and state governments to fight the onslaught of substance abuse." In fiscal year 1969, the antidrug budget was set at $86 million (Drug Abuse Council 1980). Nixon resolutely declared that illicit drugs were now "public enemy number one" (cited in Chambers and Inciardi 1974:221) and established the Special Action Office for Drug Abuse Prevention, the Office of Drug Abuse Law Enforcement, and the Office of National Narcotics Intelligence. At all appearances, the Nixon administration seemed deadly serious about fighting a full-scale war to extinguish illicit drug use in the United States.

This war has not been without effect, but as we know from our everyday experience and from a constant stream of media reports, neither during Nixon's abbreviated tenure as president nor during the terms of subsequent administrations has this war been a success. Furthermore, a closer look at the impact of the War on Drugs on drug use dynamics reveals that the war has helped to shape contemporary patterns of drug use and populations of users even though the expressed goal of the war—stopping illicit drug use—has never been accomplished.

Deconstructing the War on Drugs

In his book, *Agency of Fear*, investigative reporter Edward Epstein (1977) argues that Nixon's primary motive in creating the new criminal justice and

Antimarijuana poster from the 1930s. Courtesy of Drug Enforcement Administration.

investigative bodies noted above was not primarily to fight drug abuse but rather to gather information on his political enemies. While this allegation has never been verified, it is evident that hypersensitivity to opposition and a willingness to launch covert initiatives characterized the "Nixon years." It is notable that prior to being elected president, Nixon had been (circa 1959), as vice president of the United States, the chief political officer of the National Security Council's (NSC) Special Group, the entity that planned the failed Bay of Pigs invasion of Cuba by expatriate Cubans in Florida.

Known to the planners as Operation Mongoose, the invasion of Cuba was linked to various other covert operations, including several disastrous attempts to assassinate Fidel Castro. Notably, in 1963, a number of leaders of Operation Mongoose were caught smuggling narcotics into the United States from Cuba (Fresia 1988; Kruger 1976). This event was not unique. Rather, it was one of the schemes in an enduring pattern of using drug money to finance covert (and often illegal) U.S. government-sponsored activities against disliked foreign regimes. As Rob Schultheis (1983:237) reports, for example, from

> the 1950s through the Vietnam War era, the Nationalist Chinese (KMT) in the Golden Triangle were supplied, even advised, by the CIA; the involvement of the Chinese in the opium and heroin business was excused because of the fact that they carried out paramilitary and intelligence activities along the Burma–Chinese border and elsewhere in the Triangle.

In other words, the War on Drugs has been a most curious war, with very contradictory objectives.

The Asian Front

Exemplary is the Asian case where, beginning after World War II, the CIA used one of its front organizations, the Sea Supply Company, to give its

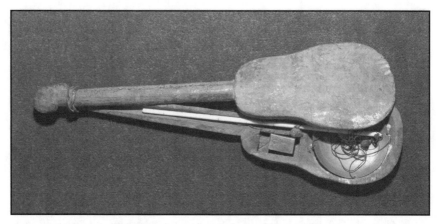

Scale used in the late 1800s to measure opium. Courtesy of Drug Enforcement Administration.

full support to Golden Triangle opium producer General Phao and helped him to become the strongest warlord in Thailand. The CIA supplied Phao with millions of dollars of support in arms, communications equipment, armored vehicles, ships, and aircraft. At the height of the CIA's involvement with Phao, at least 300 CIA agents worked directly with Phao's oppressive police force. By way of repayment, Phao allowed the CIA to develop two paramilitary organizations, the Police Aerial Reconnaissance Unit and the Border Patrol Police, with the ultimate goal of overthrowing Mao's communist regime in China. In repayment of CIA funding, Phao became the region's most outspoken anticommunist while his police force actively protected KMT opium supply shipments, marketed drugs, and solicited support for the KMT among the Southeast Asian Chinese community, the richest group in southern Asia.

During this period, U.S. Ambassador William Donovan, a senior adviser to the CIA, praised Phao's military state as "the free world's strongest bastion in Southeast Asia." By the mid-1950s, this "free world bastion" was controlled by the largest opium-trafficking cartel in the region and was deeply involved in every aspect of the narcotics trade, including providing guards for KMT opium caravans from the Thai–Burmese border until the drug shipments were safely loaded onto freighters bound for Hong Kong or Singapore.

When Operation Mongoose (which had achieved little of its expressed agenda) was shut down in 1965, its director, Theodore Shackley, and his assistant, Thomas Clines, were transferred to Laos, where Shackley became the Deputy Chief of Station for the CIA. During this period, Shackley and Clines took over management of the CIA's relationship with General Vang Pao, a Hmong warlord and former French colonial officer who controlled the main Hmong cash crop in Laos—opium. In exchange for helping him market his opium (including, as described below, to U.S. soldiers in Vietnam), Vang

Pao committed his forces to fighting a Laotian communist nationalist group, Pathet Lao, and the North Vietnamese. Vang Pao also repaid Shackley and Clines for their support by using his drug money to train Hmong tribesmen in guerrilla war tactics and by helping to organize disruptive forays into southern China (Fresia 1988).

In 1973, Shackley and Clines were sent to Vietnam under the Phoenix Project. Again, Vang Pao's drug money was used to finance secret operations, this time against village leaders who were sympathetic to the Viet Cong. During the Vietnam War one of the biggest markets for Vang Pao's opium (some of it processed as heroin) was U.S. troops.

> CIA protégé General Van[g] Pao . . . use[d] his U.S.-supplied helicopters and STOL (short take-off-and-landing) aircraft to collect the opium from the surrounding areas. It [was] unloaded and stored in hutches in Long Cheng [a CIA base built in 1962]. Some of it is sold there and flown out in Royal Laotian government C-47s to Saigon or the Gulf of Siam or the South China Sea, where it is dropped to fishing boats. . . . One of Van[g] Pao's main sources of transport, since the RLG Air Force [was] not under his control, [was] the CIA-created Xieng Khouang Airlines, which [was] supervised by an American. . . . A considerable part of the opium and heroin remain[ed] in Saigon, where it [was] sold directly to U.S. troops or distributed to U.S. bases throughout the Vietnamese countryside. (Browning and Garrett 1986:121)

In 1972, army medical personnel estimated that there were between 25,000–35,000 heroin addicts among U.S. troops in Vietnam (10–15 percent of the rank-and-file soldiers), with some combat units suffering such high levels of addiction that they were rendered useless from a military standpoint (Booth 1996). As a result, the U.S. military in Vietnam was forced to discharge between 1,000 and 2,000 GI drug addicts a month. They were flown back to the United States and released from military service, but not always from their addictions. Few of these soldiers were given follow-up drug treatment and many of those who could not get into treatment on their own—and who probably had more intense addictions than those veterans who stopped heavy drug use once they were back in the United States—continued their drug habit. Communities in the United States that had rarely had a drug problem suddenly were caught up in the drug scene, with addicted former soldiers selling drugs locally to support their own addiction. Some of the discharged GIs returned to Vietnam and set themselves up as drug dealers, recruiting active-duty soldiers to serve as couriers when they returned to the states or to ship heroin back home through military postal systems. As a result, heroin moved out of the inner city and addiction became widespread.

The dark irony of this situation as noted by Frank Browning and Banning Garrett (1986:119) is that: "While the President is declaring war on narcotics and on crime in the streets, he is widening the war in Laos, whose principal product is opium and which has now become the funnel for nearly half the world's supply of the narcotic, for which the U.S. is the chief consumer." But this fact—that at the time the Golden Triangle was the source of 80 percent of the world's supply of opium, and that the area and its drugs were controlled by U.S.-backed forces—was never acknowledged by the Nixon administration. Rather, Turkey was nominated as the primary source of most opium, and the Nixon administration and the Department of Agriculture promoted the development of a biological agent to destroy Turkey's poppy crop, although it was never used for fear it would spread to other areas of Turkish agriculture (Inciardi 1986). Argue Browning and Garrett (1986:123):

> It is no accident that Nixon has ignored the real sources of narcotics trade abroad and by so doing has effectively precluded any possibility of being able to deal with heroin at home. It is he more than anyone else who has *underwritten that trade* through the policies he has formulated, the alliances he has forged, and . . . the political appointments he has made. (emphasis added)

Similarly, in Burma, which in the mid-1970s was a recipient of U.S. State Department International Narcotics Control (INC) funding to eliminate narcotics production, investigators from the U.S. House Select Committee on Narcotics found "convincing evidence that [the] . . . antinarcotics campaign is [in fact] a form of economic welfare aimed at subjugation of . . . Minority Peoples" (U.S. Congress 1977:225). When not attacking the ethnic minority Kachin, Shan, and Karen peoples, Burmese soldiers were found to be busily engaged in harvesting minority-owned opium fields for their own profit.

The Colombian Front

The shaky Nixon blueprint for the War on Drugs in Asia was, to a degree, replicated by the Clinton administration in South America. The Clinton administration focused its chapter of the War on Drugs primarily on Colombia, a center of coca and, later, poppy growing. On August 30, 2000, Clinton visited Cartagena, Colombia (although significant security risks made his stay a very brief one), to formally begin the transfer of $1.3 billion in U.S. aid. This money was said to have three purposes: (1) to help the Colombian government fight runaway inflation; (2) to prop up Colombia's own drug war; and (3) to assist the government in its 40-year armed conflict with 17,000 leftist insurgents (Riechmann 2000). Although numerous Colombian government officials themselves have been implicated in the drug trade (Castillo 1987; Orjuela 1990), it is evident that Colombian revolutionaries have had a role in protecting drug cultivation and production from the Colombian army while collecting a tax from growers for this service. As Francisco Thoumi (1995:159) points out, this "narco-guerrilla connection" has long whetted the U.S. appetite "to kill two birds with one stone, since it could link its antidrug policies with anticommunist policies in the region."

While Clinton strongly denied a military objective in Colombia—claiming that the 60 transport and attack helicopters included in the massive U.S. aid package would be used for illicit crop elimination only—past history and the chaotic sociopolitical situation in Colombia puts this assertion in immediate doubt. It is known that right-wing paramilitary groups with very close ties to the Colombian military, such as Carlos Castaño's United Self-Defense Forces of Colombia (AUC), have been heavily involved in both drug trafficking and political assassinations (Gutierrez and Torriero 2000). In an interview in August 2000, Castaño maintained that AUC had been contacted by the DEA to build an alliance in fighting the war on drug trafficking (McInery 2000). The parallels to the contradictory events in the Golden Triangle are striking.

Drug Producers Fight Back

Drug producers have responded to the pressure put on them by the War on Drugs in ways that have had an impact on drug use dynamics. As Agar and Reisinger (2002:393) note:

> The war on drugs disrupted the conditions under which the 1960s [heroin] epidemic had flourished. But the disruption was short-lived, and supply systems and addiction returned after the early 1970s heroin drought in even stronger form. The data [do] not show the end of an epidemic; instead, they [show] the transformation of an enduring heroin system.

Among cocaine producers and traffickers, response to antidrug pressure was the development of several strategies to replace losses caused by interdic-

Hidden compartment used to smuggle drugs. Courtesy of Drug Enforcement Administration.

tion and control efforts (Clawson and Lee 1998), including increasing production efficiency to lower costs of production (e.g., drying cocaine to increase its shelf life); experimenting with cheaper production methods (e.g., finding less expensive chemicals that are still effective for drug production); controlling both "upstream" (production) and "downstream" (sales) sectors of the drug industry; and moving from a focus on a single product to the manufacture of a diverse line of products, including alternative forms of the same product (e.g., powder cocaine and crack) and alternative products (e.g., heroin and cocaine). Rather than defeat the illicit drug industry, a primary effect of the War on Drugs has been changes in specific drug availability that have had direct influence on use patterns.

The War Goes On, and On

As we have seen, the War on Drugs, *from the beginning*, was a tainted war characterized by conflicted and, from a public health standpoint, questionable and contradictory subagendas. In fact, Nixon's War on Drugs was not alone in this respect. Federal government as well as state or even judicial opposition to drugs before Nixon was no less tainted, no less "political" in nature, and no more driven by a primary concern with the health of the nation. The same types of patterns also characterize the continually renewed War on Drugs *since* the Nixon presidency. For example, after the fall of the Shah of Iran, the CIA developed a growing presence in Afghanistan, which had become one of the world's largest opium-producing areas. When the Soviet Union invaded Afghanistan in 1979, the CIA, on the authority of President Jimmy Carter, began supplying arms and logistical support to the northern tribes. As a result of "high-powered CIA largess" and a record poppy crop in the region, there appeared a new "monster source of opium production [that] . . . promise[d] to send a veritable hurricane of heroin swirling once again through the streets of Europe and America: Afghanistan" (Levins 1986:125).

That wave struck in the early 1980s. In response, presidents Reagan (who in 1986 in a major policy speech called for "a national crusade against drugs . . . to rid America of this scourge" [Courtwright, Joseph, and Des Jarlais 1989:344]) and Bush resuscitated a somewhat indolent drug war, again without any real success. During his watch, Bill Clinton joined the battle by appointing General Barry McCaffrey to lead America's charge. In the introduction to his 1996 National Drug Control Strategy, President Clinton (1996:3) claimed: "In the last few years our Nation has made significant progress against drug use and related crime. . . . [W]e have dealt serious blows to the international criminal networks that import drugs into America. . . ." Similarly, in his 2004 report to the U.S. Congress on his own National Drug Control Strategy, President George W. Bush (2004:1) announced he was

> pleased to report that we have exceeded our two-year goal of reducing drug use among young people. The most recent survey shows an 11 percent

drop between 2001 and 2003 in the use of illicit drugs by teenagers. Among teens, some drugs—such as LSD—have dropped to record low levels of use. For others, we are seeing the lowest levels of use in almost a decade.

Further, under Bush, the ONDCP (2004:123) claimed that:

> Both abroad and at home, for the past two years the [president's National Drug Control] Strategy has focused on such sectors as the drug trade's agricultural sources, its processing and transportation systems, its organizational hierarchy, and its financing mechanisms. We are now attacking the drug trade in all of its component parts, and we have made progress on all fronts. The U.S. Government's master list of targeted trafficking organizations is shorter this year, thanks to the elimination of eight major trafficking organizations during the past fiscal year. . . . Another seven organizations were weakened enough to be classified as "significantly disrupted."

A street-level view of the drug scene, however, does not support these rosy pronouncements. Drops in the levels of some kinds of drug use appeared to be unrelated to supply issues and were offset by rises in other kinds of drug use (Community Epidemiological Work Group 1998). Powder cocaine use, for example, dropped, but use of heroin, methamphetamine, and designer drugs increased significantly. Similarly, crack use rose in levels of popularity among drug users, only to later decline in many locations, as the crack epidemic ran its course among users. The War on Drugs was of little significance in this process (Golub and Johnson 1997). Among youth, LSD use declined but use of other club drugs increased. Indeed, data from the U.S. Substance Abuse and Mental Health Services Administration (SAMHSA) indicate that since 1988 there has been a significant drop in the mean age of first-time heroin users, from 27.4 years in 1988 to 17.6 years in 1997 (Dee 1999). Further, the declines in both powder and crack cocaine use appear to be a consequence of user experience with undesirable effects and shifting variables—such as a radical drop in the street price of heroin—rather than an achievement of federal or local policy initiatives (Constantine 1996). At the same time, the significant drop in marijuana use that occurred between 1979 and 1994 had little to do with changes in policy and a lot to do with changes in demographics, namely the aging of the "boomer" generation.

The notable drop in the price of heroin was a product of the response of the cocaine drug lords of South America to the War on Drugs as well as to recognition of new marketing possibilities. In recent years, Colombia and Mexico have supplanted southern Asia as the primary sources of heroin used in the U.S. Reporters Juan Forero and Tim Weiner (2002:1) describe the situation:

> Here in the lush, nearly impassable mountains of Tolima Province, rebels of Colombia's largest guerrilla group stand watch near muddy footpaths leading to opium farms that experts say help produce upward of 80 percent of the heroin that reaches American streets. . . . After steadily expanding its market in recent years, white Colombian heroin now dom-

inates east of the Mississippi; brown Mexican heroin rules to the west. The pattern signals an alliance between Colombian and Mexican traffickers, one American official said. . . . "A miscalculation in our strategy was to obviously ignore the poppy cultivation, and we paid for it with an increase in supply," stated Representative John L. Mica, Republican of Florida and a member of the House subcommittee on drug policy issues.

Facing aerial spraying of their coca fields by U.S. and Colombian forces, the drug producers switched to poppies, which could be grown in small scattered plots high in the mountains. Continue Forero and Weiner (2002:12):

> Blanca Ruby Pérez, 39, said she and her family live by poppies, which can be harvested twice a year and bring far more money than blackberries, corn, beans and lettuce. "It is much easier to grow than the other crops," she said, carefully tiptoeing around the small, green leaves. "Look, we have put no fertilizer on it, and look how pretty it is."

Law enforcement officials affirm that in the northeastern United States, the Colombian network that had controlled cocaine sales for years is now distributing heroin, which is producing greater profit than cocaine ever did. While there were lessons for cocaine dealers to learn about how to properly cut heroin to improve profits, the existence of a ready-made distribution system facilitated a rapid shift to a new product. Customers were not hard to find. Consequently:

> Optimistic reports from the White House drug control office estimate that the size of opium fields was reduced last year by 25 percent in Colombia and 40 percent in Mexico. But using new research techniques, the same American drug enforcement analysts say the amount of Colombian heroin produced last year is three times the 4.3 metric tons previously assumed. (Forero and Weiner 2002:12)

Now in its fourth decade, the War on Drugs, in short, continues to fail at achieving its goal of significantly stemming the flow of illicit drugs into the United States (Guttman 1996). In the city of El Paso, Texas, for example, a primary entry point for marijuana, cocaine, and heroin from Mexico, U.S. Customs seizures, which are believed to net only a small percentage of the illicit goods smuggled over the border, have shot up from about 40,000 pounds of illegal drugs in 1990 to almost 280,000 pounds in 1999. As Pauline Arrillaga (1999:14) notes, "Despite . . . sporadic arrests, turf wars and leads, drug activity along the border from Texas to California continues to blossom." Indeed, as Eva Bertram and Kenneth Sharpe (1996:C-1), coauthors of the book *Drug War Politics: The Price of Denial*, argued in 1996:

> There is overwhelming evidence that the centerpiece of the drug war—the fight to stop the supply of drugs into and within the United States—can never work. . . . The more drugs are seized, the more traffickers produce and ship; for every route cut off, new ones, Hydra-like, spring up. Drug law-enforcement budgets increased from $1 billion to $9 billion

annually during the past 15 years, but heroin and cocaine are cheaper and more available than ever.

In the years since Bertram and Sharpe's book was published, nothing much has changed on the supply side, except new drugs like methamphetamine and new illicit pharmaceuticals have been added to the mix.

Costs and Benefits

Notably, since 1996, the drug law enforcement price tag has jumped another $3 billion annually without any significant record of real success. Federal expenditures for the War on Drugs in 2003 were over $19 billion or about $600 per second throughout the year. Another $20 billion was spent by state and local governments. Arrests for drug law violations in 2004 exceeded the 1,579,566 drug arrests made during the year 2000, with someone in the country being arrested for a drug law violation every 20 seconds (Bush 2004).

Costs of Incarceration: Money and Lives

In other developed countries, like England, Germany, and France, the rate of incarceration is 1 per 1,000 of the world's population. By contrast, in the United States the rate is 1 per 143. While the U.S. population accounts for only about 5 percent of the world's population, 25 percent of all people in prison in the world are in U.S. prisons. According to a report from the Washington, D.C.–based Sentencing Project entitled "Young Black Americans and the Criminal Justice System: Five Years Later," "Drug policies constitute the

Police move drug buyers off of a street corner in New York. Photograph by Richard Curtis.

single most significant factor contributing to the rise in criminal justice populations in recent years, with the number of incarcerated drug offenders having risen by 510 percent from 1983 to 1993" (quoted in Muwakkil 1996:20). Radical increases in the number of individuals imprisoned for drug offenses is a consequence of changes in the wording of the drug laws that are enforced at both the federal and state levels. For example, in New York State, drug legislation pushed for by former Governor Nelson Rockefeller in 1973, which mandated sentences of 15 years to life for all persons selling two ounces of any illicit substance or possessing four ounces of such substances, resulted in a fivefold jump in the number of inmates in the state (Andrews 1995).

There are 1.7 million drug arrests per year in the U.S.—50 percent of possession arrests are for marijuana (Bureau of Justice Statistics, 2004a)—and Michael Massing (1999) reports that 400,000 people have been jailed for nonviolent drug-related crimes. In 1980, 19 out of every 1,000 people arrested for a drug-related violation served time in prison; 12 years later this figure had increased by more than 500 percent to 104 incarcerations per 1,000 drug arrests. During this period, drug arrests accounted for approximately 75 percent of the total increase in the number of federal prisoners (Chambliss 1994). Importantly, in 2003, more than 75 percent of drug law violation arrests were for possession of illegal drugs and approximately 25 percent were for the sale and manufacture of the substances (Bureau of Justice Statistics 2004b). The cost to society of incarceration is $20,000 per person, per year, producing an annual bill of $9.4 billion for the prolonged warehousing of drug offenders (Betty, Holman, and Schiraldi 2000). This bill is borne by the American taxpayer.

Not surprisingly, like programs allegedly intended to cut the supply line between producers and consumers, incarceration has not hindered the use of drugs. As James Inciardi, Duane McBride, Jerome Platt, and Sandra Baxter (1993:338) report, consistently "research studies and correctional investigations have suggested that drug use, including injection drug use . . . is likely to occur in every jail and penitentiary across the nation." As a key informant in our Building Community Responses project stated during an interview several months after getting out of prison:

> I never had like a habit like I have on the outside [while I was in prison] because it costs more [for drugs in prison] unless you have someone bring [i.e., smuggle] it to you. I had someone but then I lost her. She went to jail. So I was buying it [from other inmates] maybe once a week. I would snort a bag [of heroin] here or there. Or if I got lucky, I got a syringe.

Not only are drugs readily available in most prisons, so are the alienation and socially generated dysphoria that foster drug use to begin with (Markou, Kosten, and Koob 1998; Khantzian 1985; Khantzian, Mack, and Schatzberg 1974), to say nothing of the knowledge and networks needed to train and redeploy drug preparation and distribution workers in the underground drug market upon their release from prison, a pattern facilitated by the lack of other employment opportunities for many "ex-cons."

Also present in prisons, and of special weight from a public health perspective, is HIV and hepatitis infection. As the U.S. National Commission on AIDS (1990: 121) pointed out, "By choosing mass imprisonment as the federal and state governments' response to the use of drugs, we have created a de facto policy of incarcerating more and more individuals with HIV infection." For example, in 1989, when the incidence rate of AIDS in the total U.S. population was approximately 15 per 100,000, the aggregate incidence rate for all federal and state prisons was 202 per 100,000 and 130 for city and county jails (Moini and Hammett 1990). Findings from the National AIDS Demonstration Research projects organized by the National Institute on Drug Abuse concluded that "the seroprevalence rate among inmates will continue to increase because HIV disease is more widespread now among the pool of IDU [injection drug user] offenders than previously" (Inciardi, McBride, Platt and Baxter 1993). Already the rate of HIV infection among people in prison in the United States is 12 times higher than the general population. The same is true of the hepatitis infections, some of which are more easily and widely spread among drug users than HIV (Heimer 1998).

In light of this reassessment of somewhat hidden features of the War on Drugs, it must be asked why the program has continued, year after year, decade after decade, at great cost and with little sustained, overt success. A number of factors account for the continued War on Drugs. These factors, discussed below, can be perceived as secondary benefits derived from a failed policy.

Maintaining Face

It has never been easy for the United States to admit that it lost a war, any war. Historically and objectively it is hard to deny, for example, that the United States lost the war in Vietnam. After all, the forces the United States tried to defeat gained control and continue to rule the country. The final U.S. forces in Vietnam fled for their lives from the rooftop of the U.S. embassy in Saigon (now, tellingly, called Ho Chi Minh City). But denial about the defeat is widespread. So it goes for the War on Drugs. "It is humbling," note Patrick Clawson and Rensselaer Lee (1998:viii), "that a superpower such as the United States cannot exorcise a curse that has been laid on millions of its citizens." Rather than admit defeat, U.S. administration after administration has claimed victory, or more exactly, a partial victory here, a partial victory there. Drug monitoring statistics are watched with an eagle eye for any sign of a drop in illicit drug use of any sort.

Thus, ignoring the fact stressed in this book that drug use spreads in waves and that over time use of any single drug slopes up, plateaus, and slopes down, only to go up again at a later date, perhaps in new form, promoters of the drug war seize upon a decrease in the use of a particular drug or

Vietnamese children today. Photograph by Merrill Singer.

drug use by a particular group as a clear-cut sign that administrative determination and commitment to wipe out drugs is succeeding and total victory is just around the bend. Changes in administrations are handy because past failures can be blamed on the other party and its meek response to the massive drug threat. In the end, defeat cannot be admitted because no alternative approach has ever gained credibility in eyes of dominant groups in society. Instead, the war is pursued, victories are claimed, and drug abuse continues.

Serving Global Designs

At the international level, as has been noted, the War on Drugs serves to further U.S. geopolitical and geoeconomic interests when overt actions toward serving those ends are illegal, embarrassing, or would prove unpopular with the American people. Repeatedly, as has been noted, behind the public face of the drug war has been a backstage effort to collude with, and hence foster, drug producers/distributors and/or use the drug war as a Trojan Horse for the achievement of other political economic aims. At the same time, while targeted political enemies like Castro of Cuba or the Sandinistas of Nicaragua have been accused repeatedly by the U.S. government of having deep involvement in drug trafficking, the clear involvement of U.S. clients and intelligence personnel in the drug trade has been hidden from public view. Exploiting the drug problem in the service of international political power in this way reflects the phenomenon that Noam Chomsky (1988:169) referred to as "the reality that must be effaced."

Creating a Device for Blame

By scapegoating drug users as the nefarious cause of contemporary urban suffering and decay—a practice that is even more common among government spokespersons than making accusations against foreign heads of state—attention is diverted from the role of class and other inequalities as sources of social misery. Since the full implementation of federal laws banning the sale of some substances, and ever more so since the formal declaration of the War on Drugs, there has been an effort to paint the drug addict as the very essence of deviance and badness in U.S. society. Addicts are not simply socially devalued, they are portrayed as the reason our streets and homes are unsafe, our inner cities are eyesores that must be avoided by suburbanites at all costs, and that our ability to experience a traditional American feeling of community has been shattered.

Lost in this interpretation is any assessment of the role of corporate policy—including rampant mergers, buyouts, restructurings, overseas outsourcing, downsizing, and discriminatory hiring, training, and promotion policies, shrinking public-giving budgets, and factory closings—in reshaping American social life. The inner-city areas commonly identified in the popular imagination with drug use are the very areas that have been abandoned in corporate shifts, producing rampant unemployment, deteriorating services, failing schools, and the resulting short-term coping strategies for surviving social misery that have come to be seen as the causes and not the consequences of pressing urban problems (Bourgois 1995; Singer 1994; Waterston 1993).

Justifying Racism and Arrests

By widely promoting the image of the gangster drug user of color as a modern social bogeyman, the War on Drugs effectively reinforces divisive racist stereotypes that contribute to a well-contained labor force with negligible working-class consciousness. Consistently, the demonized image of the drug user and drug dealer presented to society through all arms of the mass media is that of the African American male nationally and the Latino male internationally. At the neighborhood level, these threatening images of color are used to justify nightly police assaults in full battle gear on minority neighborhoods, a campaign that has telling social consequences. As William Chambliss (1994:679) points out:

> The war on drugs in the United States has produced another war as well: it is a war between the police and minority youth from the "ghetto underclass." You need only listen to the words of "gangsta rap" music to get a sense of the hostility, the war mentality that permeates the ghetto. . . . For the past several years my students and I have been riding with the Rapid Deployment Unit (RDU) of the Washington, D.C. Metropolitan Police Force. . . . The typical [drug] arrest [by the RDU] is accompanied by violence, racist slurs, and disrespect for citizens and suspects alike.

Indeed, whatever its failures, one of the things that the War on Drugs has done quite well is to arrest a lot of people and put them in prison. A profile of those incarcerated on drug-related charges, however, suggests that enforcement of drug policy is a better reflection of the "politics of race" than it is of a meaningful effort to stop the sale and use of illicit drugs. While studies show that 15 percent of the nation's cocaine users are African American, they account for approximately 40 percent of those charged with powder cocaine violations and 90 percent of those convicted on crack cocaine charges (Davidson 1999). Overall, African Americans, who comprise 12 percent of the U.S. population, make up 55 percent of those convicted for illicit drug possession. One in 15 African American males currently is incarcerated, primarily as a result of drug laws. Moreover, by 1995, approximately 30 percent of African American males between the ages of 20 and 29 years were under some form of criminal justice supervision, up from 23 percent in 1990.

The significantly higher proportion of African Americans charged with crack cocaine offenses has been found to be "the single most important difference accounting for the overall longer sentences imposed on blacks, relative to other groups" according to a 1993 Justice Department report (Muwakkil 1996:21). Ironically, while still clinging to patriotic slogans about the unparalleled freedoms of U.S. society, compared to other industrialized countries, on a per capita basis the United States is now one of the most incarcerating nations in the world. Lost in the "lock 'em up" drug-war-mentality is any systematic assessment of why socially marginalized working-class youth turn to drugs and the drug trade. Left unexamined are the direct contributions of unequal access to socially valued statuses, avenues of social success, and coveted material wealth. As Bourgois (1995:320) notes, the drug trade is "the biggest equal opportunity employer" for inner-city youth. By hiding this painful reality behind demonized images of drug users of color, the War on Drugs blocks a full public consideration of real solutions to one of our most thorny social problems.

Supplying Cheap Labor

By sustaining the existence of an exploitable pariah subcaste of low-cost, drug-dependent workers, and by allowing a revolving system for warehousing segments of this labor pool behind publicly funded prison walls, the War on Drugs slashes production costs and bolsters corporate profits. While street drug users often lack steady full-time employment, they do acquire shorter-term blue-collar jobs of various sorts, often in unregulated and somewhat hidden sectors of the formal economy, including "off the books" work, day labor, and odd jobs like snow removal. Sociologists have long recognized that a sector of semi-employed workers at the bottom of the labor market—workers who are resigned to accept socially marginal, low-status jobs at minimal wages—function to competitively pull down the wage levels of other strata of labor. As Alisse Waterston (1993:241) notes, "As a special category, addicts are politically weak and disconnected from organized labor, thereby becoming a source of cheap, easily expendable labor. Moreover, the costs of daily reproduction are absorbed by addict-workers themselves." Lower labor costs, of course, mean higher profits.

Moreover, the dramatic increase in the number of imprisoned Americans has created a large pool of potentially available superexploited workers, some of whom earn as little as 17 cents an hour. As Arnold Chien, Margaret Connors, and Kenneth Fox (2000:319) point out, "[prison] employers can freely dismiss and recall workers, need not deal with unions, and do not have to pay for benefits or even work facilities, as these costs are borne by taxpayers." The prison industry, they note, which has a number of subsectors, including the building and running of prisons and the leasing of prison labor to private companies, is but one arena in which the private sector directly reaps growing profits from the War on Drugs.

Facilitating Redistribution at the Bottom

Finally, the War on Drugs helps to control those on the heavily stepped upon lower rungs of the American ladder of social success by sustaining an illicit redistribution system in which drug users steal and make available low cost "street goods" to the poor and working classes. This illicit redistribution system may play a critical role in containing the kind of wealth disparity rage that only periodically explodes into the open in the form of mass looting, burning, and attacks on individuals during overt urban rebellions. In their study in New York City, for example, Johnson and his colleagues (1985) found a wide range of illegal income-generating activities among drug users, including burglary, robbery, forgery, con games, prostitution, pimping, stripping abandoned buildings, and drug sales. Also, they found that daily heroin users had an average yearly income of $18,710 from quite diverse sources and performed various calculations to assess the economic impact of the drug-use-driven informal economy.

Unlike other researchers who have sought to demonstrate only negative effects of drug-related crime, Johnson et al. (1985) revealed the local economic benefits related to the theft and street sale of merchandise. Involvement in this informal street economy may be critical to the very survival of some households. As Bourgois (1995:3) observed, with reference to East Harlem, "The enormous, uncensused, untaxed underground economy allows the hundreds of thousands of New Yorkers in neighborhoods like East Harlem to subsist with the minimal amenities that people living in the United States consider to be basic necessities." For others, the underground economy may primarily be the difference between having and not having access to highly desired items, like gold jewelry, high-priced watches, and big-screen televisions, which are constantly paraded in the media as primary symbols of social status and personal self-worth in U.S. society and that would otherwise be unattainable.

A Health Perspective Strategy

Ultimately, there is no rational justification for why some drugs are illegal and others are paid for or otherwise supported by the government, like tobacco. Certainly, currently illegal drugs are no more addictive, dangerous, likely to provoke violence or other antisocial behavior, or even to produce pleasure and social escape than legal ones (Pollan 1999). Rather, the differentiation of socially acceptable and contemptible drugs is a product of historic events and social relationships, including international geopolitics, interclass struggles, and racial discrimination. Nonetheless, for several decades the United States has expended billions of dollars on a curious War on Drugs that contributes more toward achieving exploitative economic and political ends, nationally and internationally, than it does reductions in drug use.

As a result, enthusiasm for the War on Drugs has been flagging (Nadelmann 1989). As Chambliss (1994:675) pointed out during the Clinton administration, "almost everyone, including the Attorney General Janet Reno, acknowledges [that the War on Drugs] has been a complete and utter failure." Clear directions for a healthier policy approach to drug issues, however, have not emerged among those social sectors that recognize the current dilemma. For example, despite fairly extensive scientific research showing conclusively the value of syringe-exchange in HIV prevention (Heimer 1998; Lurie 1997; Singer, Weeks, and Himmelgreen 1995; Singer et al. 1997; Vlahov and Junge 1998), successive federal administrations have declined to make public health the basis of their drug-related policies and have repeatedly rejected broad community requests for approving the use of federal dollars to support sterile syringe exchange on the unsupported assertion that syringe exchange promotes drug use (Singer 1997). The over-the-counter pharmacy sale of syringes also has been resisted in the United States despite demonstrated risk-reduction benefits (Vlahov 1995; Singer et al. 1998), as have other harm-reduction strategies that may have a place in a health-driven approach to the drug problem (Coffin 1999; Des Jarlais 2000; Haemming 1995).

Attitudes toward drug treatment per se, which for many years have been encumbered by a punitive moralistic view of drug users, appear to be changing in a more positive but limited direction, at least in some sectors. Generally, as a past director of the National Institute on Drug Abuse has lamented, there remains "a widespread misperception that drug abuse treatment is not effective. . . . [In fact] there are now extensive data showing that addiction is eminently treatable if the treatment is well delivered and tailored to the needs of the particular patient" (Leshner 1999:1314). Rates of success in drug treatment are comparable to those for other chronic diseases such as diabetes, hypertension, and asthma. Ironically, studies of the social benefits of drug treatment support the very kinds of changes that those who demonize drug users would most support.

First, criminal activity among individuals in and after drug treatment is two-thirds of that of comparable out-of-treatment drug users (Gerstein et al. 1994). Andrew Rajkumar and Michael French (1996), for example, calculated the costs of crime averaged $47,971 per drug user per year prior to drug treatment, compared to $28,657 in the year following drug treatment. This drop would more than cover the cost of drug treatment itself, meaning that based on the drop in crime *alone*, drug treatment is highly cost-effective. Second, Michael French and Gary Zarkin (1992) found that even a 10 percent increase in the amount of time spent in a residential drug treatment program increases the subsequent legal earning of a drug user by 2.4 percent and decreases illegal earnings by 4.1 percent. Similar findings exist for outpatient methadone treatment (French and Zarkin 1992). Third, cost savings in terms of preventing AIDS infection, tuberculosis, and other diseases that are much more common among drug users who are out of treatment compared to those in treatment significantly add to the demonstrated health and cost benefits of drug treatment (French et al. 1996). Injection drug users who are not in treatment have been found to be six times more likely to be infected with HIV than those who are enrolled and stay in drug treatment (Metzger et al. 1993). Further, it consistently has been found that there is a strong association between duration of drug treatment and protection from HIV infection (Metzger, Navaline, and Woody 1998).

Nonetheless, of the billions of dollars in the federal drug budget, only one-third is directed toward prevention and treatment efforts and only 10 percent of the approximately $6 billion of federal money targeted to reduce the demand for drugs is specifically earmarked for the treatment of the estimated four million hard-core drug users in the United States (Stocker 1998). Importantly, as a widely cited 1994 RAND study found, from a cost-benefit standpoint, drug treatment is seven times more cost-effective than domestic law enforcement and incarceration, ten times more effective than interdiction programs designed to stop drugs at the U.S. border, and twenty-three times more effective than efforts to attack the sources of illicit drug production abroad (e.g., the spraying of fusarium fungus on coca bushes in Colombia) (Massing 1999). In other words, the least-funded component of the federal drug strategy—treatment—produces the greatest benefit in terms of lowering the use of illicit drugs!

One thing that is certain is that most drug users are not in drug treatment at any point in time. It is estimated, for example, that on any given day 85 percent of injection drug users are not in treatment (Needle et al. 1998). Moreover, rather than increasing during the AIDS epidemic, the availability of drug treatment has diminished; today there are fewer treatment programs in existence and they are able to provide fewer services than before the epidemic. Drug detoxification, which is merely the first step in the treatment process, and it is not really considered treatment *per se* in the drug treatment field, commonly is the only intervention that is covered in many health insurance programs (Kleber 1996). While there may be shortcomings in a fully medicalized model of drug treatment (Waterston 1993)—because it tends not to recognize and respond to the social origins of drug abuse—and sound concerns about the growing "commodification of treatment" (Murphy and Rosenbaum 1999), a radical shift toward an emphasis on treatment would nonetheless go a long way toward creating a healthier drug-abuse policy orientation.

Conclusion

One telling social product of the War on Drugs is the drug enforcement press conference. These media events are held periodically at DEA offices around the country to highlight a particularly significant "achievement" in the War on Drugs, such as a major drug bust or the seizure of an impressive quantity of drugs, drug paraphernalia, drug-related weapons, or drug profits. Sometimes these press conferences, in the vogue of a colonial era safari hunt, showcase displays of seized items or other trophies of the War on Drugs and feature celebrity speeches by key figures from the Department of Justice. The underlying message is that the War on Drugs, although a challenge of significant proportion, and therefore quite costly, is slowly but surely being won through the commitment of the administration and the gallant efforts of DEA field officers, local police departments, and other law enforcement organizations.

Despite the media spin during the War on Drugs, the National Institute on Drug Abuse has reported a steady increase in the drug abuse cost to society. Indeed, in the thick of the recent War on Drug years, from 1985 to 1992, there was a 50 percent increase in the estimated cost to society of illicit drug use in terms of the combined impact of drug-related crime, health-care expenditures, and lost wages. In 1992 alone, a year in which the drug abuse cost to society was estimated to be just under $100 billion, 25,000 premature deaths were attributed to illicit drug abuse (Swan 1998). During 1988–1993, it is estimated that Americans spent approximately $350 billion on illicit drugs (Abt Associates 1995). The current policy has not reduced the cost to or eliminated the toll on society. Many public health advocates have concluded therefore that it is time to replace the "War on Drugs" with a strategy that realistically addresses the complex problems involved with both legal and illegal drug use.

CHAPTER 9

Health Consequences of Changing Drug Use Patterns

Before 1980, concern for the health of drug users was marginal at best, which helped set the state for the subsequent explosive HIV/AIDS epidemic in this vulnerable population.

—David Metzger, Helen Navaline, and George Woody,
"Drug Abuse Treatment as AIDS Prevention"

Maggie, an injection drug user interviewed in one of the Hispanic Health Council's NIDA-funded studies on drug use and HIV infection (Project COPE), noted during an interview that since learning she is infected with HIV she sees her life as "a slow death." While she worries about loss of health, what particularly frightens her is the loss of her appearance and mobility:

That's what bothers me a lot, the appearance part of it. When I see those scars, I hope it ain't going to be all over my face . . . knowing that I won't be able to get around like I normally do. When I see people [who are HIV positive], they can't really get around. Those are the things that worry me the most. The only medication side-effect I got was the darkness of the fingernails and the dryness of the skin. I would do anything to keep my appearance; I didn't want to be sick. Some people look healthy and then there are those that really look sick. And my biggest scare is looking sick; not just feeling it but looking sick.

Juan, another HIV-infected participant in this study, had a somewhat different set of fears:

I feel like something is aching inside my body. I believe it is the HIV because sometimes I can't sleep because sometimes I just start thinking

187

about it, that I got it and I be up all night. And I don't know if it's that, why I am losing weight too because of the worries; I'm thinking, "whoa when it's going to be the day that I am going to [die] . . ." you know, and it's hard for me.

These two excerpts from our many interviews with drug users reveal some of the tremendous anguish and suffering caused by the AIDS epidemic; although, notably, we have found other reactions as well, including individuals who feel thankful for being prodded by their infection with HIV into giving up drugs and turning their life around finally. AIDS is but one of a long list of health hazards faced by drug users, many of which will be examined in this chapter.

The Spread of HIV/AIDS

The story of drug use and HIV/AIDS, of course, is not new. It is, however, increasingly painful to tell. AIDS has become the most devastating disease humankind has faced in its history. Since the existence of the epidemic was first recognized in the early 1980s, over 60 million people around the world have been infected with the virus. In 2003 alone, HIV infected a record five million people and was responsible for the deaths of an unprecedented

Drug injection site in a New York City abandoned building. Photograph by Pedro Mateau-Gelabert.

three million sufferers, according to the United Nations Joint Program on HIV/AIDS (Ross 2004). The number of people living with HIV infection continues to rise in every region of the world. At a teleconference in London in July 2004, Peter Piot, executive director of UNAIDS, the United Nations' joint program on HIV/AIDS, told reporters, "We're [only now] entering the true globalization phase" of the pandemic (Newsday 2004). Most cases of AIDS are in sub-Saharan Africa. However, eastern Europe and Asia, regions that, combined with Africa, are home to 60 percent of the world's population, are new frontlines in the spreading AIDS crisis. Notably, in both central Asia and eastern Europe, drug use is a primary cause of new infections. Indicative of how well the world is coping with the epidemic, nine of every ten people who are in urgent need of AIDS treatment do not receive it, and only one in five people engaged in high-risk behaviors receives AIDS prevention services.

HIV/AIDS and Injection Drug Use

Illicit injection drug use, now a global phenomenon, is found in highly developed countries like the United States, as well as in a growing number of developing countries, from Albania to Zambia. By 1992, drug injection had been reported in over 80 countries, jumping to 121 two years later. Russia, for example, which reports having more than three million injection drug users, is one of the worst-hit parts of eastern Europe. The insidious spread of injection drug use globally has included both urban and rural areas, men and women users, and the resulting spread of HIV and other blood-borne diseases (Stimson and Choopanya 1998).

A number of factors have contributed to the diffusion of drug injection, some of them local, others regional or international. In Vietnam, for example, somewhat different factors were critical in the north and south; both, however, stem from the U.S. war in Vietnam. In the north, lacking adequate medical supplies, including analgesics, physicians were forced to treat badly wounded North Vietnamese soldiers and civilians with opium and possibly with heroin as well. In the south, the spread of injection among U.S. soldiers created a local market, and heroin injection soon spread to (and from) bar girls, commercial sex workers, and other service workers involved with U.S. troops.

In the United States, self-injection of heroin dates to about 1915, beginning first with "skinpopping" (injecting into the skin or muscle) but leading soon to intravenous injection by about 1920. By the early 1930s, illicit injection drug use could be found in all major American cities, and by 1950 the vast majority of people seeking drug treatment for opiate addiction were injectors. Another wave of injection diffusion to new populations occurred with the 1960s drug transition, after which diffusion in the United States slowed. As Gerry Stimson and Kacjit Choopanya (1998:5) observe, "The U.S. experience . . . illustrates both that diffusion of injecting can be rapid and that the periodic diffusion of injecting (rapid incidence) may be followed by relative plateau, only to be followed later by further diffusion [and a subsequent plateau]."

The spread of the HIV epidemic among drug users is tied to four factors: (1) although under most conditions, and certainly when sterile syringes are readily available (e.g., because of the presence of syringe exchange programs or because it is possible to acquire syringes from a pharmacy without a prescription), drug users do not tend to share syringes directly with most other injectors; they will share them with certain people (e.g., spouses, other relatives, close associates), however, and they will share them with still others at certain times (e.g., when they lack another way to get high because their own syringe is clogged, broken, or otherwise unavailable); (2) drug injection practices have evolved that increase the likelihood that HIV will be transmitted when drug users share syringes, including, especially, behaviors like "registering" or injecting a vein and pulling blood back into the syringe to affirm that a good injection site has been located (but as a result potentially introducing HIV into the syringe with the blood, where it is capable, under the right conditions, of living for days outside of the body and hence available to infect the next user of the syringe); (3) even drug users who scrupulously avoid directly sharing syringes with others often share other drug paraphernalia (often called "indirect" or "drug-mediated" sharing by researchers), including "cookers" (bottle caps or other containers used to mix drugs with water), cottons (used to filter drugs), and water (used to liquefy drugs and to clean

AIDS prevention kits left for drug users at an injection site by public health workers. Photograph by Richard Curtis.

syringe needles of clogs); moreover, they use drug equipment to mix drugs (e.g., pulling out the plunger of a syringe and using it to stir drugs and water); they buy syringes, most of which are new but some of which have been found to be previously used, on the street from underground syringe sellers, and they share other noninjection equipment, like stems and pipes used to ingest drugs like crack that are smoked; and (4) they have sex with others, including other drug users, under the influence of drugs, or to acquire drugs, and often without any use of barrier protection (e.g., condoms).

All of the aforementioned behaviors are potential routes for the transmission of HIV from one drug user to another, and they have been responsible for the infection, sickness, and death of thousands of drug users since the 1980s. While risk behaviors and contexts among drug injectors vary from one part of the country to another or from one state to the next (Buchanan et al. 2004; Singer et al. 1992; Stopka et al. 2003), as do the drugs that are consumed and the ways they are prepared and used, drug injectors tend to have significantly higher rates of infection than other people in any local population.

HIV/AIDS and Noninjection Drug Use

Changing drug trends have played a critical role in HIV infection patterns. For example, in recent years an important drug use pattern that has swept across the country from the West to the Midwest to the South and beyond is the use of methamphetamine among gay and bisexual men in dance clubs. Traveling under various street names, such as Tina or Crystal, methamphetamine use and unprotected sex in gay clubs have become closely connected. Patrick, a gay man in Atlanta, for example, reported to journalists from the *Journal-Constitution* that he began using meth at age 16: "Whenever he had sex, he wanted meth. Whenever he was high on meth, he wanted sex" (McWhirter and Young 2004:1). Throughout his teen years and afterward, Patrick had anonymous, unprotected sex while high with many different partners whom he met at dance parties and at all-night sex clubs. Fellow users were not hard to find.

Meth and sex have become so linked in many gay communities that subcultural patterns have emerged. Flyers can be found advertising "PnP" gatherings, a shorthand reference to Party and Play get-togethers involving sharing meth and sharing sex. A variant is the Tina Party. A very active participant in this scene, Patrick had trouble sustaining himself economically. Low on money at one point, he even engaged in commercial sex. During these years, he was hospitalized six times for drug overdose. One morning, Patrick woke up to find that he had a bad gash in his head that was still bleeding and shattered glass was spread around the room: "My head had crashed through a glass table, and I didn't remember any of it," he told reporters (McWhirter and Young 2004:1). This experience frightened Patrick and he admitted himself into a drug rehabilitation program. While there, he was tested for HIV and found to be positive. He is not alone.

"Meth use among gay men in Atlanta is really, really insidious," said Michael Dubin, a counselor whose clients are all gay men. "From what I am hearing from friends and from clients, it is a lot more extensive than any of us would like to think, especially in the club scene. And it leads to people throwing caution to the wind—when they know better." (McWhirter and Young 2004:8)

Having spread through several southern gay centers (and into heterosexual populations as well), the drug and its accompanying behavioral practices have moved northward. Meth use and attendant HIV transmission are now a major problem in New York City. The Gay Men's Health Crisis, the largest gay HIV/AIDS prevention, support, and advocacy organization in the country, has initiated a major education campaign on the risk of meth use in sexual transmission of HIV. The sexual transmission of HIV among drug users is by no means limited to those who consume methamphetamine. Somewhat belated, researchers who studied the spread of AIDS realized that sexual contact is a significant route of infection among heroin and cocaine injectors.

Curtailing the Spread of HIV/AIDS

As a result of these multiple potential risks of infection, rates of HIV among drug users have soared in many locales. Among street drug users in some places the rapidity of HIV spread has been truly explosive, moving from 1 to 2 percent to 60 percent rates of infection within a year or so. On the West Coast of the United States, however, rates of infection among street injection drug users have remained relatively flat for years. The reason for this stability appears to be drug use dynamics, namely either the drugs people inject and the ways that they inject them, or having easy access to and using sterile syringes and other prevention services early in the local epidemic when rates of infection were still very low. The key issue usually in determining the extent of the spread of HIV among drug users is not user knowledge about HIV risk behaviors. In a country like the United States, with multiple and far-reaching mass media and health-related services, AIDS knowledge tends to diffuse widely unless hindered by social barriers, such as not speaking English or being highly marginalized. Rather, ease of access of sterile syringes and other equipment and supportive services for drug users are determinant in curtailing the spread of HIV.

Even areas that had once seen very high rates of HIV infection among drug injectors (such as the eastern seaboard from New Jersey to Massachusetts), but have since implemented programs to increase access to sterile syringes and other prevention services, have entered what has been called a "declining phase" of HIV infection, characterized by low HIV incidence and a significant drop in prevalence rates among drug users and others (Des Jarlais et al. 2000).

Other Risks Associated with Drug Use

As noted, AIDS is just one of the many threats to health found in the changing world of drug use (Brick 2003; Donoghoe and Wodak 1998). Indeed, new drug use practices involve potential health risks of at least ten different kinds: (1) drug overdose, a common cause of death among drug users, as well as other kinds of negative drug experiences (like bad trips or flashbacks); (2) mental health problems and brain damage, including exacerbating comorbid mental health disorders; (3) organ damage, malfunction, and death; (4) exposure to various infectious diseases of the body surface and internal organs other than AIDS; (5) a predisposition toward violence and victimization, as well as being a witness to violence; (6) exposure to the elements, especially freezing; (7) burns associated with the use of flammables in the manufacture or consumption of drugs, but also getting caught in building fires during drug use; (8) drug-related vehicular and nonvehicular accidents, as well as falls, cuts, or other body trauma; (9) poisoning, from either drugs themselves or adulterants used to cut drugs to increase dealer profits; and (10) destruction of the social relationships and support systems that allow people to cope with life's burdens. The following sections will examine examples of each of these kinds of risk to health associated with contemporary and changing drug use dynamics.

Overdose

Unexpectedly one day, Emilio Chavez Garcia's estranged wife Nydia in Puerto Rico received a call from her husband in Chicago saying he wanted to come home. While she had heard Emilio many times before say he was going to stop using heroin, only to resume use, it was Christmastime and she responded to his claim positively. It would be nice for their three children to have their papa back. "Maybe this time, she hoped, he would finally kick the heroin addiction that had ruined their family" (Bebow 2004:1). An army veteran, Emilio had worked steadily in a Chicago plastics factory until he developed a heroin addiction. Then everything changed, for the worse. Rafael Diaz, another drug user in Chicago, also was trying to quit using heroin that Christmas. His parole for drug sales had ended two months earlier, and he felt he could turn his life around once and for all. He kept a day planner in which he had inscribed a pledge: "If I do not build a case against myself, all goals will be accomplished" (Bebow 2004:1). Diaz had just returned to Chicago after an extended stay with his sickly father in Louisiana. While there, Diaz had worked as a management trainee at a McDonald's; he also began developing a plan to market Latin music on the Internet.

Neither man achieved his goals. Instead, on January 7, 2004, both died within minutes of each other of heroin overdoses in the Humboldt Park area of Chicago. The police reported that the heroin they used was extremely pure, and consequently they both injected a much higher quantity of the central nervous system depressant than either probably had ever experienced. Although many of the features of drug overdose are not well understood (e.g., medical criteria are not established for what constitutes an overdose), it is clear in this instance that changes in drug use dynamics—namely, the successful takeover of a large sector of the U.S. heroin market by Colombian producers by delivering high-quality heroin at low prices—was a primary cause of the death of these two men. For five consecutive years, Chicago led the nation in heroin-related emergency room visits—with 12,982 in 2002, a jump of 176 percent since 1995. During 2001 and 2002, the Cook County medical examiner recorded 628 deaths—six a week—from heroin and other opiate-related drug abuse (Bebow 2004).

As the data cited above suggest, accidental overdose is a significant cause of death among drug users. Research by Lorraine Copeland and colleagues (2004) found that prior to the AIDS epidemic, the principal cause of death among active drug users each year was overdose. Various street drugs, especially drugs that slow activity in the central nervous system, are a special risk for this life-threatening event. When heroin users, for example, inject heroin, their heartbeat and breathing slow down. When they consume a higher dose than their bodies are adapted to or capable of metabolizing, they lose consciousness. A typical lethal heroin dose ranges from 200 to 500 mg, but hard-core addicts have been known to survive doses of 1,800 mg and higher. With street heroin there really is no "safe dosage," as both drug purity and the tolerance of the individual vary greatly. A first-time user might well die of a dosage level taken daily by a seasoned user whose body has built up tolerance.

There are certain conditions that increase the likelihood of drug overdose. Experiencing a hiatus in drug use during a prison incarceration, for example, and then starting up again at the old dosage level when the body's tolerance of the drug has diminished, is a common trigger of drug overdose. Another is drug mixing. In a study of annual overdose death rates by age, gender, and race in New York City from 1990 to 1998, Phillip Coffin et al. (2003) found that opiates, cocaine, and alcohol were the three drugs most commonly associated with accidental overdose death—97.6 percent of all overdose deaths. Almost 60 percent of the overdose deaths (57.8 percent) involved the use of two or more of these drugs in combination. Trends in accidental overdose death rates suggest that different drug combinations are most commonly associated with overdose across gender and racial subgroups. In an era in which drug mixing and the use of multiple drug combinations have become standard practices among drug users, overdose is a special hazard.

Lethal drug combinations can also involve interactions between prescription medications and illicit drugs. Bruce Mirken (1997), for example, reported the death of an AIDS patient who had been prescribed the protease inhibitor drug ritonavir to fight HIV infection. Unknown to the physician in the case, the patient was also using Ecstasy and died shortly after of an

Ecstasy overdose. Mixing ritonavir and Ecstasy is extremely risky in that the former drug in some as yet unknown way significantly magnifies the dose level of the latter drug in the body.

Researchers also have pondered whether cycles of the moon or the sun have an impact on the frequency of drug overdoses. Research designed to assess whether drug overdoses are more common during a full moon have proved to be negative. Relative to the distribution of overdose by month, studies have shown some level of increase during December, as well as in August, but the findings do not suggest dramatic differences (Rocchi, Miotto, and Preti 2003; Sharfman 1980).

Finally, not all lethal illicit drug overdoses are accidental. Drug users often are familiar with their drug level tolerances. Intentional consumption of drugs in quantities exceeding these levels may reflect an attempt to commit suicide. Suicide is the eleventh leading cause of death in the United States, accounting for the deaths of about 10 of every 100,000 people. In our interviews with drug users at the Hispanic Health Council, we periodically interview individuals who report trying to kill themselves through planned drug overdose. For example, a participant in one of our studies, a man we named Charlie, told us:

> I'm looking for the drugs to kill me . . . but I'll tell you the truth . . . the way I've taken drugs, if anyone else took [so many] it would kill them, even if they took much less than me. (Singer et al. 2001:396)

Joanne Neale (2000) has reported on 78 drug users who were hospitalized with nonfatal drug overdose. Interviews with these patients found that almost half reported suicidal thoughts or feelings prior to their overdose.

While experience with drug overdose is common among drug users, it is probably most common when patterns and behaviors are changing and, as a result, user certainty about drug quality and content is diminished. A sudden spike in drug overdoses in a local setting is a sure sign that changes have occurred and users have not adjusted culturally or biologically. One of the most unfortunate examples of this pattern occurred in the small New Mexico town of Chimayo (population 5,000), located approximately 90 miles north of Albuquerque. Between 1995 and 1998, there were at least 85 overdose deaths in Chimayo, all of which were attributed to arrival of very pure black tar heroin from Mexico. During these years, 2 percent of the town's population died of drug overdose.

Mental Health Problems and Brain Damage

Overall, the role of drug use in the onset of mental disorders appears to be a chicken or egg debate. Does drug use cause mental health problems or do people with mental health problems use drugs to self-medicate their psychiatric symptoms, or both? Within this broader debate, there also is disagreement among researchers internationally about the effects of drug use on the brain.

Some believe the negative impact of drugs on the brain is profound and enduring. For example, it is well known that treatment failure is disproportionately common among cocaine users, but the exact reasons have not been clear.

Efrat Aharonovich, Edward Nunes, and Deborah Hasin (2003) have suggested that treatment of cocaine addiction is severely hobbled by cognitive impairments caused by prolonged cocaine use. These researchers assessed a number of cognitive abilities among cocaine users, including attention, learning, memory, reaction time, spatial processing, abstract reasoning, and cognitive flexibility. They found that users who had cognitive deficits were much more likely to drop out of drug treatment than those who did not have deficits. Moreover, the greater the level of cognitive impairment a patient suffered, the more likely they were to drop out.

Researchers have linked the kinds of cognitive deficits seen in cocaine users to the way cocaine affects the brain. Cocaine is known to constrict the blood vessels in the cerebral sector of the brain, with a resulting drop in the flow of blood to this area. Use of magnetic resonance imaging on the brains of cocaine users reveals the development of tiny lesions and clots in cerebral blood vessels. Moreover, prolonged cocaine use depletes the brain chemical dopamine, a neurotransmitter that facilitates cognitive work by the brain. All of these changes in brain structure are believed to contribute to the kinds of memory, performance, attention, and reaction-time loss seen in cocaine users.

Studies like the one carried out by Aharonovich and coworkers are exemplary of recent, intensified scientific focus on the way drugs, including alcohol, leave their footprint on the brain. To a great degree this work has relied on the use of various high-tech imaging machines to examine the living brain. One of the debates that this line of research has set off is whether the changes in the structure and chemicals of the brain that can be picked up with brain scans are short-term reactions to drug exposure or are enduring transformations that do not revert (or only slowly or partially revert) with drug abstinence. Some research findings do not support an enduring damage conclusion.

A study of 117 individuals (divided into four groups: current Ecstasy users, former Ecstasy users, non-drug users, and users of other drugs) by Ralph Buchert and coworkers (2004) found a significant drop in the brain chemical serotonin in several sections of the brains of current Ecstasy users (especially females) compared to the other three groups. Serotonin helps to regulate appetite, sleep, mood, and sexual arousal. In the brain and the rest of the nervous system, serotonin functions as a neurotransmitter, a chemical that carries signals from one nerve cell to another. Buchert and colleagues found a significant positive correlation between serotonin availability and the length of time since last use among former Ecstasy users. In other words, loss of serotonin among users of Ecstasy may reverse once an individual stops using the drug.

Ecstasy and other club drugs—drugs that are often said by users to be harmless—have drawn attention among brain researchers. One of the findings is that Ecstasy, like amphetamine, not only impacts serotonin but also two other brain messenger chemicals as well: dopamine and norepinephrine. Ecstasy causes these substances to be released from storage sites in brain cells, producing a significant jump in neurotransmitter activity, which is experienced by users as feelings of happiness and pleasure. Studies on animals have shown, however, that Ecstasy can produce long-lasting damage to brain cells that contain transmitter chemicals, especially serotonin-holding cells. Over time, exposure to Ecstasy damages the branches through which serotonin-producing neurons reach out and connect to other cells. As summarized by Una McCann (Check 2004:127), a researcher at Johns Hopkins University, "The bottom line is that over 15 years worth of research by us and others has clearly demonstrated that MDMA is toxic to brain serotonin neurons." This damage may account for the heightened levels of depression seen in long-term Ecstasy users (NIDA 2004).

One of the most damaging findings on Ecstasy's brain effects was published in *Science* by McCann, her husband, and other colleagues (Ricaurte et al. 2002). This laboratory research team injected a group of ten squirrel monkeys and baboons with doses of MDMA that they believed were equivalent to levels used among many club kids in a single night. Examination showed a loss of neurons that produce dopamine, resulting in a condition similar to Parkinson's disease. Two out of ten of the animals died. The article they wrote for *Science* on these findings drew widespread media attention. Then, in a development that jolted the drug research world, George Ricaurte, Una McCann, and their coworkers retracted their findings published in *Science*, having belatedly discovered that the monkeys had actually been given methamphetamine rather than MDMA. They blamed this egregious error on mislabeling of the drug by their suppliers at the National Institute on Drug Abuse.

Beyond Ecstasy, there is evidence suggesting that illicit drug use can induce psychopathology by causing physical damage to the brain. For example, stimulants like amphetamine are believed to induce psychosis in some users because they are known to increase the concentration of brain chemicals like dopamine outside of brain cells. It has not been clear, however, why in some patients psychiatric symptoms persist even after the user begins to abstain from amphetamine use. One theory is that the parts of the brain that absorb dopamine back into brain cells are damaged by amphetamine exposure, allowing high concentrations of extracellular dopamine to remain even when amphetamine is no longer present in the user's brain (Volkow 2001). Certainly, it is clear that longer-term heavy users of amphetamine frequently exhibit paranoid symptoms and other indicators of mental illness. From this vantage, the extent of persistence of psychiatric symptoms following abstinence from illicit drugs may be a reflection of the degree of damage done to brain cells, which, in turn, would be a product of the interaction of several factors, including biological individualism, the unique susceptibility of one's brain cells to drug exposure, duration of drug use, and the drugs a person has used.

One source of information on this issue is drug users themselves. In one such study on the effects of marijuana, Amanda Gruber and colleagues (2003) gathered psychological and demographic measures on 108 individuals, between 30 and 55 years of age who had smoked marijuana a minimum of 5,000 times in their lives. They then compared these heavy users to 72 individuals who were matched for age who had smoked marijuana at least once but no more than 50 times in their lives. They found that the heavy users self-reported that marijuana had damaged their cognition, memory, and overall mental health, with large majorities of heavy users (66–90 percent) reporting a negative effect of prolonged marijuana use.

Other research on marijuana has found that individuals who smoke the drug regularly undergo withdrawal symptoms that match those found among individuals who are in nicotine withdrawal, including increased cravings, sleep disruption, restlessness, decreased appetite, and increased irritability and anger, but not the dramatic pain, cramps, and nausea symptoms found among those withdrawing from addiction to an opiate (Budney et al. 2001). Additionally, with the newer, high-potency marijuana on the illicit market, there have been dramatic increases in the number of reports of marijuana use among individuals seeking help at hospital emergency rooms. Findings like these must be taken into consideration in contemporary debates about marijuana legalization, although there are many other issues to consider also in this debate.

While it is sometimes difficult to tease out whether psychiatric symptoms precede or follow abusive drug taking, it is clear that comorbidity for drug abuse and mental health problems is extremely common. For example, Karen Abram of the Department of Psychiatry at Northwestern University and coworkers (Abram et al. 2003) interviewed a group of over 1,800 adolescents who were incarcerated for various criminal violations. They found that significantly more females (56.5 percent) than males (45.9 percent) met criteria for two or more of the following psychiatric disorders: major depression, mania, psychosis, panic disorder, separation anxiety, generalized anxiety, obsessive-compulsive disorder, attention-deficit/hyperactivity, conduct disorder, or oppositional defiant behavior. Almost 14 percent of female participants and 11 percent of male participants had both a major mental disorder (i.e., psychosis, manic episode, or major depressive episode) and a drug use disorder. Compared with participants with no major mental health illnesses, those with a major mental disorder had significantly greater odds (1.8:4.1) of being a drug user. Approximately 30 percent of females and more than 20 percent of males who were drug abusers had major mental disorders. Similarly, among drug-abusing homeless youth treated at a mental health clinic in Hollywood, California, 85 percent were diagnosed as depressed, 9 percent were actively suicidal, 20 percent had attempted suicide, and 18 percent suffered from a severe mental health problem (Yates et al. 1988).

One of the issues of strong public concern about changing illicit (as well as legal) drug use patterns is the increased use of drugs during pregnancy and the consequences for the developing fetus of in utero exposure to drugs (Singer and Snipes 1992). Crack cocaine, in particular, has been a cause for concern with headline-driven fears about inconsolable "crack babies" who suffer serious life-long deficits. In this regard, Lynn Singer of the School of Medicine at Case Western Reserve University, and colleagues (L. Singer et al. 2004), tracked 376 infants identified from a high-risk population from birth to four years of age. Mothers were screened for drug exposure using a clinical interview and urine testing, while babies were tested for in utero exposure using meconium screens. Among the infants, 190 were cocaine-exposed and 186 were not. Prenatal cocaine exposure was not found to be related to lower overall IQ or to lower oral performance scores. These researchers did find a small but statistically significant relationship between cocaine exposure and the children's scores on visual-spatial, general

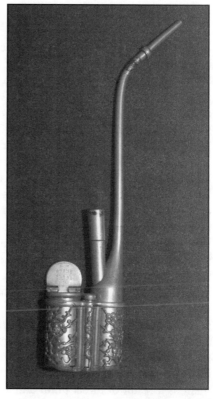

Chinese opium pipe, circa 1890. Courtesy of Drug Enforcement Administration.

knowledge, and math ability. Prenatal cocaine exposure was associated as well with a lower likelihood of achieving an IQ above normative levels.

Nevertheless, these researchers also found that the quality of caregiving to the infant was the single strongest predictor of cognitive outcomes. Cocaine-exposed children who were placed in foster care with a nonrelative or in adoptive care tended to live in homes that provided more stimulation than what their birth mothers could provide. These foster-care/adopted babies also lived with caregivers who had better vocabulary scores than caregivers in their birth families. Crack babies placed outside their birth homes attained overall and performance IQ scores that were similar to children not exposed to cocaine. These findings indicate that cocaine-exposed infants may suffer some cognitive deficits, but these can be overcome with appropriate caregiving during infancy. These findings should not be read as evidence that children should be taken away from drug-involved mothers, but rather that the latter need treatment and other supportive intervention to provide nurturing home environments for their children as they progress in their recovery.

Organ Damage and Death

Drug-related risks include damage to various organ systems of the body. Inhalant drugs, in particular, have been associated with an array of morbid outcomes. Long-term "huffing" of concentrated chemicals in solvents or aerosol sprays can cause irregular and rapid heart rhythms and lead to heart failure even during first use by an otherwise healthy individual and, under certain circumstances, cause sudden death, a condition known as "sudden sniffing death." Butane, propane, and chemicals in aerosols are the most likely to be associated with this outcome. Inhalants can also cause death due to asphyxiation. In such cases, repeated inhalations lead to the buildup of high concentrations of inhaled fumes that keep oxygen from being absorbed by the lungs. Fumes can also block air from entering the lungs, which can cause suffocation; sometimes suffocation occurs when users place a plastic bag over their heads to retain inhalant fumes. Inhalation can also trigger vomiting, which in turn has been known to cause choking in individuals whose reactions are hindered by drug effects.

Most gravely, inhalants can cause long-lasting damage to the brain and other areas of the nervous system. Both animal and human research shows that chronic exposure to volatile solvents damages the protective sheath that surrounds certain nerve fibers in the brain and peripheral nervous system. Individuals with this kind of nerve damage exhibit symptoms similar to those seen in multiple sclerosis. Other health consequences can include loss of cognitive ability (ranging from mild loss to dementia), sight, hearing, and movement as a result of direct brain damage. Chronic exposure can also damage the user's heart, lungs, liver, and kidneys.

With the advent of the youth-oriented dance club and rave scenes, a new set of drug use and health concerns has emerged. Among gay and bisexual men, hospitals are beginning to see the health consequences of using methamphetamine, including hypertension, life-threatening dehydration, rhabdoymyolysis (a breakdown of muscle tissue that can lead to lethal kidney damage), and stroke. Additionally, it has been found that mixing "meth" with certain HIV medications can produce symptoms of paranoia, as well as auditory hallucinations and, occasionally, violent behavior. Withdrawal from "meth" commonly produces depression (Urbina and Jones 2004). Similar conditions, including rhabdoymyolysis, have been found among cocaine users (Horst, Bennett, and Barrett 1991).

Ecstasy is known to cause severe dehydration among users, especially when taken during intensive dancing; Ecstasy also causes the body temperature to rise, enhancing the potential for dehydration. Individuals suffering from dehydration are unable to sweat and feel dizzy. They may have cramps in their limbs, feel exhausted, be confused and disoriented, and begin to vomit. Beyond these immediate symptoms, dehydration increases blood pressure, placing added strain on the heart. Left untreated, dehydration can be fatal. Repeated doses of Ecstasy cause some users to experience flashbacks, producing panic and anxiety.

In recent years, there have been about 20 Ecstasy/dehydration fatalities a year in the United States. In one case, Irma Perez, a 14-year-old from San Mateo County, California, took Ecstasy with two friends during a sleepover (Kim 2004). The other girls and a 17-year-old boy who was with them did not know what to do when Irma began to complain of not feeling well. At one point, they gave Irma a bath to calm her down, but no one called for emergency assistance. Irma was eventually hospitalized but she never regained consciousness. Irma's two friends were charged with child endangerment and possession of a controlled substance. The boy, who sold Ecstasy to Irma and her friends, was charged with involuntary manslaughter.

In New York City, researchers have examined the cause of death of all deceased individuals whose bodies tested positive for MDMA between January 1997 and June 2000. During this period, there were 22 Ecstasy-positive fatalities in the city. More than half, like Irma, died because of drug overdose or acute intoxication, while seven died as a result of physical trauma, such as a gunshot wound (Gill et al. 2002).

Infectious Diseases

AIDS is but one of a number of infectious diseases associated with drug use. For example, in the western U.S., the black tar form of heroin that is smuggled into the country from Mexico is responsible for frequent skin and wound infections among users, including both abscesses and cellulitis, and as a result, black tar heroin has become the most common cause of emergency room visits among drug injectors and one of the most costly causes of such visits overall (Ciccarone et al. 2001). Various pathogens can be involved in drug-related skin and soft tissue abscesses. Not uncommonly, infections involve multiple pathogens, including anaerobic organisms and aerobic gram-positive cocci. A rare but well-documented soft tissue infection in IDUs is pyomyositis, an abscess-forming infection of skeletal muscle. Intramuscular injection of black tar heroin also has been linked with deadly infections like necrotizing fasciitis and botulism.

Necrotizing fasciitis, so-called "flesh-eating" bacteria, is an insidiously advancing soft tissue infection that is being seen with increasing frequency. The infection can cause massive skin and other tissue damage that is irreversible. One population that has repeatedly been associated with this kind of infection in recent years is intramuscular illicit drug injectors. Between December 1999 and April 2000, nine IDUs in Ventura County, California, were diagnosed with necrotizing fasciitis, and four ultimately died of their infections (Kimura et al. 2004). Laboratory cultures of wound specimens from six of these cases grew the bacteria *Clostridium sordellii*. Several of the patients appeared to be suffering from toxic shock syndrome, which is known to be characteristic of toxins produced during a *C. sordellii* infection. The suspected source of this outbreak was contaminated black tar heroin that had been injected subcutaneously (just under the skin) or intramuscularly. Similarly, James Chen, Kathleen Fullerton, and Neil Flynn (2001) studied 107 patients who were diagnosed with necrotizing fasciitis at the California Davis Medical Center during the 16-year period between 1984 and 1999. Just over half of these patients (55 percent) self-reported illicit injection drug use. Fifty-four percent of the drug users reported that they had recently injected at the site of the infection. Six of the IDUs in this sample died of their infection. One line of thinking about the increase in this potentially lethal disease concerns the widespread use of nonsteroidal anti-inflammatory drugs like ibuprofen. These drugs inhibit the body's natural inflammatory response to infection, one of the ways the body has for fighting off invasive microbes. Regular use of ibuprofen can mask infection.

Botulism is another potentially fatal disease usually associated with eating foods infected with *Clostridium* bacteria or with suffering a traumatic wound. In wound botulism, a deep break in the skin's surface, including abscesses associated with drug injection, becomes infected with the bacteria, and there is a subsequent release of damaging poisons from the infected cells into the body generally. Neurological signs include respiratory paralysis. For example, in August 2003, two men and two women in Yakima County, Washington, sought medical care at the same hospital with the same complaints (Spitters et al. 2003). They told the attending doctors they were suffering from weakness, drooping eyelids, blurred vision, difficulty speaking, and inability to swallow. All four also reported that they were regular, nonintravenous injectors of black tar heroin. Hospital physicians found that all four of these patients had cranial nerve palsies, as well as headaches, diminished or absent gag reflex, weakness of the upper extremity, but no sensory deficits. Three of the patients had readily identifiable wound infections at the site of drug injection. Two of them developed respiratory failure after being admitted to the hospital even though they were given antitoxin. Nonetheless, all four survived the ordeal. Lab tests revealed botulinum toxin type A in stool cultures from all four patients; however, the cultures failed to show *Clostridium* bacteria growth. These cases are not isolated; wound botulism associated with injection drug abuse has been reported in a number of places around the country as well as in the United Kingdom (Passaro et al. 1988).

Yet another potentially lethal infectious disease that has been spreading among drug users is tetanus, which is best known because it can cause lockjaw or trimus. In fact, the earliest documented health problem associated with illicit drug injection was a case of tetanus in a female morphine injector in 1876 (Donoghoe and Wodak 1998). More recently, it is believed that the multiple cases of tetanus that have been seen since the turn of the twenty-first century, especially in the United Kingdom, are due to actual tetanus spore infections of the heroin supply (Hahne, Crowcroft, and White 2003). Infection is believed to be caused by skinpopping the infected drug. Cases have been especially common among women and older injectors who were previously intravenous injectors but had begun having difficulty accessing veins— a common experience of drug users, especially those who inject drugs diluted with various other substances. Of reported cases, very few have been immunized for tetanus within ten years prior to becoming infected.

While there are a variety of other infectious diseases, such as endocarditis (inflammation of the innermost layer of the heart), that are known to be associated with drug use, after HIV/AIDS the most significant form of infection in drug using populations is hepatitis, especially hepatitis B and hepatitis C. The latter is particularly common among injection drug users, with rates of infections surpassing 90 percent in some parts of the country. Hepatitis C virus (HCV) was first detected in the United States in the 1960s, particularly among transfusion patients and injection drug users. It is estimated that about 20 percent of individuals infected with HCV—for which there is no vaccination or fully effective treatment—will develop cirrhosis and many of these will progress to liver cancer. It is estimated that about five million people in the United States have hepatitis C, with an annual rate of 13 new cases of infection per 100,000 population, or about 230,000 new cases a year (CDC 2001). It is estimated that 8,000–10,000 people in the United States die of HCV each year.

The spread of HCV among drug users is linked, like HIV, to the direct and indirect sharing of syringes and other injection equipment (Koester and Hoffer 1994). While it is clear that a range of behaviors can be involved in direct and indirect drug equipment sharing, the relative risk or ease of HCV transmission associated with each behavior has not been clear. In an innovative study in Chicago, Lorna Thorpe and colleagues (2002) examined HCV seroconversion (moving from being uninfected to being infected) among over 700 injection drug users by drawing and testing their blood for HCV antibodies at three points in time over a one-year period. Twenty-nine participants were infected with HCV during the study. The highest rates of conversion occurred among individuals who shared drug cookers, followed by those who shared cotton filters. These two behaviors were significantly more important in this sample than the direct sharing of syringes or sharing rinse water. Other research suggests that HCV may be spread through the sharing of noninjection drug-use equipment, like crack pipes (Tortu et al. 2004). Consistently, HCV has been found to spread easier and faster than HIV; coinfection with HCV and HIV is increasingly common in drug user populations.

Beyond the level of individual knowledge and behavior, Philippe Bourgois, Bridget Prince, and Andrew Moss (2004:261), based on a study of street amphetamine and heroin injectors in San Francisco, found that most of the woman they studied were "knowledgeable about the biological transmission mechanisms of hepatitis C," however, they were not able to put this knowledge to use in protecting themselves against infection because they were "too overwhelmed by everyday gendered violence." Similarly, Louisa Gilbert and colleagues (2000:460), based on their New York study of HCV and HIV risk among women drug users, ask "how do you introduce condom use in an abusive relationship, when condom use connotes outside affairs and any hint of other lovers is a powder keg for violence?"

Drug use is also a major factor in the spread of sexually transmitted infections (STIs). The National Institute on Drug Abuse Cooperative Agreement (CA) study of drug users, with a national sample of 12,624 not-in-treatment injection drug or crack users, found that 36 percent had a history of gonorrhea infection (Paschane et al. 1998). Among men in the sample, the two drug use–related variables that predicted infection identified by Logistic Regression analysis were "ever used cocaine" and "ever used amphetamine" (p < .001), while for women, "traded sex for money" and "traded sex for drugs" in the last 30 days were the most significant variables associated with infection (p < .001). These findings—including the startlingly high levels of STIs among drug users—affirm that drug users face both *direct health risks* from specific drug use behaviors (e.g., multiperson use of the same syringe) and *indirect health risks* from behaviors that often are associated with drug use (e.g., poor nutrition). Consistently, HCV has spread faster than HIV, while coinfection of HIV/HCV is found to be common in drug-using populations.

Violence

Violence has become a common feature of contemporary life, and our society often is said to be caught in a cycle of intergenerational transmission of violence that produces ever more violent generations over time. Already, the U.S. homicide rate is between 4 and 70 times that of other countries, and for every homicide there are about 100 nonfatal intentional injuries caused by violence (Sullivan 1991). In the media and in public discourse, street violence is regularly linked to drug use. In fact, of all the psychoactive drugs, violence is most commonly associated with alcohol consumption; comparatively, lower rates of association have been found between violence and the various illicit drugs. The precise nature of the relationship between drugs and violence, however, is complex and conditioned by several factors, including not only the drug(s) used and the method of consumption but also the social context in which drug use commonly occurs (Goldstein 1985).

Several illicit drugs (or drug combinations) have been especially linked to increased aggression and resulting violence, including marijuana, heroin, cocaine, PCP, and amphetamine (Simonds and Kashani 1980). Although marijuana is commonly thought of as a suppressor of hostility, it has been tied in several studies to heightened irritability and violence under certain conditions. Barry Spunt and colleagues (1994), for example, examined marijuana use among 268 individuals imprisoned for homicide and found that one-third used the drug on the day of the homicide, and a quarter of these individuals reported that marijuana was a factor in their crime. Most of these individuals (80 percent), however, were also under the influence of alcohol at the time of the homicide.

Several studies have found a link between cocaine use and violence. A study of men who called a cocaine hotline, for example, found that 32 percent had a history of violence not associated with crime and 46 percent had a history of violent crime (Miller 1990). Crack cocaine, in particular, has been found to be associated with the perpetration of violent crime, especially felonious assault and murder. Johnson (1989), in a detailed review of violence and drug sales in the inner city, explained the rise of violence commonly associated with crack in terms of the so-

Street altar for a drug gang violence victim in New York City. Photograph by Pedro Mateau-Gelabert.

cial organization, rivalry, and citizen-intimidation strategies of crack-selling gangs. Because crack sells for such low prices, many vials of the drug must be sold to make a significant profit. Consequently, potentially promising sites for crack sales, like a particularly busy street corner with many users who live in the neighborhood, can become a highly sought-after sales location. Control of such a location can come to be violently contested by several rival groups. At the same time, efforts by residents or merchants to stop sales in such locations may produce violent backlashes by crack sellers who want to dominate the site. Of note, the low price of individual crack sales tends to support bigger dealers having many sellers out in the street dispensing the drug, producing a considerable cadre of potential soldiers to carry out violent acts. All of these factors appear to have combined to produce at least part of crack's infamous reputation as a drug of violence. Additionally, the short-term nature of the "crack high" appears to contribute to frustration among users, creating the potential for interpersonal conflict and clashes over drug ownership.

Although there were early attempts to suggest that heroin users avoid violence because the drug inhibits aggression, opiates have been linked to violence in more recent studies, especially for some subgroups of users. Crime, however, rather than violence per se, has been the focus of much of the research on the social consequences of heroin addiction. An examination of the types of crimes committed by heroin addicts suggests that acts of violence are not uncommon. In a study of 573 Miami heroin users, during a one-year period, for example, participants were found collectively to have committed 5,300 robberies (mostly at gunpoint) and 639 assaults, as well as an assortment of other crimes including arson, vandalism, and extortion (Inciardi 1986). Violence among heroin-using prostitutes has been explained in terms of impatience and irritability associated with drug withdrawal (Goldstein 1979). A multisite ethnographic study of heroin injectors in a number of eastern cities, however, found that only 10 percent regularly engaged in violent crime, and did so primarily to raise money to support their habit (Hanson et al. 1985). Still, patterns have been changing, and since the 1970s crimes among heroin users have become increasingly violent. In his restudy of an East Harlem sample of heroin users, for example, Edward Preble (1980) found that 40 percent had been murdered since his original study 15 years earlier.

Violence in the life of street drug users like those studied by Preble are exemplified by the case of Tony, an individual who began using drugs as a teenager and was still an active user in his early 40s. Tony enrolled in a Hispanic Health Council study of the relationship between drug use and HIV risk during the 1990s. He was interviewed multiple times over the course of several years. On one occasion he reported:

> When I was walking down the street, waiting for her [his girlfriend] to come back from her trick [commercial sex], I was going up towards Washington Street. . . . There's like this little alleyway. I take that alleyway because it's a shortcut, everybody knows that. That's where they got me. They started to attack me and one dude sliced me like that [indicating a jagged 12 inch slash across his chest on the left side].

In these words, Tony explained a bout with violence, a near-fatal revenge stabbing initiated by a drug dealer from whom Tony had gotten drugs to sell on consignment but had used them himself instead. As both a victim and perpetrator, Tony has known drug-related violence since childhood. The violence in his life began with harsh beatings administered by his drug-addicted father, daily punishments intended to convince him to correct his many alleged transgressions. They continued throughout adolescence as he defended his ground in the bellicose world of street-corner drug dealing, a practice he learned from his father for whom he worked as a street dealer. During his young adulthood, violence, in the form of brutal assaults of wayward gang members, was a regular part of his role as an "enforcer" in a drug-selling street gang. The threat of violence, emotional and physical preparation for violence, and enduring the agony of violence-inflicted pain were all commonplace to Tony. He accepts them as he accepts inclement weather—undesirable, but unavoidable. The intertwined worlds of drug use and violence followed Tony into the twenty-first century. In his most recent encounter, he got into a bar fight that led to a two-year prison sentence for assault. He continued to use contraband drugs that were smuggled into the prison on a weekly basis, returning to his full-blown heroin addiction shortly after his release from custody.

In our research at the HHC on the relationship between violence and drug use, we have identified a wide range of important types of violence exposure and involvement among street drug users. Seventy-four percent of the 224 drug-involved participants in one of our studies (called SAVA 1), individuals who had been recruited by street outreach workers or through their peer social networks, reported witnessing fighting in the streets of their neighborhood during the last several months. Study participants said violence in the streets was especially common, with "once or twice a week" being the median frequency. The other most common type of recently witnessed violence was domestic violence, which, notably, was reported by 54 percent of study participants. Gang violence (45 percent), robbery and muggings (42 percent), and beatings or stabbing (31 percent) were the next most common types of violence participants reported they witnessed. As these findings indicate, street drug users are exposed as spectators to a substantial amount of violence both on the streets and in their homes. Witnessing violence, it became evident in our study, is a frequent and very distressing aspect of a street drug user's life.

Additionally, 14 percent of our participants reported being the targets of physical violence and 7 percent indicated they suffered serious physical violence during the last several months. One participant reported the following example which was typical of the violence victimization incidents reported in the study:

> I was up against the corner, and I was sitting on that little bench, the little couch. A guy came up and said, "Give me everything, your watch, everything." He had a knife. . . . He had me trapped in the corner. And the way he had me, you know. It was like, "give it up, and this and that." And see, if I had seen it coming, I would grab . . . you see, I always carry a bottle. . . . I'll crack that over someone's head. They'll think twice about robbing me with a knife or not. . . . I think he was using "ready" [crack cocaine]. He probably wanted to get a hit, because I had dope on me and he came in with a girl. And he was like, "Give me the dope too!"

Significantly, nine of the drug users in our sample responded that they had been the target of attempted murder. Participants also revealed their own role as perpetrators of violence against others. Ten percent admitted committing acts of violence, while two respondents indicated that they had attempted to kill someone.

Of the incidents of violence victimization reported by our participants, 71 percent of the cases of physical violence involved the use of drugs and/or alcohol. In the reported incidents of suffering serious physical violence, the rate of drug use rose to 75 percent. In cases where the study participants were the perpetrator, the reported use of psychoactive drugs was 75 percent when they committed emotional abuse; when they were guilty of committing physical violence against another person the rate of drug use was 80 percent; and it rose to 100 percent in cases of serious physical violence and attempted deadly acts of violence. Discussing the emotional effects of being a perpetrator of violence, one participant told us:

> So then I started shooting up and that's when I started going crazy . . . you know like getting sick, real sick, starting to do bad things, stealing robbing . . . like taking money away from people . . . and I used to have a gun. My cousin had a gun and he used to give it to me so I can go rob people, like drug dealers, take their drugs. A lot of crazy stuff like that I come to think about now and I be like, damn, man, I could have been dead.

Conversely, another participant succinctly summarized the relationship between drugs and violence in his own life saying, "I am dangerous if I am not high." Indeed, using drugs to control pent up hostility is a practice claimed by a number of participants in our study (Duke et al. 2003).

Notably, over 44 percent of respondents in the SAVA 1 study reported that involvement in violence (as either victim or perpetrator) contributed to increases in their rates of drug consumption, while 47 percent stated that it affected the kinds of drugs that they used. At the same time, 14 percent reported a decrease in the frequency of drug use as a result of involvement in violence, including two participants who gave up using drugs as a result. As these findings and a wealth of other studies indicate, there is a relationship between drug use and violence, and drug users are certainly on the receiving end of a considerable amount of violence, but the precise role of drugs in causing violence is less clear. Certainly, changes in drug use patterns, such as the emergence of a new drug form like crack cocaine or the reintroduction of a previously popular drug like PCP, appear to be associated with jumps in interpersonal violence. What is not clear, however, is the degree to which drug chemistry per se is the key factor in drug-related violence, as opposed to the otherwise violent social contexts in which drug use is commonly a component as a result of criminalization. Certainly some new drugs like Ecstasy are viewed, at least by users, with intensified sociability and nonviolence.

Exposure to the Elements

In regions of the United States with cold winters, a change in season commonly is accompanied by the deaths of some number of drug users, especially homeless individuals, due to exposure to the elements. In the Northeast, for example, where homeless drug users often sleep in abandoned buildings (which lack heating or electricity) on particularly cold nights the risk of hypothermia is great. Various other weather-related symptoms and diseases, like frostbite and obstructive lung diseases, coughing, wheezing, and chronic bronchitis also are common among homeless drug users from colder climes. The term frostbite refers to frozen body tissue, usually involving part of the skin but sometimes deeper tissue as well, especially on extremities like fingers and toes. It takes only a short while for exposed skin to become frostbitten if the temperature is –20°F. Often, people with frostbite also suffer from hypothermia. The extent of the impact that exposure to the elements has on drug user health nationally is not known because it has been little studied. Nonetheless, many drug users in cold climates tell stories of almost freezing to death and of innovative strategies (e.g., sleeping on heating grates, stuffing their clothing with insulating newspapers) used to survive deadly winter conditions.

Some inhalants have been found to be associated with frostbite of internal organs. Clinical reports have appeared in recent years of drug users presenting at emergency rooms with frostbite of the lips, oral cavity, oropharynx, trachea, and other organs following inhalation of fluorinated hydrocarbons (e.g., found in airbrush propellants). In severe cases, inflammation from frostbite can block the airway and cause death.

Burns

Drug users are also vulnerable to suffering burns from several different sources. First, as noted above, drug users often make use of abandoned buildings, both to consume drugs and to escape the elements. Because of economic woes, some of which flow from the nature of the prevailing economic system and some from the reigning structure of class inequality and social disregard for the poor, many U.S. cities face the thorny paradox of having large numbers of abandoned and deteriorating buildings and growing homeless populations (Waterston 1999; Baer, Singer, and Susser 2004). During winter, abandoned buildings offer some escape from the biting winds and low temperatures. The homeless sometimes occupy these buildings and build small fires to warm themselves on particularly chilly nights. Given the amount of flammable debris that is often dumped in abandoned buildings, it is not unusual for these fires to get out of control, causing burns and other injuries. A study by Michael Greenberg and colleagues (1993) of abandoned buildings in the 15 largest U.S. cities found that they are also frequently used as crack houses and for drug dealing. Similarly, William Spelman's (1993) study of 59 abandoned residential buildings in a low-income Austin, Texas, neighborhood found that 34 percent were being used for illegal activities. As Spelman (1993) emphasizes, abandoned buildings are ideal locations to trade, conceal, and consume drugs. Activity in abandoned buildings is rarely visible from the street, and police may be reluctant to enter them because of the slight chance of making an arrest. Evidence of drug use was found in 19 percent of the abandoned buildings in Spelman's study.

In our own studies of high-risk sites (mainly abandoned buildings) in Hartford, we frequently encounter drug users who are using such sites either temporarily to get high in or as residences, having cleaned out and fixed up at least one room in what otherwise is a dilapidated building. Large quantities of drug paraphernalia (syringes, cookers, water bottles, crack pipes) as well as HIV prevention literature and an array of discarded trash and other items may be spread across of the floors of these buildings. The fire potential is significant, and each winter the newspaper reports one or more fires that burn down abandoned buildings. A typical, if particularly tragic example from the New England region was the 1999 warehouse fire in Massachusetts that killed six firefighters. The origin of the fire was a candle lit by a homeless couple who had been squatting in the building (KVG 2002:1):

> The homeless couple . . . were described as many things by the public: vagrants, drug addicts, even murderers, for six firefighters died battling the conflagration. When the papers showed pictures of the culprits, I realized they were not the usual kind of homeless couple you see in cities, bent over shopping carts with their matching coats of grime. This was a different kind of street coupling. The man, a thirty-five-year-old heroin addict, was with a 17-year-old girl who was said to be mentally challenged and on drugs. Media images showed a scraggly bearded man and a gaunt, vacant-eyed girl—not the stuff of a love story by most people's standards, but it was there anyway, like the underhanded heat of eroticism itself. They stayed inside the warehouse, in the corner room containing a makeshift bed of blankets, a candle burning in an empty soup can, and the remains of sandwiches nested in wax paper wrappers; the sound of passing sirens muffled by the brick walls and the glow of car lights that passed by.

Second, as mentioned in chapter 1, drug users may suffer burn injuries because of the use of flammables like ether during the manufacture or use of

Abandoned building used by drug users. Photograph by Pedro Mateau-Gelabert.

drugs. The popular comedian, Richard Pryor, was reported to have badly burned himself while freebasing cocaine, resulting in third-degree burns over 50 percent of his body (although it was later reported that Pryor might have intentionally lit himself on fire in a suicide attempt). Police have discovered that the children of "cookers," individuals who work in illicit meth labs converting a diverse set of flammable and explosive substances into saleable drugs, are often found with burns from sudden lab fires. Finally, certain types of drug use, such as using a stem or pipe to smoke cocaine can cause burns to the lips and hands of users, as can the traditional "roach clip" used to hold a marijuana cigarette while smoking. Crack use commonly causes bilateral burns on the thumbs and forefingers of users, a feature that has been used by physicians to confirm cocaine use by individuals who deny involvement with the drug. While many such burns may be minor, there has been public health concern voiced that burns on the lips may be transmission points for the spread of HIV or other sexually transmitted infections.

Accidents

People under the influence of drugs are disproportionately likely to be injured in vehicular and nonvehicular accidents as drivers, passengers, and pedestrians, as well as through falls, cuts, or other body trauma. Adolescents who suffer from accidental injuries often are found to have been using drugs at the time of the incident, including receiving a gunshot wound (70 percent of victims report drug use at the time they were shot), being hit by a car as a pedestrian (42 percent), and being injured during a fight (38 percent) (Spirito et al. 1997).

In a hospital-based study of patients 15 years of age and older admitted to an inner-city orthopedic service from January 1993 until December of the following year, researchers administered a urine toxicology screen for alcohol, cocaine, opiates, marijuana, barbiturates, amphetamines, benzodiazepines, and PCP. For the 628 patients who completed a drug screen, the researchers then sorted patients by diagnosis, route of injury, type of injury, length of inpatient stay, age, sex, and race. The overall incidence of a positive test for either an illicit drug or alcohol was 56 percent, with 24 percent of the patients testing positive for two or more drugs, and 9 percent for three or more. Not surprisingly, the most commonly detected drug was alcohol (25 percent of patients in the sample), followed in similar amounts by cocaine (22 percent) and marijuana (21 percent). The demographic group with the highest incidence of drug detections were males 31–40 years of age. The injuries most likely to be associated with a positive drug screen were: fractures of the tibia, gunshot wounds, injuries suffered in fights, and injuries sustained from being hit by a car. The length of stay in the hospital was 1.3 days longer for patients with positive drug screens, suggesting patients who are under the influence of psychoactive substances at the time they are injured sustain greater injury and more costly injury than those not under the influence of alcohol or drugs.

Disinhibition, loss of coordination, dulled pain sensation, and visual impairments caused by drugs probably all contribute to this heightened risk of injury. An injury of this sort befell a woman who participated in one of our studies. In addition to being high at the time of her injury (a broken leg), she was "jumping from car to car," as she put it, engaging in commercial sex transactions.

Poisoning

Drug poisoning can occur in several ways. Users may be poisoned by substances that are taken for their psychoactive properties. This type of poisoning happens periodically with the drug Datura from the plant *Datura stramonium*. A case of this sort involved a 19-year-old man who intentionally ate the seeds of the Datura plant hoping to experience the intense hallucinogenic high they can produce. The nature of his experience is unknown as two chemicals contained in the seeds of Datura plants, hyoscyamine and scopolamine, which in his case were *at the highest blood levels ever recorded for a human*, killed the man (Boumba, Mitselou, and Vougiouklakis 2004).

Another way drugs can cause poisoning is through the substances that are added to cut drugs so as to expand the quantity of drug powder available for sale. Diverse substances have been used for this purpose, including, on occasion, known poisons like strychnine (a plant-based poison used to kill rats) and thallium (a naturally occurring metal that can cause intense vomiting, diarrhea, hair loss, as well as damage to the nervous system, lungs, heart, liver, and kidneys) (Insley, Grufferman, and Ayliffe 1986). Drug user folk beliefs have been found to include the false notions that strychnine is needed to bond LSD to blotter paper and that strychnine is produced when the body metabolizes LSD. These folk ideas reflect a more general pattern of drug users not being aware of what they are actually ingesting or the potential health consequences of the drugs they use. In our studies at the HHC we have been surprised at how little some users—especially younger users—know about the drugs they take. The same lack of knowledge occurs with legal drug use as well, even though those drugs' contents are revealed on their labels.

Various studies have been done on the substances used to cut drugs, sometimes with surprising results. Longitudinal studies of this sort add to our understanding of the ways drug producers, and sellers at various levels in the hierarchical drug trade, impact drug use dynamics and their health consequences. A 12-year study of heroin seized on the street by authorities in Denmark (Kaa 1994), for example, found that while the average portion of diluents (45 percent of the total) did not change much from year to year, there was a wide unexplained range from month to month within each year. This study found that heroin seized in the early 1980s had high levels of noscapine (an anticongestion medication). By the mid-1980s, caffeine and novocaine had become the most frequent cuts, as well as sugar. During the middle and late eighties an increasing number of heroin samples were being cut with the drugs phenobarbital and methaqualone. By the early nineties, the frequency of these cuts had diminished and were being replaced by paracetamol (a drug with both analgetic and fever reduction properties) in combination with caffeine. Similar adulterants have been found in other seized heroin samples, while lidocaine has been found as a common adulterant (comprising as much 52 percent by weight) of street cocaine samples (Gomez and Rodriguez 1989).

Depending on tolerances and sensitivities, any of these substances that are added to illicit drugs could have toxic side effects. Sometimes, however, substances with significant toxicity are added to drugs as adulterants. One such case was discovered in the spring of 1995 in New York City and ultimately other mid-Atlantic cities as well. The adulterant, found in samples of heroin, was scopolamine, the substance mentioned earlier as a toxic component of Datura seeds (Hamilton et al. 2000). This adulterant caused severe toxic reactions among individuals who used the tainted heroin. Users began presenting at hospital emergency departments in great numbers. A study of 241 of them found that when naloxone was administered to assist the patients with breathing they became very upset and exhibited anticholinergic symptoms, such as disorientation, confusion, memory loss, agitation, incoherent speech, delusions, hyperactivity, and paranoia. Ninety percent required hospital admission. Why use scopolamine? It may be that psychoactive drugs are used as a cut because drug dealers hope to get the word out that their drugs are very potent. Similarly, early in 2005, a number of drug injectors along the eastern seaboard died after using a batch of heroin that had been cut with clenbuterol, an anabolic steroid sold in Europe as an asthma treatment (Blint 2005).

Poisons (e.g., solvents) also may enter drugs during the manufacturing process. Drugs reach the market at various stages of processing, with less-processed drugs being more likely to still contain toxic chemicals. Brown tar heroin, for example, is less fully refined than white powder heroin and hence is more likely to contain certain chemicals and even bits and pieces of the raw poppy plant. The manufacture of methamphetamine requires the use of several hazardous chemicals, including acids like hydrochloric acid, lye, and sulfuric acid; solvents such as toluene, xylene, acetone; as well as starter fluid, lithium removed from batteries, and hexane, a fuel used in camp stoves. The vapors given off by these chemicals during the meth manufacturing process can attack mucous membranes, skin, eyes, and the respiratory tract. When mixed with water, some of the chemicals used in the manufacture of meth are explosive. Additionally, production of meth produces a large quantity of hazardous waste and most of the by-products are carcinogenic. Production of just one pound of methamphetamine creates six pounds of waste products that contain corrosive liquids, acid vapors, heavy metals, flammable solvents, and other harmful substances that can cause disfigurement or death if they come in contact with the skin or if they are breathed. To save money and avoid detection, operators of meth labs have been known to dump their toxic waste into common sewage systems, in open fields, into the large trash dumpsters of businesses, along the sides of roads, in national parks, on beaches, or at other public sites. Clean-up of a single meth production site costs $5,000–$50,000.

Finally, poisoning with illicit drugs can occur because of the age or health of the user. A particularly tragic occurrence reported in recent years involved two very young children ingesting drugs left by their parents in accessible places. Dean Havlik and Kurt Nolte (2000) report the case of a 10-month-old infant who died of cocaine poisoning. While her parents told rescue personnel that the girl had ingested rat poison accidentally, it was discovered that she had in fact been fed crack by her 2-year-old brother. Crack samples were discovered to be scattered throughout the house and in the infant's crib. The baby was found on autopsy to have two pieces of crack in her stomach and had a high concentration of cocaine in her blood. The parents were charged with homicide for putting a child in a hazardous environment and for failing to call for emergency help until two hours after the child was found to be ill. While this distressing case is somewhat unique, there have been many occasions in which small children have been subject to passive cocaine consumption as the result of being in homes or vehicles while adults were smoking the drug.

Destruction of Social Relationships and Support Systems

The potential dangers of drug use are not limited to health risks, they also can threaten to destroy supportive social relationships. Some drugs present a bigger risk in this regard than others. Methamphetamine use can be especially hard on relationships. Users often are irritated and upset and may be obsessively focused on an issue that is bothering them (e.g., inability to find something that is missing), exhibit signs of paranoia, suffer dramatic mood swings, and have bouts of violence. All of these behaviors can be very taxing for parents, spouses, other relatives, friends, coworkers, and employers, leading to the breakdown of social relationships. Numerous studies have shown that whatever the problems people face in life, their coping skills, mental health, and physical health are better if they have genuinely supportive social relationships. Loss of such support is a significant stressor that can lead to depression and other psychiatric symptoms, which, ironically, drug users may try to treat by taking more drugs. At the same time, of course, social relationships can be the route through which individuals are subjected to their most injurious experiences. Child sexual abuse, which is often committed by relatives or family friends, has been shown to be strong predictor of subsequent drug use, risky behavior, and mental health problems.

Limiting Risk

A key issue in assessing drug-related health risks is drug user heterogeneity. There is great variation among drug users, with some falling into higher-risk categories and others who use the same or similar drugs being far less risky in their pattern of use. From a health perspective, the issue is not only which drugs are used but also the contexts, frequencies, methods, styles, and duration of drug use. For example, concerning crack users, Danielle German and Claire Sterk (2002:383) note that they are standardly "depicted as people whose lives are out of control" and "are frequently presented as a homogeneous group." Instead, based on widely acclaimed ethnographic research among crack users in Atlanta, Sterk and her colleagues found a considerable degree of diversity—a point that has been stressed frequently by anthropologists who study users of a variety of illicit drugs—and, based on this range of identified behaviors, they developed a typology of crack users. At the risky end of this typology are what they refer to as "immersed users," individuals who tend to fit the usual portrayals of out-of-control crackheads. As one of the individuals who fit this categorization told German and Sterk (2002:390):

> Sometimes I don't care if I catch a VD or not. I want dope. I want money and I have no other choice. . . . I can't worry about venereal disease when I got to eat or I want some dope and I'm on the street.

By contrast, these researchers also identified crack users who employed an assemblage of protective strategies to avoid potential harm associated with drug consumption, including taking periodic respites from crack use, structuring use temporally so that it did not interfere with life responsibilities, avoiding certain risky locations and individuals, purchasing necessities and storing money with friends and family before buying crack, and maintaining supportive relationships with non-drug-using friends. Individuals who utilize many of these protective factors and maintain structured lives that limited (but did not eliminate) access to crack were labeled "stable users." The retention of non-crack users in their social networks was identified by the stable users in German and Sterk's sample as the primary reason they could avoid becoming a "crackhead," a social designation they were quite concerned about avoiding.

As a result of mobilizing various strategies, some drug users can minimize many of the potential dangers of drug use. Similarly, in some contexts, especially where it is closely socially controlled and its use ritualized, drug use has limited negative impacts. As Ross Coomber and Nigel South (2004:18) conclude:

> Drug use *per se* is far from predictive of problematic behaviour or problematic social outcomes. Many . . . examples of normal drug use are sufficiently important and/or sacred to those that practice them that one dimensional international conventions aiming to prevent their use . . . can be seen to be both myopic and unreasonably ethnocentric. Conversely . . . there are cases where problematic behaviours and social outcomes follow from drug use that reflects, sometimes in stark relief, the consequences of post-colonial intrusion of western governmental and market economic power into formerly stable and harmonious cultural environments.

Ironically, at the centers of market influence, like the United States, as a result of using drugs often expropriated historically from the colonized world, the kinds of drug-related health problems described above are most frequent.

Syndemics

The term *syndemic* was introduced into the public health lexicon during the 1990s as a way of drawing conceptual attention to the fact that traditional ways of thinking about diseases as discrete conditions brought on by an identifiable pathogens, environmental conditions, genetic predisposition, injury, or a set of sufferer behaviors were problematic (Singer 1996). Rather than existing as distinct entities, diseases often, and particularly under certain social conditions, cluster and mingle, both within populations and within the bodies of the members of those populations. In this light, and at its simplest level, "syndemic" was introduced to label two or more epidemics (notable increases in the rate of specific diseases in a population), interacting synergistically and contributing, as a result of their interaction, to an excess burden of disease. Syndemic refers not only to the temporal or locational co-occurrence of two or more diseases or health problems, but also to the identifiable health consequences of biological interactions among copresent health conditions. In syndemics, the interaction of diseases or other adverse health conditions (e.g., malnutrition, heart conditions, and stress) occurs because of a set of social conditions (e.g., poverty, exploitative, stigmatization, oppressive social relationships in society) and puts marginalized social groups at heightened risk (Singer and Clair 2003). In the broadest sense, syndemics comprise co-occurring and potentially biologically interacting diseases that are linked to causative structural and social conditions and tend to produce higher levels of morbidity and mortality than would otherwise occur.

Drug-related syndemics involve interacting diseases, at least one of which is introduced and transmitted as a result of drug use. For example, HIV and TB are known to cluster together, and further, HIV is known to be a disease transmitted through several behaviors related to injection and noninjection drug use. Specifically, as noted earlier, these behaviors include either the sequential, multiple-person use of the same syringe or part of a syringe and/or other drug injection paraphernalia or sexual contact without the use of disease prevention methods. Moreover, studies have shown that because HIV damages human immune systems, individuals with HIV disease who are exposed to TB are more likely to develop active and rapidly progressing tuberculosis compared to those who are HIV negative, whose immune systems can keep the disease-causing tuberculosis bacteria in check and in a dormant state. HIV/TB, in other words, is a drug-related syndemic with significant health implications.

One window on the concentration of diseases among drug users—in this case, the most at-risk drug users—is a set of interviews with 988 not-in-treatment IDUs we conducted during the Hispanic Health Council's Syringe Access Study. In this sample, we found the following distribution of "ever-diagnosed" major diseases (suffered by participants):

Disease	Prevalence Percentage
Hepatitis C	32.2
Abscess	26.1
HIV	24.7
Hepatitis B	23.1
STI	22.5
Pneumonia	18.4
Liver disease	11.7
Tuberculosis	7.9
Endocarditis	5.6

Beyond the clustering of disease, syndemic theory directs research attention to an examination of the living conditions and social relations of disease-burdened populations. Exposure to violence, for example, has been found to be a condition commonly linked to drug abuse (Singer 1996). Previously, the astonishing level of violence to which street drug users are subjected was described in some detail. But even the account that was provided does not adequately summarize all of violence that shapes the day-to-day experience of this population. Missing from the account was an in-depth discussion of the significant role that childhood sexual abuse plays.

From a syndemic perspective, assessing the health consequences of changing drug use practices and conditions requires a much broader frame of reference than looking at individual health problems linked to particular drugs, drug combinations, or routes of drug consumption. For example, the emergence and spread of crack use during the 1980s became part and parcel of an interlocked set of infectious diseases, including HIV, hepatitis, and TB. The same can be said of the contemporary spread of methamphetamine. Both of these drugs not only help to drive a set of behaviors, such as unprotected sex, which facilitate the spread of diseases, they, along with the infections they promote, also damage the body's protective immune system and compromise its ability to fight off an array of other opportunistic infections that normally are held at bay by healthy immune systems.

The list of opportunistic diseases that comprise the AIDS syndemic, for example, is frighteningly long, and biologically varied, and includes various pathological bacteria and mycobacteria, fungal infections, protozoal infections, viral infections, and cancers. The entwinement of these diseases is complex. For example, Agostino Pugliese and colleagues (2002a) have conducted research showing that human papillomavirus (HPV), a cause of cervical cancer, and herpes simplex virus type 2 coinfection correlates with greater immunosuppression in HIV-positive women, compared with other sexually transmitted diseases. This same research team has investigated the effect of coinfection with human herpes virus type 8 (HHV-8) and HIV among women. They found that compared to HIV+ women who tested negative for HHV-8 infection, those who were coinfected with both viruses exhibited accelerated deterioration of their immunologic and hematologic statuses

(Pugliese et al. 2002b). Among women in the United States, drug use and sexual relations with a drug user are the most common routes of HIV infection.

The examples above point to the importance of understanding how new drug use patterns and various diseases interact with each other and with social conditions to produce new causes of morbidity and mortality in a population.

Conclusion

While this book is about emergent illicit drug use, and thus this chapter has focused on the medical, mental health, and negative social consequences of illegal drug use (especially of changing drug use behaviors), legal drugs like alcohol and tobacco take a far greater toll on the health and well-being of people in the United States than do illegal drugs. Until the rise of the AIDS syndemic, the collective damage done by alcohol and tobacco made the health and social costs of illicit drug use pale by comparison. Thus, almost half a million people die in the United States each year from tobacco-related causes. Smoking is now known to damage almost every organ of the human body.

Nonetheless, especially since the rise of AIDS, the health burden of drug abuse is considerable. AIDS, of course, is not the only new disease; the field of emergent diseases research has blossomed in recent years. Potentially, any existing or future blood-borne infection could be transmitted through drug injection as well as through sex-for-drugs/money transactions and risky or forced sex under the influence of drugs (Romero-Daza, Weeks, and Singer 1998, 2003; Weeks et al. 1998). Additionally, with the arrival of new scan technology, some of the dangers of drug use are only now being discovered. Consequently, there are multiple reasons for improving our knowledge about changing drug use patterns. Finding ways to detect quickly new patterns of drug use that are beginning to spread in society and having effective mechanisms in place to minimize the potential health consequences of these new patterns—the topic of concern in the next and final chapter—should be rated as major public health priorities.

CHAPTER 10

Emergent Drug-Related Risk and Public Health Responses

To our knowledge, a monitoring system based on the systematic collection and analysis of anecdotal data—"narrative" data, we call it—has never been tried. It certainly could be.

—Michael Agar and Heather Schacht Reisinger,
"A Tale of Two Policies"

On September 5, 1989, President George H. W. Bush went on national television to affirm his deep commitment to waging and winning the War on Drugs. During this prime-time speech, the president dramatically drew attention to a large plastic bag lying conspicuously on the desk in the Oval Office and solemnly said, "This is crack cocaine, seized a few days ago by Drug Enforcement Administration agents in a park just across the street from the White House" (*New York Times* 1989). As discussed in chapter 7, this was not the nation's first introduction to this new drug. As early as 1985, the *New York Times* had carried an article on drug treatment that made reference to crack, and soon afterward both CBS and NBC broadcasted major documentaries on the dramatic impact crack was having on the streets. Notably, the moment of emergence of the drug and its rapid spread among drug users were not captured by the systems that were in place to monitor emergent drug use trends. As Bruce Jacobs (1999:3) points out, "Scientific data concerning the use, abuse, and sale of crack were virtually absent until 1990—fully five [actually probably seven or eight] years after the drug's appearance on the street scene." In other words, the horse was far out of the barn and causing great havoc before anyone realized it, or was able to close the barn doors.

The causes of this kind of failure and approaches for avoiding similar public health breakdowns in the future are the primary topics discussed in this chapter. In brief, the chapter focuses on the development of systems for identifying new drug use practices, tracking their rate and range of proliferation, assessing their potential health and social impacts, and implementing community and public health responses early in the game before the horse has gotten so far from the barn that it will be years, if ever, before it can be herded back inside. An authentic response to the drug problem must be evidence-based and be aimed at nonjudgmentally assisting drug users to avoid the health consequences frequently associated with drug use; this assistance includes bridging the path to low-threshold, easily accessed drug treatment. Unfortunately, as stressed in chapter 8, the approach usually taken in the public response to illicit drugs leaves much to be desired, including candor.

Fear: An Unauthentic Response

Returning to the scene at the opening of this chapter, of President George H. W. Bush in the Oval Office of the White House holding up a bag of crack during a nationally televised statement to the American people, we have an example of the usual pattern of duplicity when it comes to the topic of drug use in U.S. society. The plan to have Bush show off a bag of crack purchased in Lafayette Park across from the White House was developed by Bush's speechwriters, and the president enthusiastically approved. Through the chain of command, the DEA was instructed by the White House to arrest a crack dealer in the park and seize a bag of drugs in time for broadcasting Bush's speech. But the plan hit a snag unforeseen by Bush's public relations team; no crack dealers (or any drug dealers for that matter) could be found in the park. Consequently, agents of the DEA were sent out to find a crack dealer elsewhere in the city and entice him to come to the park for the sale. They finally found Keith Jackson, an 18-year-old high school senior selling crack in another part of the city, but he had no idea where the White House was located and had to be given instructions. To avoid a charge of entrapment, the DEA did not arrest Jackson, they merely purchased the crack from him for $2,400 and let him go.

Subsequent interviews conducted by National Public Radio with a number of men arrested for selling drugs in Washington, D.C., revealed that none would have tried to sell crack in the park because it tended to be visited by out-of-town tourists and not by local crack users, who happen to live in the poorest neighborhoods of the District at some distance from the White House. As Reinarman and Levine (1997:23) observe, "This incident illustrates how a drug scare distorts and perverts public knowledge and policy. The claim that crack was threatening every neighborhood in America was not based on the evidence."

Scare tactics rather than evidence-based, health-driven approaches have remained the norm in the U.S. response to illicit drug use. One further expression of this pattern is seen in a series of television, radio, and newspaper advertisements developed by the U.S. Office of National Drug Control Policy (ONDCP) beginning in 2002. The splashy ads, targeted to teenagers, had a pointed message: buying drugs funds terrorism. In one of the ads, a young man grimly states, "Yesterday afternoon, I did my laundry, went out for a run, and helped torture someone's dad." In another, a youth reports, "Last weekend I washed my car, hung out with a few friends, and helped murder a family in Colombia." Somberly, the ads conclude, "Drug money helps support terror. Buy drugs and you could be supporting it, too." The goal of these ads is clear: if you can link drugs to absolute evil you can prevent drug use. To support that assertion, $10 million went into making the first two, 30-second TV ads and print versions that appeared in hundreds of newspapers around the country. According to the ONDCP, the ads are fair, accurate, and justified. In the words of John Walters, ONDCP director (and, hence, the U.S. drug czar), who approved the ads: "These ads are among the most powerful and effective prevention messages this office has ever released." The George W. Bush administration aggressively latched onto this new message with the president asserting, "Terrorists use drug profits to fund their cells to commit acts of murder. If you quit drugs, you join the fight against terror in America" (Singer 2002:3).

The claims directly tying drug use to terrorism are bold, innovative, and clearly speak to widespread fears. But what does the scientific evidence say? A number of social scientists, drug policy advocates, and drug control experts have questioned the accuracy of the ads. "It's despicable and dangerous," argued Ethan Nadelmann (2003), executive director of the Drug Policy Alliance, an education and advocacy group that supports the development of alternatives to the War on Drugs. "When you start labeling tens of millions of Americans as accomplices to terrorists or de facto murderers, you are creating and stirring an atmosphere of intolerance and hate-mongering that ends up being destructive and dangerous to the broader society." Similarly, Peter Reuter, a drug policy expert at the University of Maryland asserted, "You have to stretch a long way to make that plausible. . . . Marijuana, which is what the vast majority of drug users use, is grown primarily in the United States and Mexico and has no connection with terrorism" (Trafford 2002). This is but one example Reuters (1996:64) notes of a larger pattern of "reckless disregard for the truth" in the War on Drugs.

Other critics of the ads pointed out that even the Bush administration linked the sale of honey and other legal commodities to fund-raising efforts by organizations that have been labeled as terrorist. Critics of the ads asked whether buyers of these items will be labeled as supporters of terrorism as well. Rather than paving the way for accurate, research-supported conclusions, critics pointed out that closely linking drug use to terrorism does nothing other than shore up the ever-stumbling War on Drugs, as well as foster a disingenuous way for drug control entities to grab a slice of the multibillion dollar antiterrorism pie created by the Bush administration and Congress. Most importantly, some researchers believe that from a public health standpoint the ads may be quite harmful. "This is an effort to demonize drug users," remarks Eric Sterling (2004), president of the Criminal Justice Policy Foundation. "At a time when many are talking about the importance of drug treatment," he laments, "this rhetoric sends the message that drug users are not people with chemical dependencies, they are aiding and abetting terrorists and need to be locked up."

Ultimately, there is grim irony in the fact that in the same era in which the National Institute on Drug Abuse, under the leadership of Alan Leshner, went to considerable lengths to make the point that drug addiction is a bona fide disease of the brain caused by drug-induced biological changes in brain structure, we are witnessing a return to the old mantra of drug user demonization. As many anthropologists and other social scientists know from direct experience, the unintended consequences of social decisions can be far more telling in the long run than their intended purpose. In this instance, we see a typical policy practice in which a course of action is embraced, not because it has been validated by rigorous research, but rather because it is in harmony with what some people—those who make decisions and set policy—would like to believe. It is the assertion of this chapter that what is needed is the political commitment to make use of the rigorous assessment of real behavior the formulation of national and local drug policy.

Thinking about Trends

In the public health world, there is a growing interest in the development of strategies for tracking and understanding longer-range trends in illicit drug use practice. One expression of this mounting attention, as noted in chapter 1, is a set of articles published by Michael Agar and Heather Reisinger (1999; 2002) on the use of "trend theory" to explain the several waves of heroin use that have been discussed in previous chapters, beginning with the period of legal heroin use in the nineteenth century and continuing through the late twentieth/early twenty-first-century jump in heroin snorting among younger users. Agar and Reisinger situate their approach within a broader orientation to history developed by three anthropologists who have also been significant influences on the Critical Medical Anthropology perspective that guides this book: Sidney Mintz (1985), especially his work on the cultural construction and diffusion of sugar as a commodity; Eric Wolf (1982), who developed a sweeping, global approach to culture writ large and small; and William Roseberry (1991), who was concerned with how multiple histories interact in local settings.

These anthropologists contributed to the theoretical tradition known as political economy, seeking through their studies to demonstrate the importance of linking local cultures and histories to broader, global trends in economic production and the distribution of both goods and political power. In addition to being friends, all three shared a recognition of the fundamental importance of social inequality in historic social process, as well as an appreciation of the interplay of global and local processes that creates the social worlds of human experience and action, including the role of drug use in those worlds. As Agar and Reisinger (2002:272) note:

> Explanation of a phenomenon of interest is not available in the location where that phenomenon takes place. Instead, events—most of them at remote social locations—unfold and interact over time, and the local phenomenon is only one of a number of factors involved.

In other words, to take the case of crack cocaine as an example, the appearance and rapid adoption of this drug at roughly the same time on both the East (New York) and West (L.A.) Coasts cannot be fully explained in terms of the unique features of either of these sites or their local drug scenes and drug using populations. Rather, while local social and cultural differences were at play creating variation and degrees of contrast, something bigger, cross-cutting, and powerful appears to have been at work influencing local events and behaviors in the same general direction at otherwise distant locations. In this instance, several factors, including markedly unequal social class and racial relations, contributed to the emergence and continuation of a far-flung, marginalized underclass in U.S. cities (Bowser, Quimbey, and Singer in press).

Social inequality helped to create an extensive market for a drug like crack, with its low-cost escape from the brutality of everyday discrimination, street violence, and economic hardship. All of the other elements of the Critical Medical Anthropology model were important as well, including: (1) social networks, which were used to recruit and control the workforce for crack distribution and the customer-based street dealers served; (2) culture, especially sets of knowledge used to facilitate drug distribution, acquisition, and use; to lubricate interactions in the dealer hierarchy, as well as among fellow users and between dealers and users; to allow successful coping with often harsh street realities; and to increase the likelihood of avoiding detection by the police; and (3) biology, including the rapid brain effects produced by crack smoking, quick extinction of intensely pleasurable experiences, and intense and compelling craving for repeated exposure to the drug. Working in tandem with the socioeconomic context described above, these factors shaped the biopsychosocial profile of the crack wave that began in the early 1980s.

Once launched, the spread of crack was not detected by the public health system for a number of years. Drug monitoring devices tended to focus on school-enrolled youth and dispersed community samples but missed harder-to-reach street drug users who were neither going to school nor waiting behind residential doors to answer interviewers' survey questions (Singer 1999d). In light of these factors, how might crack use have been spotted early and its effects possibly minimized?

Studying Change:
Methods for Monitoring Emergent Drug-related Risk

Drug researchers have recognized for some time that it is necessary to build broadly based public health surveillance mechanisms that allow "early bird" identification of emergent behavioral trends in drug use while evaluating their potential health and other consequences. As Lawrence Ouellet, Wayne Wiebel, and Antonio Jimenez (1995:182) effectively argue, "Given the potential impact of substance abuse on matters as grave as health, education, and crime, intelligent policy formation often requires that accurate information be produced quickly." Some researchers and policy makers began to point to the need for ongoing monitoring capable of quickly spotting new behaviors or new health and social consequences of older behaviors performed under changed conditions. While traditional public health surveillance analyzed trends in mortality and, to a somewhat lesser extent, morbidity, such an approach is inadequate when there is a significant time lag between preventable exposure and the clinical manifestations of disease, as is the case with AIDS, in which the lag can be ten years or longer. As Alfredo Morabia (1996:625) emphasizes, under these circumstance, "monitoring distributions of *risk factors* in populations provides short-term indicators to identify prevention strategies, assess their effectiveness, and predict emerging epidemics" (emphasis added).

Surveillance of risk factors, including the various behaviors involved in drug use and the social processes and contexts that shape these behaviors, as opposed to the statistical monitoring of drug-related mortality and morbidity, requires a dramatic shift in focus from outcome to onset, from ultimate consequences to actual, on-the-ground behaviors. This conceptual and methodological shift creates the opportunity for *ethnoepidemiology*, the productive integration of traditional ethnographic and epidemiological strategies for the definition of research questions and the collection, analysis, and interpretation of findings. As a result, field research in natural settings takes on a conspicuous new importance in public health surveillance research, as does "technique triangulation," which is the collection of different kinds of data, such as field observations of behavior, answers to survey questions, and participant-kept diaries of experiences, in a multimethod research design with the intention of comparing findings across methods. By way of analogy, if researchers were trying to understand the layout and furnishing of the interior of a home without actually entering it, they might peek through the windows, interview the residents, and look at photographs of the interior. They would then assemble their findings to create an as accurate picture as possible of the inside of the house. A similar approach, in which the findings produced by several different methods are assembled to get a sense of the whole picture, has become typical of drug use and health risk monitoring studies.

While movement toward the public health monitoring of risk began in the 1970s, the effort really picked up steam with the onset of the AIDS epidemic and recognition of the important connection between drug use patterns and HIV transmission. In 1994, the Committee on Substance Abuse and Mental Health Issues in AIDS Research of the Institute of Medicine, in response to a congressional directive to the Alcohol, Drug Abuse and Mental Health Administration, initiated a study of AIDS, which concluded that among injection drug users it is "critical to develop effective epidemiologic surveillance mechanisms for identifying new drug injectors within populations, to be able to track trends in drug injection over time" (Auerbach, Wypijewski, and Brodie 1994:71). The committee recommended that the National Public Health Service coordinate new interagency efforts "to monitor and respond to concurrent epidemics (such as drug use, violence, and infectious diseases) that will alter the course of the HIV epidemic" (Auerbach, Wypijewski, and Brodie 1994:6). The committee explicitly emphasized the value of expanding the role of behavioral and social science research, including cultural and ethnographic studies, as part of these efforts. A similar conclusion was reached by the National Research Council:

> Monitoring changes in risk-associated behaviors that can lead to subsequent acquisition and spread of infection is . . . critically important. During the first decade of the [AIDS] epidemic, investigators who considered the risks associated with drug use focused primarily on injection practices. As the epidemic has matured, however, greater appreciation of the role of other drugs, such as crack, has emerged. . . . (Miller, Turner, and Moses 1990:69)

This recognition further supported the development of new surveillance approaches capable of drawing "attention to the appearance of new drugs whose use may pose additional risk to [the drug using] population" and beyond to their romantic and other sexual partners and children (Miller, Turner, and Moses 1990:71).

Responding to the new recognition were several efforts by the National Institute on Drug Abuse, including the 29-site National AIDS Demonstration Research (NADR) projects, and the 23-site Cooperative Agreement for AIDS Community-based Outreach Intervention Research (CA), two large-scale studies in which the Hispanic Health Council participated. Through these projects, ethnographer/indigenous outreach worker field teams were deployed in varying configurations in local communities to identify, recruit, interview, and provide intervention to active, not-in-treatment drug users. At the same time, these fieldworkers—many of whom were themselves in recovery from drug addiction—were in a position to identify new or emergent drug use trends and related health risks and to monitor the changing drug scene locally. In the work of our Hispanic Health Council research team through NADR and the CA, we were able to develop a profile of street drug use patterns in Hartford, including, among other findings, a notable tendency toward high frequency drug injection compared to IDUs in other cities,

Disease-prevention material developed for drug users. Photograph by Delia Easton.

important ethnic differences (African American vs. Puerto Rican) in drugs of consumption and injection frequencies, an absence of methamphetamine injection locally, notable levels of injection equipment sharing, comparatively high rates of arrest and homelessness, and very high rates of HIV and hepatitis infection compared to IDUs elsewhere in the country. What these studies did not register was the risky tide of club drug use, again because it was not focused on the population—club kids—among whom club drugs were rapidly spreading. For the same reason, neither study identified the emergence of social circles of high-potency marijuana or illy users.

Another important expression of the growing awareness of the benefits of broad *perpetual monitoring* across diverse social groups, reflecting an appreciation of the public health value of learning about all levels and sectors of the heterogeneous drug user population, is an ongoing project known as the Community Epidemiology Work Group (CEWG) of the National Institute on Drug Abuse. The CEWG is a loosely affiliated network of field researchers from not only major urban areas across the United States but also from other countries. The network meets semiannually

> with the primary objective of providing ongoing community-level public health surveillance of drug use and abuse, principally through collection and analysis of epidemiologic and ethnographic research data. Through this program, the CEWG provides current descriptive and analytical information regarding the nature and patterns of drug abuse, emerging trends, and characteristics of vulnerable populations. (Kozel 1997:iii)

A primary goal of systematic behavioral monitoring of this sort is to "get out ahead" of shifting patterns of drug use through the expeditious implementation of research-driven educational, treatment, or other efforts designed to minimize the negative health effects of drug use shifts. One example of a community-based initiative of this sort is the Hispanic Health Council and Institute for Community Research collaborative Drug Monitoring Study, which was designed to monitor emergent drug use and linked HIV risk patterns among drug users in Hartford, Connecticut. The project grew out of a Northeast regional initiative supported by the Centers for Disease Control and Prevention (CDC) to enhance coordination of AIDS prevention in high prevalence cities in New Jersey, Pennsylvania, New York, and Connecticut.

The CDC effort to build multicity collaborative programs in response to AIDS dates back to 1984, when it funded a U.S. Conference of Mayors program to enhance information exchange on AIDS-prevention activities. In 1985, the CDC, the nation's premier institution for understanding disease emergence and patterning and for implementing public health responses, began funding community-based HIV prevention demonstration projects. Initially, only public health programs like local city government departments of health could apply for funding. Two years later, the CDC began to enter into cooperative agreements with nongovernment organizations focused on AIDS prevention and soon launched its AIDS Community Demonstration Projects initiative (O'Reilly and Higgins 1991).

By 1994, over 500 organizations were directly or indirectly funded by CDC. That same year, CDC's HIV prevention strategies were assessed through an external review by health professionals, social scientists, and prevention experts organized by the CDC Advisory Committee on the Prevention of HIV Infection (ACPHI). One recommendation of this review was that CDC's AIDS/HIV surveillance be expanded from "counting cases" of disease or infection to include the monitoring of behaviors like drug use that facilitate acquisition and transmission of HIV. In the language of the review committee, "Moving the focus of surveillance to the 'front end' of the epidemic is a critical prerequisite to the identification, development and evaluation of prevention interventions" (ACPHI 1994:34).

An initial step in this direction was CDC support of an eight-city, two-year community assessment process (CAP). Year one involved a series of qualitative interviews with injection drug users and youth in high-risk situations (e.g., homeless youth who support themselves through the illicit street economy) followed in year two by a survey with representative samples of these two target populations. The CAP was designed to learn: (1) the distribution of prevention materials and messages; (2) the locations of intervention delivery by street outreach workers; and (3) the delivery of other services to the target populations. In the CDC-supported AIDS Community Demonstration Projects (Corby and Wolitski 1997; Higgins et al. 1996), formative research to identify sources of HIV information, such as community experts knowledgeable about local risk patterns in targeted populations like injection drug users, was a prerequisite for the development of community-level HIV prevention efforts.

In the Northeast, the CDC-supported initiative that led to the Hispanic Health Council's entrée into drug monitoring urged participating cities to organize local consortia of AIDS-involved organizations, including city and state public health departments, and to mount needs-based local and regional initiatives to respond to the particular profile of the local AIDS epidemic. Emphasis in the meetings of local consortia teams was on finding ways to ground prevention efforts in experience-based awareness of specific risk patterns and populations. Drug use behavioral monitoring was identified by participating organizations as a pressing need by representatives from Hartford, Connecticut, a city in which, at the time, 51.6 percent of males and 57.1 percent of females with AIDS were IDUs (CDC 1996) and in which drug use had long been the single most important local source of new HIV infections. Several years later—and after much frustration on the part of local researchers eager to begin tracking drug-related HIV risk behavior—the funding finally became available to implement drug monitoring in Hartford.

The drug monitoring study (1997–98) included four components: (1) a baseline ethnographic and key informant exploration of emergent drug use behaviors; (2) a literature and computer search for drug use trends nationally; (3) a survey of drug use and related behaviors among approximately 100 street-recruited, out-of-treatment drug users; and (4) the sharing of project findings with providers to facilitate prevention/intervention or treatment. Individuals in the sample reported a range of drugs they had used, including illy, the use of which in Hartford was first identified by this study (Singer, Juvalis, and Weeks 2000).

Overall, in terms of "drugs ever used," the drug use patterns of the sample differed notably from our prior studies in Hartford in that monitoring study participants tended to have broader, less injection-focused drug use patterns. This is precisely the difference we expected in the sample, in that the drug-use criteria for inclusion in the study was "illicit drug use during the last 30 days," whereas in our prior HIV-focused studies of street drug users the criteria were either drug injection or crack cocaine use during the last 30 days. In short, the drug monitoring study succeeded in tapping broader layers of street drug users than our past, more narrowly focused studies. In addition to the research component, the study assembled a team of frontline healthcare providers to discuss project findings.

One product of this discussion was the shared recognition that an action team be formed to develop research-based public health intervention in response to monitoring initiatives that newly identified risky drug-related behaviors. Unfortunately, one year is an insufficient time to effectively monitor changing drug use patterns. During any given year, drug-related behaviors may not change much, if at all. Nonetheless, the project suggested the definite utility of a monitoring methodology for understanding drug use emergence and related social change. Our desire was to find longer-term funding for a multiyear monitoring initiative, a goal that took several years to achieve.

Rapid Assessment and Monitoring

In the meantime, the U.S. Department of Health and Human Services' Office of HIV/AIDS Policy (OHAP) adopted a rapid ethnographic assessment model called RARE (Rapid Assessment, Response, and Evaluation) for use by U.S. cities in identifying, targeting, and implementing effective interventions to deal with emergent or unresolved risk patterns driving local HIV epidemics, especially in African American and Latino communities. Rapid assessment as a quick-paced, applied research methodology was first fully described in the late 1980s and early 1990s (Scrimshaw, Carballo, and Ramos 1991), along with other types of accelerated assessment and evaluation models that were developed during the same period.

The multi-methods mixture found in RARE parallels that adopted in other rapid assessment and response programs. This methodological toolset includes: (1) direct field observation of behavior; (2) brief on-the-street intercept interviews of people in targeted sites (such as places where illicit drugs are sold and commercial sex work occurs); (3) in-depth interviews of individuals usually recruited from these sites; and (4) focus groups. RARE has been implemented in several dozen U.S. cities coast-to-coast, including in the Virgin Islands, and has produced numerous evidence-based, locally grounded recommendations for improved HIV prevention, as well as invigorated commitment among local AIDS-prevention workers who are highly subject to emotional fatigue because so many of the people they try to help become infected, get sick, and die of AIDS-related causes (Bowser, Quimbey, and Singer in press).

Not surprisingly, there has been an uneven response to project-recommended changes in public health practices/policies, in part reflecting local political structures, histories, and challenges, as well as traditional tensions between research and practice. For example, a recommendation to fund prevention efforts with a specific population may be resisted by decision makers who want AIDS prevention and intervention dollars to go to their own community.

As with the NADR and CA projects noted above, Hartford was one of the cities selected to participate in the RARE initiative, with the Hispanic Health Council coordinating data collection and analysis. Specifically, the Hartford RARE project, like parallel RARE projects in other cities, concentrated on identifying and assessing late-night drug- and sex-related HIV risk behaviors (Singer and Eiserman in press). The project sought to answer four key questions:

1. What types of risk behavior are going on in the streets of Hartford during the late-night hours (from 11 PM to 2 AM)?

2. What are the characteristics of the populations that are engaged in these behaviors?

3. Where are the critical locations for late-night risk?

4. What are the unmet HIV/AIDS prevention and service needs of these individuals?

In order to identify potential venue for recruitment of study participants engaged in late-night risk behavior, the RARE Hartford field team engaged in a brain-storming exercise to identify known high-traffic, late-night sites in Hartford. Based on the experience of field team members in various parts of the city, 17 initial sites were identified, including the sidewalk areas and parking lots outside of bars, downtown dance clubs, certain fast-food restaurants, several adult bookstores, stores, a few motels, several street corners, and local parks. Field team members drove to the sites after midnight, walked around the area, and carefully watched the behavior of individuals on the street, recording field notes based on these observations.

At sites that proved to be activity points for late-night social interaction and risk behaviors, field team members recorded detailed field notes based on their observations. Drawing on the field team's experiences, sites were added or dropped from the original list. Although fieldworkers occasionally entered businesses in order to recruit individuals for rapid street-intercept interviews, they primarily conducted observation in outdoor locations around the city.

Throughout the study period (August–November 2003), the field team revised the list of target sites to reach more individuals, locate additional high-risk "hot spots," and contact populations that were not being found at other sites, such as men who have sex with men (MSM). Our fieldwork and discussions with community members revealed that Hartford has many public locations at which HIV risk behaviors are conducted during late-night hours. Ultimately, the team identified six hot spots in six different target neighborhoods or neighborhood intersections for focused study. These areas were selected because they were consistently frequented by individuals who engaged in HIV high-risk behaviors, and in most cases, were effective sources for the recruitment of participants for focus groups, one-on-one short interviews, and in-depth interviews.

One of the neighborhoods selected for focus in RARE Hartford, for instance, is called Asylum Hill. Since the 1960s, Asylum Hill has claimed the infamous distinction of consistently holding a high spot on the city's frequent crime location list. Many streets, pockmarked with abandoned buildings, have taken on a run-down appearance, telltale signs of the faltering local economy, which is now bereft of the factories that once made Hartford a regional industrial center, as well as the lack of national commitment to maintaining the once-bustling cores of U.S. cities.

Today, the neighborhood has a number of halfway houses and group homes, as well as various social service agencies. Residentially, the neighborhood is dominated by low-income African American and Puerto Rican households in the north and somewhat wealthier condo-dwellers in the south. As of 1990, the population of the neighborhood was about 52 percent African American, 25 percent white, and 20 percent Hispanic (Asylum Hill Problem Solving Revitalization Association 1998). Female-headed households constituted 31 percent of the family units. The incomes of 23 percent of the families living in Asylum Hill fell below the federal poverty line.

Over the years, Asylum Hill has been a regular recruitment site for our research projects on drug use and HIV risk. In our NADR study, Asylum Hill was found to have one of the highest sexually transmitted disease rates in the city. In RARE, the hot spot in Asylum Hill was the area outside of a neighborhood bar, where drug sellers, drug users, and commercial sex workers congregated late into the night.

Based on the observations, interviews, and focus groups conducted with participants living in neighborhoods like Asylum Hill and encountered in late-night hot spots, the project produced a set of findings on risk after dark in the city. Individuals who are out on the street, late into the night, appear to be at considerably greater risk than those who are out on the street during the day because there is more open drug selling, drug using, hustling, and prostitution that occurs in the protective darkness of the night. Moreover, many of the "late-night" individuals we interviewed reported that they see themselves as being at high risk for HIV transmission. During the interviews, we asked participants, "On a scale of 1 to 10, with 10 being the most and 1 being the least, how much at risk do you think you are for contracting HIV?" Most of the drug users and sex workers interviewed by the field team replied that they are 6 or higher.

The majority of the individuals we interviewed reported participation in risk behaviors; indeed, most reported two or more types of risk that they regularly engaged in. For example, many of the participants were both drug users *and* sex workers; others were drug users, sex workers, and MSM who did not use condoms. We also interviewed sex workers, primarily males, who were also customers of other sex workers, a pattern we had previously discovered in an earlier study but one that continues to surprise us. Additionally, we interviewed drug users who reported having multiple sex partners as well as being customers of sex workers. In short, many of our participants were at risk for both sex- and drug-related HIV infection, a feature of all the identified hot spots around the city. Additionally, it is likely that after-hours sex exchange and drug use hot spots are transmission sites for information about and acquisition of new or renewed drugs and premixed drug combinations. Frequented by individuals who do not put a high premium on avoiding risk, hot spots attract receptive audiences for the gilded promises of an exciting new high.

Many of the commercial sex workers, male and female, encountered by the RARE field team at late-night sites were crack cocaine addicts, although more than half of the crack users who were interviewed also reported heroin injection (further affirming the problem of drug user labels in an era of drug mixing). Given the fleeting if intense high conferred by crack cocaine, and the rapid need to smoke again just to avoid a post-crack letdown, participants reported spending hundreds of dollars a day to get high. Accordingly, users must turn many "tricks" in one night to support their demanding crack habit. Many of the male crack users and one female crack user we interviewed reported that they have both male and female customers.

On a positive note, most of our participants reported that they had been tested for HIV at some point during their lives. At the same time, they also indicated that fear often prevents them and their associates from getting tested regularly or even returning to learn their results (a common problem in HIV testing). Three out of the 31 individuals who completed rapid street interviews told us they were HIV+. All were sex workers. Although we did not ask about HIV status in the focus groups, two out of the 31 individuals who participated in one of our focus groups mentioned that they were HIV+. Even if only these five individuals were in fact infected, which is unlikely, they still constitute 8 percent of these samples, a startlingly high percentage compared to the general population, suggesting just how risky participation in late-night hot spots can be.

While most of the RARE Hartford participants reported that they have received HIV/AIDS prevention information at some point in the past, only three reported ever having seen an HIV prevention outreach worker late at night in Hartford, and one of those participants stated that this sighting occurred in a bar. The experiences of the RARE fieldworkers while performing late-night ethnography in Hartford support the assessment that late-night HIV prevention outreach is not readily apparent. None of the fieldworkers ever saw an outreach worker while they were out in the field over an eight-week period. In short, one of the findings of the study was that in the locations and time period when risk is greatest in the city, prevention efforts are at the lowest. By monitoring risk behavior during hours of the night when HIV-prevention programs have closed and their staffs have gone home, RARE Hartford was able to identify one of the reasons existing prevention efforts have failed to stem the epidemic in the city.

Ethnography as a Monitoring Method

Among the range of available research methods for monitoring emergent drug use practice, ethnography has proven to be especially useful. Ethnography is a type of firsthand, immersion-based research that is conducted in "natural settings" in which the researcher(s) directly observes and, at least to some degree within ethical, safety and legal limits, participates in the everyday life of members of the group under study. The term "natural settings" is used in contrast to laboratory or other experimental conditions constructed and to some degree controlled by the researcher. In a contemporary vernacular, ethnography is like reality TV, except that it is *about* reality. Ethnography is especially useful for the detection of emergent drug use practices and the monitoring of the diffusion of drug-related behaviors because it is a highly porous approach that imposes little in the way of researcher control over the domain of study. This emergent feature of ethnographic research makes it an especially important tool in the study of new trends in drug use; in the accessing of the often hidden, time/place locations and settings of drug consumption; and in the assessment of some of the potential health consequences of these behaviors. As a result, there has developed a renewed recognition of the contributions of ethnography to drug use and public health research.

Ethnographers commonly enter the field with a set of issues of primary concern. As a result of contingencies encountered in the field, however, they have been known to carry out studies very different from but locally more salient than the ones that brought them to the field in the first place. This has certainly been the case where drug use is involved because so few ethnographers are trained in this area. To learn about the exact beliefs, behaviors, and "material culture" of drug users, ethnographers at the Hispanic Health Council routinely visit shooting galleries, "get-off" houses, crack houses, abandoned buildings, homeless encampments, wooded areas in otherwise urban settings, alleyways, drug users' homes, rooftops, and other illicit drug use locations, as well as drug copping (acquiring) sites, homeless shelters, soup kitchens, street corners, and other places where active drug users can be found, observed, and engaged in conversation. In the course of this kind of work, ethnographers are in a position to spot new drug-related behaviors, recently created or introduced "cultural" objects (e.g., drug use paraphernalia), new drug-using populations, and the consumption of new (or newly combined or packaged) mind-altering drugs.

As a process, ethnography has been described as an approach to research in which the researcher "closely observes, records, and engages in the daily life of another culture . . . and then writes an account of this culture, emphasizing descriptive detail" (Marcus and Fischer 1986:44) While ethnographers can and do collect quantitative data, qualitative data collection and analysis—including regularly netting the kind of anecdotal or narrative data referred to by Agar and Reisinger at the outset of the chapter—certainly is a fundamental component of ethnography.

The qualitative aspects of ethnography stem from its emphasis on: (1) situating the behaviors or beliefs of concern within their natural contexts; (2) developing observation-based descriptions of these contexts, the social groups who occupy them, and the daily social processes and relationships that unfold within them; and (3) attending to the cultural meanings, insider understandings, and the signs/symbols used to express them in any given cultural context. As Miles and Huberman (1994:25) indicate, "the hallmark of qualitative research is that it goes beyond how much there is of something to tell us about its essential qualities." As a result, ethnography is an ideal method to incorporate in drug-use behavioral monitoring programs.

Multiyear Monitoring

The project design for the Hispanic Health Council's multiyear monitoring of changing drug use patterns in Hartford, a CDC-funded project known as Building Community Responses to Risks of Emergent Drug Use, which has been referred to multiple times in previous chapters, has three major components. The first involves three waves of surveys among active drug users about existing and new drug use behaviors, with approximately 250 participants per survey. The second builds on the strengths of ethnography to add in-depth information on changing and emergent drug use behaviors through observations of drug use and open-ended interviews with key informants, including drug users, frontline providers of services to drug users, and other individuals who are in a position to observe changing drug use patterns (e.g., police, public health officials). During the study drug tests have been administered to assess the actual contents of drugs in use. The final component of the study involves the convening of a community advisory board composed of state and city public health officials, drug treatment providers, emergency room physicians, HIV program staff, and the personnel of community-based organizations that work with drug using populations.

Findings from the data collection are presented at regular intervals to the advisory team (and shared with local public health officials), followed by discussion with project research staff about the public health consequences of identified behaviors and appropriate public health responses to prevent harm. The ultimate objective of the project is the implementation of prevention programs based on research findings. The first of these programs, for example, involved a community forum, an op-ed article published in the local newspaper, and a press conference to warn of the great potential for a methamphetamine epidemic in the city.

An alternative statewide drug monitoring model is provided by the Ohio Substance Abuse Monitoring (OSAM) network. The purpose of the OSAM network is to gather timely information on substance abuse trends statewide, including data from individual and focus group interviews with drug users, treatment providers, and law enforcement officials, as well as statistical data from county coroners, local law enforcement offices, and regional crime labs for use by Ohio public health officials and policy makers. In this program, ten key informants dispersed across Ohio collect both qualitative and quantitative data on substance abuse trends in their respective regions and submit biannual reports. Additionally, the OSAM network has a rapid response capability through which the ten key informants can investigate special issues identified by the Ohio Department of Alcohol and Drug Addiction Services. Reports prepared in the project have been well received by policy makers (Siegal et al. 2000).

While there are other models, it appears that key features in effective community response to the health risks of emergent drug use behaviors include: (1) implementation of a locally grounded system for monitoring changes on the drug scene; (2) assurance that this monitoring system includes the collection of quantitative data from existing data collection sources, periodic interviews with active drug users, and ethnographic observation of drug use behaviors and social interactions; (3) a mechanism for transferring and translating findings from drug monitoring for rapid use by public health officials, clinical personnel, drug treatment providers, and community organizations; (4) adequate funding to sustain monitoring over the long haul; and (5) periodic evaluation to identify strengths and weaknesses in the monitoring and referral systems, thereby insuring a basis for continued growth and development.

Conclusion

New drugs, old drugs in new forms, new drug combinations, new ways of using drugs, new drug-using populations, and new drug use environments will continue to appear over time. It is likely that many of the new psychoactive drugs on the street will have their origin in the high-technology laboratories of wealthy mainstream pharmaceutical companies. A few will first be produced in amateur laboratories, in foul-smelling basements, or through the locating and harvesting of plants used by indigenous populations. While many of the changes that occur will not significantly enhance the risks and consequences of drug use, others may have devastating effects on users and others. As is seen in the cases of HIV or HCV, some pathogens can be readily transmitted through syringes, and it is not inconceivable that other pathogens will also begin to be transmitted through drug use behaviors. For this reason alone, emergent drug use monitoring and drug use tracking generally are critically important public health practices that merit prioritization by public health officials.

There is a Greek expression credited to Persius who lived from AD 34–62: *Venienti occurrite morbo*. It means "confront disease at its onset." As Persius apparently knew almost 2,000 years ago, the failure to identify new disease outbreaks early can lead to disastrous consequences later. Drug use has already contributed enormously to the sorrows and woes of many individuals, families, and communities. Through effective emergent drug monitoring programs designed to identify and investigate changing drug use behaviors, it is possible to confront new drug-related diseases early. Unfortunately, standing between the possible and the actual there is the political.

Drug users, as has been noted, are treated often as pariahs in American society. This attitude, however unjust, inhumane, and misguided from the standpoint of public health and ultimate public good, is nonetheless politically convenient—for some. It provides a rationale for laying blame for many of the ills of society on the shoulders of a group that can rarely speak out in its own defense. Yet drug users can hardly be blamed for being the real causes of the "new social landscape of unemployment, poverty and despair" (Pappas 1989:124). Nor can they be blamed for the loss of urban jobs that were once the bedrock of city life but are now exported to South America, southern Asia, and elsewhere.

Drug abuse did not cause the restructuring of the American economy. If anything, it is a consequence. As Rubin, a participant in our CDC-funded drug monitoring study stated: "I had a car, I helped my father pay the mortgage, but from one day to the next we had touched the bottom, and there was nothing and nobody that could pull us up." Drugs certainly could not pull up Rubin and his family. All they could do was offer respite from the misery and the disappointment he felt when the loss of his father's job condemned the family to economic ruin. Ramon, another participant in this study, stated:

> One needs higher doses of dope to really feel it and avoid reality . . . all that I have been through and that I am going through right now . . . the drama of seeing my children and not being able to take them with me . . . the fact that I am a *tecato* [a scum, slang term for heroin addict] . . . that I feel embarrassed . . . [and] that I try to go unnoticed. (Santelices, Singer, and Nicolaysen 2003:24)

Noticing people like Ramon is precisely the goal of drug-related behavioral monitoring—not to accuse, but to try and make sure that, unlike Emilio and Rafael (who died of drug overdoses in Chicago's Humboldt Park area), Ramon lives. Through research-initiated contact with him to begin a process of intervention, Ramon can regain personally meaningful reasons to go on living.

References

Abram, K., L. Teplin, G. McClelland, and M. Dulcan
2003   Comorbid Psychiatric Disorders in Youth in Juvenile Detention. *Archives of General Psychiatry* 60(11):1097–1108.

Abt Associates, Inc.
1995   *What America's Users Spend on Illegal Drugs, 1988–1993*. Boston: Abt Associates.

Abu-Lughod, L.
1991   Writing Against Culture. In *Recapturing Anthropology: Working in the Present*. Richard Fox, ed. Pp. 137–162. Santa Fe: School of American Research Press.

Adler, P.
1993   *An Ethnography of a Upper-Level Drug Dealing and Smuggling Community*. 2nd edition. New York: Columbia University Press.

Advisory Committee on the Prevention of HIV Infection (ACPHI)
1994   *External Review of CDC's HIV Prevention Strategies*. Washington, DC: U.S. Department of Health and Human Services.

Agar, M.
1973   *Ripping and Running*. New York: Academic Press.

Agar, M., and H. S. Reisinger
1999   Numbers and Patterns: Heroin Indicators and What They Represent. *Human Organization* 58(4):365–374.

Agar, M., and H. S. Reisinger
2002   A Tale of Two Policies: The French Connection, Methadone and Heroin Epidemics. *Culture, Medicine and Psychiatry* 26:371–396.

Aharonovich, E., E. Nunes, and D. Hasin
2003   Cognitive Impairment, Retention and Abstinence among Cocaine Abusers in Cognitive-Behavioral Treatment. *Drug and Alcohol Dependence* 71(2):207–211.

Andrews, D.
1995   Altered State. *In These Times*, May 15: 26–28.

Anslinger, H., and K. Chapman
1957   Narcotic Addiction. *Modern Medicine* 25:180–191.

Arrillaga, P.
1996   Drug Trade Undeterred by Tales of Murder. *Hartford Courant*, December
            12: A14.
Associated Press
2004   Smokable Heroin Pushed on Middle Class. *Hartford Courant*, March 3: A8.
Asylum Hill Problem Solving Revitalization Association
1998   *Asylum Hill Neighborhood Strategic Plan For Revitalization*. Hartford, CT:
            Asylum Hill Problem Solving Revitalization Association.
Audrain-McGovern, J., K. Tercyak, A. Shields, A. Bush, C. Espinel, and C. Lerman
2003   Which Adolescents are Most Receptive to Tobacco Industry Marketing?
            Implications for Counter-advertising Campaigns. *Health Communication*
            15(4):499–513.
Auerbach, J., C. Wypijewski, and K. Brodie, eds.
1994   *AIDS and Behavior*. Washington, DC: National Academy Press.
Baer, H., M. Singer, and I. Susser.
2004   *Medical Anthropology and the World System*. 2nd edition. Westport, CT:
            Greenwood.
Baggott, M.
2002   Preventing Problems in Ecstasy Users: Reduce Use to Reduce Harm.
            Journal of Psychoactive Drugs 34(2):145–162.
Barnet, R., and J. Cavanagh
1994   *Global Dreams: Imperial Corporations and the New World Order*. New York:
            Simon and Schuster.
Baum, L. F.
1990[1900]   *The Wonderful Wizard of Oz*. New York: Books of Wonder.
Bebow, J.
2004   Flood of Heroin Ravaging City. *Chicago Tribune*, January 30: 1.
Beck, J., and M. Rosenbaum
1994   *Pursuit of Ecstasy: The MDMA Experience*. New York: State University of
            New York.
Becker, H.
1963   *Outsiders: Studies in the Sociology of Deviance*. London: Free Press of Glencoe.
Becker, H.
1967   History, Culture, and Subjective Experience: An Exploration of the
            Social Bases of Drug-Induced Experiences. *Journal of Health and Social
            Behavior* 8:163–176.
Bell, R.
1971   *Social Deviance: A Substantive Analysis*. Homewood, IL: The Dorsey Press.
Bemmers, H., and D. Radler
1958   Teenage Attitudes. *Scientific American* 198(6):28–29.
Bennett, L., and P. Cook
1996   Alcohol and Drug Studies. In *Medical Anthropology*. C. Sargent and T.
            Johnson, eds. Pp. 235–251. Westport, CT: Praeger.
Bertram, E., and K. Sharpe
1996   Drug Abuse: Is the Cure Worse than the Crime—Candidates Lack
            Answers to Questions. *Hartford Courant*, September 26: C1, C4.

Best, J.
1983   Economic Interests and the Vindication of Deviance: Tobacco in Sev-
            enth-Century Europe. In *Drugs and Society*. M. Kelleher, B. MacMurray,
            and T. Shapiro, eds. Pp. 173–183. Dubuque, IA: Kendall/Hunt.
Betty, P., B. Holman, and V. Schiraldi
2000   *Poor Prescription: The Cost of Imprisoning Drug Offenders in the United States.*
            San Francisco: Center on Juvenile and Criminal Justice.
Bibeau, G.
1989   For a Biocultural Approach to AIDS, Dead Ends and New Leads.
            Paper presented at the Fifth International Conference on AIDS, Mont-
            real, Canada.
Blint, D.
2005   Teenager's Death Linked to Heroin. *Hartford Courant*, February 15, p. 1.
Bonné, J.
2001   Scourge of the Heartland. *MSNBC News*, January 2.
Bonnie, R., and C. Whitebread
1970   The Forbidden Fruit and the Tree of Knowledge: An Inquiry into the
            Legal History of American Marijuana Prohibition. *Virginia Law Review*
            56(6):971–1203.
Booth, M.
1996   *Opium: A History.* New York: St. Martins.
Booth, M.
1999   *The Dragon Syndicates: The Global Phenomenon of Triads.* New York: Car-
            roll & Graf.
Boumba, V., A. Mitselou, and T. Vougiouklakis
2004   Fatal Poisoning from Ingestion of Datura Stramonium Seeds. *Veterinary
            and Human Toxicology* 46(2):81–82.
Bourgois, P.
1995   *In Search of Respect: Selling Crack in El Barrio.* Cambridge: Cambridge Uni-
            versity Press.
Bourgois, P., M. Lettiere, and J. Quesada
1997   Social Misery and the Sanctions of Substance Abuse: Confronting HIV
            Risk among Homeless Heroin Addicts in San Francisco. *Social Problems*
            44(2):155–173.
Bourgois, P., B. Prince, and A. Moss
2004   The Everyday Violence of Hepatitis C among Young Women Who
            Inject Drugs in San Francisco. *Human Organization* 63(3):253–264.
Bovelle, E., and A. Taylor
1985   Conclusions and Implications. In *Life with Heroin: Voices from the Inner
            City*. B. Hanson, G. Beschner, J. Walters, and E. Bovelle, eds. Pp. 175–
            186. Lexington, MA: Lexington Books.
Bowser, B., E. Quimbey, and M. Singer
in press   *Communities Accessing Their AIDS Epidemics.* Lanham, MD: Lexington
            Books.
Brecher, E.
1972   *Licit and Illicit Drugs.* Boston: Little, Brown.
Brick, J.
2003   *Handbook of the Medical Consequences of Alcohol and Drug Abuse.* Bingham-
            ton, NY: The Haworth Press.

Brook, J., D. Brook, M. De La Rosa, M. Whiteman, and I. Montoya
1990   The Psychosocial Etiology of Adolescent Drug Use: A Family Interactional Approach. *Genetic, Social, and General Psychology Monographs* 116(2):111–267.

Brook, J., L. Richter, and M. Whiteman
2001   Risk and Protective Factors of Adolescent Drug Use: Implications for Prevention Programs. In *Handbook of Drug Abuse Prevention Theory and Practice*. W. Bukowski and Z. Sloboda, eds. Pp. 128–139. New York: Plenum Press.

Brook, J., M. Whiteman, and A. Gordon
1983   States of Drug Use in Adolescence. *Developmental Psychology* 19:269–277.

Brooks, J.
1952   *The Mighty Leaf.* Boston: Little, Brown.

Brown, C.
1965   *Manchild in the Promised Land.* New York: Penguin Books.

Brown, T.
2005a   Police Bust UP Crack Ring. *Hartford Courant,* February 1: 1–2.

Brown. T.
2005b   City Drug Ring Traced to Mexico. *Hartford Courant,* February 2: B3–B4.

Browning, F., and B. Garrett
1986   The CIA and the New Opium War. In *Culture and Politics of Drugs*. P. Park and W. Matveychuk, eds. Pp. 118–124. Dubuque, IA: Kendall/Hunt.

Buchanan, D., M. Singer, S. Shaw, W. Teng, T. Stopka, K. Khoshnood, and R. Heimer
2004   Syringe Access, HIV Risk, and AIDS in Massachusetts and Connecticut: The Health Implications of Public Policy. In *Unhealthy Health Policy: A Critical Anthropological Examination*. A. Castro and M. Singer, eds. Walnut Creek, CA: Altamira Press.

Buchert, R., R. Thomasius, F. Wilke, K. Petersen, B. Nebeling, J. Obrocki, O. Schulze, U. Schmidt, and M. Clausen
2004   A Voxel-Based PET Investigation of the Long-Term Effects of "Ecstasy" Consumption on Brain Serotonin Transporters. *American Journal of Psychiatry* 161(7):1181–1189.

Buckland, F.
2002   *Impossible Dance Club Culture and Queer World-Making.* Middletown, CT: Wesleyan University Press.

Budney, A., J. Hughes, B. Moore, and P. Novy
2001   Marijuana Abstinence Effects in Marijuana Smokers Maintained in their Home Environment. *Archives of General Psychiatry* 58(10):917–924.

Bureau of Justice Statistics
2004a   Drug Law Violations. Electronic document, http://www.ojp.usdoj.gov/bjs/dcf/enforce.htm, accessed December 21.

Bureau of Justice Statistics
2004b   Drug Law Violations. Electronic document, http://www.ojp.usdoj.gov/bjs/dcf/tables/salespos.htm, accessed December 21.

Bush, G. W.
2004   Message to the Congress of the United States. In *The National Drug Control Strategy*. Washington, DC: Office of National Drug Control Policy.

Byron, K.
2000   Trinity Students: Drug Issues Overlooked, Death of Senior a "Wake Up Call." *The Hartford Courant*, March 19: B1.

Byron, K., and D. Stacom
2004   Houses Held Forests of Pot. *The Hartford Courant*, September 17: 1, 8.

Calafat, A., P. Stocco, F. Mendes, J. Simon, G. van de Wijngaart, M. Suresa, A. Palmer, N. Maaiste, and P. Zavatti
1999   *Characteristics and Social Representations of Ecstasy in Europe.* Valencia, Spain: IREFREA.

Carlson, R., R. Falck, and H. Siegal
2000   Crack Cocaine Injection in the Heartland: An Ethnographic Perspective. *Medical Anthropology* 18(4):305–323.

Castillo, F.
1987   *Los Jinetes de la Cocaina.* Bogotá: Editorial Documentos Periodisticos.

Castro, A., and M. Singer, eds.
2004   *Unhealthy Health Policy: A Critical Anthropological Perspective.* Walnut Creek, CA: Altamira Press.

Centers for Disease Control and Prevention (CDC)
2001   *National Hepatitis C Prevention Strategy: A Comprehensive Strategy for the Prevention and Control of Hepatitis C Infection and its Consequences.* Atlanta: CDC, Division of Viral Health.

Chambers, C., and J. Inciardi
1974   Forecasts for the Future: Where We Are and Where We Are Going. In *Drugs and the Criminal Justice System.* J. Inciardi and C. Chambers, eds. Beverly Hills: Sage.

Chambliss, W.
1994   Why the U.S. Government is not Contributing to the Resolution of the Nation's Drug Problem. *International Journal of Health Services* 24(4):675–690.

Check, E.
2004   Psychedelic Drugs: The Ups and Downs of Ecstasy. *Nature* 429:126–128.

Chen J., K. Fullerton, and M. Flynn
2001   Necrotizing Fasciitis Associated with Injection Drug Use. *Clinical Infections and Diseases* 33(1):6–15.

Chien, A., M. Connors, and K. Fox
2000   The Drug War in Perspective. In *Dying for Growth.* J. Kim, J. Millen, A. Irwin, and J. Gershman, eds. Pp. 293–327. Monroe, ME: Common Courage Press.

Chien, I., D. Gerard, R. Lee, and E. Rosenfeld.
1964   *Road to H: Narcotics, Juvenile Delinquency, and Social Policy.* New York: Basic Books.

Chomsky, N.
1988   *The Culture of Terrorism.* Boston, MA: The South End Press.

Ciccarone, D., J. Bamberger, A. Kral, B. Edlin, C. Hobart, A. Moon, E. Murphy, P. Bourgois, H. Harris, and D. Young
2001   Soft Tissue Infections among Injection Drug Users—San Francisco, California, 1996–2000. *Morbidity and Mortality Weekly Review* 50:381–384.

Ciccarone, D., and P. Bourgois
2003   Explaining the Geographical Variation of HIV among Injection Drug Users in the United States. *Substance Use and Misuse* 38(14):2049–2063.

Clawson, P., and R. Lee
1998   *The Andean Cocaine Industry.* New York: St. Martin's Griffin.

Clinton, W.
1996   Transmittal Letter From the President. In *The National Drug Control Strategy: 1996*. Washington, DC: The White House.
Coffin, P.
1999   *Safer Injection Rooms*. New York: The Lindesmith Center.
Coffin, P., S. Galea, J. Ahern, A. Leon, D. Vlahov, and K. Tardiff
2003   Opiates, Cocaine and Alcohol Combinations in Accidental Drug Overdose Deaths in New York City, 1990–98. *Addiction* 98(6):739–747.
Cohen, R.
1999   *Tough Jews: Fathers, Sons and Gangster Dreams*. New York: Vintage Books.
Community Epidemiological Work Group
1998   *Epidemiologic Trends in Drug Abuse, vol. 1: Highlights and Executive Summary*. Rockville, MD: National Institute on Drug Abuse.
Community Epidemiology Work Group
2000   *Epidemiologic Trends in Drug Abuse, vol. 1: Proceedings*. Washington, DC: National Institutes of Health, Department of Health and Human Services.
Community Epidemiology Work Group
2001   *Epidemiologic Trends in Drug Abuse, vol. 1: Proceedings*. Washington, DC: National Institutes of Health, Department of Health and Human Services.
Community Epidemiology Work Group
2002   *Epidemiologic Trends in Drug Abuse, vol. 1: Proceedings*. Washington, DC: National Institutes of Health, Department of Health and Human Services.
Conrad, P., and J. Schneider
1980   *Deviance and Medicalization: From Badness to Sickness*. St. Louis: C. V. Mosby.
Constantine, T.
1996   Testimony before the Senate Caucus on International Narcotics Control, and the House Subcommittee on Coast Guard and Maritime Transportation, September 12.
Coomber, R., and N. South
2004   Drugs, Cultures and Controls in Comparative Perspective. In *Drug Use and Cultural Contexts "Beyond the West."* R. Coomber and N. South, eds. Pp. 13–26. London: Free Association Books.
Copeland, L., J. Budd, J. Robertson, and R. Elton
2004   Changing Patterns in Causes of Death in a Cohort of Injecting Drug Users, 1980–2001. *Archives of Internal Medicine* 164(11):1214–1220.
Corby, N., and R. Wolitski
1997   *Community HIV Prevention*. Long Beach, CA: Statewide Technical Books.
Courtwright, D.
1982   *Dark Paradise*. Cambridge: Harvard University Press.
Courtwright, D.
2001   *Forces of Habit: Drugs and the Making of the Modern World*. Cambridge: Harvard University Press.
Courtwright, D., H. Joseph, and D. Des Jarlais
1989   *Addicts Who Survived: An Oral History of Narcotic Use in America, 1923–1965*. Knoxville: University of Tennessee Press.
Dai, B.
1937   *Addiction in Chicago*. Montclair, NJ: Patterson Smith.

Davidson, J.
1999   The Drug War's Color Line: Black Leaders Shift Stances on Sentencing. *The Nation* 269(8):42–43.

Dee, J.
1999   New Face of Heroin: First-Time Users Getting Younger. *Hartford Courant*, November 15: A1, A6.

Dei, K.
2002   *Ties that Bind: Youth and Drugs in a Black Community.* Prospect Heights, IL: Waveland Press.

De Quincey, T.
1822   *Confessions of an Opium Eater.* New York: F. M. Lupton.

Des Jarlais, D.
2000   Prospects for a Public Health Perspective on Psychoactive Drug Use. *American Journal of Public Health* 90:335–337.

Des Jarlais, D., H. Hagen, S. Friedman, P. Friedmann, D. Goldberg, M. Frischer, S. Green, K. Tunving, B. Ljungberg, A. Wodak, M. Ross, D. Purchase, M. Millson, and T. Myers
1995   Maintaining Low HIV Seroprevalence in Populations of Injecting Drug Users. *Journal of the American Medical Association* 274(15):1226–1231.

Des Jarlais, D., M. Marmor, P. Friedmann, S. Titus, E. Aviles, S. Deren, L. Torian, D. Glebatis, C. Murrill, E. Monterroso, and S. Friedman
2000   HIV Incidence among Injection Drug Users in New York City, 1992–1997: Evidence for a Declining Epidemic. *American Journal of Public Health* 90(3):352–359

Díaz, R.
1998   *Latino Gay Men and HIV.* New York: Routledge.

Donoghoe, M., and A. Wodak
1998   Health and Social Consequences of Injecting Drug Use. In *Drug Injecting and HIV Infection.* G. Stimson, D. Des Jarlais, and A. Ball, eds. Pp 42–57. London: UCL Press.

Drake, St. C., and H. Cayton
1970   *Black Metropolis: A Study of Negro Life in a Northern City, vol. 2.* New York: Harcourt, Brace and World.

Drug Abuse Council
1980   *The Facts About "Drug Abuse."* New York: Free Press.

Drug Abuse Warning Network
1997   *Drug Abuse Warning Network Survey.* Rockville, MD: DHHS Publications.

Drug Enforcement Administration (DEA)
2002   *Drug Intelligence Brief: OxyContin Pharmaceutical Diversion.* Washington, DC: Office of Domestic Intelligence, U.S. Drug Enforcement Administration.

Duke, M., W. Teng, S. Clair, H. Salaheen, and M. Singer
2004   Patterns of Intimate Partner Violence among Drug Using Women. *Journal of Free Inquiry in Creative Sociology* (in press).

Duke, M., W. Teng, J. Simmons, and M. Singer
2003   Structural and Interpersonal Violence among Puerto Rican Drug Users. *Practicing Anthropology* 25(3):28–31.

Duzan, M.
1994   *Death Beat.* New York: Harper-Collins.

Eaton, V.
1888   How the Opium Habit is Acquired. *Popular Science* 33:665–666.
Eiserman, J., S. Diamond, and J. Schensul
in press   "Rollin' on E": A Qualitative Analysis of Ecstasy Use among Inner-City
             Adolescents and Young Adults. *Journal of Ethnicity and Substance Abuse* 4(2).
Eiserman, J., M. Singer, J. Schensul, and L. Broomhall
2003   Methodological Challenges to Club Drug Research. *Practicing Anthropol-
             ogy* 25(3):19–22.
Elkin, D.
1978   Understanding the Young Adolescent. *Adolescence* 13:127–134.
Ellison, M.
2003   Authoritative Knowledge and Single Women's Unintentional Pregnan-
             cies, Abortions, Adoptions, and Single Motherhood: Social Stigma and
             Structural Violence. *Medical Anthropology Quarterly* 17(3):322–347.
Elwood, W.
1998   *"Fry": A Study of Adolescents' Use of Embalming Fluid with Marijuana and
             Tobacco.* Austin: Texas Commission on Alcohol and Drugs.
Emboden, W.
1974   *Narcotic Plants: Hallucinogens, Stimulants, Inebriants, and Hypnotics, Their
             Origins and Uses.* London: Studio Vista.
Engels, F.
1969[1845] *The Condition of the Working Class.* London: Granata.
Epele, M.
2003   Changing Cocaine Use Practices: Neo-liberalism, HIV-AIDS, and Death
             in an Argentine Shantytown. *Substance Use and Misuse* 38(9):1189–1216.
Epstein, E.
1977   *Agency of Fear.* New York: G. P. Putnam's.
Farmer, P.
1999   *Infections and Inequality: The Modern Plagues.* Berkeley: University of Cali-
             fornia Press.
Farmer, P., M. Connors, and J. Simmons
1996   *Women, Poverty and AIDS.* Monroe, ME: Common Courage Press.
Feldman, H., and M. Aldrich
1990   The Role of Ethnography in Substance Abuse Research and Public Pol-
             icy: Historical Precedent and Future Prospects. In *The Collection and
             Interpretation of Data from Hidden Populations.* E. Lambert, ed. Pp. 12–30.
             NIDA Research Monograph #98. Rockville, MD: National Institute on
             Drug Abuse.
Fischer, B.
1995   Drugs, Communities and "Harm Reduction" in Germany: The New
             Relevance of "Public Health" Principles in Local Responses. *Journal of
             Public Health Policy* 16(4):389–411.
Fleisher, M.
1995   *Beggars and Thieves: Lives of Urban Street Criminals.* Madison: The Univer-
             sity of Wisconsin Press.
Fleisher, M.
1998   *Dead End Kids: Gang Girls and the Boys They Know.* Madison: The Univer-
             sity of Wisconsin Press.

Forero, J., and T. Weiner
2002   Latin American Poppy Fields Undermine U.S. Drug Battle. *New York Times*, June 8: 1.
French, M., J. Mauskopf, J. Teague, and E. Roland
1996   Estimating the Dollar Value of Health Outcomes from Drug Abuse Interventions. *Medical Care* 34:890–910.
French, M., and G. Zarkin
1992   Effects of Drug Abuse Treatment on Legal and Illegal Earnings. *Contemporary Policy Issues* 10:98–110.
Fresia, J.
1988   *Toward an American Revolution: Exposing the Constitution and Other Illusions*. Boston: South End Press.
Friedman, S., B. Jose, B. Stephenson, A. Neaigus, M. Goldstein, P. Mota, R. Curtis, and G. Ildefonso
1998   Multiple Racial/Ethnic Subordination and HIV among Drug Injectors. In *The Political Economy of AIDS*. M. Singer, ed. Pp. 105–128. Amityville, NY: Baywood.
Friedman, S., R. Curtis, A. Neaigus, B. Jose, and D. Des Jarlais
1999   *Social Networks, Drug Injectors Lives, and HIV/AIDS*. New York: Kluwer Academic.
Frontline
2000a   Drug Wars. Electronic document, http://www.pbs.org/wgbh/pages/frontline/shows/drugs/interviews/ochoajorge.html
Frontline
2000b   Drug Wars. Electronic document, http://www.pbs.org/wgbh/pages/frontline/shows/drugs/interviews/toro.html.
Frontline
2000c   Drug Wars. Electronic document, http://www.pbs.org/wgbh/pages/frontline/shows/drugs/interviews/ochoajdo.html.
Gamella, J.
1994   The Spread of Intravenous Drug Use and AIDS in a Neighborhood in Spain. *Medical Anthropology Quarterly* 8(2):131–160.
German, D., and C. Sterk
2002   Looking Beyond Stereotypes: Exploring Variations among Crack Users. *Journal of Psychoactive Drugs* 34(4):383–400.
Gerstein, D., R. Johnson, H. Harwood, D. Fountain, N. Suter, and K. Mallory
1994   *Evaluating Recovery Services: The California Drug and Alcohol Treatment Assessment (CALDATA)*. Sacramento: State of California, Health and Welfare Agency, Department of Alcohol and Drug Programs, Contract No. 92–00110.
Gilbert, L., N. El-Bassel, V. Rajah, A. Foleno, J. Fontdevila, V. Frye, and B. Richman
2000   The Converging Epidemics of Mood-Altering-Drug Use, HIV, HCV, and Partner Violence. *The Mount Sinai Journal of Medicine* 67(5 & 6):452–464.Gill, J., J. Hayes, I. deSouza, E. Marker, and M. Stajic
Gill, J., J. Hayes, I. deSouza, E. Marker, and M. Stajic
2002   Ecstasy (MDMA) Deaths in New York City: A Case Series and Review of the Literature. *Journal of Forensic Science* 47(1):121–126.

Girodin, P., and T. Groat
1989   AIDS among Adolescent Subgroups: Inferences from Research and
            Theory on Delinquency and Sexuality. In *Troubled Adolescents and HIV
            Infection*. J. Woodruff, D. Doherty, and J. Athey, eds. Pp. 14–36. Wash-
            ington, DC: Child and Adolescent Services System.
Gladwell, M.
2000   *The Tipping Point*. Boston: Little Brown and Company.
Glick, R.
1983   Demoralization and Addiction: Heroin in the Chicago Puerto Rican
            Community. *Journal of Psychoactive Drugs* 15:281–292.
Glick, R.
1990   Survival, Income, and Status: Drug Dealing in the Chicago Puerto
            Rican Community. In *Drugs in Hispanic Communities*. R. Glick and J.
            Moore, eds. Pp. 77–102. New Brunswick, NJ: Rutgers University Press.
Goldstein, P.
1979   *Drugs and Prostitution*. Lexington, KY: Lexington Press.
Goldstein, P.
1985   The Drugs-Violence Nexus: a Tripartite Conceptual Framework. *Journal
            of Drug Issues* 14:493–506.
Golub, A., and B. Johnson
1966   The Crack Epidemic: Empirical Findings Support an Hypothesized Dif-
            fusion of Innovation Process. *Socioeconomic Planning Science* 30:221–231.
Golub, A., and B. Johnson
1997   *Crack's Decline: Some Surprises Across U.S. Cities*. Research in Brief (NCJ
            165707). Washington, DC: National Institute of Justice.
Gomez, J., and A. Rodriguez
1989   An Evaluation of the Results of a Drug Sample Analysis. *Bulletin of Nar-
            cotics* 41(1–2):121–126.
Goode, E.
1984   *Drugs in American Society*. New York: Alfred A. Knopf.
Goode, E.
2005   *Drugs in American Society*. 6th edition. New York: McGraw-Hill.
Gorman, M., and R. Carroll
2000   Substance Abuse and HIV: Considerations with Regard to Methamphet-
            amines and Other Recreational Drugs for Nursing Practice and
            Research. *Journal of the Association of Nurses in AIDS Care* 11(2):51–62.
Gosch, M., and R. Hammer
1974   *The Last Testament of Lucky Luciano*. Boston: Little, Brown.
Grant, B.
1997   The Influence of Comorbid Major Depression and Substance Use Dis-
            orders on Alcohol and Drug Treatment: Results of a National Survey. In
            Treatment of Drug-Dependent Individuals with Comorbid Mental Disorders.
            NIDA Monograph 172:4–15.
Gray, M.
2000   *Drug Crazy*. New York: Routledge.
Green, E.
1914   Psychoses among Negroes—A Comparative Study. *Journal of Nervous
            and Mental Disease* 41:697–708.

Greenberg, M., F. Popper, D. Schnieder, and B. West
1993   Community Organizing to Prevent TOADS in the United States. *Community Development Journal* 28:55–65.

Gruber, A., H. Pope, J. Hudson, and T. Yurgelun-Todd
2003   Attributes of Long-term Heavy Cannabis Users: A Case-control Study. *Psychological Medicine* 33(8):1415–1422.

Gutierrez, P., and E. Torriero
2000   Amid Coca Wars: In Colombia, Plant a Way of Life, and a U.S. Target. *Hartford Courant*, September 17: 1, 14, 16.

Guttman, W.
1996   The War No One Wants to Win. *Z Magazine*, January: 1–5.

Haemming, R.
1995   Harm Reduction in Bern: From Outreach to Heroin Maintenance. *Bulletin of the New York Academy of Medicine* 72(2):371–379.

Hahne, S., N. Crowcroft, and J. White
2003   Cluster of Cases of Tetanus in Injecting Drug users in England: European Alert. *Eurosurveillance Weekly*, November 7: 1.

Hall, S.
2002   Teen Abuse of Cold Drug on the Rise. *The Detroit News*, March 12: 1.

Hamilton, R., J. Perrone, R. Hoffman, F. Henretig, E. Karkevandian, S. Marcus, R. Shih, B. Blok, and K. Nordenholz
2000   A Descriptive Study of an Epidemic of Poisoning Caused by Heroin Adulterated with Scopolamine. *Journal of Toxicology and Clinical Toxicology* 38(6):597–608.

Hammersley, R., F. Kahn, and J. Ditton
2002   *Ecstasy and the Rise of the Chemical Generation*. Reading: Harwood.

Hanson, B., G. Beschner, J. Walters, and E. Bovelle
1985   *Life with Heroin*. Lexington, MA: Lexington Books.

Harrison, P. M., and A. J. Beck
2003   *Prisoners in 2002* (NCJ 200248). Washington, DC: Bureau of Justice Statistics.

Harrison, P. M., and J. C. Karberg
2004   *Prisoners and Jail Inmates at Midyear 2003* (NCJ 203947). Washington, DC: National Institute of Justice.

Havlik, D., and K. Nolte
2000   Fatal "Crack" Cocaine Ingestion in an Infant. *American Journal of Forensic Medical Pathology* 21(3):245–248.

Hayner, G.
2002   MDMA Misrepresentation: An Unresolved Problem for Ecstasy Users. *Journal of Psychoactive Drugs* 34(2):195–198.

Haynie, D. L.
2001   Delinquent Peers Revisited: Does Network Structure Matter? *American Journal of Sociology* 106(4):1013–1057.

Heath, D.
1988   Emerging Anthropological Theory and Models of Alcohol Use and Alcoholism. In *Theories on Alcoholism*. C. Douglas, B. D. Chaudron, and A. Wilkinson, eds. Pp. 353–410. Toronto: Addiction Research Foundation.

Heilig, S.
2002   The State of Ecstasy: MDMA—Science and Policy. *Journal of Psychoactive Drugs* 34(2):129–131.
Heimer, R.
1998   Syringe Exchange Programs: Lowering the Transmission of Syringe-Borne Diseases and Beyond. *Public Health Reports* 113(Supplement 1):67–74.
Helmer, J.
1983   Blacks and Cocaine. In *Drugs and Society.* M. Kelleher, B. MacMurray, and T. Shapiro, eds. Pp. 14–29. Dubuque, IA: Kendall/Hunt.
Heston, L., and R. Heston
2000   *The Medical Casebook of Adolf Hitler.* New York: Cooper Square Press.
Higgins, D., K. O'Reilly, N. Tashima, C. Crain, C. Beeker, G. Goldbaum, C. Elifson, C. Galavotti, and C. Guenther-Grey
1996   Using Formative Research to Lay the Foundation for Community-Led HIV Prevention Efforts. *Public Health Reports* 111(Supplement 1):28–35.
Hills, S.
1980   *Demystifying Social Deviance.* New York: McGraw-Hill.
Holland, J., L. Nelson, P. Ravikumar, and E. William
1998   Embalming Fluid-Soaked Marijuana: New High or New Guise for PCP? *Journal of Psychoactive Drugs* 30(2):215–219.
Horst, E., R. Bennett, and O. Barrett Jr.
1991   Recurrent Rhabdomyolysis in Association with Cocaine Use. *South Medical Journal* 84(2):269–270.
Iiyama, P., S. Nishi, and B. Johnson
1976   *Drug Use and Abuse among U.S. Minorities: An Annotated Bibliography.* New York: Praeger.
Inciardi, J.
1986   *The War on Drugs: Heroin, Cocaine, Crime, and Public Policy.* Mountain View, CA: Mayfield.
Inciardi, J.
1992   *The War on Drugs II.* Mountain View, CA: Mayfield.
Inciardi, J.
1993   *The War on Drugs: Heroin, Cocaine, Crime, and Public Policy.* 2nd edition. Mountain View, CA: Mayfield.
Inciardi, J., D. Lockwood, and A. Pottieger
1993   *Women and Crack-Cocaine.* New York: Macmillan.
Inciardi, J., D. McBride, J. Platt, and S. Baxter
1993   Injection Drug Users, Incarceration, and HIV: Some Legal and Social Service Delivery Issues. In *Handbook on Risk of AIDS: Injection Drug Users and Sexual Partners.* B. Brown and G. Beschner, eds. Pp. 336–351. Westport, CT: Greenwood Press.
Insley, B., S. Grufferman, and H. Ayliffe
1986   Thallium Poisoning in Cocaine Abusers. *American Journal of Emergency Medicine* 4(6):545–548.
Institute of Medicine
1982   *Marijuana and Health.* Washington, DC: National Academy Press.
Jacobs, B.
1999   *Dealing Crack.* Boston: Northeastern University Press.

James, W., and S. Johnson
1996 *Doin' Drugs: Patterns of African American Addiction.* Austin: University of Texas Press.

Jansen, K.
2000 A Review of the Nonmedical Use of Ketamine: Use, Users, and Consequences. *Journal of Psychoactive Drugs* 32(4):419–433.

Jatlow, P., J. Elsworth, C. Bradberry, G. Winger, J. Taylor, R. Russell, and R. Roth
1991 Cocaethylene: A Neuropharmacologically Active Metabolite Associated with Concurrent Cocaine-ethanol Ingestion. *Life Sciences* 48:1787–1794.

Jessor, R.
1979 Marijuana: A Review of Recent Psychosocial Research. In *Handbook of Drug Abuse.* R. DuPont, A. Goldstein, and J. McDonnell, eds. Washington, DC: U.S. Government Printing Office.

Jessor, R., and S. Jessor
1977 *Problem Behavior and Psychological Development, a Longitudinal Study of Youth.* New York: Academic Press.

Johnson, B.
1973 *Marihuana Users and Drug Subcultures.* New York: John Wiley and Sons.

Johnson, B.
1989 Drug Abuse in the Inner City: Impact on Hard-drug Users and the Community. In *Drugs and Crime.* J. Wilson and M. Tonry, eds. Chicago: University of Chicago Press.

Johnson, B., P. Goldstein, E. Preble, J. Schmeidler, D. Lipton, B. Spunt, and T. Miller
1985 *Taking Care of Business: The Economics of Crime by Heroin Abusers.* Lexington, MA: Lexington Books.

Johnson, B., and A. Golub
1998 Trends in Heroin Use among Manhattan Arrestees from the Heroin and Crack Eras. In *Heroin in the Age of Crack-Cocaine.* J. Inciardi and L. Harrison, eds. Pp. 109–130. Thousand Oaks, CA: Sage.

Johnson, B., and A. Manwar
1991 Towards a Paradigm of Drug Eras: Previous Drug Eras Help to Model the Crack Epidemic in New York City during the 1990s. Presented at the American Society of Criminology, San Francisco.

Johnston, L., P. O'Malley, and J. Bachman
1997 *National Survey Results on Drug Use from the Monitoring the Future Study.* Rockville, MD: National Institute on Drug Abuse.

Join Together
2001 Report: Heroin Use on the Rise. Electronic document, http://www.jointogether.org/sa/news/summaries/reader/0,1854,266290,00.html.

Joselit, J.
1983 *Our Gang: Jewish Crime and the New York Jewish Community (1900–1940).* Bloomington: Indiana University Press

Kaa, E.
1994 Impurities, Adulterants and Diluents of Illicit Heroin. Changes During a 12-year Period. *Forensic Science International* 64(2–3):171–179.

Kandel, D., and R. Jessor
2002 The Gateway Hypothesis Revisited. In *Stages and Pathways of Drug Involvement.* D. Kandel, ed. Pp. 365–372. Cambridge: Cambridge University Press.

Kandel, D., and K. Yamaguchi
1993   From Beer to Crack: Developmental Patterns of Drug Involvement. *American Journal of Public Health* 83(6):851–855.
Katcher, L.
1959   *The Big Bankroll: The Life and Times of Arnold Rothstein.* New York: Arlington House.
Kaufman, M.
2003   Worried Pain Doctors Decry Prosecutions. *Washington Post*: A1.
Kent, J.
1996   The Ketamine Konundrum. Electronic document, http://www.erowid.org/chemicals/ketamine/ketamine_info3.shtml.
Khantzian, E.
1985   The Self-Medication Hypothesis of Addictive Disorders: Focus on Heroin and Cocaine Dependence. *American Journal of Psychiatry* 142:1259–1264.
Khantzian, E., J. Mack, and A. Schatzberg
1974   Heroin Use as an Attempt to Cope: Clinical Observation. *American Journal of Psychiatry* 131:160–164.
Kim, R.
2004   Manslaughter Charge in Girl's Ecstasy Death. *San Francisco Chronicle*, June 25: 14.
Kimura, A., J. Higa, R. Levin, G. Simpson, Y. Vargas, and D. Vugia
2004   Outbreak of Necrotizing Fasciitis Due to Clostridium Sordellii among Black-tar Heroin Users. *Clinical and Infectious Disease* 38(9):87–91.
Kleber, H.
1996   Outpatient Detoxification from Opiates. *Primary Psychiatry* 1:42–52.
Knipe, E.
1995   *Culture, Society and Drugs.* Prospect Heights, IL: Waveland Press.
Koester, S., and L. Hoffer
1994   "Indirect Sharing": Additional HIV Risks Associated with Drug Injection. *AIDS and Public Policy Journal* 2:100–104.
Kozel, N.
1997   Foreword. *Epidemiologic Trends in Drug Abuse.* Vol. II. Proceedings. Community Epidemiological Work Group. Rockville, MD: National Institute on Drug Abuse.
Kozel, N., Z. Sloboda, and M. De La Rosa, eds.
1995   *Epidemiology of Inhalant Abuse: An International Perspective.* NIDA Research Monograph 148, pp. 8–28. DHHS Publication No. NIH 95-3831. Washington, DC: U.S. Government Printing Office.
Kruger, H.
1976   *The Great Heroin Coup.* Boston: South End Press.
KVG
2002   Love in Abandoned Buildings. *Real Change: Puget Sound's Newspaper of the Poor and Homeless*, June 8: 1.
Lankenau, S., and M. Clatts
2002   Ketamine Injection among High-risk Youth: Preliminary Findings from New York City. *Journal of Drug Issues* 32(3):893–905.
Leary, T.
1988   *Politics of Psychopharmacology.* Berkeley: Ronnin Press.

Leshner, A.
1999   Science-based Views of Drug Addiction and its Treatment. *Journal of the American Medical Association* 282(14):1314–1316.
Leshner, A.
2001   Addiction is a Brain Disease. *Issues in Science and Technology* 17(3):75–80.
Levins, H.
1986   The Shifting Source of Opium. In *Culture and Politics of Drugs*. P. Park and W. Matveychuk, eds. Pp. 124–125. Dubuque, IA: Kendall/Hunt.
Liebow, E.
1967   *Tally's Corner.* Boston: Little, Brown.
Lilly, J.
1978   *The Scientist: A Novel Autobiography.* New York: Bantam Books.
Lindesmith, A.
1968   *Addiction and Opiates.* Chicago: Aldine.
Lindesmith, A., A. Strauss, and N. Denzin
1975   *Social Psychology.* Hinsdale, IL: The Dryden Press.
Logan T. K., C. Leukefeld, and D. Farabee
1998   Sexual and Drug Use Behaviors among Women Crack Users: Implications for Prevention. *AIDS Education and Prevention* 10(4):327–340.
Lupsha, P.
1992   Drug Lords and Narco-Corruption: The Players Change but the Game Continues. In *War on Drugs: Studies in the Failure of U.S. Narcotics Policy.* A. McCoy and E. Block, eds. Pp. 177–195. Boulder: Westview Press.
Lurie, P.
1997   An Opportunity Lost: HIV Infections Associated with Lack of a National Needle-Exchange Programmes in the USA. *Lancet* 349:604–608.
Lynskey, M., A. Heath, K. Bucholz, W. Slutske, P. Madden, E. Nelson, D. Statham, and N. Martin
2003   Escalation of Drug Use in Early-onset Cannabis Users vs. Co-twin Controls. *Journal of the American Medical Association* 289(4):427–433.
MacDonald, J.
2004   White House Battling Medical Marijuana Bids. *Hartford Courant*, October 24: 1, 6.
Malcolm X
1965   *The Autobiography of Malcolm X.* New York: Grove Press.
Mansergh, G., G. Colfax, G. Marks, M. Rader, R. Guzman, and S. Buchbinder
2001   The Circuit Party Men's Health Survey: Findings and Implications for Gay and Bisexual Men. *American Journal of Public Health* 91:953–958.
Marcus, G., and M. Fischer
1986   *Anthropology as Cultural Critique.* Chicago: The University of Chicago Press.
Markou, A., T. Kosten, and G. Koob
1998   Neurobiological Similarities in Depression and Drug Dependence: A Self-Medication Hypothesis. *Neuropsychopharmacology* 18:135–174.
Massing, M.
1999   It is Time for Realism. *The Nation*, September 20: 11–15.
Matthee, R.
1995   Exotic Substances: The Introduction and Global Spread of Tobacco, Coffee, Cocoa, Tea, and Distilled Liquor, Sixteenth to Eighteenth Cen-

turies. In *Drugs and Narcotics in History.* R. Porter and M. Teich, eds. Pp. 24–51. Cambridge: Cambridge University Press.

Mauss, M.
2000   *The Gift: The Form and Reason for Exchange in Archaic Societies.* New York: W. W. Norton.

McCoy, A., C. Read, and L. Adams
1986   The Mafia Connection. In *Culture and Politics of Drugs.* P. Park and W. Matveychuk, eds. Pp. 110–118. Dubuque, IA: Kendall/Hunt.

McGee, L., and M. Newcomb
1992   General Deviance Syndrome: Expanded Hierarchical Evaluations at Four Stages from Early Adolescence to Adulthood. *Journal of Consulting and Clinical Psychology* 60(5):766–776.

McInerney, A.
2000   Colombia: Death Squads "Defend Business Freedom." *Workers World*, September 21: 14.

McWhirter, C., and J. Young
2004   Meth Abuse Elevates HIV Crisis for Gays. *Atlanta Journal-Constitution*: 1, 8.

Merline, A., P. O'Malley, J. Schulenberg, J. Bachman, and L. Johnston
2004   Substance Use among Adults 35 Years of Age: Prevalence, Adulthood Predictors, and Impact of Adolescent Substance Use. *Journal of the American Public Health Association* 94(1):96–102.

Metropolitan News-Enterprise
2002   Undercover Officers Arrest 136 Drug Dealers at Local High Schools: 8.

Metzger, D., H. Navaline, and G. Woody
1998   Drug Abuse Treatment as AIDS Prevention. *Public Health Reports* 113(Supplement 1):97–106.

Metzger, D., G. Woody, A. McLellan, C. O'Brien, P. Druly, and H. Navaline
1993   Human Immunodeficiency Virus Seroconversion among In- and Out-of-Treatment Intravenous Drug Users: An 18-month Prospective Follow-Up. *Journal of Acquired Immune Deficiency Syndromes* 6:1049–1056.

Miles, M., and A. Huberman
1994   *Qualitative Data Analysis: An Expanded Sourcebook.* 2nd edition. Thousand Oaks, CA: Sage.

Miller, J.
1983   *National Survey on Drug Abuse: Main Findings.* Rockville, MD: National Institute on Drug Abuse.

Miller, N.
1990   A Study of Violent Behaviors Associated with Cocaine Use. *Annals of Clinical Psychiatry* 2:67–71.

Miller, H., C. Turner, and L. Moses
1990   *AIDS: The Second Decade.* Washington, DC: National Academy Press.

Mintz, S.
1985   *Sweetness and Power.* New York: Penguin Books.

Mirken, B.
1997   Danger: Possibly Fatal Interactions Between Ritonavir and "Ecstasy," and Some Other Psychoactive Drugs. *AIDS Treat News*, February 21: 5.

Moini, S., and T. Hammett
1990   *1989 Update: AIDS in Correctional Facilities.* Washington, DC: Office of Justice Programs, National Institute of Justice.

Monitoring the Future Study
1997   *National Survey Results from The Monitoring the Future Study.* Washington, DC: U.S. Department of Health and Health and Human Services.

Moore, J.
1978   *Homeboys: Gangs, Drugs, and Prison in the Barrios of Los Angeles.* Philadelphia: Temple University Press.

Morabia, A.
1996   From Disease Surveillance to the Surveillance of Risk Factors. *American Journal of Public Health* 86(5):625–627.

Murphy, S., and M. Rosenbaum
1999   *Pregnant Women on Drugs.* New Brunswick: Rutgers University Press.

Musto, D.
1987   *The American Disease: Origins of Narcotic Control.* New York: Oxford University Press.

Muwakkil, S.
1996   Politics By Other Means. *In These Times*, March 18: 20–21.

Nadelmann, E.
1989   Drug Prohibition in the United States: Costs, Consequences and Alternatives. *Science* 245:939–947.

Nadelmann, E.
2003   Speech, Wilson School, Princeton University, October 2.

National Institute on Drug Abuse
2001   *Teen Drug Abuse: High School and Youth Trends—2000 Monitoring the Future Study.* Washington, DC: U.S. Government Printing Office.

National Institute on Drug Abuse
2004a   *2003 Monitoring the Future Study* (revised April 2004). Electronic document, http://www.nida.nih.gov/Infofax/pcp.html.

National Institute on Drug Abuse
2004b   *MDMA Abuse (Ecstasy): What Does MDMA Do to the Brain?* NIDA Research Report Series. Washington, DC: U.S. Government Print Office.

Neaigus, A.
1998   Trends in the Noninjected Use of Heroin and Factors Associated with the Transition to Injection. In *Heroin in the Age of Crack Cocaine.* J. Inciardi and L. Harrison, eds. Pp. 131–159. Thousand Oaks, CA: Sage.

Neale, J.
2000   Suicidal Intent in Non-fatal Illicit Drug Overdose. *Addiction* 95(1):85–93.

Needle, R., S. Coyle, J. Normand, E. Lambert, and H. Cesari
1998   HIV Prevention with Drug-Using Populations—Current Status and Future Prospects: Introduction and Overview. *Public Health Reports* 113(Supplement 1): 4–18.

Nemoto, T., D. Operario, and T. Soma
2002   Risk Behaviors of Filipino Methamphetamine Users in San Francisco: Implications for Prevention and Treatment of Drug Users. *Public Health Reports* 117(1):30–38.

New York Times
1989   Text of President's Speech on National Drug Control Strategy. September 6: B6.

New York Times Magazine
1975   Cocaine the Champagne of Drugs. January 6: 14.

Newsday
2004   AIDS Infections Soaring, U.N. Says. *Hartford Courant*, July 7: 5.
O'Donnell, J., and J. Jones
1968   Diffusion of Intravenous Techniques among Narcotic Addicts in the
            U.S. *Journal of Health and Social Behavior* 9:120–130.
Offer, D., E. Ostrov, and K. Howard
1981   *The Adolescent: A Psychological Self-Portrait*. New York: Basic Books.
Office of the National Drug Control Policy (ONDCP)
2001   *The National Drug Control Strategy: 2001*. Annual Report. Washington,
            DC: The White House.
Office of National Drug Control Policy (ONDCP)
2004   *The National Drug Control Strategy: 2004*. Annual Report. Washington,
            DC: The White House.
O'Reilly, K., and D. Higgins
1991   AIDS Community Demonstration Projects for HIV Prevention among
            Hard-to-Reach Groups. *Public Health Reports* 106:714–720.
Orjuela, L.
1990   Nacotrafico y Poltica en la Decada de los Ochenta: Entre la Represion y
            el Dialogo. In *Nacotrafco en Colombia: Demensiones Politicas, Economicas,
            Juridicas e Internacionales*. C. Arrieta, ed. Pp. 199–276. Bogota: Tercer
            Muno Editores-Ediciones Uniandes.
Ortner, S.
1991   Reading America: Preliminary Notes on Class and Culture. In *Recaptur-
            ing Anthropology: Working in the Present*. R. Fox, ed. Pp. 163–190. Santa
            Fe: School of American Research Press.
Ouellet, L., W. Wiebel, and A. Jimenez
1995   Team Research Methods for Studying Intranasal Heroin Use and its
            HIV Risks. In *Qualitative Methods in Drug Abuse and HIV Research*. E.
            Lambert and R. Ashery, eds. Pp. 182–211. NIDA Research Monograph
            157. Rockville, MD: National Institute on Drug Abuse.
Page, J. B.
2004   Drug Use. In *Encyclopedia of Medical Anthropology*. C. Ember and M.
            Ember, eds. Pp. 374–383. New York: Kluwer Academic.
Pappas, G.
1989   *The Magic City*. Ithaca, NY: Cornell University Press.
Paschane, D., D. Fisher, H. Cagle, and A. Fenaughty
1998   Gonorrhea among Drug Users: An Alaskan Versus a National Sample.
            The American Journal of Drug and Alcohol Use 24(2):285–298.
Passaro, D., S. Werner, J. McGee, W. MacKenzie, and D. Vugia
1988   Wound Botulism Associated with Black Tar Heroin among Injecting
            Drug Users. *Journal of the American Medical Association* 280(17):1479–1480.
Partridge, W.
1973   *The Hippie Ghetto: The Natural History of a Subculture*. New York: Holt,
            Rinehart and Winston.
People
1978   In Showbiz, the Celebs with a Nose for What's New Say the New High
            is Cocaine, January 6: 16.
Pepper, A., and L. Pepper
1994   *Straight Life*. New York: Da Capo Press.

Pollan, M.
1999   A Very Fine Line. *New York Times Magazine*, September 12: 27–28.
Preble, E.
1980   El Barrio Revisited. Paper presented at the annual meeting of the Society for Applied Anthropology, Denver.
Preble, E., and J. Casey
1969   Taking Care of Business: The Heroin User's Life on the Streets. *International Journal of the Addictions* 4(1):1–24.
Price, J.
1964   The Economic Growth of the Chesapeake and the European Market, 1697–1775. *Journal of Economic History* 24:496–511.
Pugliese, A., L. Andronico, L. Gennero, G. Paliano, F. Gallo, and D. Torre
2002a   Cervico-Vaginal Dysplasia-Papillomavirus-Induced and HIV-1 Infection: Role of Correlated Markers for Prognostic Evaluation. *Cell Biochemistry and Function* 20(3):233–236.
Pugliese, A., D. Torre, A. Saini, G. Pagliano, G. Gallo, P. Pistono, and G. Paggi
2002b   Cytokine Detection in HIV-1/HHV-8 Co-Infected Subjects. *Cell Biochemistry and Function* 20(3):191–194.
Rajkumar, A., and M. French
1996   Drug Abuse, Crime, Costs and the Economic Benefits of Treatment. Unpublished Manuscript, University of Maryland.
Ratner, M.
1993   Sex, Drugs, and Public Policy: Studying and Understanding the Sex-for-Crack Phenomenon. In *Crack Pipe as Pimp: An Ethnographic Investigation of Sex-for-Crack Exchanges*. M. Ratner, ed. Pp. 1–36. New York: Lexington Books.
Reinarman, C., and H. Levine, eds.
1997   The Crack Attack: Politics and Media in the Crack Scare. In *Crack in America: Demon Drugs and Social Justice*. Pp. 18–51. Berkeley: University of California Press.
Rettig, R.
1999[1977]   *Manny: A Criminal-Addict's Story.* Prospect Heights, IL: Waveland Press.
Reuter, P.
1996   The Mismanagement of Illegal Drug Markets. In *The Underground Economy.* S. Pozo, ed. Kalamazoo, MI: Upjohn Institute for Employment Research.
Reuters News Service
2004   Inhalant Abuse Rebounds among U.S. youths: Teens Experimenting with Glue, Nail Polish, Report Finds, March 18.
Ricaurte, G., J. Yuan, G. Hartzidimitriou, B. Cord, and U. McCann
2002   Severe Dopaminergic Neurotoxicity in Primates after a Common Recreational Dose Regimen of MDMA ("Ecstasy"). *Science* 297(5590): 2260–2263.
Riechmann, D.
2000   Clinton Lends Hand to Colombia: Drug War Targeted; Bombs Found in Area. *Hartford Courant*, August 31: A17.
Rocchi, M., P. Miotto, and A. Preti
2003   Distribution of Deaths by Unintentional Illicit Drug Overdose in Italy Based on Periodicity Over Time, 1984–2000. *Drug and Alcohol Dependence* 72(1):23–31.

Rogers, E.
1962   *Diffusion of Innovations.* The Free Press. New York.
Romero-Daza, N., M. Weeks, and M. Singer
1998   Much More Than HIV! The Reality of Life on the Streets for Drug-Using Sex Workers in Inner-City Hartford. *International Quarterly of Community Health Education* 18(1):107–119.
Romero-Daza, N., M. Weeks, and M. Singer
2003   "Nobody Gives a Damn if I Live or Die." Violence, Drugs, and Street-level Prostitution in Inner-City Hartford, CT. *Medical Anthropology* 22:233–259.
Roper, A.
2002   National Survey: Ecstasy Use Continues Rising among Teens. Electronic document, http://www.drugfreeamerica.com.
Roseberry, W.
1991   *Anthropologies and Histories.* New Brunswick, NJ: Rutgers University Press.
Rosenbaum, M.
1998   "Just Say Know" to Teenagers and Marijuana. *Journal of Psychoactive Drugs* 30(2):197–203.
Rosenbaum, M.
2002   Ecstasy: America's New "Reefer Madness." *Journal of Psychoactive Drugs* 34(2):137–144.
Ross, E.
2004   HIV Infections Hit Record High in 2003. Associated Press File Story, July 7.
Rounsaville, B., M. Weissman, K. Crits-Christoph, and C. Wilber
1982a   Diagnosis and Symptoms of Depression in Opiate Addicts. *Archives of General Psychiatry* 39:151–156.
Rounsaville, B., M. Weissman, H. Kleber, and C. Wilber
1982b   Heterogeneity of Psychiatric Disorders in Treated Opiate Addicts. *Archives of General Psychiatry* 39:161–166.
Rudgley, R.
1993   *Essential Substances: A Cultural History of Intoxicants in Society.* New York: Kodansha International.
Saluter, A., and T. Lugaila
1998   *Marital Status and Living Arrangements: March 1996.* Washington, DC: U.S. Bureau of the Census.
Santelices, C., M. Singer, and A. M. Nicolaysen
2003   Risky and Precarious Dependencies of Puerto Rican IDUS in El Barrio: An Ethnographic Glimpse. *Practicing Anthropology* 25(3):23–27.
Scharf, T.
1967   *History of Maryland: From the Earliest Periods to the Present Day.* Hatboro, PA: Tradition Press.
Schensul, J., S. Diamond, B. Disch, R. Pino, R. Bernudez, and J. Eiserman
in press   The Diffusion of Ecstasy through Urban Youth Networks. *Journal of Ethnicity and Substance Abuse* 4(2).
Schensul, J., C. Huebner, M. Singer, M. Snow, P. Feliciano, and L. Broomhall
2000   The High, the Money and the Fame: The Emergent Social Context of "New Marijuana" Use among Urban Youth. *Medical Anthropology* 18(4):389–414.

Schultheis, R.
1983   Chinese Junk. In *Drugs and Society*. M. Kelleher, B. MacMurray, and T.
            Shapiro, eds. Pp. 234–241. Dubuque, IA: Kendall/Hunt.
Scott, J.
1969   *The White Poppy*. New York: Harper and Row.
Scrimshaw, S., M. Carballo, and L. Ramos
1991   The AIDS Rapid Anthropological Assessment Procedures: A Tool for
            Health Education Planning and Evaluation. *Health Education Quarterly*
            18(1):111–123.
Sennett, R., and J. Cobb
1973   *The Hidden Injuries of Class*. New York: Vintage Books.
Sharfman, M.
1980   Drug Overdose and the Full Moon. *Perceptual Motor Skills* 50(1):124–126.
Sheridan, B.
1995   Fed's Big Catch: Man at Center of Cali Cartel. *Miami Herald*, October
            5: 24A.
Sherlock, K.
1997   Psycho-Social Determinants of Ecstasy Use. Doctoral Thesis.
Shulgin, A.
1978   Characterization of Three New Psychotomimetics. In *The Psychopharma-
            cology of the Hallucinogens*. R. Stillman and R. Willete, eds. New York:
            Pergamon Press.
Siegal, H., R. Carlson, D. Kenne, S. Starr, and R. Stephens
2000   The Ohio Substance Abuse Monitoring Network: Constructing and
            Operating a Statewide Epidemiologic Intelligence System. *American
            Journal of Public Health* 90(12):1835–1837.
Siegel, B.
1970   Defensive Structuring and Environmental Stress. *American Journal of
            Sociology* 76:11–32.
Simonds, J., and J. Kashani
1980   Specific Drug Use and Violence in Delinquent Boys. *American Journal of
            Drug and Alcohol Abuse* 7:305–322.
Singer, L., S. Minnes, E. Short, R. Arendt, K. Farkas, B. Lewis, N. Klein, S. Russ, M.
Min, and H. Kirchner
2004   Cognitive Outcomes of Preschool Children with Prenatal Cocaine
            Exposure. *Journal of the American Medical Association* 291(20):2448–2456.
Singer, M.
1994   AIDS and the Health Crisis of the U.S. Urban Poor: The Perspective of
            Critical Medical Anthropology. *Social Science and Medicine* 39(7):931–948.
Singer, M.
1996   A Dose of Drugs, A Touch of Violence, A Case of AIDS: Conceptualiz-
            ing the SAVA Syndemic. *Free Inquiry in Creative Sociology* 24(2):99–110.
Singer, M.
1997   Needle Exchange and AIDS Prevention: Controversies, Policies and
            Research. *Medical Anthropology* 18(1):1–12.
Singer, M.
1999a   Why Do Puerto Rican Injection Drug Users Inject So Often? *Anthropol-
            ogy and Medicine* 6(1):31–58.

Singer, M.
1999b   Toward a Critical Biocultural Model of Drug Use and Health Risk. In
             *Cultural, Observational, and Epidemiological Approaches in the Prevention of
             Drug Abuse and HIV/AIDS*. P. Marshall, M. Singer, and M. Clatts, eds.
             Pp. 26–50. Bethesda, MD: National Institute on Drug Abuse.

Singer, M.
1999c   The Ethnography of Street Drug Use Before AIDS: A Historic Review.
             In *Cultural, Observational, and Epidemiological Approaches in the Prevention
             of Drug Abuse and HIV/AIDS*. P. Marshall, M. Singer, and M. Clatts, eds.
             Pp. 228–264. Bethesda, MD: National Institute on Drug Abuse.

Singer, M.
1999d   Studying Hidden and Hard-to-Research Populations. In *Mapping Net-
             works, Spatial Data and Hidden Populations, vol. 4: The Ethnographer's Tool-
             kit*. J. Schensul, M. LeCompte, R. Trotter, E. Cromley, and M. Singer,
             eds. Walnut Creek, CA: Altamira Press.

Singer, M.
2002   From Immorality to Illegality to Terrorism: A Dangerous New Wrinkle
             in the Demonization of Drug Users. *Newsletter of the Society for Applied
             Anthropology* 13(2):3–4.

Singer, M.
2004a   Critical Medical Anthropology. In *Encyclopedia of Medical Anthropology*.
             C. Ember and M. Ember, eds. Pp. 23–30. New York: Kluwer Academic.

Singer, M.
2004b   Why is it Easier to Get Drugs Than Drug Treatment? In *Unhealthy Health
             Policy*. A. Castro and M. Singer, eds. Walnut Creek, CA: Altamira Press.

Singer, M., and H. Baer
1995   *Critical Medical Anthropology*. Amityville, NY: Baywood Publishing Co.

Singer, M., H. Baer, S. Horowitz, G. Scott, and B. Weinstein
1998   Pharmacy Access to Syringes among Injection Drug Users: Follow-Up
             Findings from Hartford, CT. *Public Health Reports* 113(Supplement 1):81–89.

Singer, M., and S. Clair
2003   Syndemics and Public Health: Reconceptualizing Disease in Bio-Social
             Context. *Medical Anthropology Quarterly* 17(4):423–441.

Singer, M., S. Clair, J. Schensul, C. Huebner, J. Eiserman, R. Pino, and J. Garacia
in press(a) Dust in the Wind: The Growing Use of Embalming Fluid among Youth
             in Hartford. *Substance Use and Misuse*.

Singer, M., and J. Eiserman
in press   Twilight's Last Gleaning: Rapid Assessment of Late Night HIV Risk in
             Hartford, CT. In *Communities and Their AIDS Epidemics*. B. Bowser, E.
             Quimbey, and M. Singer, eds. Lanham, MD: Lexington Books.

Singer, M., D. Himmelgreen, M. Weeks, K. Radda, and R. Martinez
1997   Changing the Environment of AIDS Risk: Findings on Syringe
             Exchange and Pharmacy Sale of Syringes in Hartford, CT. *Medical
             Anthropology* 18(1):107–130.

Singer, M., and Z. Jia
1993   AIDS and Puerto Rican Injection Drug Users in the U.S. In *Handbook on
             Risks of AIDS: Injection Drug Users and Their Sexual Partners*. B. Brown and
             G. Beschner, eds. Pp. 227–255. Westport, CT: Greenwood Press.

Singer, M., Z. Jia, J. Schensul, M. Weeks, and J. B. Page
1992   AIDS and the IV Drug User: The Local Context in Prevention Efforts. *Medical Anthropology* 14:285–306.
Singer, M., J. Juvalis, and M. Weeks
2000   High on Illy: Studying an Emergent Drug Problem in Hartford, CT. *Medical Anthropology* 18:365–388.
Singer, M., G. Mirhej, S. Shaw, H. Salaheen, J. Vivian, E. Hastings, L. Rohera, D. Jennings, J. Navarro, A. Wu, A. Smith, and A. Perez
in press(b) When the Drug of Choice is a Drug of Confusion: Embalming Fluid Use in Inner-City Hartford. *Journal of Ethnicity and Substance Abuse* 4(2).
Singer, M., J. Simmons, M. Duke, and L. Broomhall
2001   The Challenges of Street Research on Drug Use, Violence, and AIDS Risk. *Addiction Research and Theory* 9(4):365–402.
Singer, M., and C. Snipes
1992   Generations of Suffering: Experiences of a Pregnancy and Substance Abuse Treatment Program. *Journal of Health Care for the Poor and Underserved* 3(1):325–239.
Singer, M., T. Stopka, C. Siano, K. Springer, G. Barton, K. Khoshnood, A. Gorry de Puga, and R. Heimer.
2000   The Social Geography of AIDS and Hepatitis Risk: Qualitative Approaches for Assessing Local Differences in Sterile Syringe Access among Injection Drug Users. *American Journal of Public* 90(7):1049–1056.
Singer, M., M. Weeks, and D. Himmelgreen.
1995   Sale and Exchange of Syringes. *Journal of Acquired Immunodeficiency Disease Syndromes and Human Retrovirology* 10: 104.
Sorensen, J., L. Wermuth, D. Gibson, K-H Choi, J. Guydish, and S. Batki
1991   *Preventing AIDS in Drug Users and their Sexual Partners.* New York: Guilford Press.
Spector, I.
1985   AMP: A New Form of Marijuana. *Journal of Clinical Psychiatry* 46:498–499.
Spelman, W.
1993   Abandoned Buildings: Magnets for Crime. *Journal of Criminal Justice* 21:481–495.
Sperry, K.
1988   An Epidemic of Intravenous Narcoticism Deaths Associated with the Resurgence of Black Tar Heroin. *Journal of Forensic Science* 33(5):1156–1162.
Spirito, A., D. Rasile, L. Vinnick, E. Jelalian, and M. Arrigan
1997   Relationship Between Substance Use and Self-reported Injuries among Adolescents. *Journal of Adolescent Health* 21(4):221–224.
Spitters, C., J. Moran, D. Kruse, N. Barg, M. Leslie, J. Hofmann, M. Moore, and G. Macgregor-Skinner
2003   Wound Botulism among Black Tar Heroin Users—Washington, 2003. *Morbidity and Morality Weekly Review* 52(37):885–886.
Spunt, B., P. Goldstein, H. Brownstein, and M. Fendrich
1994   The Role of Marijuana in Homicide. *The International Journal of the Addictions* 29(2):195–213.
Starmer, G., and K. Bird
1984   Investigating Drug-Ethanol Interactions. *British Journal of Clinical Pharmacology* 18(Supplement 1):27S–35S.

Steinberg, L.
2002   *Adolescence.* New York: McGraw-Hill.
Sterk, C.
1999   *Fast Lives: Women Who Use Crack Cocaine.* Philadelphia: Temple Univer-
            sity Press.
Sterk, C.
2000   *Tricking and Tripping: Prostitution in the Era of AIDS.* Putnam Valley, NY:
            Social Change Press.
Sterling, E.
2004   Speech, New Alliance, Hartford, CT, November 17.
Stimson, G., and K. Choopanya
1998   Global Perspectives on Drug Injecting. In *Drug Injecting and HIV Infec-
            tion.* G. Stimson, D. Des Jarlais, and A. Ball, eds. Pp 1–21. London:
            UCL Press.
Stocker, S.
1998   Drug Addiction Treatment Conference Emphasizes Combining Thera-
            pies. *NIDA Notes* 13(3):1, 13.
Stopka, T., M. Singer, C. Santelices, and J. Eiserman
2003   Public Health Interventionists, Penny Capitalists, or Sources of Risk?
            Assessing Street Syringe Sellers in Hartford, Connecticut. *Substance Use
            & Misuse* 38(9):1339–1370.
Substance Abuse and Mental Health Services Administration
1997   *National Household Survey on Drug Abuse. Main Findings.* Washington,
            DC: Department of Health and Human Services.
Substance Abuse and Mental Health Services Administration
1998   *National Household Survey on Drug Abuse.* Washington, DC: Department
            of Health and Human Services.
Substance Abuse and Mental Health Services Administration
2001   *National Household Survey on Drug Abuse.* Washington, DC: Department
            of Health and Human Services.
Substance Abuse and Mental Health Services Administration
2003   *Emergency Department Trends from the Drug Abuse Warning Network, Final
            Estimates 1995–2002.* Electronic document, http://www.DAWNinfo.
            samhsa.gov/, accessed November 4.
Sullivan, L.
1991   Violence as a Public Health Issue. *Journal of the American Medical Associa-
            tion* 265(21):2778–2786.
Swan, N.
1998   Drug Abuse Cost to Society Set at $97.7 Billion, Continuing Steady
            Increase Since 1975. *NIDA Notes* 13(4):1, 12–13.
Tercyak K., and J. Audrain-McGovern
2003   Personality Differences Associated with Smoking Experimentation
            among Adolescents with and without Comorbid Symptoms of ADHD.
            Substance Use and Misuse 38(14):1953–1970.
Thomas, P.
1967   *Down These Mean Streets.* New York: Knopf.

Thorpe, L., L. Ouellet, R. Hershow, S. Bailey, I. Williams, J. Williamson, E. Monterroso, and R. Garfein
2002   Risk of Hepatitis C Virus Infection among Young Adult Injection Drug Users Who Share Injection Equipment. *American Journal of Epidemiology* 155(7):645–653.

Thoumi, F.
1995   *Political Economy and Illegal Drugs in Colombia*. Boulder: Lynne Reinner Publishers.

Tortu, S., J. McMahon, E. Pouget, and R. Hamid
2004   Sharing of Noninjection Drug-use Implements as a Risk Factor for Hepatitis C. *Substance Use and Misuse* 39(2):211–224.

Trafford, A.
2002   Health Talk: The War on Drugs. Electronic document, http://discuss. washingtonpost.com/wp-srv/zforum/02/health0212.htm, accessed November 12.

Tuohy, L.
2004   Parents Want Answers in Son's Death. *The Hartford Courant*, September 17:7.

U.S. Congress, House, Select Committee on Narcotics Abuse and Control
1977   *Southeast Asian Narcotics*. Hearings, 95th Congress, 1st Session. Washington, DC.

U.S. National Commission on AIDS
1990   *Report: HIV Disease in Correctional Facilities*. Washington, DC: National Institute of Justice.

Urbina, A., and K. Jones
2004   Crystal Methamphetamine, Its Analogues, and HIV Infection: Medical and Psychiatric Aspects of a New Epidemic. *Clinical and Infectious Diseases* 38(6):890–894.

Vivian, J., H. Salaheen, M. Singer, J. Navarro, and G. Mirhej
in press   Under the Counter: The Diffusion of Narcotic Analgesics to the Inner-City Street. *Journal of Ethnicity and Substance Abuse* 4(2).

Vlahov, D.
1995   Deregulation of the Sale and Possession of Syringes for HIV Prevention among Injection Drug Users. *Journal of Acquired Immune Deficiency Syndromes and Human Retrovirology* 10:71–72.

Vlahov, D., and B. Junge
1998   The Role of Needle Exchange Programs in HIV Prevention. *Public Health Reports* 113(Supplement 1):75–80.

Volkow, N.
2001   Drug Abuse and Mental Illness: Progress in Understanding Comorbidity. *American Journal of Psychiatry* 158:1181–1183.

Volkow, N.
2005   *NIDA Community Drug Alert Bulletin—Inhalants*. Bethesda, MD: National Institute on Drug Abuse.

Waterston, A.
1993   *Street Addicts in the Political Economy*. Philadelphia: Temple University Press.

Waterston, A.
1999   *Love, Sorrow and Rage: Destitute Women in a Manhattan Residence*. Philadelphia: Temple University Press.

Weeks, M., M. Grier, N. Romero-Daza, M. Puglisi, and M. Singer
1998   Streets, Drugs, and the Economy of Sex in the Age of AIDS. *Women and Health* 27(1/2):205–228.
West, C.
1999   *The Cornel West Reader.* New York: Basic Civitas Books.
Whyte, W.
1956   *The Organization Man.* New York: Simon and Schuster.
Wolf, E.
1982   *Europe and the People without History.* Berkeley: University of California Press.
Wolfenstein, M.
1975   Fun Morality. In *Culture and Commitment.* W. Sussman, ed. New York: Braziller.
Yacoubian, G., B. Urbach, K. Larsen, R. Johnson, and R. Peters
2002   Exploring Benzodiazepine Use among Houston Arrestees. *Journal of Psychoactive Drugs* 34(4):393–399.
Yang, C.
2001a   Baltimore is the Heroin Capital of the United States. Electronic document, http://www.abcnews.go.com/sections.us/DailyNews/heroin 010314_baltimore.html, accessed August 21.
Yang, C.
2001b   Holding the Line in Heroin City. Electronic document, http://www.abcnews.go.com/sections/us/DailyNews/heroin010314_cops.html, accessed March 21.
Yates, G., R. MacKenzie, J. Pennbridge, and E. Cohen
1988   A Risk Profile Comparison of Runaway and Non-runaway Youth. *American Journal of Public Health* 78:820–821.

Index

Abram, K., 198
Abu-Lughod, L., 31
Accidental injury, 211
Adams, L., 58, 156
Addiction
    colonial-early American, 44
    cultural aspects of, 155
    heroin-morphine, 48
    nineteenth-century, 55
    opium, Chicago study on, 59–60
    soldier's disease, 47
Addicts, as cheap source of labor,
    181–182
Adler, P., 160
Adolescence, 105–106. *See also* Youth
    Drug use
Adolescent behavior
    changing cultural patterns and,
        109–110
    coming of age, 107–108
    developmental processes and,
        108–109
    egocentrism, 108
    oppositionalism, 110–111
    syndrome assumption, 107
Adult drug users, social relationships
    among, 154–155
Adulteration, 14, 212–213
Aerosols, 119
Afghanistan, as heroin/opium source,
    146, 173
African Americans
    addiction, factors contributing to,
        60–61

arrests and racism, 60, 181
community risk patterns of, 229
demonized drug-use image of, 180
drug use dynamics and, 10–12
drug-user stereotype of, 51–52, 180
factors contributing to addiction,
    59–61
post-World War II drug scene, 65–71
Agar, M., 24, 61, 145, 147, 160, 172,
    219, 222–223
Agency of Fear (Epstein), 167
Aharonovich, E., 196
AIDS. *See* HIV/AIDS
Alcohol, 1, 3, 35, 41, 49, 79, 94, 96–97,
    101, 104–105, 107, 151–152, 194,
    196, 204, 207, 211, 218
Aldrich, M., 37, 62, 83
American Disease, The (Musto), 56
Amphetamine, in 1960s–1970s, 84–87.
    See also Methamphetamine
Andrews, D., 177
Angel dust, 83–84, 141–143
Anslinger, H., 74
Anterograde amnesia, 135
Arrest(s)
    Asian racism and, 45
    BZD-related, 93
    effect of War on Drugs on, 176–178
    increased incarceration resulting
        from, 177
    justifying racism in, 180–181
    narcotics, for African Americans, 60
    twenty-first-century rates of, 176
Arrillaga, P., 175

Assessment, rapid, 229–232
Attention Deficit Disorder (ADD), 137
Attention Deficit/Hyperactive Disorder
    (ADHD), 137
Auerbach, J., 133, 225
Availability, 9, 32, 52, 117–118, 138,
    146, 173
Ayliffe, H., 212

Bachman, J., 83
Baer, H., 25, 28, 137, 209
Baggott, M., 112, 114
Barnet, R., 27
Barrett, O., 200
Baxter, S., 177–178
Bebow, J., 193–194
Beck, A., 11
Beck, J., 127
Becker, H., 22, 94
Bell, R., 62
Bemmers, H., 75
Bennett, L., 113
Bennett, R., 200
Benzedrine, 84–85
Benzodiazepines (BZDs), 93
Bertram, E., 175–176
Best, J., 39
Betty, P., 177
Bibeau, G., 62
Biological factors affecting drug use,
    33–34
Biomedicine, as source for street drugs,
    136
Bird, K., 120
"Black tar" heroin, 12–13, 201
Blint, D., 213
Bogus innovations, 128–129
Bonne, J., 89
Bonnie, R., 45
Booth, M., 37, 44, 153, 170
Botulism, 13, 202
Boumba, V., 212
Bourgois, P., 11–13, 28, 31–33, 111,
    180–182, 203
Bovelle, E., 63, 155
Bowser, B., 223, 229
Brain damage, 195–198
Brain disease model of drug use, 23

Brecher, E., 55
Brick, J., 193
Brodie, K., 133, 225
Brook, J., 117–118
Brown, C., 65–66
Brown, T., 163
Browning, F., 170–171
Buchanan, D., 191
Buchert, R., 196
Buckland, F., 120
Budney, A., 198
Building Community Responses to
    Risks of Emergent Drug Use, 6
Burns, 209–211
Bush, G. H. W., 219–220
Bush, G. W., 173–174, 176, 221
Byron, K., 140

Cacao, 38
Calafat, A., 127
Cannabis. *See* Marijuana
Carroll, R., 90
Cartels, Colombian, 157–159
Carter, J., 173
Casey, J., 61
Castillo, F., 171
Castro, A., 25
Cavanagh, J., 27
Cayton, H., 61
Centers for Disease Control and Preven-
    tion, 6, 227–228
Chambers, C., 167
Chambliss, W., 177, 180, 183
Chapman, K., 74
Chen, J., 202
Chicano youth gangs, 116–117
Chien, A., 64, 182
Chomsky, N., 179
Choopanya, K., 189
Ciccarone, D., 12–13, 201
Circuit parties, 133–134
Clair, S., 216
Clatts, M., 99
Clawson, P., 158, 173, 178
Clinton, W. J., 171–173
Club drugs, 123–146
    ecstasy, 90, 116, 126–130, 196–197,
    200–201

GHB, 133–135
illy (embalming fluid), 140–144
ketamine, 99, 131–132, 134
marketing online, 163–164
MDMA, 112, 114, 121, 126–130,
134, 165, 197
CMA approach
biological factors, 33–34
cultural factors, 30–33
social factors, 29–30
structural factors, 26–29
Coca-Cola, cocaine-infused, 50
Cocaine
1970s popularity of, 78
cognitive deficits caused by, 196
drug producer defensive strategies,
172–173
evolutionary use pathway of, 95
history of use of, 50–52
sex and, 132–133
sex for crack, 18–20
South American, 157–160
treatment, 196
violence and, 205
See also Crack cocaine
Cocktailing, 120
Coffin, P., 183, 194
Cognitive impairment, 195–199
Cohen, R., 151
Colombia
cocaine and heroin production in,
157, 174–175
drug cartels, 157–160
War on Drugs and, 171–172
Comadrona Program, 16–17
Community Antidrug Coalitions of
America, 123
Community Epidemiology Work
Group, 226
Connectors, 113–115, 124
Connors, M., 28, 182
Conrad, P., 48, 55, 64
Constantine, T., 174
Consumption, social shifts in, 110
Controlled Substance Act, 135–136
Cook, P., 113
Coomber, R., 215
Copeland, L., 194

Corby, N., 227
Counterculture, middle-class, 74–79
Courtwright, D., 48, 52, 55, 60, 64, 71,
73, 78, 153, 173
Crack cocaine
accidental burning from, 211
crack babies, 199
distribution of, 157–160
marketing of, 161
production of, 161–162
sex in exchange for, 18–20
violence and, 205
Crack houses, 209–210
Criminalization and racism, 56–57
Critical medical anthropology (CMA)
approach to drug use, 25–34
Crowcroft, N., 202
Culture
changing patterns in, and drug use,
109–111
club drug use and, 125–126
diseases reflective of, 136–137
factors affecting drug use, 30–33
subcultural model of drug use, 23–24

Dai, B., 59, 61–62, 154–155
Dance clubs, 60, 90, 120, 123–126, 129,
132, 135–136, 143, 191, 200
Date rape drugs, 134–135
Datura, 212–213
Davidson, J., 10, 181
De La Rosa, M., 119
De Quincey, T., 42
Deaths. *See* Fatalities, drug-related
Dee, J., 174
Defensive adaptation, 75
Dehydration, 200–201
Dei, K., 29, 111
Denzin, N., 62, 154
Des Jarlais, D., 22, 55, 60, 64, 71, 73,
78, 153, 173, 183, 192
Designer drugs, 21–22
Detoxification, 184
Deviance model of drug use, 22–23, 62
Diaz, R., 90
Diffusion, 59, 90, 111–116, 120
Diffusion of innovation model, 114–116
Discontinuance, 115

Diseases, 7, 136–137, 201–204, 216–218. *See also* Sexually transmitted diseases
Distribution, 89, 157–160, 182
Diversification, 97, 115–116, 136
Diversion, pharmaceutical, 91–93
Divorce, 109–110
Doblin, R., 129–130
Doctor shopping, 91
Donoghoe, M., 193, 202
Drake, St. C., 61
Drug Abuse Warning Network (DAWN), 92, 121
Drug classifications, 79, 136
Drug cutting, 14, 212–213, 152–154
Drug eras, development stages of, 94–95
Drug laws and enforcement
  Controlled Substance Act, 135–136
  cost effectiveness of, 176–178
  Hague Convention of 1912, 57
  Harrison Narcotic Act of 1914, 10, 57–58
  Illicit Drug Anti-Proliferation Act (RAVE Act), 129
  Marijuana Tax Act of 1937, 65
  Methamphetamine Control Act, 89
  United States v. Behrman, 58
  Volstead Act, 151
  Webb v. United States, 58
Drug scares, politically motivated, 219–222
Drug use dynamics
  1930–1940, 59–63
  1960s transition, 73–97
  changing social awareness, 11–12
  club drug transition, 11, 90
  defined, 10
  diffusion, 59, 90, 111–116, 120
  disenchantment, 115
  diversification, 97, 115–116, 136
  drug mixing, 61, 90, 93, 101, 117, 120, 127, 133, 140–143, 153– 154, 194–195, 200
  evolutionary aspects of, 94–97
  explanatory models of, 22–34
  factors affecting, 13–14
  gateway hypothesis, 81, 105
  heterogeneity and, 63, 77, 155, 214
  innovation and diffusion in, 111–116

  patterns of, 100–111, 187–218
  pharmaceutical diversion, 91–93
  post–World War II, 63–71
  rejection, 115
  replacement, 115
  risks involved. *See* Risks
  significance of, 10
  smuggling, 89, 151, 155, 157, 158, 160
  stepping-stone theory, 105
  typology of, 14–16
  War on Drugs and, 172
Drug War Politics: The Price of Denial (Bertram & Sharpe), 175
Drugs
  colonial era, 35–53
  criminalization and racism, 56–57
  dilution (cutting) of, 14, 152–153, 212–213
  distribution, 89, 157–160, 182
  history of use of, 35–52
  pattern of use. *See* Patterns of drug use
  role of, in social relationships, 155
  sex, predation and, 132–136
  social relations among adult users, 154–155
  switching, 95–96
  War on. *See* War on Drugs
  See also Drug use dynamics
Duke, M., 17, 208
Dust. *See* PCP; Embalming fluid
Duzan, M., 159

Eaton, V., 44
Ecstasy, 90, 112, 116, 124–130, 133–134, 161, 163, 196–197, 200– 201
Endocarditis, 203
Eiserman, J., 123–125, 229
Elkin, D., 108
Ellison, M., 26
Elwood, W., 141–142
Embalming fluid (illy), 140–144
Emboden, W., 79
Emergency room episodes, 121, 134
Engels, F., 69
Epele, M., 95
Ephedrine, 85, 125, 135
Epidemics, syndemic, 216–218

Epstein, E., 167
Ethnoepidemiology, 224
Ethnography, as monitoring method, 229, 232–233
Exposure, 208–209

Families, redefining, 109–110
Farabee, D., 20
Farmer, P., 25, 28
Fatalities, drug related
  dehydration-induced, 201
  ecstasy-related, 201
  inhalant-related, 200
  other drug-related, 201
  overdose, 193–195
Feldman, H., 37, 62, 83
Fischer, M., 233
Fleisher, M., 22, 142
Flynn, N., 202
Forero, J., 174–175
Fox, K., 182
Freebase, 18, 132, 210
French, M., 184
Fresia, J., 168, 170
Friedman, S., 28, 113, 154
Fullerton, K., 202
Fun morality, 110, 125

Gamella, J., 29
Gangs. *See* Street gangs
Garrett, B., 170–171
Gases, classification of, 119
Gateway hypothesis, 81, 105
Gay Men's Health Crisis, 192
Gays, 90, 133–134, 191–192, 200. *See also* HIV/AIDS
Generation X, 109, 125
German, D., 214
Gerstein, D., 184
GHB (gamma hydroxybutyric acid), 133–135, 164
Gift, The (Mauss), 155
Gilbert, L., 203
Gill, J., 201
Girodin, P., 107
Gladwell, M., 112–114, 124
Glick, R., 117
Golden Triangle, 155, 168–169, 171

Goldstein, P., 204, 206
Golub, A., 94, 114, 174
Gomez, J., 212
Goode, E., 23, 30, 51, 58, 76, 79, 82, 86
Gordon, A., 118
Gorman, M., 90
Gosch, M., 150
Grant, B., 22
Gray, M., 78, 81
Greenberg, M., 209
Greenberg, T., 151
Groat, T., 107
Gruber, A., 198
Grufferman, S., 212
Gutierrez, P., 172
Guttman, W., 175

Haemming, R., 183
Hague Convention of 1912, 57
Hahne, S., 202
Halcion, 93
Hallucinogens, 37, 73–74, 79, 82, 101, 126, 132, 212
Hamilton, R., 213
Hammer, R., 150
Hammersley, R., 126
Hammett, T., 178
Hanson, B., 62, 154, 206
Harlem, drug use and addiction in, 60
Harrison Narcotic Act of 1914, 10, 57–58
Harrison, P., 11
Hasin, D., 196
Havlik, D., 214
Hayner, G., 129
Haynie, D., 29
Health and drug use
  botulism, 13, 202
  burns, 209–211
  emergent public health issues, 12–13, 16
  HIV/AIDS. *See* HIV/AIDS
  hypothermia, 208–209
  injury, accidental, 211
  organ damage, 200–201
  poisoning, 212–214
  pregnancy, 16–18
  public responses to, 12–13, 16, 219–235

tetanus, 202–203
tuberculosis, 216–217
Health perspective, and War on Drugs, 183–185
Health
    CMA definition of, 25
    social science of, 4–7, 13–14
Heart disease, 203
Heath, D., 94
Heilig, S., 126
Heimer, R., 178, 183
Helmer, J., 46, 58
Hepatitis C, 203–204
Heroin
    "black tar," 12–13, 201
    current status of production/distribution, 174–175
    early research on, 62–63
    history of use of, 48, 144–146
    marketing to the middle class, 163
    Mexican trafficking of, 174–175
    OxyContin and, 93
    transition from snorting to injection, 152–153
    in Vietnam, 170
    violence and, 205–206
    See also Opium
Heroin Lifestyle Study, 62–63, 154
Heston, L., 86
Heston, R., 86
Higgins, D., 227
High schools, drug use in, 106
Hills, S., 32
Himmelgreen, D., 183
Hispanic Health Council, 2–4, 12, 70, 101, 116, 124, 132, 140, 154, 195, 206, 216, 225, 227–229, 233–234
Hispanics, 50. See also Latinos, Puerto Ricans
HIV/AIDS
    as biological factor of drug use dynamics, 13, 33
    black tar heroin use and, 13
    CDC Advisory Committee on Prevention of, 227
    drug use dynamics and, 87
    injection drug use and, 189–191
    noninjection drug use and, 191–192

pharmaceutical diversion and, 93
preventing, 232
in prison populations, 178
spread of, 188–192
syringe sharing and, 33, 183, 190–192, 203–204, 216
Hoffer, L., 203
Hoffman, A., 82
Holland, J., 83, 141–142
Holman, B., 177
Homicide, 204, 214
Horst, E., 200
Howard, K., 109
Huberman, A., 233
Huffing, 119–120, 200
Hypnotics, 79
Hypothermia, 208

Iiyama, P., 61
Illicit Drug Anti-Proliferation Act (RAVE Act), 129
Illicit drug capitalism
    Chinese Triads, 153
    club drug marketing online, 163–164
    for-profit business, 156–157
    heroin marketing to the middle class, 163
    Italian connection, 152
    Jewish connection, 150–151
    Mafia, 152–153
    origins of, 58
    players and practices, 149–153
    production and marketing dynamics of, 160–163
    South American cocaine, 79, 157–160
Illy (embalming fluid), 140–144
Incarceration, costs of, 176–178
Inciardi, J., 9–10, 19, 44, 47–48, 62, 64, 88, 161, 167, 171, 177–178, 206
Inebriants, 79
Infectious diseases, 7, 136–137, 201–204, 216–218
Inhalants, 119–120, 200, 209
Injection. See Intravenous drug injection; Syringe use
Injuries, accidental, 211
Innovation, drug use, 111–112

Insley, B., 212
Intergenerational drug amnesia, 144
International Narcotics Control Board,
   163
Intravenous drug injection, 13, 152–153,
   177, 184, 189, 203. *See also* Syringe
   use
Italian gangsters, 152

Jacobs, B., 128, 219
James, W., 11, 60–61, 141, 154
Jansen, K., 132
Jatlow, P., 120
Jessor, R., 74, 107
Jessor, S., 107
Jewish gangsters, 150–151
Jia, Z., 70
Jimenez, A., 9, 224
Jimsonweed, 38
Johnson, B., 61, 80, 94, 114, 128, 174,
   182, 205
Johnson, S., 11, 60–61, 141, 154
Johnston, L., 83
Jones, J., 153
Jones, K., 200
Joselit, J., 150
Joseph, H., 55, 60, 64, 71, 73, 78, 153,
   173
Junge, B., 183
Juvalis, J., 141, 228

Kaa, E., 212
Kandel, D., 118
Kashani, J., 204
Katcher, L., 152
Katzenberg, J., 151
Kaufman, M., 91
Kefauver Committee on Crime, 64
Kent, J., 131
Ketamine, 99–100, 125, 131–132, 134
Khantzian, E., 177
Kim, R., 201
Kimura, A., 201
Kleber, H., 185
Knipe, E., 24
Koester, S., 203
Koob, G., 177
Kosten, T., 177

Kozel, N., 119, 226
Kruger, H., 168

Lankenau, S., 99
Lansky, M., 152
Latinos
   community risk patterns of, 229
   demonized drug-use image of, 180
   drug use patterns of, 70, 87
   gay, meth use among, 90
   Hispanic Health Council, 2, 4
   marijuana use among, 80
   school dropout rate of, 111
   social networks and drugs, 116
Leary, T., 82
Lee, R., 158, 173, 178
Leshner, A., 23, 183, 222
Lettiere, M., 28
Leukefeld, C., 20
Levine, H., 161, 220
Levins, H., 173
Liebow, E., 32
Lifestyle, drug-related, 154–155
Lilly, J., 131
Lindesmith, A., 62–63, 154–155
Lockwood, D., 9, 161
Logan, T. K., 20
LSD, 81–83, 212
Luciano, Lucky, 152, 156
Lugaila, T., 109
Lurie, P., 183
Lynskey, M., 101
Lysergic acid diethylamide. *See* LSD

MacDonald, J., 139
Mack, J., 177
Macrostructural model of drug use,
   24–25
Mafia, control of heroin distribution,
   152–156
Malcolm X, 65
Mansergh, G., 133
Manwar, A., 94, 128
Marcus, G., 233
Marijuana
   1960s–1970s use, 80–81
   anti-Mexican bigotry and, 50
   high-potency, 138–139

homicide and, 204
longer-term drug patterns and, 101
medical purposes of, 139
normalization of, 114
production of, 139–140
study on effects of, 198
violence and, 204
Marijuana Tax Act of 1937, 65
Marketing
club drugs online, 163–165
crack cocaine, 161
dynamics of, 160–163
heroin, to the middle class, 163
online, of club drugs, 163–164
players and practices, 150–153
Markou, A., 177
Massing, M., 177, 184
Matthee, R., 52
Mauss, M., 155
Mavens, role in social epidemics, 113–115
McBride, D., 177
McCann, U., 197
McCoy, A., 58, 156
McGee, L., 62
McInery, A., 172
McWhirter, C., 191–192
MDMA, 112, 114, 121, 126–130, 134,
    164, 197
Medicinal marijuana use, 139
Merline, A., 110
Methamphetamine, 88–90, 96, 191–192,
    200
Methaqualone, 87
Methedrine, 90
Metzger, D., 184
Mexico-based drug trafficking, 88–89,
    92, 174–175
Michalski, T., 139
Miles, M., 233
Miller, H., 225
Miller, J., 80
Miller, N., 205
Minorities, oppositionalism and, 111
Mintz, S., 39–40, 222
Miotto, P., 195
Mirken, B., 194
Mithoefer, M., 129–130
Mitselou, A., 212

Moini, S., 178
Monitoring
ethnography as, 229, 232–233
history of, 225–229
importance of, 224–225
multiyear, 234–235
perpetual, 226
public health, history of, 224
rapid assessment and, 229–232
tracking longer-range trends, 222–223
Moore, J., 92, 116
Moore, M., 131
Morabia, A., 224
Morality, fun, 110, 125
Morphine, 46–49, 59, 63. *See also*
    Heroin, Opium
Moses, L., 225
Moss, A., 203
Mules, drug, 157
Multiyear monitoring, 234–235
Murphy, S., 17, 185
Musto, D., 7, 26–27, 50–52, 56, 167
Muwakkil, S., 11, 177, 181

Nadelmann, E., 183, 221
National Institute on Drug Abuse, 123,
    225–226
Native Americans, 119
Navaline, H., 184
Neaigus, A., 146
Neale, J., 195
Necrotizing fasciitis, 201
Needle, R., 184
Nemoto, T., 89–90
Netherlands, Ecstasy production in, 161
Networks, social. *See* Social networks
Newcomb, M., 62
Nicolaysen, A., 236
Nishi, S., 61
Nitrites, 119
Nixon, R., 167–168, 171, 173
Nolte, K., 214
Normality, pursuit of, 63, 154
Novelty seeking, and drug use, 102–104
Nunes, E., 196

O'Donnell, J., 153
O'Malley, P., 83

O'Reilly, K., 227
Ochoa, J., 157, 159
Offer, D., 109
Operario, D., 90
Operation Mongoose, 168–169
Opium
    anti-Asian sentiment and, 10, 45–46
    early research on, 61–62
    Golden Triangle, 169–171
    Golden Triangle production, 155
    history of use of, 36–38, 42–48
    See also Heroin, Morphine
Opium Addiction in Chicago (Dai), 59
Oppression illness, 28–29
Organ damage, 200–201
Orjuela, L., 171
Ortner, S., 31
Ostrov, E., 109
Ouellet, L., 9, 224
Overdose, 193–195
OxyContin, 92–93

Page, J., 113
Parental concern/involvement, 11–12,
    109
Park, R. E., 59
Partridge, W., 76–77, 81
Paschane, D., 204
Passaro, D., 202
Patterns of drug use
    differences for minorities, 225–226
    established in teen years, 101
    HIV/AIDS and, 188–192, 225
    identifiable, 100–111
    methods for monitoring, 224–235
PCP (phencyclidine, "angel dust"),
    83–84, 141–143
Pedestrian-oriented drug injection
    neighborhoods, 155
Peer interaction, 116
Pepper, A., 70–71, 85
Pepper, L., 70–71, 85
Perpetual monitoring, 226
Personality disorders, addiction theory
    of, 64
Peyote, 38
Pharmaceutical diversion, 91–93
Phencyclidine. See PCP

Phenethylamines I Have Known and Loved:
    A Chemical Love Story (Shulgin &
    Shulgin), 163
Phenylethylamines, 21
Platt, J., 177–178
Poisoning, 212–214
Politics of Psychopharmacology, The
    (Leary), 126
Pollan, M., 183
Polydrug use, 61, 90, 93, 101, 117, 120,
    127, 133, 140–143, 153– 154,
    194–195, 200
Pottieger, A., 9, 161
Preble, E., 61, 206
Predation, sexual, 132–136
Pregnancy, drug use during, 16–18,
    198–199
Prescription forging, 91
Preti, A., 195
Price, J., 40
Prince, B., 203
Prohibition and bootlegging, 151
Psychiatric disorders, 195–199
Psychological model of drug use, 22
Public health responses
    fear (an unauthentic response),
        220–222
    tracking long-range trends, 222–223
Puerto Ricans
    1940–1959 drug use patterns, 67–69
    drug switching among, 96
    ethnic differences in consumption/
        injection frequencies, 226
    Hispanic Health Council, 2
    post–World War II drug scene, 69–71
    pregnancy and drug use among, 16
    racist societal concern levels and, 12
    rapid assessment, response and eval-
        uation of, 231
    trajectory of use study on, 117
Pugliese, A., 217–218

Quesada, J., 28
Quimbey, E., 223, 229

Racism
    arrest and, 45
    criminalization and, 56–57

drug legislation and, 10–12, 45, 56
drug stereotyping and, 50–52, 61
oppression illness and, 28–29
War on Drugs and, 180–181
Radler, D., 75
Rajkumar, A., 184
Rapid assessment, 229–232
Ratner, M., 19
Raves, 125–126. *See also* Dance clubs
Read, C., 58, 156
Reagan, R., 173
Reinarman, C., 161, 220
Reisinger, H., 24, 145, 147, 160, 172,
     219, 222–223
Rejection, process of, 115
Research, early, 59, 61–62
Rettig, R., 62, 68–70
Ricaurte, G., 197
Richter, L., 117
Riechmann, D., 171
Risks
     accidents, 211
     behavior, risk-taking, 113, 117
     burns, 209–211
     destruction of social relationships,
        214
     exposure to the elements, 208–209
     infectious diseases, 201–204
     limiting, 214–215
     linkages in social networks, 154
     mental health problems and brain
        damage, 195–199
     methods for monitoring. *See* Moni-
        toring
     organ damage and death, 200–201
     overdose, 193–195
     poisoning, 212–214
     sexually transmitted diseases, 204
Ritalin, 137–138
Rocchi, M., 195
Rodriguez, A., 212
Rogers, E., 114–115
Rohypnol, 134–135
Romero-Daza, N., 218
Roseberry, W., 222
Rosenbaum, M., 17, 105, 125–127, 185
Ross, E., 189
Rothstein, A., 150–151

Rounsaville, B., 22
Rudgley, R., 37

Salerno, R., 73
Salesmen, in social epidemics, 113–115,
     124
Saluter, A., 109
Salvia, 147
Santelices, C., 236
Scharf, T., 40
Schatzberg, A., 177
Schensul, J., 100, 124, 138
Schiraldi, V., 177
Schneider, J., 48, 55, 64
Schultheis, R., 168
Scientist, The (Lilly), 131
Scott, J., 36, 42
Self-esteem, lowered, 110
Sennett, R., 29
Serotonin, 196–197
Sex
     cocaine and, 132–133
     ecstasy, 133
     methamphetamine use and, 191
     miscellaneous club drugs and, 134
     predation and drugs, 132–136
Sexually transmitted diseases, 5, 204
     marijuana use and, 81
     sex for crack and, 20
     See also HIV/AIDS
Sharfman, M., 195
Sharpe, K., 175–176
Sheridan.B., 159
Sherlock, K., 127
Shulgin, A., 126, 163
Siegal, H., 234
Siegel, B., 75
Simmons, J., 28
Simonds, J., 204
Singer, L., 199
Singer, M., 11, 17, 25, 28, 61, 70, 137,
     141–142, 180, 183, 199, 209,
     216–217, 223, 228–229, 236
Skinpopping, 189
Sloboda, Z., 119
Snipes, C., 17, 199
Snorting, transition to injection from,
     152–153

Social deviance model, 62–63
Social epidemic model, 112–114
Social factors influencing drug use, 29–30
Social movements, counterculture, 76–77
Social networks, 59
    drug switching and, 96
    emergent drug use and, 29–30, 154
    ethnic-specific nature of, 87
    functions of, 116–117
Social order, and drug problems, 69
Social pathology model of drug use, 22–23
Social relationships
    among adult drug users, 155
    destruction of, 214
Social science of health, 4–7, 13–14
Social suffering, 28–29
Soldier's disease, 47
Solvents, 213
Soma, T., 90
Sorensen, J., 22
South, N., 215
Spector, I., 141
Speed. See Amphetamine; Methamphetamine
Spelman, W., 209
Sperry, K., 13
Spirito, A., 211
Spitters, C., 202
Spunt, B., 204
Stacom, D., 140
Starmer, G., 120
Steinberg, L., 108, 110
"Stepping stone" theory, 105
Stereotypes, drug-related, 50–52, 61
Sterk, C., 19–20, 214
Sterling, E., 222
Stimson, G., 189
Stimulants, 79, 86, 197
Stocker, S., 184
Strauss, A., 62, 154
Street gangs, 56, 58, 89, 92, 116–117
Structural factors affecting drug use, 26–29
Structural violence, 23, 28
Strychnine, 14, 212

Subcultural model of drug use, 23–24
Substance Abuse and Mental Health Services Administration, 174
Suicide, 46, 195, 198
Sullivan, L., 204
Support systems, destruction of, 214
Susser, I., 25, 28, 137, 209
Swan, N., 185
Syndemics, 216–218
Syndrome assumption, 107
Syringe use, 33, 47, 87, 183, 190–192, 203–204, 216. See also Intravenous drug injection

Taylor, A., 63, 155
Terry, C., 149
Tetanus, 202–203
Thailand, 169
Thomas, P., 67–68
Thorpe, L., 203
Thoumi, F., 24, 157, 171
Tobacco, 38–41, 96, 104, 107, 218
Torres, M., 68–70
Torriero, E., 172
Tortu, S., 203
Toxicology screens, 211
Treatment, 4–5, 196
    commodification of, 185
    cost-effectiveness of, 184
    criminal activity after, 184
    difficulty in obtaining, 184–185
    moralistic attitude toward, 183
    resistance to change in, 10
Trends
    setting, in social epidemics, 113
    tracking longer-range, 222–223
    trend theory model of drug use, 24
Tuberculosis, 216–217
Turner, C., 225

Underground narcotics industry, birth of, 58
United States v. Behrman, 58
Urbina, A., 200

Valium, 93
Viagra, mixing with ecstasy, 133
Victimization, 132–136, 207–208

Vietnam, 76, 170, 178, 189
Violence
    cocaine and, 205
    drug-associated risk of, 204–208
    heroin and, 205–206
    marijuana and, 204
    structural, 23, 28
    victimization, 207–208
Vivian, J., 91
Vlahov, D., 183
Volatile solvents, 119
Volkow, N., 120, 197
Volstead Act, 151
Vougiouklakis, T., 212

Walters, J., 221
War on Drugs
    Asian front, 168–171
    cheap labor, supplying, 181
    Colombian front, 171–172
    costs of incarceration, 176–178
    deconstructing, 167–173
    drug producers fight back, 172–173
    duration and effectiveness of,
      173–176
    federal expenditures for, 176
    global designs and, 179
    health perspective strategy, 183–185
    history of, 167
    maintaining face, 178–179
    politically motivated drug scares,
      219–222
    racism and arrest, justification of,
      180–181
    redistribution, facilitating at the bot-
      tom, 182
    scapegoating and, 180
    shortcomings of, 175
Waterston, A., 25, 62, 154, 180–181,
    185, 209

Webb v. United States, 58
Weeks, M., 141, 183, 218, 228
Weiner, T., 174–175
West, C., 157
Wexler, I., 150–151
White, J., 202
Whitebread, C., 45
Whiteman, M., 117–118
Whyte, W., 76
Wiebel, W., 9, 224
Withdrawal, 198
Wodak, A., 193, 202
Wolf, E., 31, 39, 109, 222
Wolfenstein, M., 110
Wolitski, R., 227
Women
    drug abuse dynamics and, 17
    pregnancy and drug use, 16–18
    sex for crack, 18–20
Woody, G., 184
World War II, impact on drug produc-
    tion, 155
World Wide Web, marketing club drugs
    on, 163–164
Wypijewski, C., 133, 225

Xanax, 93

Yacoubian, G., 93
Yamaguchi, K., 118
Yates, G., 198
Young, J., 191–192
Youth drug use
    identifiable patterns of, 100–111
    innovation and diffusion in, 111–116
    oppositional pockets, 110–111
    trends in, 117–120

Zarkin, G., 184